Judicial Review in EU Law

ELGAR EUROPEAN LAW

Series editor: John Usher, *formerly Professor of European Law and Head, School of Law, University of Exeter, UK*

European integration is the driving force behind constant evolution and change in the laws of the member states and the institutions of the European Union. This important series will offer short, state-of-the-art overviews of many specific areas of EU law, from competition law to consumer law and from environmental law to labour law. Whilst most books will take a thematic, vertical approach, others will offer a more horizontal approach and consider the overarching themes of EU law.

Distilled from rigorous substantive analysis, and written by some of the best names in the field, as well as the new generation of scholars, these books are designed both to guide the reader through the changing legislation itself, and to provide a firm theoretical foundation for advanced study. They will be an invaluable source of reference for scholars and postgraduate students in the fields of EU law and European integration, as well as lawyers from the respective individual fields and policymakers within the EU.

Titles in the series include:

EU Consumer Law and Policy
Stephen Weatherill

EU Private International Law
Harmonization of Laws
Peter Stone

EU Public Procurement Law
Christopher H. Bovis

EU Criminal Law and Justice
Maria Fletcher and Robin Lööf with Bill Gilmore

Judicial Review in EU Law
Alexander H. Türk

Judicial Review in EU Law

Alexander H. Türk

School of Law, King's College London, UK

ELGAR EUROPEAN LAW

Edward Elgar

Cheltenham, UK • Northampton, MA, USA

Published by
Edward Elgar Publishing Limited
The Lypiatts
15 Lansdown Road
Cheltenham
Glos GL50 2JA
UK

Edward Elgar Publishing, Inc.
William Pratt House
9 Dewey Court
Northampton
Massachusetts 01060
USA

A catalogue record for this book
is available from the British Library

Library of Congress Control Number: 2008943822

PEFC
PEFC/16-33-111
CATG-PEFC-052
www.pefc.org

ISBN 978 1 84542 203 5

Printed and bound in Great Britain by MPG Books Ltd, Bodmin, Cornwall

For Elena

The Author and Publisher are grateful to the late John Usher for his support for this book and the Elgar European Law series

Contents

Preface

The aim of this book is to provide a comprehensive assessment of avenues for judicial review of EU action by presenting an account of the vast and, some would argue, complex case-law of the Court of Justice and the Court of First Instance, but also of the academic opinion which has accompanied their rulings over the years. While initially supportive, academic opinion has increasingly taken a more hostile attitude towards the approach pursued by the Community courts in this field, in particular in respect of the treatment of applications for judicial review by private parties. I have tried to provide a more balanced picture.

This book also endeavours to provide the reader with an understanding of the changes which the Lisbon Treaty might bring about. While the Irish 'No' vote prevented the planned entry into force of the Lisbon Treaty on 1 January 2009, at the time of publication of this book the ratification process has not been abandoned and it cannot be excluded that the Lisbon Treaty will enter into force, albeit at a later date.

I would like to take this opportunity to thank Itai Rabinovitz and Cian Murphy for their research assistance and the Centre of European Law at King's College London for its generous financial support. Finally, I owe a great debt to my wife, Elena, whose patience I have surely tested with writing this book, but I hope I will be able to come up with something to repay it.

Please note that the book states the law as at 1 August 2008.

Table of cases

EUROPEAN COURT OF JUSTICE

COURT OF FIRST INSTANCE

CIVIL SERVICE TRIBUNAL

EUROPEAN COURT OF HUMAN RIGHTS

Introduction

Judicial review constitutes an important aspect of any legal system operating under the rule of law. It allows individuals to protect their rights and legitimate interests, maintains the balance between the political branches of government and provides the courts with a greater or lesser opportunity to shape the process of the making and application of the law. Judicial review hence contributes to the accountability of government and the protection of individuals. Each legal system has, however, different conceptions as to the extent to which courts are involved in the review of acts adopted by the other branches of government.[1] Member States in the European Union provide extensive review of administrative acts of individual application, but often also of those of general application. Courts have asserted greater control over the administration in part to counteract the dominance of the executive and to provide a means of accountability.[2] On the other hand, for reasons of democratic legitimacy constitutional review of parliamentary acts is the exception in the Member States and, where it exists, is entrusted to constitutional courts or tribunals, mainly to uphold constitutionally entrenched values and principles.[3]

The rationales of judicial review are also pertinent in the European Union.[4] The necessity of judicial review as a means of preserving the institutional balance in disputes between the political institutions, and, due to its federal nature, of maintaining the balance between the EU and its Member States in disputes relating to the existence and exercise of EU competence is not seriously disputed. Nor is there any doubt as to the need to protect the rights of individuals. All the same, it is with regard to the

---

[1] See R. Gavison, 'The Role of Courts in Rifted Democracies' (1999) 33 *Israel Law Review* 216.

[2] De Smith, Woolf and Jowell, *Judicial Review of Administrative Action* (Sweet & Maxwell, 5th edn., 1995), p. 1.

[3] See the discussion on judicial review by constitutional courts in V.C. Jackson and M. Tushnet, *Comparative Constitutional Law* (Foundation Press, 2nd edn., 2006), chapter VII.

[4] See the general works on judicial review in EU law, M. Brealey and M. Hoskins, *Remedies in EC Law* (Sweet & Maxwell, 2nd edn., 1998); D. O'Keeffe and A. Bavasso (eds.), *Judicial Review in European Union Law* (Kluwer Law International, 2000); H.G. Schermers and D.F. Waelbroeck, *Judicial Protection in the European Union* (Kluwer, 6th edn., 2001); A. Ward, *Judicial Review and the Rights of Private Parties in EU Law* (OUP, 2nd edn., 2007).

latter that serious concerns have been raised as to whether the European Court of Justice[5] adequately performs this function, in particular because of its restrictive approach of allowing individuals direct access to the Community Courts in case of a challenge against normative acts. Greater demand for a liberalisation of the standing requirements for individuals is considered specifically justified on the basis that the EU does not have the same democratic credentials as Member States.[6]

The proper function of judicial review in the EU is to a large extent dependent on how one views the nature of the EU. Those who see the EU as an administrative entity exercising delegated powers[7] would perhaps argue that EU acts should be subject to judicial review analogous to that applicable in the Member States for administrative acts. This would have as a consequence that direct access to the Community Courts be granted on more liberal terms and that judicial review be undertaken with greater intensity. On the other hand, those who consider the EU as an autonomous legal system of a constitutional nature,[8] like the author of this book, might be more inclined to apply a more differentiated view. Acts akin to legislation could be reviewed directly in the Community Courts in more restrictive circumstances, while direct access to challenge administrative acts would be more readily available and review would apply stricter standards.[9] A discussion about judicial review in the EU is therefore also a discussion about the nature of the EU and the nature of the acts which it adopts.

Judicial review in the EU is most extensive under the EC Treaty, where direct actions are available for the annulment of Community acts under Article 230 EC and for failure to act under Article 232 EC. Member States and EU institutions enjoy privileged access to the Community Courts to avail themselves of these remedies. Private parties, on the other hand, have

---

[5] The European Court of Justice of the European Communities consists of the Court of Justice, the Court of First Instance and the Civil Service Tribunal. References to the European Court of Justice or ECJ can therefore relate, depending on the context, to the Court of Justice of the European Communities as an umbrella term for all three courts, or only to the Court of Justice. The term Community Courts is used in this book to refer to the Court of Justice and the Court of First Instance. The term Court refers to the Court of Justice as one of the Community Courts.

[6] J.H.H. Weiler and N.J.S. Lockhart, '"Taking Rights Seriously" Seriously: the European Court and its Fundamental Rights Jurisprudence' (1995) 32 *CMLRev.* 51, at p. 66.

[7] P.L. Lindseth, 'Democratic Legitimacy and the administrative Character of Supranationalism: the Example of the European Community' (1999) *Columbia Law Review* 628.

[8] See the discussion in A. Türk, *The Concept of Legislation in European Community Law* (Kluwer Law International, 2006), at pp. 193–195.

[9] See also A. Ward, '*Locus Standi* under Article 230(4) of the EC Treaty: Crafting a Coherent Test for a "Wobbly Policy"' (2003) 22 *YEL* 45–77, at pp. 48–49.

to meet more restrictive conditions to bring a direct action in the Court of First Instance. While these conditions would usually allow individuals to challenge individual administrative acts, they generally make it impossible to bring a direct action against acts of general application.[10] The validity of such general Community acts would normally only be open to indirect review under Article 234 EC through the national courts, where individuals have brought an action against national authorities which have applied them, or, exceptionally, in the CFI under Article 241, where Community institutions were entrusted with their application. In this respect the system of judicial remedies provided in the Community legal system is a consequence of the logic of executive federalism,[11] in which the implementation and application of general and abstract Community rules would be mainly the responsibility of Member States. In addition to the remedies of judicial review, Article 235 grants the Court jurisdiction to award damages under the conditions of Article 288(2).

The Court has insisted that '[b]y Articles 230 EC and Article 241 EC, on the one hand, and by Article 234, on the other, the Treaty has established a complete system of legal remedies and procedures designed to ensure review of the legality of acts of the institutions'[12] and has given responsibility for such review to the Community Courts. Behind the claim of a robust system of judicial review is hidden the enormous task of adapting this system to the challenges it has had to face since its inception. The Court's task goes in this respect beyond the mere interpretation and in some cases, such as the non-contractual liability of the Community under Article 288(2), the creation of the principles and rules governing the remedies available under the EC Treaty. It is the transformation that has taken place within the Community's legal system[13] and through consecutive Treaty amendments the conferral of ever more competences to the Community which have posed the most profound challenges to the Community's system of judicial review. First, the increase of Community competence and the loss of national influence at EC level, be it through greater recourse in the Council of Ministers to qualified majority voting for the adoption of basic acts or the expansion of the comitology system by which implementing powers

---

[10] See A. Türk, supra note 8, at p. 173.

[11] For a description of the classic model of executive federalism, see, for example, K. Lenaerts, 'Some Reflections on the Separation of Powers in the European Community', (1991) 28 *CMLRev*, 11–35 at 11 *et seq.*; B. Dubey, 'Administration indirecte et fédéralisme d'exécution en Europe', (2003) *CDE* 87–133.

[12] Case C-263/02 P *Jégo Quéré v Commission* [2004] ECR I-3425, para. 30.

[13] See J.H.H. Weiler, 'The transformation of Europe', in J.H.H. Weiler, *The Constitution of Europe* (CUP, 1999), pp. 10–101; P. Craig, 'Constitutions, Constitutionalism, and the European Union' (2001) *ELJ* 125–150, pp. 128–135.

are delegated to the Commission,[14] has led to a more litigious approach by the Member States to protect their competences. Second, the dynamic nature of the Community's institutional balance has had to adjust to the growth in powers of the European Parliament, whose status as applicant and defendant in judicial proceedings before the Court had to be defined accordingly. Third, the increased role of the European Parliament in the law-making process within an autonomous constitutional system makes it possible to consider certain acts adopted by the Community as legislative acts which are functionally equivalent to national legislation.[15] This necessitates a reflection on the role of judicial review in relation to such acts. Fourth, the expansion of Community competence and the corresponding increase in Community acts led to a proliferation of direct challenges in the Community Courts by private parties affected by such acts. The restrictive standing requirements for private parties to challenge acts of general application directly in the Community Courts have focused attention on the availability of indirect means of review of such acts through the national courts and whether Community law provides individuals with an effective judicial remedy in this respect.[16] This seems all the more justified when the cautious approach of the Community Courts in respect of judicial review of Community acts is compared with the more radical inroads the Court has made into the autonomy of the national legal systems to provide individuals with effective remedies to enforce Community rights in national courts.[17] Finally, the development of the Community legal order has led to a more complex system of EU administrative governance[18] than the simple model of executive federalism might suggest. EU administrative governance is today characterised by intensive co-operation between administrative actors from the national and Community level.[19]

---

[14] See C.F. Bergström, *Comitology – Delegation of Powers in the European Union and the Committee System* (OUP, 2005).

[15] A. Türk, supra note 8, p. 228.

[16] See Opinion of AG Jacobs in Case C-50/00P *Unión de Pequeños Agricultores v Council* [2002] ECR I-6677; Case T-177/01 *Jégo Quéré v Commission* [2002] ECR II-2365. See also P. Ragolle, 'Access to justice for private applicants in the Community legal order: recent (r)evolutions' (2003) *ELRev* 90–101; J. A. Usher 'Direct and individual concern – an effective remedy or a conventional solution?' (2003) 28 *ELRev* 575–600; José Manuel Cortés Martin, 'Ubi uis, Ibi Remedium? – *Locus Standi* of Private Applicants under Article 230(4) EC at a European Crossroads' (2004) *MJ* 233–261; C. Koch, '*Locus standi* of private applicants under the EU Constitution: preserving gaps in the protection of individual's right to an effective remedy' (2005) *E.L.Rev.* 511–527, at p. 515; A. Ward, supra note 4, chapter 6 F.

[17] A. Ward, supra note 4.

[18] See H. Hofmann and A. Türk (eds.), *EU Administrative Governance* (Elgar Publishing, 2006).

[19] See H. Hofmann and A. Türk , 'The Development of Integrated Administration in the EU and its Consequences' (2007) 13(2) *European Law Journal* 253–271.

The involvement of national administrations in the decision-making processes of the Community and the participation of Community actors in the implementation of Community law in the national legal systems have added to the difficulties which individuals face within the current judicial architecture.

While the Court of Justice was asked to adapt the Community's system of judicial review to these challenges, it became clear that the increase in litigation also required a reform of the judicial architecture.[20] The Court of First Instance, established in 1988,[21] was given limited jurisdiction only, but by 1994[22] was competent to hear direct actions brought by natural and legal persons subject to an appeal to the Court. The growing delay in actions before the Court made further transfers of jurisdiction inevitable. The amendment to Article 225(1) EC in the Nice Treaty gives the CFI jurisdiction to hear at first instance actions or proceedings referred to in Articles 230, 232, 235, 236 and 238 EC unless they are assigned to a judicial panel or are reserved to the Court in the Statute for the Court of Justice. Article 225a EC was inserted in the Nice Treaty and provides for the possibility of judicial panels being established by Council decision. The Council made use of this possibility by setting up the European Civil Service Tribunal which has jurisdiction to hear staff cases.[23] With the amendment of Article 51 of the Court's Statute the Court has reserved jurisdiction for actions under Articles 230 and 232 EC brought by a Member State against the European Parliament and/or against the Council (with the exception of those which are heard by the CFI) or by one EC institution against another.[24] Consequently, the CFI now has jurisdiction to hear direct actions brought by natural or legal persons under Articles 230 and 232 EC; actions brought by Member States against the Commission; actions brought by Member States against the Council in the field of state aid and anti-dumping as well as against implementing acts; actions for damages; actions based on contracts which give the CFI jurisdiction; and actions relating to Community trade marks. An appeal lies against rulings of the CFI to the Court of Justice, however, only on a point of law. While Article 225(3) EC, inserted by the Nice Treaty, also provides for the CFI to hear preliminary

---

20 See A. Arnull, *The European Union and its Court of Justice* (OUP, 2nd edn., 2006), pp. 25–27 and chapter 5; P. Craig, *EU Administrative Law* (OUP, 2006), chapter 9.

21 Council Decision 88/591, [1988] OJ L 319/1, as corrected.

22 Additional transfers occurred with Council Decision 93/350, [1993] OJ L 144/21 and Council Decision 94/149, [1994] OJ L 66/29.

23 Council Decision 2004/752, [2004] OJ L 333/7. An appeal against a ruling by the Civil Service Tribunal lies with the CFI, but only on a point of law, and in exceptional cases to the Court.

24 Council Decision 2004/407, [2004] OJ L 132/5.

rulings, the necessary amendment of the Statute for this purpose has not yet been made. It should, however, not be forgotten that national courts play an increasingly important role in the system of judicial review of Community acts. While national courts are not empowered to set aside Community acts[25] their role as *fora* for the scrutiny of Community acts, and in particular those of general application, for the purpose of Article 234 EC has assumed greater importance with the rulings of the Court in *UPA*[26] and *Jégo Quéré*.[27]

Judicial supervision of EU acts is considerably more restricted outside the Community pillar.[28] While Article 46 EU does not provide the Court with any jurisdiction under the second pillar, Article 46(b) EU states that the Court of Justice has jurisdiction in the third pillar under the conditions set out in Article 35 TEU. Direct actions can be brought under Article 35(6) TEU by a Member State or the Commission against a framework decision or a decision. Article 35(1) TEU provides for an indirect way of challenging third pillar acts by providing the Court jurisdiction to give preliminary rulings, *inter alia* on the validity of framework decisions and decisions. However, the jurisdiction of the Court under this provision must first be accepted by the Member States,[29] which under Article 35(3) EU have a choice as to whether to limit the possibility of making a reference to the national court of last instance or to allow any national court to make a reference.

Despite the criticism in academic literature of the restrictive nature of direct access by private parties to the Community Courts, the reform of the system of judicial review played only a minor role on the recent reform agenda. It was discussed within the Convention on the Future of Europe first by Working Group II[30] and then by a Discussion Circle, which had

---

25 See Case 314/85 *Foto-Frost* [1987] ECR 4199.

26 Case C-50/00P *Unión de Pequeños Agricultores v Council* [2002] ECR I-6677.

27 Case C-263/02P *Commission v Jégo Quéré* [2004] ECR I-3425.

28 Article 46(f) TEU entrusts the Court of Justice, however, with jurisdiction to apply Article 47 TEU, which states that 'nothing in this Treaty [on European Union] shall affect the Treaties establishing the European Communities or the subsequent Treaties and Acts modifying or supplementing them'. Under Article 47 TEU the Court has therefore the task 'to ensure that the acts which, according to the Council, fall within the scope of Title V of the EU Treaty and which are capable of having legal effects do not encroach upon the powers conferred by provisions of the EC Treaty on the Community', see Case C-91/05 *Commission v Council*, judgment of 20 May 2008, para. 56. Similar considerations apply in relation to third pillar acts, see Case C-176/03 *Commission v Council* [2005] ECR I-7879, at para. 39 and Case C-440/05 *Commission v Council* [2007] ECR I-9097, at para. 53.

29 See Article 35(2) EU. For a list of Member States which have accepted the jurisdiction of the Court, see OJ [2005] L 327/19.

30 Working Group II was concerned with the incorporation of the Charter of Fundamental Rights of the EU and with the accession to the European Convention. On the positions within

been set up rather belatedly as an *ad hoc* working group to discuss matters related to the Community Courts. Given the divisions amongst the group[31] only modest amendments resulted from its discussions. At the same time reforms in other parts of the Constitutional Treaty also had repercussions for judicial review. The Lisbon Treaty[32] has incorporated many of the amendments of the now abandoned Constitutional Treaty, including the ones pertaining to judicial review.

This book aims at providing a comprehensive discussion of the various avenues for judicial review of EU action. It will first assess actions for annulment (Chapter 1) and failure to act (Chapter 2) before turning to incidental forms of review under Articles 241 and 234 (Chapter 3). The focus of the discussion will then shift to the remedy of compensation for damages (Chapter 4) and a study of interim relief proceedings (Chapter 5). The changes brought about by the Lisbon Treaty will be set out in the book in the context of the specific remedy under discussion and again in the conclusions to give as accurate a picture as possible on the impact of the reform and the potential issues facing judicial review in the European Union.

---

the working group on a reform of judicial review, see Final Report of Working Group II under 'C. Access to the Court of Justice' (CON 354/02). See also J. A. Usher, supra note 16.

[31] On the various proposals advanced within the group, see Final Report of the Discussion Circle on the Court of Justice under 'on question (d) of the framework' (CONV 636/03). See also C. Koch, supra note 16; P. Craig, supra note 20, p. 344.

[32] [2007] OJ C 306. This book will refer to the Treaty on European Union and Treaty on the Functioning of the European Union in their consolidated versions, see Council document 6655/08 of 15 April 2008.

1 Action for annulment

The action for annulment under Article 230 constitutes the main avenue to challenge Community acts directly in the Community Courts.[1] In contrast to the more relaxed admissibility conditions which EU institutions and Member States have to meet, access to the Community Courts by private parties is more restrictive.[2] Article 230(4) provides that natural and legal

---

[1] See the more general works on annulment actions: A. Albors-Llorens, *Private Parties in European Community Law* (1996); M. Brealey and M. Hoskins, *Remedies in EC Law* (Sweet & Maxwell, 2nd edn., 1998), chapter 13; H.G. Schermers and D.F. Waelbroeck, *Judicial Protection in the European Union* (Kluwer, 6th edn., 2001), pp. 406–463; P. Craig and G. DeBúrca, EU Law (OUP, 4th edn., 2007), pp. 502–528 and chapter 15; T.C. Hartley, *The Foundations of European Community Law* (OUP, 2nd edn., 2007), chapters 11, 12 and 15; A. Ward, *Judicial Review and the Rights of Private Parties in EU Law* (OUP, 2nd edn., 2007), chapter 6.

[2] See in particular A. Barav, 'Direct and Individual Concern: An Almost Insurmountable Barrier to the Admissibility of Individual Appeal to the EEC Court' (1974) 11 *CMLRev* 191–198; C. Harding, 'The Private Interest in Challenging Community Action' (1980) 5 *ELRev* 354–361; H. Rasmussen, 'Why is Article 173 Interpreted against Private Plaintiffs?' (1980) 5 *ELRev* 112; R. Greaves, 'Locus Standi under Article 173' (1986) 11 *ELRev* 119–133; C. Harlow, 'Towards a Theory of Access for the European Court of Justice' (1992) 12 *YEL* 213–248; P. Craig, 'Legality, standing and substantive review in Community law' (1994) 14 *OJLS* 507; P. Nihoul, 'La recevabilité des recours en annulation' (1994) 30 *RTDE* 171–194; A. Arnull, 'Private Applicants and the Action for Annulment under Art. 173 of the EC Treaty' (1995) 32 *CMLRev* 7; A. Albors-Llorens, supra note 1; M. Hedemann-Robinson, 'Article 173 EC, General Community Measures and *Locus Standi* for Private Persons: Still a Cause for Individual Concern?' (1996) 2 *EPL* 127; M. Nettesheim, 'Article 173 of the EC Treaty and Regulations: Towards the Development of Uniform Standing Requirements', in W. Micklitz and N. Reich (eds.), *Public Interest Litigation Before European Courts* (1996) 225; A. Adinolfi, 'Admissibility of action for annulment by social partners and "sufficient representativity" of European agreements' (2000) 25 *ELRev* 165; A. Arnull, 'Private Applicants and the Action for Annulment since Codorniu' (2001) 38 *CMLRev* 7–52; A. Albors-Llorens, 'The Standing of Private Parties to Challenge Community Measures: Has the European Court Missed the Boat?' (2003) *CLJ* 72–92; P. Craig, 'Standing, Rights and the Structure of Legal Argument' (2003) 9 *EPL* 493; P. Ragolle, 'Access to justice for private applicants in the Community legal order: recent (r)evolutions' (2003) *ELRev* 90–101; J. A. Usher 'Direct and individual concern – an effective remedy or a conventional solution?' (2003) 28 *ELRev* 575–600; A. Ward, '*Locus Standi* under Article 230(4) of the EC Treaty: Crafting a Coherent Test for a "Wobbly Policy"' (2003) *YEL* 45–77; J.M. Cortés Martin, 'Ubi uis, Ibi Remedium? – *Locus Standi* of Private Applicants under Article 230(4) EC at a European Crossroads' (2004) *MJ* 233–261; E. Berry and S. Boyes, 'Access to justice in the Community courts: a limited right?' (2005) *Civil Justice Quarterly* 224–245; S. Enchelmaier, 'No-One Slips Through the Net? Latest Developments and Non-Developments in the European Court of Justice's Jurisprudence on Article 230(4) EC' (2005) 24 *YEL* 173–221; C. Koch, 'Locus Standi of private applicants under the EU

persons can challenge decisions, unless they are addressed to them, only if they are of direct and individual concern to them. It is in particular the narrow interpration of individual concern by the Community Courts encapsulated in the *Plaumann*[3] formula which poses considerable problems for individuals to gain direct access to the Community Courts for administrative acts of general application. In addition, the ever more integrated nature of administrative governance in the Community in which national authorities and Community institutions intensively interact makes it difficult for private parties to satisfy the requirement that the act is reviewable and of direct concern to them.[4]

An action for annulment is also available in the third pillar under Article 35(6) EU against framework decisions and decisions. Such an action can, however, only be brought by a Member State or the Commission, thereby excluding the possibility for private parties to have third pillar acts reviewed directly. An action can be brought on grounds of lack of competence, infringement of an essential procedural requirement, infringement of the Treaty or of any rule of law relating to its application, or misuse of powers. The action has to be brought within two months of the publication of the measure.

With the entry into force of the Lisbon Treaty, annulment actions will be governed by Article 263 TFEU, which will replace Article 230 EC. This provision would lead to an extension of the jurisdiction of the Court in the review of Union acts and would bring with it a liberalisation of standing rules for private parties.

This chapter will first discuss the regime applicable before the entry into force of the Lisbon Treaty.[5] It will therefore present the EU institutions and bodies against whom an action can be brought. It will then study the case-law on when an act is considered as reviewable before examining the standing requirements which have to be met by applicants for the action to be considered as admissible as well as the legal interest which they must show in bringing the action. After assessing the two-month time limit, this chapter will present the grounds of review and will give an overview of the effects of a judgment declaring a Community act void. The final section of

---

Constitution: preserving gaps in the protection of individuals' right to an effective remedy' (2005) *ELRev* 511–527; P. Craig, *EU Administrative Law* (OUP, 2006), pp. 314–322 and pp. 331–347; T.C. Hartley, supra note 1, chapter 12; A. Ward, supra note 1, chapter 6.

3 Case 25/62 *Plaumann v Commission* [1963] ECR 95.

4 See A. Türk, 'Judicial Review of Integrated Administration', in H.H. Hofmann and A. Türk (eds.), *Legal Challenges in EU Administrative Law: Towards an Integrated Administration* (Edward Elgar Publishing, forthcoming).

5 While the main focus will be on Article 230 EC, this part will also discuss Article 35(6) TEU where this appears relevant.

this chapter will be devoted to an assessment of the effects of the reform undertaken in the Constitutional Treaty as they are now reflected in the Lisbon Treaty in relation to the action for annulment.

1. EU INSTITUTIONS OR BODIES AS DEFENDANTS

An action under Article 230 EC can be brought against an act adopted by the European Parliament and the Council. As many legislative acts are now adopted under the co-decision procedure by the European Parliament and the Council, actions against these acts will increase in importance. Actions can also be brought against the Council, the Commission and the ECB. Actions can also be initiated against acts of the European Parliament, but only where such acts are intended to produce legal effects *vis-à-vis* third parties.

Moreover, the Court has jurisdiction to review measures adopted by the Board of Governors of the European Investment Bank under Article 237(b) and measures adopted by the Board of Directors of the European Investment Bank under Article 237(c). In *Commission v EIB* the Court pointed out that 'although it is not a European Community institution, the EIB none the less is a Community body established and endowed with legal personality by the EC Treaty [. . .] and it is on that account that the EIB is subject to judicial review by the Court, in particular as provided for in Article 237(b) EC.'[6] This ruling, in particular the Court's reference to the rule of law,[7] could be understood as demonstrating the Court's willingness to review acts of other Community bodies, in particular agencies.

The EC Treaty does not contain provisions which specifically deal with judicial review of actions taken by European agencies. Such provisions can, however, be found in the regulations which establish the agencies.[8] Different approaches exist in relation to the review of the legality of agency action. While some agencies do not contain any provisions on legality review of acts of the agency, others allow for the referral of any act of the agency to the Commission for a review of legality.[9] Agencies with decision-making powers have more elaborate mechanisms for legality review,

[6] Case C-15/00 *Commission v EIB* [2003] ECR I-7281, at para. 75

[7] Ibid., para. 75.

[8] See P. Craig (2006), supra note 2, pp. 164–165.

[9] See Article 18 of Regulation 337/75 (Cedefop); Article 22 of Regulation 1365/75 (Eurofound); Article 22 of Regulation 2062/94 (EU-OSHA); Article 28 of Regulation 851/2004 (ECDC).

usually involving an internal appeal, which can be followed by an appeal to the CFI.[10] Other agencies make reference to review of their decisions by the Court of Justice.[11] Most agencies, however, do not contain any provisions on legality review.[12]

While the ruling in *Commission v EIB* does not exclude the possibility of review of agency measures, the Lisbon Treaty would remove any doubt in this respect by providing in Article 263(1) TFEU that the Community Courts 'shall also review the legality of acts of bodies, offices or agencies of the Union intended to produce legal effects vis-à-vis third parties.' Moreover, the practice of agency regulations to provide for judicial review provisions would be officially sanctioned in Article 263(5) TFEU, which stipulates that 'acts setting up bodies, offices and agencies of the Union may lay down specific conditions and arrangements concerning actions brought by natural or legal persons against acts of these bodies, offices or agencies intended to produce legal effects in relation to them.' It is submitted that these provisions would have rather limited effect, given that most agencies would not produce acts with 'legal effects' as interpreted by the case-law of the Community courts.

Acts adopted by EU institutions under the second pillar or by agencies set up under the second pillar are not subject to review by the Court. Direct actions can be brought under Article 35(6) EU against framework decisions and decisions adopted by the Council in the third pillar.[13] In case of third pillar agencies only Eurojust provides an appeal procedure to a joint supervisory body, whose decision is final, in cases of denial of access or correction of data by Eurojust.[14] In *Eurojust* the Court found that a measure adopted by Eurojust could not be reviewed under Article 230 EC.[15] This latter position might, however, have to be reviewed if and when the Lisbon Treaty enters into force.

---

[10] See Articles 57–63 of Regulation 40/94 (OHIM); Articles 67–73 of Regulation 2100/94 (CPVO); Articles 31–41 of Regulation 1592/2002 (EASA). In Case T-95/06 *Federación de Cooperativas Agrarias de la Comunidad Valenciana v OCVV*, judgment of 31 January 2008, at para. 79, the CFI held that the terms direct and individual concern in Article 68 of Regulation 2100/94 had to be regarded as identical to those in Article 230(4) EC.

[11] See Article 17 of Regulation 302/93 (EMCDDA); Article 27(3) of Regulation 168/2007 (FRA).

[12] As in case of the ETF, the EEA, the EMEA, the CdT, the EAR, the EFSA, the EMSA, the ENISA, FRONTEX, CFCA, ERA.

[13] In light of the Court's recent judgment in Case C-354/04 P *Gestoras Pro Amnistia and Others v Council* [2007] ECR I-1579, at para. 53, it no longer seems to be excluded to challenge other third pillar acts provided they produce legal effects in relation to third parties.

[14] See Articles 19(8), 20(2) and 23(7) of Decision 2002/187/JHA (Eurojust).

[15] See Case C-160/03 *Spain v Eurojust* [2005] ECR I-2077.

2. REVIEWABLE ACTS[16]

Article 230(1) stipulates that the Court shall review 'acts . . . other than recommendations and opinions'. The Court has refused to interpret this provision as including only legally binding acts laid down in Article 249 EC and has opted instead for a wider approach. The definition for a reviewable act was developed in the *ERTA* case, where the Court held that an action for annulment is available against 'all measures adopted by the institutions, whatever their nature or form, which are intended to have legal effects'.[17] In *IBM* the Court found that such legal effects occur, when the measure is 'binding on, and capable of affecting the interests of, the applicant by bringing about a distinct change in his legal position'.[18]

The *ERTA* definition places emphasis on the substance of an act and not its form.[19] The concept of reviewable acts is therefore considerably wider than that laid down in Article 249 and includes 'conclusions' by the Member States adopted in Council for negotiations concerning an international agreement,[20] letters written by Commission staff,[21] and even oral decisions.[22] On the other hand, the requirement that the measure must affect the applicant's 'legal position' often constitutes a considerable hurdle of access to the Community Courts.

The Court has made it clear that only the operative part of a measure can produce legal effects.[23] This means that 'the assessments made in the recitals to a decision are not in themselves capable of forming the subject of

---

16 See A. Arnull (2001), supra note 2, at pp. 14–23; T.C. Hartley, supra note 1, chapter 11.

17 Case 22/70 *Commission v Council* [1971] ECR 263 at para. 42.

18 Case 60/81 *IBM v Commission* [1981] ECR 2639 at para. 9. While the Court uses this formula usually also in cases brought by Member States (see Case C-163/06P *Finland v Commission*, [2007] ECR I-5127, at para. 40), the CFI has recently questioned this approach in Case T-233/04 *Netherlands v Commission*, judgment of 20 April 2008, when it stated in para. 37 that a Member State as privileged applicant need not prove 'that an act of the Commission which it is contesting produces legal effects with regard to that Member State in order for its action to be admissible'. This approach was also supported by AG Jacobs in Case C-301/03 *Italy v Commission* [2005] ECR I-10217, at paras. 52 and 53, and footnote 15. The ruling of the CFI in Case T-233/04 is currently under appeal in Case C-279/08.

19 Case 60/81 *IBM v Commission* [1981] ECR 2639, at para. 9. See also Case C-521/06 P *Athinaïki Techniki v Commission*, judgment of 17 July 2008, at paras. 42 and 43.

20 Case 22/70 *Commission v Council* [1971] ECR 263.

21 See Case T-84/97 *BEUC v Commission* [1998] ECR II-795, para. 48; Case T-113/00 *DuPont and others v Commission* [2002] ECR II-3681, para. 45.

22 See Joined Cases 316/82 and 40/83 *Kohler v Court of Auditors* [1984] ECR 641, at paras. 9–13; Case T-3/93 *Air France v Commission* [1994] ECR II-121, at paras. 57–59; Case T-85/03R *Government of the Cayman Islands Commission*, order of 26 March 2003, at para. 60.

23 Case C-164/02 *Netherlands v Commission* [2004] ECR I-1177, at para. 21. Case T-251/00 *Lagardère and Canal+ v Commission* [2002] ECR II-4825, at para. 67.

an application for annulment'.[24] However, the Court has consistently held that 'the statement of reasons is indispensable for determining the exact meaning of what is stated in the operative part'.[25] Consequently, a decision amending the grounds of an earlier decision can be a reviewable act, even if it does not alter the terms of the operative part of the earlier decision, where the amendment changes 'the substance of what was decided in the operative part, thus affecting the applicants' interest'.[26] In *Lagardère v Commission*[27] the CFI found that a decision under Regulation 4064/89 which modifies the assessment as to whether certain restrictions are ancillary to the concentration to the detriment of the notifying parties, constituted such a change.[28] On the other hand, in *Coca-Cola v Commission*[29] the Court held that the findings of dominance, the definition of the relevant market and the exercise of decisive influence in a Commission decision which considers a concentration compatible with the common market under Article 8(2) of Regulation 4064/89 (Merger Regulation) were not reviewable. The grounds must, however, 'constitute the essential basis for the operative part'[30] of an act.

The approach of the Court as to the relevant effects necessary for an act to be considered as reviewable under Article 230 has become as complex, if not more, than the assessment of *locus standi* for private parties under Article 230(4). The following survey therefore groups the case-law into categories which have caused difficulties in the assessment as to whether an act is reviewable or not.

Refusal to Comply With a Request

Under what circumstances a refusal by a Community institution to accede to a request can be a reviewable act is not always entirely clear. In *Greencore v Commission*, the Court argued that silence did not constitute an implied refusal.[31] And in *Arizona Chemicals* the CFI rejected the argument that it was sufficient for an act to be reviewable merely because the Commission addresses a letter to the person making a request, as 'an act

---

[24] Case C164/02 *Netherlands v Commission* [2004] ECR I-1177, para. 21.

[25] Case T-251/00 *Lagardère and Canal+ v Commission* [2002] ECR II-4825, para. 67. See also Case C-355/95 P *TWD v Commission* [1997] ECR I-2549, at para. 21; Joined Cases T-213/95 and T-18/96 *SCK and FNK v Commission* [1997] ECR II-1739, at para. 104.

[26] Case T-251/00 *Lagardère and Canal+ v Commission* [2002] ECR II-4825, para. 68.

[27] Case T-251/00 *Lagardère and Canal+ v Commission* [2002] ECR II-4825.

[28] Ibid., at paras. 110–112.

[29] Joined Cases T-125/97 and T-127/97 *Coca-Cola v Commission* [2000] ECR II-1733.

[30] Case C164/02 *Netherlands v Commission* [2004] ECR I-1177, para. 21.

[31] See Case C-123/03 P *Commission v Greencore* [2004] ECR I-11647, at para. 45.

of the Commission which amounts to a rejection must be appraised in the light of the nature of the request to which it constituted a reply'.[32] A Community institution's refusal is therefore only reviewable 'where the act which the Community institution refuses to withdraw or amend could itself be challenged'[33] under Article 230. Consequently, where the act which the individual requests the institution to adopt is itself not reviewable, the refusal to adopt the act is not reviewable.

This does not mean that where the requested act is reviewable, the refusal to adopt such an act is also reviewable. In *Miethke*, the Court ruled that the rejection of a request by an individual to review the mandates of German MEPs after German unification in 1990 was not a reviewable act, as the EP had no competence to act on the request.[34] In *T-Mobile Austria*,[35] the applicant brought an action against the Commission for refusing to find that Austria had infringed its obligations under Articles 86(1) and 90. The CFI found that the Commission was under a duty to examine the complaint diligently and impartially.[36] The CFI argued that the fulfilment of this obligation was subject to judicial review allowing individuals to challenge the refusal of their request in order to protect their legitimate interests. However, the review by the Community Courts in such a case was limited 'to a circumscribed review in which it merely checks, first, that the contested measure includes a statement of reasons which is prima facie consistent and reflects due consideration of the relevant aspects of the case, second, that the facts relied on are materially accurate and, third, that the prima facie assessment of those facts is not vitiated by any manifest error.'[37] On appeal the Court[38] overturned the judgment of the CFI and held that the refusal by the Commission to take action against Austria under Article 86(3) was not a reviewable act. The Court acknowledged that individuals might be entitled, under certain circumstances, to bring an action against a Commission decision addressed to a Member State under

---

[32] Case T-369/03 *Arizona Chemical and Others v Commission* [2005] ECR II-5839, at para. 64. See also Joined Cases C-15/91 and C-108/91 *Buckl and Others v Commission* [1992] ECR I-6061, para. 22; Joined Cases T-93/00 and Case T-46/01 *Alessandrini Srl and Others v Commission* [2003] ECR II-1635, at para. 59.

[33] Case T-369/03 *Arizona Chemical and Others v Commission* [2005] ECR II-5839, at para. 64.

[34] Case C-25/90 *Miethke v European Parliament* [1993] ECR I-473.

[35] Case T-54/99 *max.mobil Telekommunikation Service GmbH v Commission* [2002] ECR II-313.

[36] See also Case T-52/00 *Coe Clerici Logistics SpA v Commission* [2003] ECR II-2123, at para. 94. The CFI rejected, however, the claim that the Commission had failed to undertake a diligent and impartial examination of the applicant's complaint.

[37] Case T-54/99 *max.mobil Telekommunikation Service GmbH v Commission* [2002] ECR II-313, para. 58.

[38] Case C-141/02 P *Commission v T-Mobile Austria GmbH* [2005] ECR I-1283.

Article 86(3).[39] The Court also admitted that the applicant had 'a direct and individual interest in annulment of the Commission's decision to refuse to act on its complaint'.[40] All the same, the Court argued that such a refusal could not be regarded as producing legal effects, as the Commission was not obliged to bring proceedings against a Member State under Article 86(3). The Court's dictum in *T-Mobile Austria* is, however, difficult to reconcile with other judgments. In *DuPont*[41] the CFI had to assess whether the rejection by the Commission of the applicants' request to open an investigation as to the withdrawal of the benefit of the general tariff preference system for PET film originating in India constituted a reviewable act. Under the system of generalised tariff preferences laid down in Council Regulation 3281/94 the Member States or certain third parties can bring to the Commission's attention information which warrants a temporary withdrawal of the preferences granted. The Commission is obliged to communicate the information immediately to the Member States which may then initiate consultations. The CFI stated that '[a] third party demonstrating an interest in a temporary withdrawal measure is, accordingly, entitled to expect that the Commission will examine the information supplied to it in order to ascertain whether that information falls within one of the abovementioned cases and, if it does, that the Commission will forward it to the Member States'.[42] The limited right which the third party has would be denied if the Commission could refuse to act on the information provided. The CFI considered the Commission's letter in which it rejected the applicants' complaint as a reviewable act, as the letter 'can be read only as giving the Commission's definitive reply to the information received by it [. . .] and as bringing to a close, in its first stage, a procedure which might otherwise have led to the initiation of consultations [. . .] and, consequently, to the investigation requested by the applicants.'[43] The Commission's definitive rejection without examination of the information submitted by the applicants therefore altered their legal position.[44] In *Lilly Industries*[45] the applicant had submitted a request under Article 6 of Regulation 2377/90[46] for the inclusion of somidobove in Annex II of the regulation. The CFI found that the rejection by the Commission of this

---

39 See Case C-107/95 *Bundesverband der Bilanzbuchhalter v Commission* [1997] ECR I-947.

40 Case C-141/02 P *Commission v T-Mobile Austria GmbH* [2005] ECR I-1283, para. 70.

41 Case T-113/00 *DuPont and others v Commission* [2002] ECR II-3681.

42 Ibid., para. 51.

43 Ibid., para. 54.

44 Ibid., para. 55.

45 Case T-120/96 *Lilly Industries v Commission* [1998] ECR II-2571.

46 [1990] OJ L224/1.

request amounted to a reviewable act, as it 'constitutes the final stage in the procedure initiated by the applicant [. . .]'.[47] Similarly, in *Alessandrini*,[48] the CFI found that the Commission's refusal to exercise its power to adopt measures under Article 20d of Regulation 404/93[49] constituted a reviewable act, as it 'definitively determined the Commission's position concerning the adoption of such measures'.[50] In *Eurocoton*,[51] the Court on appeal had to decide whether the Council's failure to adopt a regulation imposing a definitive anti-dumping duty constituted a reviewable act. The CFI had answered the question in the negative on the ground that the applicants had no right to the adoption of an anti-dumping regulation.[52] The Court came to the opposite conclusion and argued that the Council's failure to adopt the Commission's proposal to adopt the regulation was an implied rejection of the proposal and this rejection became definitive at the end of the 15-month period, within which the Council could have adopted the regulation.[53] Moreover, this failure affected the appellants' interests as complainants.[54] This latter decision can be contrasted with the ruling in *Commission v Council*[55] (Stability Growth Pact). In this case the Commission recommended to the Council to decide under Article 104(8) that France and Germany had not undertaken any effective action to reduce their excessive deficits and to require France and Germany under Article 104(9) to take certain measures to reduce their deficits. The Court rejected the Commission's assertion that the Council's inaction amounted to a reviewable act. The Court pointed out that 'where the Commission recommends to the Council that it adopt decisions under Article 104(8) and (9) EC and the required majority is not achieved within the Council, no decision is taken for the purpose of those provisions.'[56] The Court made it clear that there was no 'provision of Community law prescribing a period on the expiry of which an implied decision under Article 104(8) or (9) EC is deemed to arise and establishing the content of that decision.'[57] While it

---

[47] Case T-120/96 *Lilly Industries v Commission* [1998] ECR II-2571, para. 53.
[48] Joined Cases T-93/00 and Case T-46/01 *Alessandrini Srl and Others v Commission* [2003] ECR II-1635.
[49] [1993] OJ L 47/1.
[50] Joined Cases T-93/00 and Case T-46/01 *Alessandrini Srl and Others v Commission* [2003] ECR II-1635, para. 65.
[51] Case C-76/01 P *Eurocoton and Others v Council* [2003] ECR I-10091. See also Case T-177/00 *Philips v Council* [2005] ECR II-5, at paras. 29–33.
[52] Case T-213/97 *Eurocoton and Others v Council* [2000] ECR II-3727, at paras. 46–52.
[53] Ibid., at paras. 64–65.
[54] Ibid., para. 66.
[55] Case C-27/04 *Commission v Council* [2004] ECR I-6649.
[56] Ibid., para. 31.
[57] Ibid., para. 32.

acknowledged that Regulation 1467/97[58] laid down deadlines for Council action, the Court found that 'expiry of those deadlines does not preclude the Council from adopting the acts recommended by the Commission.'[59] The Court argued that the purpose of those deadlines was to 'ensure expeditious and effective implementation of the excessive deficit procedure'.[60] This objective could not be achieved if the Council lost its competence to adopt the necessary measures.

Preparatory Acts

Where the Commission conducts a procedure which involves several stages before the institution arrives at a final decision, the Court would consider an act as reviewable 'only if it is a measure definitively laying down the position of the Commission or the Council in the conclusion of that procedure, and not a provisional measure intended to pave the way for the final decision'.[61] Consequently, intermediate steps in competition, antidumping, staff cases and other administrative procedures cannot be subject to annulment proceedings in the European Court.

In *IBM*,[62] the Commission opened an investigation against IBM to find out whether IBM had violated Article 82 (ex Article 86). After several years of investigation, the Commission decided to initiate a procedure under Article 3 of Regulation 17/62. In a letter it informed IBM that it was about to decide that IBM had violated Article 82 and explained its view in a statement of objections. IBM was requested to respond in writing and was also given the possibility to refute the allegations in a hearing. IBM challenged the letter under Article 230. The Court pointed out that an act was subject to review under Article 230 'only if it is a measure definitively laying down the position of the Commission or the Council in the conclusion of that procedure, and not a provisional measure intended to pave the way for the final decision'.[63] The Court concluded that neither the initiation of the procedure nor the statement of objections[64] could be considered as reviewable acts, as they only prepare the final decision of the Commission. Similarly, in *Guérin automobiles*[65]

---

58 [1997] OJ L 209/6.

59 Case C-27/04 *Commission v Council* [2004] ECR I-6649, para. 33.

60 Ibid., para. 33.

61 Case 60/81 *IBM v Commission* [1981] ECR 2639, para. 10.

62 Case 60/81 *IBM v Commission* [1981] ECR 2639.

63 Ibid., at para. 10.

64 See also Joined Cases T-10/92 R etc. *Cementeries CBR and others v Commission* [1992] ECR II-1571, at paras. 47–48.

65 Case C-282/95 P *Guérin automobiles v Commission* [1997] ECR I-1503.

the Commission notified the appellant under Article 6 of Regulation 99/63[66] that there were insufficient grounds to pursue his complaint of a breach by Volvo of Article 81 and invited the appellant to submit further comments. The Court found that the notification under Article 6 was only a provisional measure and therefore not reviewable. The Court pointed out that the appellant could only challenge a definitive decision rejecting the complaint and 'in the context of such an action the complainant may rely on any legal defects in the provisional measures preceding the definitive decision'.[67]

Similarly, in *Satellimages TV 5*[68] the CFI found that a letter in which the Director in charge informed the applicant that the Commission did not share the applicant's view that Deutsche Telekom's pricing policy against satellite broadcasting companies for access to its cable distribution system was an abuse in the sense of Article 82 did not constitute a reviewable act. The CFI argued that the assessments contained in the letter were merely provisional and that the measure could therefore only be regarded as 'a preparatory statement of position'.[69] The CFI placed particular emphasis on the fact that the Commission expressly invited the applicant to provide further information. Given that the applicant maintained that it had submitted all the information it had, the Commission could thereby *de facto* terminate the complaint without having to give a final decision.

The Court made it clear in *Gestetner Holdings*[70] that the rejection by the Commission of a proposed undertaking in anti-dumping proceedings is merely 'an intermediate measure whose purpose is to prepare for the final decision, and is not therefore a measure which may be challenged.'[71] The Court pointed out that applicants could raise any irregularity of the rejection of their proposed undertakings as part of their challenge against the regulation introducing definitive anti-dumping duties.

Decisions in staff cases are usually also preceded by several preparatory steps. In *Huber*[72] the Court made it clear that the integration procedure and the Opinion of the Establishment Board which preceded the disputed decision to terminate the applicant's contract was not a reviewable act

---

66 OJ, English Special Edition 1963–64, p. 47.

67 Case C-282/95 P *Guérin automobiles v Commission* [1997] ECR I-1503, para. 36. See also Case T-25/04 *González y Díez v Commission*, judgment of 12 September 2007, at para. 91.

68 Case T-95/99 *Satellimages TV 5 v Commission* [2002] ECR II-1425.

69 Ibid., para. 38.

70 Case C-156/87 *Gestetner Holdings v Council and Commission* [1990] ECR I-719.

71 Ibid., para. 8. See also Joined Cases C-133/87 and C-150/87 *Nashua Corporation v Commission and Council* [1990] ECR I-719, at para. 9.

72 Case 78/63 *Huber v Commission* [1964] ECR 367.

under Article 91(1) of the Staff Regulations.[73] In *Bossi*[74] the Court found that an action against the lists drawn up during the course of the promotion procedure was inadmissible, as the lists constituted merely 'a preparatory act which is a necessary preliminary to the final decision on the promotions'.[75] Also in *Marcopoulos*[76] the CFI held that the decision appointing the members of a selection board was only a preparatory measure within the competition procedure to establish a reserve for the recruitment of Greek-language interpreters within the Court of Justice. The CFI found that '[o]nly in an action against the decision adopted on the conclusion of that procedure may the applicant contest the legality of earlier acts which are closely linked to it'.[77]

And in *Co-Frutta*[78] the CFI found that a partial refusal by DG Agriculture of access to the documents sought by the applicant in connection with the arrangements for importing bananas was not a reviewable act, as 'under the procedure established by Decision 94/90 the decision of the Secretary-General of the Commission constitutes the final statement of the institution's position on the application for access to documents made by the applicant.'[79]

Similar considerations apply in cases where the procedure at EC level involves the interaction of the Commission, national authorities and committees. The CFI in *Olivieri*[80] rejected as inadmissible an action brought against the revised opinion of the Committee for Proprietary Medicinal Products (CPMP) acting for the European Agency for the Evaluation of Medicinal Products (EMEA). Despite the doubts raised by the applicant, the CPMP retained in its revised opinion its initial opinion in favour of granting marketing authorisation for a medicinal product. The CFI argued that the revised opinion was 'an intermediate measure whose purpose is to prepare for the marketing authorisation decision'[81] taken by the Commission. The opinion was merely a preparatory measure 'which does not definitively lay down the Commission's position'[82] and was therefore not reviewable. In the same way, a Commission proposal

---

[73] See also Case 11/64 *Weighardt v Commission* [1965] ECR 285, at p. 298.
[74] Case 346/87 *Bossi v Commission* [1989] ECR 303.
[75] Ibid., para. 24.
[76] Joined Cases T-32/89 and T-39/89 *Marcopoulos v Court of Justice* [1990] ECR II-281.
[77] Ibid., para. 22.
[78] Case T-47/01 *Co-Frutta v Commission* [2003] ECR II-4441.
[79] Ibid., para. 29.
[80] Case T-326/99 *Olivieri v Commission and European Agency for the Evaluation of Medicinal Products* [2003] ECR II-6053.
[81] Ibid., para. 53.
[82] Ibid., para. 53.

to a comitology committee could not be considered as reviewable act.[83] And in *Pfizer*[84] the CFI held that the referral by the Commission to the EMEA under Article 30 of Directive 2001/83[85] because of divergences between the summaries of product characteristics (SPCs) for Lopid did not amount to a reviewable act, as the referral merely 'sets a consultative procedure in motion and does not in itself entail any harmonisation of the Lopid SPCs.'[86]

In *Netherlands v Commission*[87] the Netherlands challenged a letter by the Commission, in which the latter informed the Prime Minister of the Netherlands Antilles that its country could for the time being not be included in the provisional list of third countries under Article 23(3)(a) of Council Directive 92/46.[88] The applicant argued that dairy products from the Netherlands Antilles could not be imported into the EC until and unless the country was included in the list. The Court considered the Commission letter not a definitive position, but merely as a preparatory act, as the Commission had pointed out in the letter that it was awaiting further documents from the Netherlands Antilles government before making a final decision, which at all events had to be preceded by an opinion of the veterinary committee.[89] In contrast the Court held in *Portugal v Commission*[90] that the letter by the Director General of Agriculture reducing the advances paid to Portugal under the European Agricultural Guidance and Guarantee Fund (EAGGF) was intended to have legal effects, as it 'constitutes the only measure which clearly determines the content and scope of the disputed financial correction'.[91]

Also contributions by the Commission to administrative or judicial proceedings at national level are frequently considered as not reviewable. In *Van Parys*[92] the CFI had the opportunity to decide whether a measure adopted by the Commission in a procedure that ended with a final decision taken by a Member State authority could be a reviewable act. The CFI found that only the competent national authority was entitled under

---

[83] Case T-369/03 *Arizona Chemical and others v Commission* [2005] ECR II-5839, at para. 65, upheld on appeal in Case C-150/06 P *Arizona Chemical and Others v Commission* [2007] ECR I-39*. See also Case T-454/05R *Sumitomo Chemical and Another v Commission* [2006] ECR II-31.

[84] Case T-123/03 *Pfizer v Commission* [2004] ECR II-1631.

[85] [2001] OJ L 311/67.

[86] Ibid., para. 32.

[87] Case C-147/96 *Netherlands v Commission* [2000] ECR I-4723.

[88] [1992] OJ L 268/1.

[89] Ibid., para. 35.

[90] Case C-249/02 *Portugal v Commission* [2004] ECR I-10717.

[91] Ibid., para. 42.

[92] Case T-160/98 *Van Parys and Another v Commission* [2002] ECR II-233.

Article 6(2) of Regulation 1442/93[93] to determine the quantity of bananas to be allocated to each operator. A measure by which the Commission reduced the quantity of bananas marketed by the applicants was therefore 'no more than an intermediary measure forming part of the preparatory work leading to determination, by the national authorities, of the quantity referred to in the second paragraph of Article 6 of Regulation No 1442/93'.[94] The CFI interpreted the reduction by the Commission of the applicants' reference quantity as amounting to 'no more than a proposal'[95] which could be modified by the competent national authority.

Also the commencement of legal proceedings in national courts could not be considered as reviewable act. The CFI ruled in *Philip Morris*[96] that two decisions by the Commission to commence legal proceedings against the applicant before a federal court in the USA could not be considered as reviewable acts. The CFI found that the commencement of legal proceedings was an indispensable step for obtaining a judgment, but did not in itself modify the legal position of the applicants. Such a modification would only result from the final judgment given by the court seized.[97]

A preparatory decision can only be considered as a reviewable act, where it affects the applicant independently from the final decision. In *AKZO*,[98] the Commission opened an investigation against AKZO on a complaint by a competitor that AKZO had violated Article 82. During the procedure against AKZO, the Commission adopted a decision to show documents belonging to AKZO to the complainant. The Court held that this decision had to be considered as a reviewable act, as it affected AKZO's right of confidentiality independently of the final decision, whether or not AKZO had violated Article 82. Were the Court to decide in an action against the final decision that the Commission's decision to show the documents to AKZO's competitor was illegal, the damage to AKZO could not be undone.

Similarly, the Court ruled in *Cimenteries*[99] that a measure by which

---

93 [1993] OJ L142/6.

94 Case T-160/98 *Van Parys and Another v Commission* [2002] ECR II-233, para. 64.

95 Ibid., para. 66.

96 Joined Cases T-377/00, T-379/00, T-380/00, T-260/01 and T-272/01 *Philip Morris and Others v Commission* [2003] ECR II-1, at paras. 79, 97 and 99.

97 Ibid., para. 79. See also Case C-191/95 *Commission v Germany* [1998] ECR I-5449, at para. 47, where the Court pointed out that the commencement of proceedings against a Member State under Article 226 does not *per se* alter the legal position in question.

98 Case 53/85 *AKZO Chemie v Commission* [1986] ECR 1965. See also Case T-198/03 *Bank Austria v Commission* [2006] ECR II-1429, at paras. 34–36; Joined Cases T-125/03 and T-253/03 *Akzo Nobel Chemicals and Another v Commission*, judgment of 17 September 2007.

99 Joined Cases 8 to 11/66 *Cimenteries and others v Commission* [1967] English Special Edition, p. 75.

the Commission notified the undertakings which formed part of the 'Noordwijks Cement Accoord' that the exemption from fines which they had previously enjoyed after notification of their agreement would cease to exist was a reviewable act. The Court found that the effect of the measure was that the undertakings would no longer be protected from fines. Despite its preliminary nature, 'the measure by which the Commission takes a decision in such a case constitutes the culmination of a special procedure which is distinct from the procedure under which [. . .] a decision on the substance of the case can be taken.'[100] The Court emphasised that if the undertakings had to wait until the Commission had reached the final decision, they would be forced either to face 'the risk of a serious threat of a fine or to terminate against their own interests an agreement which, if proceedings had been instituted, might have had a chance of escaping the prohibition.'[101] In such a case the Commission might not proceed to a final decision as it could rely on the mere threat of a fine.

In *Cimenteries*[102] the CFI stated that the Commission's refusal to grant access to the file constituted a reviewable act. The CFI found that 'inasmuch as they unequivocally refuse to allow the undertakings and associations of undertakings to which the statement of objections is addressed the advantage of a protection to which they claim to be entitled under Community law, the contested acts cannot be regarded by this Court as manifestly incapable of producing legal effects and affecting the applicant's interests'.[103]

The Court also held in *Rendo*[104] that 'an institution empowered to find that there has been an infringement and to impose a sanction in respect of it and to which private persons may make complaint, as is the case with the Commission in the field of competition, necessarily adopts a measure producing legal effects when it terminates, wholly or in part an investigation initiated upon a complaint by such a person.'[105] This means that where an individual is entitled to bring a complaint to find an infringement of Articles 81 or 82,[106] the Commission's decision to terminate the investigation is a reviewable act.

---

[100] Ibid., p. 92.

[101] Ibid., p. 92.

[102] Joined Cases T-10/92 R etc. *Cimenteries CBR and others v Commission* [1992] ECR II-1571.

[103] Ibid., para. 54.

[104] Case C-19/93 P *Rendo and Others v Commission* [1995] ECR I-3319.

[105] Ibid., para. 28 overruling thereby in part the judgment of the CFI in Case T-16/91 *Rendo and others v Commission* [1992] ECR II-2147, which had held in para. 61 that part of the Commission's decision did not have legal effects.

[106] The complaint was brought under Regulation 17/62 (OJ, English Special Edition 1959–62, p. 87). However, the reasoning of the Court seems equally applicable to a complaint lodged under Regulation 1/2003, [2003] OJ L1/1, which has replaced Regulation 17/62.

In *Assicurazioni Generali and Unicredito*[107] the CFI found that a decision, in which the Commission held that the agreements notified to it by the applicants did not constitute a concentration within the meaning of Regulation 4064/89,[108] constituted a reviewable act. The CFI held that by finding that the notified joint venture could not be considered as a concentration, the Commission terminated the procedure under Regulation 4064/89 and opened the way for the application of Article 81 under the procedure provided for in Regulation 17/62. The termination of the procedure under Regulation 4064/89 was therefore not merely a preparatory measure, but 'affects the legal position of the applicants by depriving them of the opportunity of having the lawfulness of the operation in question reviewed purely from a structural point of view under the accelerated procedure introduced by Regulation No 4064/89, with a view to securing a definitive decision on compatibility with Community law'.[109]

A similar approach was taken in *Spain v Commission*[110] concerning state aid. The Commission decided to open proceedings under Article 88(2) (ex Article 93(2)) to establish whether aid intended by the Spanish authorities for a group of electrical equipment producers was in accordance with the EC rules on state aid. The Commission took the view that the aid was new aid, which meant that by virtue of Article 88(3) the recipients of the aid were not allowed to receive the aid. The Court decided that such a decision was not merely a preparatory act, as it affected the right of the recipient to receive the aid in question independently of the final decision whether the aid is compatible or not with the common market. The consequences of the delay in paying the subsidy would have irreversible consequences, which could not be eradicated by the final decision.[111]

Provision of Information

Opinions which merely provide the applicant with information do not produce legal effects.[112] In *Italy v Commission*,[113] the Commission had informed the Italian State Agency for Intervention in Agricultural Markets of its position

---

107 Case T-87/96 *Assicurzioni Generali and Unicredito v Commission* [1999] ECR 223.

108 [1990] OJ L 257/14.

109 Ibid., para. 42.

110 Case C-312/90 *Spain v Commission* [1992] ECR I-4117.

111 See also Case C-47/91 *Italy v Commission* [1992] ECR I-4145; Case C-99/98 *Austria v Commission* [2000] ECR I-1101, Opinion of AG Jacobs at para. 44; Case C-400/99 *Italy v Commission* [2001] ECR I-7303 and Joined Cases T-195/01R and T-207/01R *Government of Gibraltar v Commission* [2001] ECR II-3915.

112 See Joined Cases T-3/00 and T-337/04 *Pitsiorlas v Council and ECB*, judgment of 27 November 2007, at para. 61.

113 Case 151/88 *Italy v Commission* [1989] ECR 1255.

on the application of the Community rules on aid for the production of soya beans. The Court considered the Commission's message as mere opinion without legal effects, as 'the application of Community provisions on aid for soya bean production is a matter for the national agencies appointed for that purpose and none of the provisions of the aforesaid regulations adopted in this field confers on the Commission power to adopt decisions on their interpretation; the Commission merely has the possibility, which is always open to it, of expressing an opinion which is not binding on the national authorities'.[114] Similarly, in *Sucrimex and Westzucker v Commission*[115] the Court found that the application of EC provisions on export refunds was a matter for the national authorities. Consequently, when the Commission informed the national authority that there were no grounds for paying the refund in issue, this could not be considered as reviewable act. On the other hand, a legally binding instruction by the Commission to a Member State constitutes a reviewable act.[116] And finally, in *Tillack*,[117] OLAF forwarded to the Belgian authorities information which contained the results of its internal investigation concerning the leak of Commission and OLAF documents implicating the applicant, a reporter, in the payment of money to obtain those documents. As a result the Belgian authorities opened an investigation for breach of professional secrecy, searched the applicant's home and seized numerous documents in his possession. The Court found that the transmission by OLAF was not a reviewable act, as it was not intended 'to have binding legal effects on those to whom it is addressed'.[118]

Internal Rules and Guidelines

Measures which have only internal effects are not considered as having legal effects and are therefore not reviewable. The Court considered the motion in the European Parliament to set up an inquiry as having merely internal effects.[119] Likewise the decision of the European Parliament to hold an urgent debate[120] or the transmission of confidential information

---

[114] Ibid., para. 22. See also Case C-308/95 *Netherlands v Commission* [1999] ECR I-6513, at paras. 27–29; Case T-234/04 *Netherlands v Commission*, judgment of 7 November 2007, at para. 61; Case C-163/06 P *Finland v Commission* [2007] ECR I-5127, at paras. 40–41; Cases T-393/06 R I, T-393/06 R II and T-393/06 R III *Makhteshim-Agan Holding BV and Others v Commission* [2007] ECR II-32*, at para. 40.

[115] Case 133/79 *Sucrimex and Westzucker v Commission* [1980] ECR 1299.

[116] See Case C-46/03 *UK v Commission* [2005] ECR I-10167, at para. 24.

[117] Case C-521/04 P(R) *Tillack v Commission* [2005] ECR I-3103.

[118] Ibid., para. 31. See also Case T-193/04 *Tillack v Commission* [2005] ECR II-3995 and Case T-309/03 *Grau v Commission* [2006] ECR II-1173.

[119] Case 78/85 *Group of the European Right v Parliament* [1988] ECR 1753.

[120] Cases 358/85 and 51/86 *France v Parliament* [1988] ECR 4821 at para. 17.

by the Commission to specific bodies in the European Parliament[121] was held to have only internal effects. On the other hand, the Court found in *Les Verts*[122] that the allocation of appropriations entered in the budget of the EP to cover the cost of preparations for the 1984 elections 'govern the rights and obligations both of political groupings which were already represented in the European Parliament in 1979 and of those which were to take part in the 1984 elections'.[123] As they determine the proportion of the appropriations for each of these groupings, the measures in issue 'were designed to have legal effects vis-à-vis third parties'.[124] Similarly, a measure laid down in the European Parliament's Rules of Procedure that imposes obligations on MEPs concerning internal investigations by OLAF (European Anti-fraud Office) goes beyond the internal organisation of the work of the European Parliament and constitutes a reviewable act.[125]

The Court found in *France v Commission* that in principle internal instructions given by the Commission to its officials have 'effects only within the administration itself and give rise to no rights or obligations on the part of third parties'.[126] The Commission's internal instructions were based on Article 9 of Council Regulation 729/70, which allowed the Commission to exercise supervisory powers with regard to an agricultural fund. The Court found that the Commission in its 'internal instructions' had not merely concretised its powers given under Article 9 of the regulation, but had extended its supervisory powers beyond the scope of that provision. Where the Commission creates new rights and obligations in internal rules without authority, they are subject to review.

Despite these dicta, it is still not clear whether guidelines which do not lay down any rights and obligations for third parties are reviewable acts within the meaning of Article 230(1). In many areas the Commission has laid down guidelines in which it sets out how it intends to exercise its discretion. In particular in the field of antitrust and state aid[127] the Commission has adopted numerous guidelines which are of great

---

121 See Case T-236/00 *Stauner and Others v EP and Commission* [2002] ECR II-135.

122 Case 294/83 *Les Verts v European Parliament* [1986] ECR 1339.

123 Ibid., para. 27.

124 Ibid., para. 27.

125 See Case T-17/00 *Rothley and Others v European Parliament*, [2002] ECR II-579. See also Case T-345/05 R *V v European Parliament* [2007] ECR II-25*, at paras. 45–49, in which the CFI held that the decision to waive the immunity of an MEP was a reviewable act.

126 Case C-366/88 *France v Commission* [1990] ECR I-3571 at para. 9. See also Case C-443/97 *Spain v Commission* [2000] ECR I-2415, at para. 28.

127 See H. Hofmann, 'Administrative governance in state aid policy', in H. Hofmann and A. Türk (eds.) *EU Administrative Governance* (Edward Elgar Publishing, 2006), at pp. 185–214.

importance for individuals and Member States. The Court[128] has confirmed the Commission's competence to adopt such guidelines, as 'such measures reflect the Commission's desire to publish directions on the approach it intends to follow'.[129] The Court found that 'the adoption of such guidelines by the Commission is an instance of the exercise of its discretion and requires only a self-imposed limitation of that power when considering the aids to which the guidelines apply, in accordance with the principle of equal treatment'.[130] Such guidelines must respect the Treaty rules[131] and are not capable of affecting the scope of primary or secondary legislation.[132] The institution is bound by the guidelines it has adopted. The Court, which is not bound by such guidelines,[133] will 'verify whether [. . .] the requirements which the Commission has itself laid down, as mentioned in those guidelines, have been observed'.[134] Where they do not determine rights and obligations of third parties, guidelines seem therefore only capable of internal effects, in that they are binding only on the institution which adopted them. However, the Court has in several judgments cast doubt on this assumption. The Court has allowed certain internal measures to be challenged under Article 241 EC.[135] In *Libéros*[136] the Court recalled this approach by stating that 'although such measures may not be regarded as rules of law which the administration is always bound to observe, they nevertheless form rules of practice from which the administration may not depart without giving the reasons which led it to do so, which must be compatible with the principle of equal treatment.'[137] Similarly, in *Dansk Rørindustri*[138] the Court confirmed this line of reasoning also in relation to the Commission's Guidelines on the calculation of fines under Regulation

---

128 Case C-382/99 *Netherlands v Commission* [2002] ECR I-5163, para. 24. See also Case T-214/95 *Het Vlaamse Gewest v Commission* [1998] ECR II-717, para. 79; Case T-35/99 *Keller and another v Commission* [2002] ECR II-261, para. 77; Case C-310/99 *Italy v Commission* [2002] ECR I-2289, para. 52; Case C-242/00 *Germany v Commission* [2002] ECR I-5603, para. 27.

129 Case T-187/99 *Agrana Zucker und Stärke v Commission* [2001] ECR II-1587, para. 56.

130 Case T-214/95 *Het Vlaamse Gewest v Commission* [1998] ECR II-717, para. 89.

131 Ibid., para. 79; Case C-310/99 *Italy v Commission* [2002] ECR I-2289, para. 52; Case C-382/99 *Netherlands v Commission* [2002] ECR I-5163, para. 24.

132 Case T-187/99 *Agrana Zucker und Stärke v Commission* [2001] ECR II-1587, para. 56.

133 Case C-310/99 *Italy v Commission* [2002] ECR I-2289, para. 52.

134 Case T-35/99 *Keller and another v Commission* [2002] ECR II-261, para. 77.

135 See Case 148/73 *Louwage and another v Commission* [1974] ECR 81, at para. 12; Joined Cases 80 to 83/81 and 182 to 185/82 *Adam and others v Commission* [1984] ECR 3411, at para. 22; Joined Cases 181/86 to 184/86 *Del Plato and others v Commission* [1987] ECR 4991, at para. 10.

136 Case C-171/00 P *Libéros v Commission* [2002] ECR I-451.

137 Ibid., para. 35.

138 Joined Cases C-189/02 P etc. *Dansk Rørindustri and others v Commission* [2005] ECR I-5425.

17/62,[139] which the Court considered as 'rules of conduct designed to produce external effects'.[140] The Court argued that:

> in adopting such rules of conduct and announcing by publishing them that they will hence forth apply to the cases to which they relate, the institution in question imposes a limit on the exercise of its discretion and cannot depart from those rules under pain of being found, where appropriate, to be in breach of the general principles of law, such as equal treatment or the protection of legitimate expectations. It cannot therefore be excluded that, on certain conditions and depending on their conduct, such rules of conduct, which are of general application, may produce legal effects.[141]

The Court further found in *CIRFS*[142] that 'the rules set out in the discipline and accepted by the Member States themselves have the effect, inter alia, of withdrawing from certain aid falling within its scope the authorization previously granted and hence of classifying it as new aid and subjecting it to the obligation of prior notification.'[143] The Court concluded from this that the 'discipline' had binding legal effects.[144] The 'discipline' was contained in a letter sent by the Commission to the Member States in which it stated that the Member States should desist from granting regional aid to the synthetic fibre industry.

Confirmatory Acts

The Court has consistently held that acts that merely confirm previous acts do not have legal effects of their own and are therefore not subject to review.[145] This is particularly relevant in those cases, where an earlier decision, the confirmation of which is sought by the applicant, can no longer be challenged due to the expiry of the time-limit laid down by Article 230(5).

---

[139] Guidelines on the method of setting fines imposed pursuant to Article 15(2) of Regulation No 17 and Article 65 of the ECSC Treaty, [1998] OJ C 9/3.

[140] Joined Cases C-189/02 P etc. *Dansk Rørindustri and others v Commission* [2005] ECR I-5425, para. 210.

[141] Ibid., para. 211. See also Opinion of AG Tizzano, at para. 59.

[142] Case C-313/90 *CIRFS and others v Commission* [1993] ECR I-1125.

[143] Ibid., at para. 35.

[144] Ibid., para. 36. See also Case C-242/00 *Germany v Commission* [2002] ECR I-5603, at para. 35.

[145] Cases 42, 49/59 *SNUPAT v High Authority* [1961] ECR 53 at p 75; Case C-12/90 *Infortec v Commission* [1990] ECR I-4265, at para. 10; Case C-480/93 P *Zunis Holding and others v Commission* [1996] ECR I-1, at para. 14; Case T-235/95 *Goldstein v Commission* [1998] ECR II-523, at para. 42; Joined Cases T-121/96 and T-151/96 *MAAS v Commission* [1997] ECR II-1355, at para. 48; Joined Cases T-83/99 to T-85/99 *Ripa di Meana and others v European Parliament*, order of 26 October 2000 (not published), at para. 33; Case C-521/03 P *Internationaler Hilfsfonds v Commission*, order of 7 December 2004 (not published), at para. 47.

The CFI made it clear in *Cobrecaf*[146] that 'where an applicant lets the time-limit for bringing an action against a decision unequivocally laying down a measure with legal effects affecting his interests and binding on him expire, he cannot start time running again by asking the institution to reconsider its decision and bringing an action against the refusal confirming the decision previously taken'.[147] And in *SIC*[148] the CFI held that in state aid cases 'it is the decision addressed to the Member State which must form the subject-matter of any action for annulment which the complainant may bring, and not the letter to the complainant'.[149] A mere confirmation can also exist where the Community institution merely takes notice of a decision producing legal effects in the Community legal order by a national authority without having any discretion in the matter.[150]

However, a later act which refers to an earlier act can, under certain circumstances, be reviewable. This is the case where the institution approves an act adopted by a person that was not competent to adopt such an act. In the *FAO* case[151] the Court held that the Council's approval of a *COREPER* decision to give the Member States the right to vote within the United Nations Food and Agriculture Organisation (FAO) on an agreement was not merely a confirmation, as *COREPER* had no competence to take such a decision.[152] Similarly, the later act is reviewable if it does not merely confirm an earlier decision, but constitutes a significant amendment[153] or creates new rights and obligations. In *France v Commission*,[154] the Court found that a communication by the Commission did not merely confirm Article 5(2) of Directive 80/723,[155] but that the Commission had added new obligations 'by requiring Member States annually to report to it, on a general, systematic basis, data relating to the financial relations of a particular category of undertaking achieving a specified turnover'.[156]

---

146 Case T-514/93 *Cobrecaf v Commission* [1995] ECR II-621.

147 Ibid., para. 44. See also Case T-35/00 *Goldstein v Commission* [2000] ECR II-2917, at para. 10; Case T-186/98 *Inpesca v Commission* [2001] ECR II-557, at para. 44.

148 In Case T-46/97 *SIC v Commission* [2000] ECR II-2125.

149 Ibid., para. 45.

150 See Case C-208/03 P *Le Pen v EP* [2005] ECR I-6051, in which the EP took notice of the French government's declaration that Jean-Marie Le Pen was barred from holding office as MEP.

151 Case C-25/94 *Commission v Council* [1996] ECR I-1469.

152 Ibid., para. 28.

153 See Case C-299/05 *Commission v Parliament and Council* [2007] ECR I-8695, at para. 32.

154 Case C-325/91 *France v Commission* [1993] ECR I-3283.

155 [1980] OJ L 195/35.

156 Case C-325/91 *France v Commission* [1993] ECR I-3283, para. 22. See also Case C-303/90 *France v Commission* [1991] ECR I-5315, the Court found at para. 24 that a Code adopted by the Commission went beyond Article 23(1) of Regulation 4253/88 ([1988] OJ

In *Ca'Pasta*[157] the Commission had granted the applicant financial aid under Regulation 4028/86 for a project for the modernisation of an aquaculture unit in Italy. As the applicant had sold its business without the Commission's consent, the Commission informed the applicant in June 1997 of its intention to initiate the procedure for the discontinuance of the aid and also the recovery of the first instalment it had already paid. In response to submissions by the applicant, the Commission confirmed the continuation of the procedure for discontinuing the aid and the recovering of the first instalment. The CFI had come to the conclusion that the measures taken by the Commission were merely preliminary in nature and therefore not reviewable. On appeal the AG supported the CFI's judgment and found it appropriate 'in cases such as the present one that only definitive decisions can be subject to judicial review, and not intermediate or preparatory decisions. Moreover, in the present case it might well be thought that there was not even an intermediate decision, but only the provision of information that a procedure was being continued which was liable to result in a decision.'[158] All the same, the Court found on appeal that the Commission's letter of August 1997 was not just a confirmation of the continuance of the procedure for discontinuing the aid, but amounted to an implied decision to suspend the aid in question. The Court argued that this suspension affected the applicant's legal position.[159]

Also where the new act contains a new factor, the Community Courts will consider it as reviewable act.[160] In *Lestelle*[161] the CFI found that the payment notice of 25 January 1969, which the applicant had received from the Commission's Pension Department, constituted not merely a confirmation of earlier salary statements, as it contained for the first time the Commission's opinion that the applicant's pension contributions were compulsory rather than optional. The payment notice of 25 January therefore constituted a new factor.[162]

L374/1) 'by imposing on Member States specific obligations concerning the content of the information to be provided to the Commission and the frequency and means of communicating it'. Similarly, in Case C-57/95 *France v Commission* [1997] ECR I-1627, the Commission sought to introduce by way of a communication obligations which were contained in a proposal for a Directive on pension funds, which the Commission had to withdraw because of a deadlock in Council. The Court found that these obligations went beyond a mere confirmation of certain Treaty freedoms.

157 Case C-359/98P *Ca'Pasta v Commission* [2000] ECR I-3977.

158 Ibid., Opinion of AG Jacobs, para. 19.

159 Ibid., at paras. 30–32.

160 See Case 24/69 *Nebe v Commission* [1970] ECR 145, at para. 8; Case 33/72 *Gunella v Commission* [1973] ECR 475, at para. 10; Case 23/80 *Gresselli v Commission* [1980] ECR 3709, at para. 18.

161 Case T-4/90 *Lestelle v Commission* [1990] ECR II-689.

162 Ibid., at para. 25.

A later act can also have legal effects, where a fundamental change in the circumstances after the first act has been adopted takes place.[163] In the *ERTA* case[164] the Court found that 'the proceedings of 20 March 1970, however, cannot be regarded as simply a confirmation of previous discussions, since Regulation No 543/69 of 25 March 1969 brought about a decisive change in the allocation of powers between the Community and the Member States on the subject-matter of the negotiations.'[165] Similarly, where the institution reconsiders its position due to substantial new facts, the later act would be reviewable, as it contains a new factor. In *Inpesca*[166] the CFI had to decide whether the rejection of a request for financial aid was merely the confirmation of an earlier rejection or constituted a reviewable act. Council Regulation 4028/86[167] provided a system for improving structures in the fisheries sector by authorising the Commission to distribute grants to provide financial aid for investments relating to the purchase and construction of new fishing vessels. If the aid was rejected in one year due to lack of funds, the applicant could apply once more in the next year. In 1989, the applicants applied to the Commission for a grant in 1990, which was rejected due to lack of funds and was carried forward to 1991, when it was again rejected for the same reason. The applicant brought an action against the Commission decisions, which was rejected as inadmissible, as it was brought after the time limit under Article 230(5) had expired. In 1994, the Commission adopted decisions against some companies to repay a grant provided for them by the Commission. The CFI rejected challenges against those decisions in 1996. In 1998 the applicant requested that as the grants repaid by these companies made funds available, the Commission should grant it financial assistance. As the Commission rejected this, the applicants brought the action in issue. After recalling that a merely confirmatory decision was not a reviewable act, the CFI held that 'if the measure constitutes the reply to a request in which substantial new facts are relied on, and whereby the administration is requested to reconsider its previous decision, that measure cannot be regarded as merely confirmatory in nature, since it constitutes a decision taken on the basis of those facts and thus contains a new factor as compared with the previous decision.'[168] For a fact to be new 'it is essential that neither the applicant nor the administration was aware

163 See Cases 42, 49/59 *SNUPAT v High Authority* [1961] ECR 53 at p. 76.
164 Case 22/70 *Commission v Council* [1971] ECR 263.
165 Ibid., para. 66.
166 Case T-186/98 *Inpesca v Commission* [2001] ECR II-557.
167 [1986] OJ L 376/7.
168 Case T-186/98 *Inpesca v Commission* [2001] ECR II-557, at para. 46.

of, or in a position to be aware of, the fact in question when the previous decision was adopted.'[169] This is mainly the case where the fact comes to light after the earlier decision has been taken. The fact is substantial if it is 'capable of substantially altering the applicant's situation forming the basis of the initial request which gave rise to the previous decision'.[170] In the case in hand the CFI found that none of the factors cited by the applicant could be considered as substantially new facts. The CFI rejected as irrelevant a Commission proposal for a regulation, as 'a preparatory measure which has not yet become definitive, cannot alter the applicant's situation'.[171] Equally unsuccessful was the applicant's attempt to rely on new judgments, as 'a judgment given by the Court of First Instance and containing a legal determination in relation to facts which might be categorised as new could never, by itself, constitute a new fact'.[172] Finally, the recovery of financial aid by the Commission relating to the year in which the applicant made his request was not helpful for the applicant for budgetary reasons.[173]

However, it is clear from the case law that an act adopted after the reconsideration by the institution, even in the absence of any new factors, might be considered as reviewable.[174] In *IPK-München*[175] the Commission had refused to pay the balance of the aid which it had granted to the applicant. All the same the Commission subsequently arranged a meeting to explain its refusal. The CFI considered this step as a reconsideration of its earlier measure. Crucially, the CFI found that 'that meeting did not reveal any new information and was not such as to prompt the Commission to adopt a different position'.[176] All the same, the fact that a meeting was held to discuss the same issues as those already dealt with meant that the initial refusal 'did not definitively close the administrative procedure'.[177] This also helps one to understand the misleading formula that 'a decision is a mere confirmation of an earlier decision where it contains no new factors as compared with the earlier measure and is not preceded by any

---

169 Ibid., para. 50.
170 Ibid., para. 51.
171 Ibid., para. 58.
172 Ibid., para. 62.
173 Ibid., paras. 65–69.
174 See Case 54/77 *Herpels v Commission* [1978] ECR 585, at paras. 13 and 14; Case 44/81 *Germany v Commission* [1982] ECR 1855, at paras. 8–12.
175 Case T-331/94 *IPK-München v Commission* [1997] ECR II-1665. The appeal in Case 433/97 P *IPK v Commission* [1999] ECR I-6795, did not concern the admissibility of the action, see Case T-331/94 *IPK v Commission* [2001] II-779, at para. 32.
176 Case T-331/94 *IPK-München v Commission* [1997] ECR II-1665, para. 26.
177 Ibid., para. 26.

re-examination of the situation of the addressee of the earlier measure'.[178] The case-law suggests that the two elements in the formula (new factor and reconsideration) should be understood as alternative rather than cumulative conditions for a later act to be considered as reviewable.

A fundamental change might also result from a judgment of the Court, which might oblige the institution to reconsider its first act.[179] In *SNUPAT*[180] the applicant had challenged before the Court the refusal by the High Authority to grant it an exemption from the equalisation levy on ferrous scrap on the ground that the scrap it had bought from Renault should be considered as coming from 'own resources'. The Court[181] rejected the applicant's interpretation of 'own resources' and ruled that 'group scrap' was also subject to the equalisation levy. This prompted the applicant to request the High Authority to withdraw the exemptions the latter had granted to two companies from paying contributions to the equalisation scheme. When the High Authority failed to comply the applicant challenged this implied decision of refusal under Article 35 ECSC. The Court rejected the argument that the refusal by the High Authority amounted to a mere confirmation of its earlier decisions to grant the exemptions. It found that the Court's earlier judgment 'showed the exemptions in a new light; this should have led, after a fresh examination of their legal basis, to a decision concerning their legality.'[182] The Court found that 'the High Authority's refusal to withdraw the exemptions, far from simply confirming its previous point of view, therefore contains the implied decision that the judgment of the Court does not require a different attitude and that the considerations which, in the Court's opinion, prevent the exemption of group scrap do not cover the case of local integration.'[183] This approach was also invoked in *AssiDomän*,[184] where the Commission had adopted a first decision against several companies on the ground that they had infringed Article 81(1) and had imposed fines on those companies. Some, though not all, companies made a successful application for annulment of that decision to the Court. The Court also annulled the fines imposed on those applicants. Subsequently, the companies who had not made an application to the Court requested the Commission to review their case and

---

[178] Ibid., para. 24. See also Case T-84/97 *BEUC v Commission* [1998] ECR II-795, para. 52 and Case T-235/95 *Goldstein v Commission* [1998] ECR II-523, at para. 42.

[179] Cases 42, 49/59 *SNUPAT v High Authority* [1961] ECR 53 at p 76. See in this context Case C-332/98 *France v Commission*, [2000] ECR I-4833.

[180] Cases 42, 49/59 *SNUPAT v High Authority* [1961] ECR 53.

[181] Joined Cases 32/58 and 33/58 *SNUPAT v High Authority* [1959] ECR 127.

[182] Cases 42, 49/59 *SNUPAT v High Authority* [1961] ECR 53, at p. 79.

[183] Ibid., p. 79.

[184] Case T-227/95 *AssiDomän v Commission* [1997] ECR II-1185.

return the fines imposed on them. As the Commission confirmed its earlier position and rejected the request, those companies applied to the CFI for annulment of the second decision of the Commission. The CFI took the view that a confirmation of an earlier decision could not be regarded as a reviewable act. However, the second decision of the Commission had to be regarded as a new, and therefore reviewable, decision, as Article 233[185] required the Commission to review its earlier decision in the light of the annulment of that decision. The later decision would then have been adopted 'in a new legal context'[186] compared with the earlier decision. The CFI's judgment was, however, overturned on appeal by the Court of Justice.[187] The ECJ held that in such a situation the principle of legal certainty precluded any necessity for the institution that adopted the decisions to re-examine them at the request of other addressees which had not challenged the acts. In other words, where an addressee of a decision does not challenge the decision within the time limit laid down in Article 230(5), this decision is binding on the addressee and it is irrelevant that the decision had been annulled by the Court with regard to other addressees.

Expression of Future Conduct

Where the institution makes a statement as to its future conduct, one could argue that this should be considered as a preparatory measure and not be reviewable. The case law is not entirely clear on this point. Earlier decisions indicate that the Court considers such statements as reviewable, where the institution 'unequivocally determined the attitude which it had decided to take'[188] or where it 'makes sufficiently clear'[189] the action it intends to take. A vacancy notice given under Article 29(1)(a) of the Staff Regulations has been considered as reviewable act 'insofar as the effect of those conditions is to rule out the candidature of officials who are eligible for transfer or promotion'.[190]

This contrasts with the position taken by the Court in *United Kingdom v Commission.*[191] The Commission announced that it would (again) take

---

185 See infra, pp. 155–164.

186 Case T-227/95 *AssiDomän v Commission* [1997] ECR II-1185 at para. 33.

187 Case C-310/97P *Commission v AssiDomän and Others* [1999] ECR I-5363.

188 Case 8/55 *Fédération Charbonière Belgique v High Authority* [1956] ECR 245 at p. 257.

189 Joined Cases 7/56 and 3 to 7/57 *Algera v Common Assembly* [1957] ECR 39 at p. 54.

190 Case 25/77 *De Roubaix v Commission* [1978] ECR 1081, para. 8. See also Case 15/63 *Lassalle v European Parliament* [1964] ECR 31 and Case 79/74 *Küster v European Parliament* [1975] ECR 725, at paras. 5–7.

191 Case 114/86 *United Kingdom v Commission* [1988] ECR 5289.

into account the nationality of candidates for drawing up a short list for the award of service contracts under the Second Lomé Convention. The Court found that an action against the announcement was inadmissible, as it was not 'the announcement of that intention but the drawing-up of the lists themselves which is capable of having legal effect'.[192] This case might, however, be distinguished from the earlier judgments of the Court on the ground that the Commission's list and the final allocation of service contracts did not entirely correspond with the announced intention of considering the nationality of the candidates. It could therefore be said that the Commission's intention did not unequivocally determine its future attitude. Similarly in *United Kingdom v Commission*[193] the Court found that 'an act of the Commission which reflects its intention, or that of one of its departments, to follow a particular line of conduct'[194] could not be considered as having legal effects. The Court therefore regarded various statements by the Commission made in relation to the export ban on British beef as not reviewable.

International Agreements

In 1991, the Commission and the government of the USA signed an agreement with regard to the application of their competition laws. France brought an action against the agreement. The Commission argued that only the decision of the Commission to authorise one of its members to sign the agreement could be reviewed under Article 230, but not the agreement itself. The Court decided that 'the act whereby the Commission sought to conclude the Agreement must be susceptible to an action for annulment'.[195] This means that it is not the international agreement that can be challenged but the act adopted by an EC institution to authorise its conclusion.[196]

Non-existent Acts

Where acts adopted by an EC institution have such serious defects that they will be considered as non-existent, an action under Article 230 to have such acts declared void will be declared as inadmissible by the Court,

---

[192] Ibid., at para. 13. See also Case T-212/99 *Intervet International BV v Commission* [2002] ECR II-1445.

[193] Case C-180/96 *United Kingdom v Commission* [1998] ECR I-2265.

[194] Ibid., para. 28. See also Case T-0554/93 *Saint and Another v Council and Commission* [1997] ECR II-563, at para. 43.

[195] Case C-327/91 *France v Commission* [1994] ECR I-3641.

[196] See also Case C-122/95 *Germany v Council* [1998] ECR I-973.

as such acts do not produce any legal effects whatever.[197] However, such a finding reflects the outcome of a balancing of two, often conflicting, principles, namely that of legal certainty, which presumes the existence of an act, and that of legality, which seeks the removal of unlawful acts.

In *Société usines à tubes de la Sarre*,[198] the Court held that the statement of reasons for an opinion was 'an essential, indeed constituent element of such an act, with the result that in the absence of a statement of reasons the act cannot exist.'[199] However, in later cases the Court abandoned this position.[200] In *Lemmerz-Werke*[201] the Court found that 'any measure, therefore, which in particular, does not appear to have been debated and adopted by the High Authority and authenticated by the signature of one of its members, cannot be regarded as a decision'.[202] In *Commission v France*,[203] the Court seemed to have indicated that if a matter fell within the exclusive jurisdiction of the Member States the Community act was non-existent, as the decision 'would lack all legal basis in the Community legal system'.[204] In *Schots*,[205] the Court refused to accept that the regulation in issue was non-existent, as it was adopted by 'the competent authority and taken with due regard to the procedural and formal conditions laid down by the Treaty'.[206]

In *Consorzio Cooperative d'Abruzzo*[207] the Court discussed the concept of non-existent acts in greater detail. The Court pointed out that 'an administrative measure, even though it may be irregular, is presumed to be valid until it has been properly repealed or withdrawn by the institution which adopted it.'[208] Where an act is, however, non-existent, the absence of any legal effects can be found by the Court at any time. The Court made it clear that the classification of an act as non-existent had to be limited, in the interest of legal certainty, 'to measures which exhibit particularly serious and manifest defects'.[209] The Court found that the alleged irregularities of the

---

[197] See T.C. Hartley, supra note 1, p. 335.

[198] Joined Cases 1/57 and 14/57 *Société des usines à tubes de la Sarre v High Authority* [1957] ECR 105.

[199] Ibid., p. 112.

[200] See T.C. Hartley, supra note 1, p. 336.

[201] See Cases 53, 54/63 *Lemmerz-Werke v High Authority* [1963] ECR 239. This does not necessarily mean that the applicant has to pay the costs for the proceedings.

[202] Ibid, p. 248.

[203] Joined Cases 6 and 11/69 *Commission v France* [1969] ECR 523.

[204] Ibid., para. 13.

[205] Joined cases 15/73 etc. *Schots and others v Council, Commission and European Parliament* [1974] ECR 177.

[206] Ibid., para. 33.

[207] Case 15/85 *Consorzio Cooperative d'Abruzzo v Commission* [1987] ECR 1005.

[208] Ibid., para. 10.

[209] Ibid., para. 10. See also Case 226/87 *Commission v Greece* [1988] ECR 3611, at para. 16.

decision in issue were not manifest, as they could not be detected by reading the decision. One of these irregularities concerned the alleged breach of internal rules, the other consisted in the discrepancy between the draft decision submitted to the management committee and the decision finally adopted. In *Mordt*[210] the CFI emphasised the exceptional nature of the finding of non-existence by holding that 'the irregularity must be so gross and so obvious that it goes far beyond a "normal" irregularity resulting from an erroneous assessment of the facts or from a breach of the law'.[211]

What constitutes such a serious defect is, however, not entirely clear. In *Commission v BASF*[212] the CFI found a measure in which the Commission had found an infringement of Article 81 by various companies operating in the PVC market to be non-existent. As the Commission could not produce a copy of the original measure which was authenticated in accordance with the Commission's rules of procedure, the CFI found that it was not possible to specify the date when the measures were adopted, nor their precise and certain content and consequently even the authority which adopted the measures in their final version.[213] The CFI held that 'such a measure is vitiated by particularly serious and manifest defects rendering it non-existent in law.'[214] However, the Court[215] reversed that decision on appeal. The Court pointed out that 'acts tainted by irregularity whose gravity is so obvious that it cannot be tolerated by the Community legal order must be treated as having no legal effect, even provisional, that is to say that they must be regarded as legally non-existent.'[216] The Court made it clear that the purpose of this exception was to find a proper balance between the, sometimes conflicting, principles of the stability of legal relations and the respect for legality. However, the Court stated that the finding of the non-existence of a Community act was the exception by making it clear that 'from the gravity of the consequences attaching to a finding that an act of a Community institution is non-existent it is self-evident that, for reasons of legal certainty, such a finding is reserved for quite extreme situations.'[217] In the case in issue, the Court held that the Commission's minutes showed that the Commission had adopted the operative part of the decision 'whatever defects may have affected that decision'.[218] The Court therefore held

---

210 Case T-156/89 *Mordt v Court of Justice* [1991] ECR II-407.
211 Ibid., at para. 84.
212 Joined Cases T-79/89 etc. *BASF and others v Commission* [1992] ECR II-315.
213 Ibid., at paras. 93–95.
214 Ibid., para. 96.
215 Case C-137/92P *Commission v BASF* [1994] ECR I-2555.
216 Ibid., para. 49.
217 Ibid., para. 50.
218 Ibid., para. 51.

that the irregularities which the CFI had noted 'do not appear to be of such gravity that the decision must be treated as legally non-existent.'[219]

Where an act is declared non-existent the Community Courts will dismiss the action as inadmissible. This does, however, not mean that the applicant will have to pay the costs. In this case the Community Courts will impose the costs on the institution whose act was declared non-existent.

Impact on Legal Position

The Community Courts have made it clear that an act is reviewable only if it brings about a change in the applicant's legal position. However, the case-law is not entirely consistent on this point. In *STS*[220] the applicant challenged the Commission's approval of public works contracts to be financed out of resources provided by the fifth European Development Fund. The Court found that the measures which the Commission's representative adopted during the procedure for the award of the contracts, 'whether approvals or refusals to approve, endorsements or refusals to endorse',[221] were merely determinations as to whether or not the conditions for Community financing were met. On the other hand, the Court pointed out that 'the contracts in question remain national contracts which the ACP states alone are responsible for preparing, negotiating and concluding'.[222] The companies which participated in the tendering process are not involved in the relationship between the Commission and the ACP states and 'have legal relations only with the ACP state which is responsible for the contract, and measures adopted by the representatives of the Commission cannot substitute in relation to them a Community decision for the decision of the ACP state, which has sole power to conclude and sign the contract.'[223] Even though the Court concluded from this assessment that the applicant was not directly concerned by the act, it is clear from its reasoning that the act did not affect the legal position of the applicant and arguably was not even a reviewable act. This was at least the conclusion which the CFI later drew in *Geotronics*.[224] The case concerned the Commission's rejection of the applicant's tender for the supply of electronic tacheometers to the Romanian ministry of agriculture to be financed under the PHARE programme on the basis that it had not fulfilled the conditions applicable to the tender.

---

219 Ibid., para. 52.

220 Case 126/83 STS *Consorzio per Sistemi di Telecomunicazione via Satellite v Commission* [1984] ECR 2769.

221 Ibid., para. 16.

222 Ibid., para. 16.

223 Ibid., para. 18.

224 Case T-185/94 *Geotronics v Commission* [1995] ECR II-2795.

Following the reasoning of the Court in *STS*, the CFI found that the rejection was not a reviewable act as 'no legal relationship arises between the tenderers and the Commission, since the latter restricts itself to taking funding decisions on behalf of the Community, and its measures cannot have the effect, in relation to tenderers, of substituting a Community decision for the decision of the beneficiary country under the PHARE programme'.[225] However, on appeal the ECJ[226] reversed the CFI's judgment. Interestingly, the Court defined reviewable acts as 'acts or decisions which have binding legal effects such as to affect the interests of the applicant'[227] thereby leaving out the usual requirement that the act had to change the applicant's legal position. The Court held that the reasoning employed in *STS* could not be applied in the present case. The Commission's decision could be severed from the contractual procedure 'inasmuch as, first, it was adopted by the Commission in the exercise of its own powers and, secondly, it was specifically directed at an individual undertaking, which lost any chance of actually being awarded the contract simply because that act was adopted'.[228] It is difficult to see how the reasoning employed by the Court in *Geotronics* could leave its earlier ruling in *STS* intact, as the latter included refusals to approve the contract in the list of Commission measures that did not affect the relationship between applicant and national authority. Moreover, the Court in *Geotronics* quite conspicuously avoided discussing how the Commission's decision affected the applicant's legal position.

Similar problems arise in state aid and merger proceedings. In state aid cases, even though usually they do not discuss the issue of reviewable act in cases of a Commission decision affecting the beneficiary of state aid, the Community Courts seem to consider the beneficiary's legal position affected. This is clear in *Mitteldeutsche Erdoel-Raffinerie*,[229] where the CFI, in the context of discussing whether the applicant was directly concerned, found that the Commission's decision obliged Germany to amend its law with the effect that the deadline for the completion of investment projects in East Germany qualifying for a premium was brought forward by two years. As a result Germany had to recover the premium from investors, such as the applicant, who had not completed the projects within the modified deadline. The CFI therefore held that 'the legal position of the applicant was directly affected by the contested decision'.[230]

---

225 Ibid., para. 32.
226 Case C-395/95 P *Geotronics v Commission* [1997] ECR I-2271.
227 Ibid., para. 10.
228 Ibid., para. 14.
229 Case T-9/98 *Mitteldeutsche Erdoel-Raffinerie v Commission* [2001] ECR II-3367.
230 Ibid., para. 52.

On the other hand, it is doubtful whether competitors of an undertaking benefiting from state aid are affected in their legal position by a Commission decision concerning such aid, which is addressed to the Member State which granted the aid. In *Cofaz*[231] the Commission adopted a decision declaring the tariff structure for national gas prices in the Netherlands compatible with the Common Market. The decision produced legal effects for the Netherlands, as it allowed the latter to apply a preferential tariff system to Dutch producers of nitrate fertilizers for the supply of natural gas intended for the manufacture of ammonia. It is, however, difficult to see how the Commission's decision could affect the legal position of the applicants, which as the French producers of nitrate fertilizers seemed to be affected only in their competitive situation.[232] It seems that in state aid cases brought by competitors the Court does not apply the requirement that the applicant's legal position be affected and instead focuses its attention on direct and individual concern,[233] which seems to be concerned mainly with procedural and economic considerations.[234]

Similarly, in merger cases, while the parties to the merger as addressees of the Commission decision are undoubtedly affected in their legal position, the situation is less clear for competitors. In *Air France*[235] the CFI found admissible the applicant's action against the Commission's decision which declared that the merger between British Airways and TAT posed no serious competition concerns. The CFI did not raise the issue of whether the decision changed the applicant's legal position. The CFI found that it was common ground that the applicant was directly concerned and highlighted the applicant's procedural involvement and the impact of the decision on its competitive situation as sufficient to find the applicant to be individually concerned.[236] In *BaByliss*[237] the CFI stated that the Commission's decision which declared the merger between SEB and Moulinex compatible with the common market brought about 'an immediate change in the situation in the markets concerned'.[238] This reference to the economic impact of the measures falls short of the requirement that the act affects the legal

---

231 Case 169/84 *Cofaz and others v Commission* [1986] ECR 391.

232 The Commission expressly raised this point in para. 13 of the judgment, ibid.

233 See Case T-380/94 *AIUFFASS and another v Commission* [1996] ECR II-2169, at paras. 44–52; Case T-442/93 *AAC and others v Commission* [1995] ECR II-1329, at paras. 44–53; Case T-149/95 *Ducros v Commission* [1997] ECR II-2031, at paras. 32–42.

234 For a more detailed discussion on individual concern in state aid cases, see infra, pp. 82–85.

235 Case T-2/93 *Air France v Commission* [1994] ECR II-323.

236 Ibid., at paras. 40–48.

237 Case T-114/02 *BaByliss v Commission* [2003] ECR II-1279.

238 Ibid., para. 89 with a reference to para. 80 of *Air France*, supra. See also Case T-158/00 *ARD v Commission* [2003] ECR II-3825, at para. 60.

situation of the applicant, which as competitor of the merging undertakings was merely affected in its competitive position on the market.

3. *LOCUS STANDI* OF PRIVILEGED AND SEMI-PRIVILEGED APPLICANTS

The right to bring an action, usually referred to as *locus standi*, is not the same for all applicants in Article 230. Three groups of applicants can be distinguished: privileged applicants face no standing restrictions, semi-privileged applicants need to demonstrate that the action is intended to protect their prerogatives, and non-privileged applicants have to show that, unless a decision is addressed to them, they are directly and individually concerned by a Community act. This section will discuss standing of privileged and semi-privileged applicants, while the next section will consider the standing requirements of private parties.

Privileged Applicants

Privileged applicants are the Member States,[239] the Council, the Commission and the European Parliament. These applicants can – within the time limit laid down in Article 230(5) – bring an action for annulment against any reviewable act before the Court without having to show any interest in the case. Problems of *locus standi* do not arise for such applicants.

The European Parliament (EP) did not have any right to bring an action under the original Rome Treaties. As the EP had few rights that could be infringed this was not considered necessary. However, when its powers increased, the EP could not bring an action to prevent other institutions from infringing these rights. This position was confirmed by the Court in the *Comitology* case.[240] In a dramatic change of heart the Court reversed this ruling in the *Chernobyl* case,[241] where it held – against the wording

---

[239] The Court has given the concept of Member State a narrow interpretation in that it 'only applies to the government authorities of the Member States of the European Communities and cannot be extended to regional governments or self-governing communities, regardless of the extent of their powers', see Joined Cases T-32/98 and T-41/98 *Netherlands Antilles v Commission* [2000] ECR II-201, at para. 43. See also Joined Cases T-132/96 and T-143/96 *Freistaat Sachsen v Commission* [1999] ECR II-3663, at para. 73, where the CFI found that the status of 'Land' under the German Constitution was not sufficient for being considered as privileged applicant. For a critique of this approach, see J. Wakefield, 'The plight of the regions in a multi-layered Europe' (2005) *ELRev* 406–419 and A. Arnull (2001), supra note 2, at pp. 10–14.

[240] Case 302/87 *European Parliament v Council* [1988] ECR 5615.

[241] Case C-70/88 *European Parliament v Council* [1990] ECR I-2041.

of Article 146 Euratom[242] – that the EP could bring an action, however, only to safeguard its prerogatives. This was confirmed by the Maastricht Treaty in Article 230(3) EC. The Nice Treaty finally conferred the status of privileged applicant on the EP, mainly in recognition of its enhanced institutional position.

Semi-privileged Applicants

Initially, this category of applicants did not exist. It only came about through the Court's ruling in the *Chernobyl*[243] case, which granted the EP the right to bring an action, but only to protect its prerogatives. The Court did not take this route easily, but had to acknowledge in the end that the arguments that it had presented in the *Comitology*[244] case were less than convincing. The Court had concluded there that Article 230(1) could not be interpreted as granting the EP a right to bring an annulment action.[245] After recalling the EP's political, budgetary and legislative powers, the Court refused to accept that 'because it is entitled to have a failure to act established[246] and to intervene in proceedings before the Court, the Parliament must be recognized as having the possibility of bringing actions for annulment'.[247] The Court denied the existence of a link between the action for annulment and that for failure to act, as the latter could be used to request measures which could not in all cases be challenged in an annulment action. The Court also added that a 'refusal to act, however explicit it may be, can be brought before the Court under Article 175 [now 232] since it does not put an end to the failure to act.'[248] This view was, however, controversial at the time and has never been referred to since by the Court in Article 232 cases.[249] The Court also saw no connection between the EP's intervention right before the Court and an action for annulment. The Court went on to refute a link between the EP's passive capacity, which the Court had established in *Les Verts*,[250] and its active capacity in annulment actions. Finally, the Court did not accept the EP's argument that without being able to bring an action for annulment it would be left

242 Article 146 Euratom is identical with Article 230 EC.

243 Case C-70/88 *European Parliament v Council* [1990] ECR I-2041.

244 Case 302/87 *European Parliament v Council* [1988] ECR 5615.

245 The Court also discussed whether the EP could bring an action as non-privileged applicant under Article 173(2) [now 230(4)] but found in para. 10 that this provision 'would be inappropriate to an action by the European Parliament for annulment'.

246 Under Article 175, which is now Article 232.

247 Case 302/87 *European Parliament v Council* [1988] ECR 5615, para. 15.

248 Ibid., para. 17.

249 See Chapter 2.

250 Case 294/83 *Parti écologiste 'Les Verts' v European Parliament* [1986] ECR 1339.

without remedy to defend its prerogatives. The Court pointed out that the EC Treaty did not grant the EP such a right despite having provided it with certain, limited, powers to participate in the legislative process. The Single European Act did not alter that position, despite an increase in the EP's legislative powers. The Court found that even though it could not itself defend its prerogatives, other applicants could do so. An annulment action to protect the EP's prerogatives was open to the Member States, the Commission, for which the Court even created a responsibility in that respect, and individuals. And also national courts could refer a Community act allegedly infringing the EP's prerogatives under Article 234.

As clearly as the position taken by the Court in *Comitology* was defensible on the ground of a strictly textual interpretation of Article 230, some of the legal arguments invoked were more than questionable. More importantly, the support from other parties, which the Court so promisingly held out to the EP, proved illusory already in the very next case presented by the EP. Ultimately, the *Comitology* ruling amounted to a *déni de justice* by the Court. And indeed the *Comitology* ruling was short-lived, as the Court took the opportunity to reverse the decision in the *Chernobyl* case, which had already been lodged even before the *Comitology* judgment was delivered. In the *Chernobyl* case[251] the Court admitted that the alternative routes for the protection of the EP's prerogatives were not workable. The Court held that 'the existence of those various legal remedies is not sufficient to guarantee, with certainty and in all circumstances, that a measure adopted by the Council or the Commission in disregard of the Parliament's prerogatives will be reviewed.'[252] As clear as it was that the *Comitology* decision was untenable in terms of judicial policy, given the textual silence, which was clearly by no means an accidental omission, in Article 173 [now 230], it was difficult to find a convincing legal basis for including the EP amongst those with active capacity to bring an action for annulment. The Court argued that the EP's prerogatives formed part of the institutional balance set up by the Community Treaties. Each institution had to respect this balance and should be penalised for a breach of it. The Court found that, as it was its task to ensure that the law was observed in the interpretation and application of the Treaties, it had to be able to maintain the institutional balance and 'review the observance of the Parliament's prerogatives when called upon to do so by the Parliament, by means of a legal remedy which is suited to the purpose which the Parliament seeks to achieve.'[253] The Court made it clear that this did not mean that the EP could be included

---

[251] Case C-70/88 *European Parliament v Council* [1990] ECR I-2041.
[252] Ibid., para. 20.
[253] Ibid., para. 23.

amongst the privileged applicants. On the other hand, observance of the institutional balance required that the EP be granted a remedy, 'which may be exercised in a certain and effective manner'.[254] The Court therefore decided that 'an action for annulment brought by the Parliament against an act of the Council or the Commission is admissible provided that the action seeks only to safeguard its prerogatives and that it is founded only on submissions alleging their infringement.'[255] The Court acknowledged that the absence of the right for the EP in the Treaties constituted a procedural gap, but was adamant that such a gap 'cannot prevail over the fundamental interest in the maintenance and observance of the institutional balance laid down in the Treaties establishing the European Communities'.[256]

The Maastricht Treaty formally acknowledged the Court's position by providing the EP with the right to bring an action for annulment for the protection of its prerogatives. A third paragraph was inserted in Article 173 [now 230], which gave the same right to the European Central Bank. The Court of Auditors joined the club of semi-privileged applicants in the Treaty of Amsterdam. After the Treaty of Nice when the EP was finally upgraded to a privileged applicant, the third paragraph of Article 230 now comprises the European Central Bank and the Court of Auditors as semi-privileged applicants. It is interesting to note that the Committee of the Regions and the Social and Economic Committee are not included in Article 230(3) despite the fact that both are given certain rights to participate in the legislative process. On the basis of the Court's dictum in *Chernobyl* this seems hardly justifiable.

The Court's case-law on the protection of the prerogative as condition of standing of semi-privileged applicants has so far exclusively concerned actions brought by the EP while it was still a semi-privileged applicant.[257] The rationale of these rulings can, however, also be applied for actions by the Court of Auditors and the ECB.

The Court considered an action by the EP as admissible, where 'the Parliament indicated in an appropriate manner the substance of the prerogative to be safeguarded and how that prerogative is allegedly infringed'.[258] The Court found that the EP's prerogatives include 'participation in the

---

254 Ibid., para. 25.

255 Ibid., para. 27.

256 Ibid., para. 26.

257 It is interesting to note that to date neither the Court of Auditors nor the European Central Bank have brought an action under Article 230(3).

258 Case C-316/91 *Parliament v Council* [1994] ECR 625 at para. 13. See also Case C-156/93 *European Parliament v Commission* [1995] ECR I-2019, para. 10; Case C-303/94 *European Parliament v Council* [1996] ECR I-2943, para. 17; Case C-189/97 *European Parliament v Council* [1999] ECR I-4741, para. 13.

drafting of legislative measures'.[259] This means that the right to be consulted in accordance with a provision of the Treaty is a prerogative of the EP.[260] Consequently, its prerogative was liable to be infringed where the EP alleged that the Council had adopted an act on a legal basis which did not provide for such consultation, even if the EP had been consulted anyway.[261] The Court also considered an action admissible in which the EP argued that the Council should have consulted it a second time.[262] The Court[263] also regarded as admissible an action brought by the EP against an implementing act adopted by the Commission which the EP claimed amended Council Regulation 2092/91.[264] The EP argued that the amendment could only have been carried out on the basis of Article 43 [now 37], which provided for the consultation of the EP. Similarly, the Court[265] held admissible an action by the EP, in which it claimed that the Council could not have amended Directive 91/414[266] by way of an implementing act but only on the basis of provisions in the EC Treaty which provided for its consultation. On the other hand, the Court declared as inadmissible an action by the EP which alleged that the Council should have chosen a legal basis which did not contain any consultation of the EP.[267]

Actions of the EP were also considered admissible, where the Council chose a legal basis which did not provide for any participation of the EP instead of the legal basis requested by the EP which contained the co-operation[268] or co-decision procedure,[269] or which provided for the consultation procedure instead of the co-operation[270] or assent procedure.[271] This suggests that whenever a semi-privileged applicant claims that a different legal basis for the adoption of an act based on the Community Treaties should have been chosen, it has *locus standi*, provided that the legal basis actually chosen provides less participation for the applicant. On the other hand

---

[259] Case C-70/88 *European Parliament v Council* [1990] ECR I-2041, para. 28.
[260] See Case C-316/91 *Parliament v Council* [1994] ECR 625, at para. 16.
[261] Case C-316/91 *Parliament v Council* [1994] ECR 625, at para. 16.
[262] Case C-65/90 *European Parliament v Council* [1992] ECR I-4593, at para. 14.
[263] See Case C-156/93 *European Parliament v Commission* [1995] ECR I-2019, at paras. 12 and 13.
[264] [1991] OJ L 198/1.
[265] Case C-303/94 *European Parliament v Council* [1996] ECR I-2943, at paras. 19 and 20.
[266] [1991] OJ L 230/1.
[267] Case C-187/93 *European Parliament v Council* [1994] ECR I-2587, at para. 15.
[268] Case C-360/93 *European Parliament v Council* [1996] ECR I-1195, at paras. 18 and 19.
[269] Case C-259/95 *European Parliament v Council* [1997] ECR I-5303.
[270] Case C-70/88 *European Parliament v Council* [1990] ECR I-2041, at para. 28; Case C-295/90 *European Parliament v Council* [1992] ECR I-4193; Case C-187/93 *European Parliament v Council* [1994] ECR I-2857, at para. 16; Joined Cases C-164/97 and C-165/97 *European Parliament v Council* [1999] ECR I-1139.
[271] Case C-189/97 *European Parliament v Council* [1999] ECR I-4741.

the EP failed to convince the Court that an infringement of Article 253 (ex Article 190) to give adequate reasons could impair the EP's prerogative.[272]

4. *LOCUS STANDI* OF NON-PRIVILEGED APPLICANTS

Natural and legal persons are non-privileged applicants, as they can bring an action only under restricted conditions. The Court considers an applicant as a legal person 'if, at the latest by the expiry of the period prescribed for proceedings to be instituted, it has acquired legal personality in accordance with the law governing its constitution [. . .] or if it has been treated as an independent legal entity by the Community institutions'.[273] The term also encompasses territorial units of a Member State, such as regions or autonomous communities, which have to bring an action under Article 230(4).[274]

Article 230(4) provides that 'any natural or legal person may . . . institute proceedings against a decision addressed to that person or against a decision which, although in the form of a regulation or a decision addressed to another person, is of direct and individual concern to the former.' *Locus standi* under the restrictive conditions of Article 230(4) has developed into a complex body of law[275] and has proven to be a considerable obstacle for private litigants to challenge EC acts directly in the Community Courts.[276]

Statutory Requirements under Article 230(4)

The wording of Article 230(4) distinguishes between three situations, in which private parties can challenge Community acts. The first deals with a

---

[272] Case C-156/93 *Parliament v Commission* [1995] ECR I-2019, at para. 11; Case C-303/94 *European Parliament v Council* [1996] ECR I-2943, at para. 18; Case C-189/97 *European Parliament v Council* [1999] ECR I-4741, at paras. 14–16.

[273] Case T-161/94 *Sinochem Heilongjiang v Council* [1996] ECR II-695, para. 31. See also A. Arnull, supra note 2, at p. 10.

[274] See Joined Cases T-32/98 and T-41/98 *Netherlands Antilles v Commission* [2000] ECR II-201, at paras. 43 to 45; Case C-142/00 P *Commission v Nederlands Antillen* [2003] ECR I-3483, para. 59; Case C-15/06 P *Regione Siciliana v Commission* [2007] ECR I-2591, at para. 29; Case T-37/04 *Região autónoma dos Açores v Council*, judgment of 1 July 2008, at para. 53. For a detailed analysis of the case-law, see A. Arnull (2001), supra note 2, at pp. 10–14; J. Wakefield, supra note 239.

[275] A. Arnull (2001), supra note 2, at p. 52, has claimed that 'it has become extremely difficult to give a concise account of the standing requirements which private applicants must satisfy under Article 230'.

[276] For a detailed discussion of the case-law, see the literature, supra note 2.

decision addressed to the applicant. Private parties have *locus standi* where acts are addressed to them. In this case, the applicant does not have to demonstrate direct and individual concern. This does not mean, however, that the requirement that the act be reviewable is also dispensed with. The second case is concerned with an act addressed to a third party. In this case the applicants have standing if the act is a decision and is of individual and direct concern to them. The third case gives private parties *locus standi* where they can show that even though the act was adopted in the form of a regulation it is a decision of individual and direct concern to them.

It is apparent that the three cases have in common that they provide for challenges to decisions only.[277] This leaves the impression that the drafters only wanted natural and legal persons to challenge administrative acts, rather than legislative acts.[278] This is most obvious for allowing private parties to challenge acts which EC institutions have addressed to them or to third parties. These classical types of administrative acts are employed at Community level in limited fields, such as competition law and state aid. By also encompassing regulations in form only the drafters wanted to ensure that a Community institution, by labelling the administrative act they adopted as regulation, could not circumvent the drafters' intention of including also administrative acts in substance, though not form, in the ambit of Article 230(4). Article 230(4) therefore establishes a difference between the form and the substance of legal acts.[279] In all three cases, we can assume that the term 'decision' is used in its substantive meaning. This means that even where the act in question is not called a decision it can be challenged, if it is in substance a decision.

It is also obvious from the text of Article 230(4) that the drafters did not want private parties to challenge legislative acts. This gap should be filled by Article 234, which allows the Court to rule on the validity of Community acts on referral by a national court. This approach assumed that private parties could challenge Community legislation incidentally by bringing an action against the national administrative acts which applied such Community legislation to them. This also explains why Article 230(4) does not mention directives. The assumption seems to have been that private parties could mount a challenge against directives indirectly by bringing an action in the national court against the implementing measures adopted by national authorities to transpose the directive into national law. As the Community was based on a system of executive federalism, in which Community law was applied by and large by national authorities,

---

[277] T.C. Hartley, supra note 1, p. 343.
[278] See C. Harding, supra note 2, at p. 355.
[279] T.C. Hartley, supra note 1, pp. 343–344.

Article 234 seemed to have been envisaged as the main procedural vehicle for private parties to challenge Community acts with Article 230(4) as complementary procedure where Community law was exceptionally applied by Community institutions. It is difficult to speculate why the drafters chose such an approach to judicial review for private parties. The drafters might have considered that the challenge to Community acts should be performed in the judicial forum that is closest to those affected by the act. As Community acts are mainly applied by national authorities, it seemed desirable to provide private parties with a judicial forum with which they were familiar, that of their national court.[280]

Whatever the rationale for the narrow approach to judicial review in Article 230(4), the provision left the Court of Justice with some unenviable technical problems and also ones of policy. The Court first had to define the concept of decision in substance, which seemed to underlie Article 230(4). It is clear from the case-law that where the act is adopted in the form of a decision, the Court seems not to be concerned to ascertain whether the act is also in substance a decision. If the decision has been addressed to a third party the Court seems more to be concerned with whether the applicant is directly and individually concerned. The substantive nature of the act is therefore mainly relevant in cases where the act was adopted in form of a regulation. Second, the Court had to determine the concept of individual concern, in particular in its relationship with the nature of the act. If only administrative acts in substance could be challenged then the concept of individual concern could not go beyond that of decision in substance. As a matter of policy, the Court had to ensure that the initial division between judicial review of administrative acts under Article 230(4) and Community rules under Article 234 did not leave any gaps in the review of Community acts and provided private parties with adequate judicial protection. Finally, the development of the Community legal order has, however, led to a more complex system of EU administrative governance.[281] This system of integrated administration is characterised by its intensive co-operation between administrative actors from the national and Community level.[282] The involvement of national administrations in the decision-making processes of the Community and the participation of Community actors in the implementation of Community law in the national legal systems have

---

280 In this sense also S. Enchelmaier, supra note 2, at p. 203. On a critical discussion of the concept of 'legal subsidiarity', see also J.M. Cortés Martin, supra note 2, at pp. 251–253.

281 See H. Hofmann and A. Türk (eds.), *EU Administrative Governance* (Edward Elgar Publishing, 2006).

282 See H. Hofmann and A. Türk , 'The Development of Integrated Administration in the EU and its Consequences' (2007) 13(2) *ELJ* 253–271.

added to the difficulties which individuals already face within the current judicial architecture.

The following sections will therefore deal with the definition of decision in substance and its relevance for the standing of private parties before assessing the issues of direct and individual concern.

Determining the Nature of an Act

The Court pronounced on the distinction between decisions and regulations in substance[283] for the purpose of Article 230(4) for the first time in *Producteurs*.[284] The Court pointed out that the terms had to be interpreted in the same way as in Article 249. Article 249(2) stipulates that 'a regulation shall have general application. It shall be binding in its entirety and directly applicable in all Member States'. On the other hand, Article 249(4) provides that 'a decision shall be binding in its entirety upon those to whom it is addressed'. The Court found that 'it is inconceivable that the term "decision" would be used in Article 173 [now 230] in a different sense from the technical sense as defined in Article 189 [now 249]'.[285] In accordance with the definitions provided in Article 249 for regulation and decision it held that the relevant criterion to distinguish them was therefore the general application or otherwise of an act.

The Court then proceeded to a more precise definition of the nature of decisions and regulations by finding that 'the essential characteristics of a decision arise from the limitation of the persons to whom it is addressed, whereas a regulation, being essentially of a legislative nature, [is] applicable not to a limited number of persons, defined or identifiable, but to categories of persons viewed abstractly and in their entirety'.[286] The Court then linked the distinction between regulation and decision with individual concern, by pointing out that 'in doubtful cases [. . .] it is necessary to ascertain whether the measure in question is of individual concern to specific individuals'.[287] The Court then provided a definition of a regulation by finding that:

> 'a measure which is applicable to objectively determined situations and which involves immediate legal consequences in all Member States for categories of persons viewed in a general and abstract manner cannot be considered as

---

[283] For a detailed discussion on the distinction between acts of individual and general application, see A. Türk, *The Concept of Legislation in European Community Law – A Comparative Perspective* (Kluwer, 2006), at pp. 77–185.

[284] Joined Cases 16 and 17/62 *Producteurs de Fruits v Council* [1962] ECR 471.

[285] Ibid., p. 478.

[286] Joined Cases 16 and 17/62 *Producteurs de Fruits v Council* [1962] ECR 471, p. 478.

[287] Ibid., at p. 478.

constituting a decision, unless it can be proved that it is of individual concern to certain persons.'[288]

Definition of addressees of an act

It has first to be noted that the nature of the act is determined by reference to the legal effects on persons who might be affected by it (its addressees) and not in relation to the products that fall within its scope of application. In *Zuckerfabrik Watenstedt* the Court refused to consider an act as a decision because it only concerned a certain product and therefore affected the producers thereof by reason of circumstances in which they are differentiated from all other persons. The Court held that 'the concept of a decision would thereby be expanded to such an extent as to imperil the system of the Treaty which only allows individuals to bring applications for annulment against individual decisions addressed to them or against measures which affect them in a similar manner'.[289] With this argument the Court rejected the approach taken by German courts, which was suggested by the AG in his Opinion,[290] which considered an act that concerned a specific product as a decision, albeit of a general nature (*Allgemeinverfügung*), even though it affected an indeterminate number of persons.

However, despite the importance of the legal effects on persons for the determination of the nature of an act, it is not clear from *Producteurs* how the relevant persons should be defined. As has been discussed elsewhere in greater detail,[291] addressees can be defined as those natural or legal persons whose legal position is directly modified by a Community act.[292] Such a modification is brought about where the act grants rights or imposes obligations.[293] Even though the discussion on the concept of right has not yet produced any clear results,[294] such rights can be identified where a Community act defines with sufficient clarity the beneficiary and the content of the right or where it imposes obligations on a third

---

288 Ibid., at p. 479.

289 Case 6/68 *Zuckerfabrik Watenstedt v Council* [1968] ECR 409, at p. 415; see also Case 101/76 *KSH v Council and Commission* [1977] ECR 797 at para. 25.

290 Opinion of AG Roemer in Case 6/68 *Zuckerfabrik Watenstedt v Council* [1968] ECR 409, at pp. 418–9.

291 For a detailed discussion of the concept of 'addressee', see A. Türk, supra note 283, pp. 82–120.

292 Ibid., p. 115.

293 Ibid., p. 115.

294 See J. Coppel, 'Rights, Duties, and the End of Marshall' (1994) *MLRev* 859–879; M. Ruffert, 'Rights and Remedies in European Community Law: A Comparative View' (1997) *CMLRev* 307–336; C. Hilson and T. Downes, 'Making Sense of Rights: Community Rights in E.C. Law' (1999) 24 *ELRev* 121–138; W. Van Gerven, 'Of Rights, Remedies and Procedures' (2000) 37 *CMLRev* 501–536; S. Prechal, *Directives in EC Law* (OUP, 2nd edn., 2005), pp. 97–130.

party provided that the act was adopted with the intention of protecting an individual interest on which the beneficiary of the right can rely.[295] The notion of addressee requires in addition that the Community act directly modifies the legal situation of a person.[296] This requires that the act 'must directly affect the legal situation of the person concerned and its implementation must be purely automatic and result from Community rules alone without the application of other intermediate rules'.[297] Even though regulations and decisions will usually comply with this requirement, it cannot be excluded that directives can also have such direct legal effects.[298]

Criteria for determining the nature of the act

A second issue which arises from the definition in *Producteurs de Fruits* is that one could conclude that where a measure applies to a limited number of persons who can be defined or identified it has to be qualified as a decision. This view was, however, rejected by the Court in *Zuckerfabrik Watenstedt* where the Court held that 'a measure does not lose its character as a regulation simply because it may be possible to ascertain with a greater or lesser degree of accuracy the number or even the identity of the persons to which it applies at any given time.'[299] The Community Courts consider an act of general application as one that is 'applicable to objectively determined situations'.[300] Such objectively determined situations have invariably been found to exist in the situation of an open class, that is where the number of addressees is not fixed at the time the act is adopted, but is subject to fluctuation thereafter.[301] This is the case even where such fluctuation is less likely to occur due to the narrow personal or temporal scope of the act[302] and even where some addressees are affected

---

[295] M. Ruffert, supra note 294, at pp. 324 *et seq.*; S. Prechal, supra note 294, pp. 118–124.

[296] A. Türk, supra note 283, pp. 117–120.

[297] Case T-69/99 *DSTV v Commission* [2000] ECR II-4039, at para. 24.

[298] See A. Türk, supra note 283, pp. 118–120. On Directives see J. Coppel, supra note 294, p. 875 or more generally S. Prechal, supra note 294.

[299] Case 6/68 *Zuckerfabrik Watenstedt v Council* [1968] ECR 409, p. 415. See also Case 147/83 *Binderer v Commission* [1985] ECR 257.

[300] Joined Cases 16 and 17/62 *Producteurs de Fruits v Council* [1962] ECR 471, p. 479.

[301] For a detailed discussion of the case-law, see A. Türk, supra note 283, pp. 123–130.

[302] Case 6/68 *Zuckerfabrik Watenstedt v Council* [1968] ECR 409; Case 101/76 *KSH v Council and Commission* [1977] ECR 797; Case 123/77 *Unicme v Council* [1978] ECR 845; Joined Case 789 and 790/79 *Calpak v Commission* [1980] 1949; Case 231/82 *Spijker v Commission* [1983] ECR 2559; Case 147/83 *Binderer v Commission* [1985] ECR 257; Case T-37/04 *Região autónoma dos Açores v Council*, judgment of 1 July 2008, at para. 33. For a critical discussion of this approach, see M. Hedemann-Robinson, supra note 2, pp.141–142; A. Türk, supra note 283, pp. 123–130.

by the act in a way which distinguishes them from other addressees.[303] Where the act applies to a closed class, that is where the number of addressees is fixed at the time the act is adopted and cannot be extended after the act is adopted, a rather more careful analysis seems to be required as to whether 'the measure is applicable as the result of an objective situation of law or of fact which it specifies and which is in harmony with its ultimate objective.'[304] The fact that a class is closed is therefore a necessary, but not sufficient precondition for an act to be considered as decision in substance.[305] An act is not of general application only where it has been adopted on the basis of and with exclusive application to the situation of a closed class of addressees.[306] The act is then not adopted on the basis of an objectively determined situation, but on the basis of the individual situation and with exclusive application to those addressees.[307] However, even though they do not merely classify an act as a regulation simply because it is drafted in abstract terms, but examine the purpose and framework of the measure in issue,[308] the Community Courts can in some instances be justly criticised for not taking sufficient account of the economic reality of the market. Too strict a legal analysis is difficult to reconcile with the normative requirement of achieving equality through legislation in substance.

---

303 Case 6/68 *Zuckerfabrik Watenstedt v Council* [1968] ECR 409, p. 415. See also A. Türk, supra note 283, pp. 130–153.

304 Case 6/68 *Zuckerfabrik Watenstedt v Council* [1968] ECR 409, p. 415. See also Case 101/76 *KSH v Council and Commission* [1977] ECR 797, at para. 23; Case 250/81 *Greek Canners v Commission* [1982] ECR 3535; Case 307/81 *Alusuisse v Commission* [1982] ECR 3463; Case 147/83 *Binderer v Commission* [1985] ECR 257; Case 160/88R *Fédération Européenne de la Santé v Council* [1988] ECR 4121; Case C-209/94P *Buralux v Council* [1996] ECR I-615; AG Cosmas in Case C-321/95P *Greenpeace v Commission* [1997] ECR I-1651.

305 See Case 64/69 *Compagnie Française Commerciale et Financière v Commission* [1970] ECR 221; Case 100/74 *CAM v Commission* [1975] ECR 1393; Cases 103–109/78 *Beauport v Council and Commission* [1979] ECR 17; Cases 97, 99, 193, 215/86 *Asteris v Commission* [1988] ECR 2181; Case T-139/01 *Comafrica SpA and Another v Commission* [2005] ECR II-409. For a detailed analysis of the case law, see A. Türk, supra note 283, pp. 153–161. The case law does therefore not support the view that the Court automatically considers an act which applies to a closed class as a decision; see, however, A. Arnull (1995), supra note 2, p. 26; M. Nettesheim, supra note 2, p. 226; P. Craig and G. DeBúrca, supra note 1, pp. 512–513.

306 See Cases 41–44/70 *International Fruit Company v Commission* [1971] ECR 411; Case C-354/87 *Weddel v Commission* [1990] ECR I-3847; Case 138/79 *Roquette v Council* [1980] ECR 3333.

307 See A. Türk, supra note 283, p. 162. See also A. Albors-Llorens, supra note 1, p. 223.

308 See Case 45/81 *Moksel v Commission* [1982] ECR 1129, at para. 19; Case T-243/01 *Sony Computer Entertainment Europe v Commission* [2003] ECR II-4189. See also Case T-82/06 *Apple Computer International v Commission*, order of 19 February 2008.

Relationship between nature of the act and individual concern

A third point of contention arises from the Court's dictum in *Producteurs* that in doubtful cases individual concern should be used as a criterion to determine whether an act would have to be considered as a decision in substance. This view was shared by AG Lagrange when he asked whether one could really admit 'that a decision "of individual concern" to someone is not an individual decision'.[309] This assumption is however, not unproblematic, as the test for individual concern would then be the same as that for establishing whether a measure was a decision.

It might therefore not come as a surprise that the relationship between the nature of an act and individual concern has greatly troubled the Court and the case-law displays different, not always harmonious, approaches to determine the issue.[310] In some cases, the Court used the test of general applicability to determine the nature of the act with the result that the measure was considered a regulation in substance and the action brought by non-privileged applicants declared inadmissible without a discussion of individual concern.[311] Conversely, the Court came to the conclusion that the act even though it was adopted in the form of a regulation was a decision with individual concern.[312] In other cases, which represent a more liberal approach to standing, the Court proceeded to the test of individual concern without considering the nature of the act or leaving it expressly open.[313] In yet another set of cases, even though it found that the act was of individual concern to some persons, the Court expressly accepted that the act was of a legislative nature.[314]

---

[309] Opinion of AG Lagrange in Joined Cases 16 and 17/62 *Producteurs de Fruits v Council* [1962] ECR 471, p. 485.

[310] See A. Arnull (1995), supra note 2, pp. 35–36; T.C. Hartley, supra note 1, p. 348.

[311] See Case 64/69 *Compagnie Française Commerciale et Financière v Commission* [1970] ECR 221; Case 101/76 *KSH v Council and Commission* [1977] ECR 797; Cases 103–109/78 *Beauport v Council and Commission* [1979] ECR 17; Joined Cases 789 and 790/79 *Calpak v Commission* [1980] ECR 1949; Case 250/81 *Greek Canners v Commission* [1982] ECR 3535; Case 231/82 *Spijker v Commission* [1983] ECR 2559; Case 147/83 *Binderer GmbH v Commission* [1985] ECR 257; Case 26/86 *Deutz & Geldermann v Council* [1987] ECR 941; Cases 97, 99, 193, 215/86 *Asteris v Commission* [1988] ECR 2181; Case 160/88R *Fédération Européenne de la Santé Animale v Council* [1988] ECR 4121; Case T-472/93 *Campo Ebro Industrial SA and Others v Council* [1995] ECR II-421; Case C-209/94P *Buralux SA v Council* [1996] ECR I-615.

[312] Joined Cases 41–44/70 *International Fruit v Commission* [1971] ECR 411; Case 113/77 *NTN Toyo Bearing Company v Council* [1979] ECR 1185, at para. 11; Case 118/77 *I.S.O. v Council* [1979] ECR 1277, at para. 24; Case C-354/87 *Weddel v Commission* [1990] ECR I-3847.

[313] Case 232/81 *Agricola Commerciale Olio v Commission* [1984] ECR 3881, at para. 11; Case 11/82 *Piraiki-Patraiki v Commission* [1985] ECR 207, at para. 5; Case C-152/88 *Sofrimport v Commission* [1990] ECR I-2477.

[314] See Case 100/74 *Société CAM v Commission* [1975] ECR 1393; Cases 239 and 275/82 *Allied Corporation v Commission* [1984] ECR 1005; Case C-156/87 *Gestetner Holdings v Council and Commission* [1990] ECR I-781.

This ambiguous attitude seemed to have ceased with the Court's ruling in *Codorniu*.[315] The Court found that 'although it is true that according to the criteria in the second paragraph of Article 173 [now Article 230(4)] of the Treaty the contested provision is, by nature and by virtue of its sphere of application, of a legislative nature in that it applies to the traders concerned in general, that does not prevent it from being of individual concern to some of them.'[316] This seems to indicate that, even where the measure is a true regulation, it can nevertheless be of individual concern to the applicant. The abstract terminology test seems, therefore, to be no longer relevant.[317] The decisive criteria for *locus standi* in this case are individual and direct concern. All the same, in the case of acts of general application the Community Courts seem to consider private parties as individually concerned only in exceptional circumstances.[318]

Directives

Article 230(4) EC allows an action against an act that is in substance a decision, 'although in the form of a *regulation*'[319] thereby seemingly excluding challenges to directives.[320] And indeed, the CFI in *Asocarne* came to the conclusion that Article 230(4) EC does not allow for challenges against directives. It argued that 'the justification for that exclusion lies in the fact that, in the case of directives, the judicial protection of individuals is duly and sufficiently assured by the national courts which review the transposition of directives into the domestic law of the various Member States'.[321] On appeal, the Court left the question expressly open. It examined, however, the nature of the directive and came to the conclusion that the directive was of a general and abstract nature and could not be considered as a decision in the substantive sense. Moreover, it considered whether the appellants were individually concerned and came to the conclusion

---

315 Case C-309/89 *Codorniu SA v Council* [1994] ECR I-1853.

316 Ibid., para. 19.

317 The CFI still seems to analyse acts that were adopted as regulations as to whether they are of general applicability. This is usually followed by an examination of whether the act could nevertheless be of individual concern, see Case T-268/99 *Fédération national d'agriculture biologique des régions de France and Others v Council* [2000] ECR II-2893, paras. 34–56. See, however, Case T-472/93 *Campo Ebro and Others v Council* [1995] ECR II-421 at para. 29, where the CFI found that the act was of general applicability, but did not supplement this finding by the usual reminder that the measure could nevertheless be of individual concern.

318 See A. Türk, supra note 283, at p.164.

319 Emphasis added.

320 See A. Arnull (2001), supra note 2, pp. 22–23.

321 Case T-99/94 *Asocarne v Council* [1994] ECR II-871, para. 17.

that this was not the case.[322] An action against a directive is, therefore, in principle admissible.[323] Problems arise here, however, in relation to direct concern.

Direct Concern

Where the measure is not addressed to the applicant, standing under Article 230(4) is only granted if the measure is of direct concern to the applicant.[324] This can be doubtful, in particular in cases where a Community act requires further implementation at Community or national level, where a Community act authorises a Member State to take a particular course of action, where the Community grants Member States funds which benefit private parties, or in the case of a directive addressed to Member States. Given that the implementation and enforcement of Community acts is normally a matter for the Member States, this requirement often determines whether an action can be brought in the Community Courts under Article 230(4) or whether the individual has to bring an action in the national courts.

In order for an applicant to be directly concerned by an EC measure the Community Courts require that 'that measure must directly affect the legal situation of the person concerned and its implementation must be purely automatic and result from Community rules alone without the application of other intermediate rules'.[325] This seems to be obviously the case for acts adopted as regulations, is sometimes problematic for decisions and seems to be excluded in case of directives.

---

[322] See also Case 160/88R *Fédération Européenne de la Santé Animale and Others v Council* [1988] ECR 4121 and Case C-298/89 *Government of Gibraltar v Council* [1993] ECR I-3605, where the Court came in both cases to the conclusion that the acts in question were not decisions in substance. See also Joined Cases T-172/98 and T-175/98 to T-177/98 *Salamander AG and Others v European Parliament and Council* [2000] ECR II-2487.

[323] See Opinion of AG Colomer in Case C-23/00P *Council v Boehringer* [2002] ECR I-1873, at para. 47. The CFI has recently confirmed this position in Case T-213/02 *SNF SA v Commission* [2004] ECR II-3047, at para. 54, and in Case T-94/04 *EEB v Commission* [2005] ECR I-4919, at para. 34.

[324] On direct concern, see generally A. Albors-Llorens, supra note 1, pp. 63–75; A. Arnull (2001), supra note 2, pp. 25–30; T.C. Hartley, supra note 1, pp. 363–366; A. Ward, supra note 1, pp. 317–321.

[325] Case T-69/99 *DSTV v Commission* [2000] ECR II-4039, at para. 24. Compare with the definition of AG Verloren van Themaat in Case 11/82 *Piraiki-Patraiki v Commission* [1985] ECR 207 at p. 216, where he considers an EC measure of direct concern 'if, even though it requires the adoption of a further national implementing measure, it is possible to foresee with certainty or with a high degree of probability that the implementing measure will affect the applicant and the manner in which it will do so'.

Regulations[326]

As regulations are directly applicable in the legal systems of the Member States, they directly concern 'the legal situation of the person concerned', where their implementation is 'purely automatic and result[s] from Community rules alone without the application of other intermediate rules'.[327] The Court found such a situation to exist in *International Fruit*.[328] Each week the Member States would communicate to the Commission the quantities of dessert apples from third countries for which import licences into the EC had been applied. The Commission would then take a decision with regard to those licences. On the basis of that decision each Member State should issue the licence to any interested party applying for it. The Court found that 'the national authorities do not enjoy any discretion in the matter of the issue of licences and the conditions on which applications by the parties concerned should be granted'.[329] The duty of the national authorities was merely to collect the data necessary so that the Commission could take its decision, which the national authorities had to carry out. The Court consequently concluded that the 'measure whereby the Commission decides on the issue of the import licences directly affects the legal position of the parties concerned.'[330] Similarly, the Court found in *Weddel*[331] that 'it is sufficient to state that Regulation No 2806/87 fixes in great detail the criteria on the basis of which import licences must be granted, without leaving any discretion to the agencies of the Member States responsible for issuing licences. Consequently, the regulation is of direct concern to the applicant.'[332]

However, the direct applicability of regulations does not always lead to individuals being directly concerned by them. In *Beauport*[333] the Court did not consider the applicants, sugar producers from Guadeloupe and Martinique, as directly concerned, as 'only the measures adopted by the French Republic under the derogating rule laid down by Regulation 298/78 could be of direct . . . concern to the applicants.'[334] The link of direct concern and 'immediate legal consequences' was made clear by AG Warner in that case, when he argued that in accordance with the 'clear and consistent'

---

326 The term regulation is here used with reference to the form in which the act was adopted, and not its substance.

327 Case T-69/99 *DSTV v Commission* [2000] ECR II-4039, para. 24.

328 Cases 41 to 44/70 *NV International Fruit Company v Commission* [1971] ECR 411.

329 Ibid., para. 25. See also Case C-152/88 *Sofrimport v Commission* [1990] ECR I-2477, at para. 9.

330 Ibid., para. 28.

331 Case C-354/87 *Weddel v Commission* [1990] ECR I-3847.

332 Ibid., para. 19.

333 Joined Cases 103 to 109/78 *Société des Usines de Beauport v Council* [1979] ECR 17.

334 Ibid. para. 22.

case law of the Court 'where an act of a Community Institution does not itself have an immediate effect on a person's rights, but merely empowers a Member State to take action that may have such an effect, it is not the act of the Community, but the action, if any, of the Member State, that may be of direct concern to that person'.[335] However, it is not always easy to determine whether a provision of a regulation is of direct concern or not.[336]

Decisions[337]

The early cases before the Court were dominated by the question of under what circumstances authorisations granted by the Commission to a Member State could directly concern private parties. In *Plaumann*[338] AG Roemer found that where a Member State took action following an authorisation by the Commission a private party could not be directly concerned, as 'only when the Member State avails itself of the authorization, which is left to its discretion, are legal effects created for the individual'.[339] This approach was followed by the Court in *Alcan*[340] where the Commission refused to grant Belgium and Luxembourg authorisation to open a tariff quota for unwrought aluminium for the year 1968. The Court found that a decision concerning the authorisation of such quotas 'has thus no effect other than to create a power in favour of the Member States concerned, and does not confer any rights on possible beneficiaries of any measures to be taken subsequently by the said States'.[341] The Court argued that it did not matter that the decision was a refusal rather than an authorisation, as the benefits of a reduced tariff would only result from the national decision. The Court concluded that '[t]he decision rejecting the request does not therefore concern the applicants in any other manner than would the positive decision which they wish to obtain.'[342] Hence the applicants were not directly concerned by the refusal to grant the authorisation.

In *Bock*[343] and *Piraiki-Patraiki*[344] the concept of direct concern was

---

335 Opinion of AG Warner of Joined Cases 103 to 109/78 *Société des Usines de Beauport v Council* [1979] ECR 17, p. 31. See also Case T-127/05 *Lootus v Council* [2007] ECR II-1*, at paras. 39–48; Case C-441/05 *Roquette Frères*, [2007] ECR I-1993, at paras. 43–47.

336 See Case C-73/97P *France v Comafrica and Others* [1999] ECR I-185, where the Court of Justice on appeal rejected the Court of First Instance's finding that the regulation in issue was of direct concern to the applicants.

337 The term decision refers here to the form and not the substance of the act.

338 Case 25/62 *Plaumann v Commission* [1963] ECR 95.

339 Ibid., p. 115. See also the Opinion of AG Roemer in Case 1/64 *Glucoseries réunies v Commission* [1964] ECR 813, at p. 421.

340 Case 69/69 *Alcan Aluminium v Commission* [1970] ECR 385.

341 Ibid., para. 8.

342 Ibid., para. 16.

343 Case 62/70 *Bock v Commission* [1971] ECR 897.

344 Case 11/82 *Piraiki-Patraiki v Commission* [1985] ECR 207.

more liberally construed[345] by also including cases where the Member State concerned had made it expressly or implicitly clear how to exercise its discretion once the authorisation was granted. In *Bock*[346] the German authorities made it clear to the applicant that they would reject its application, as soon as the Commission had given its authorisation. Once the Commission had authorised Germany to take protective measures, the German authorities rejected the application. The fact that the German authorities had discretion to use the authorisation would have meant that the Commission's decision could not directly concern the applicant. All the same, the Court considered the applicant directly concerned by holding that 'the appropriate German authorities had nevertheless already informed the applicant that they would reject its application as soon as the Commission had granted them the requisite authorisation. They had requested that authorisation with particular reference to the applications already before them at that time'.[347] In *Piraiki-Patraiki*[348] the Court went even further and accepted direct concern where the authorised Member State had made it implicitly clear how it would exercise its discretion. The Court remarked that 'without implementing measures adopted at the national level the Commission decision could not have affected the applicants'.[349] This, however, in the Court's view, did not 'prevent the decision from being of direct concern to the applicants if other factors justify the conclusion that they have a direct interest in bringing the action'.[350] Even before being authorised to do so by the Commission, France had applied a very restrictive system of licences for imports of cotton yarn from Greece. The Court therefore found that 'in those circumstances the possibility that the French Republic might decide not to make use of the authorization granted to it by the Commission decision was entirely theoretical, since there could be no doubt as to the intention of the French authorities to apply the decision'.[351] For the applicants to be directly concerned it was obviously not necessary to be actually affected, but that such impact was a practical certainty. AG Verloren Van Themaat seemed to have come to the same conclusion, even though he proposed a different test for direct concern.[352] He found the applicants directly concerned, as 'the legal

---

[345] See A. Albors-Llorens, supra note 1, p. 68.
[346] Case 62/70 *Bock v Commission* [1971] ECR 897.
[347] Ibid., para. 7.
[348] Case 11/82 *Piraiki-Patraiki v Commission* [1985] ECR 207.
[349] Ibid., para. 7.
[350] Ibid., para. 7.
[351] Ibid., para. 9.
[352] Ibid., Opinion of AG Verloren Van Themaat, p. 216, where he stated that '[a] measure taken by the Community is defined as being of direct material concern to an interested party

consequences for the parties concerned, as well as their identity, can be deduced from the contested decision with certainty or with a high degree of probability'.[353]

The above cases concern prior authorisations, which are not of direct concern to third parties unless the Member State has made it expressly or implicitly clear how it would use the authorisation. The Community Courts had to decide however also on Commission decisions taken to confirm or reject measures already adopted by a Member State. Direct concern depends in these cases on the effect of such *ex post* authorisations. In *Toepfer*[354] the Commission adopted a decision by which it authorised Germany to maintain the protective measure already taken by Germany. AG Roemer found the applicants not to be directly concerned, as the Commission decision to authorise, in contrast to one that abolished or amended, the protective measures adopted by Germany did not affect Germany's discretion. The AG argued that 'even after the Commission has given its authorization, the Member State retains its complete freedom of action in the sense that it can revoke the protective measure which has been adopted'.[355] The Court differed in its analysis from the AG and considered the applicants directly concerned. The Court stated that a measure which allowed Germany to retain its protective measures had the same effect as a decision which amended or abolished protective measures as that 'decision does not merely approve such measures, but renders them valid'.[356]

In contrast, in *DSTV*[357] the Court made it clear that a Commission decision which found an order made by the UK Government to be compatible with Community law was not of direct concern to the applicant. The order effectively banned the 'Eurotica-Rendevouz-Vous' programme broadcast in the UK by the Danish television company DSTV. The Court stated that the Commission decision was 'limited merely to pronouncing ex post facto on the compatibility with Community law of the Order, which was adopted, independently, by the United Kingdom in the exercise of its discretionary power'.[358] The Court held that unlike the situation in *Toepfer* 'the Commission did not, in the present case, retrospectively authorise the

---

if, even though it requires the adoption of a further national implementing measure, it is possible to foresee with certainty or with a high degree of probability that the implementing measure will affect the applicant and the manner in which it will do so.'

353 Ibid., Opinion of AG Verloren Van Themaat, p. 219.

354 Joined Cases 106 and 107/63 *Toepfer v Commission* [1965] ECR 405.

355 AG Roemer, ibid., at p. 418.

356 Ibid., p. 411.

357 Case T-69/99 *DSTV v Commission* [2000] ECR II-4039.

358 Ibid., para. 27.

Member State concerned to retain a national measure'.[359] And in contrast to *Bock* the Commission did not 'give the Member State concerned prior authorisation to adopt national measures'.[360] *DSTV* makes it clear that *ex post* authorisations, whether positive or negative, are only of direct concern if they have retroactive effect.[361] The complexity of such an assessment is apparent in *Infront*.[362] The CFI considered a decision by the Commission, by which it approved and published a list notified to it by the UK of events of major importance under Council Directive 89/552,[363] as being of direct concern to the applicant, which had obtained the broadcasting rights for these events. The CFI made it clear that the Commission decision was not of direct concern to the applicant in relation to the effect of the UK measures in the UK,[364] but only insofar as it enabled the implementation of the mechanism of mutual recognition by the other Member States provided for in the Directive.[365]

The Community Courts also seem to have difficulties in assessing direct concern, where the Community adopts decisions on the provisions of funds to Member States to finance certain projects carried out by third parties. As the Member States are the formal addressees of these measures, direct concern of third parties is doubtful.

In *Interhotel*[366] the Commission adopted a decision, addressed to Portugal, which reduced the assistance which had originally been granted by the European Social Fund for a training programme submitted on behalf of the applicant. The Court found that even though the decision was addressed to Portugal, it 'deprived the applicant of part of the assistance which had originally been granted to it, the Member State not having any discretion of its own in that respect'.[367] Consequently, the Court considered the applicant directly and individually concerned.

In contrast, Commission decisions concerning funds made available

---

359 Ibid., para. 28.

360 Ibid., para. 29.

361 See also Case T-130/06 *Drax Power Ltd. and Others v Commission* [2007] ECR II-67*; Case T-13/07 *Cemex UK cement v Commission*, order of 6 November 2007; Case T-27/07 *U.S. Steel Košice v Commission*, order of 1 October 2007, upheld on appeal in Case C-6/08 P *U.S. Steel Košice v Commission*, order of 19 June 2008.

362 Case T-33/01 *Infront v Commission* [2005] ECR II-5897; upheld on appeal in Case C-125/06 P *Commission v Infront*, judgment of 13 March 2008.

363 [1989] OJ L 298/23, as amended.

364 Case T-33/01 *Infront v Commission* [2005] ECR II-5897, at para. 135, in which the CFI made it clear that the Commission decision did not constitute a retroactive authorisation of the British measures, which existed independently from the Commission decision.

365 Ibid., para. 150.

366 Case C-291/89 *Interhotel v Commission* [1991] ECR I-2257.

367 Ibid., para. 13. See also Case C-304/89 *Oliveira v Commission* [1991] ECR I-2283, para. 13.

to the Member States from the European Agricultural Guidance and Guarantee Fund (EAGGF) only seem to concern the Member States to which they are addressed, but not the third parties which carry out the projects. In *CNTA*[368] the applicant applied to the competent national authority for subsidies provided for by Community agricultural law. The national authority was not convinced that the applicant was eligible and made the payment of the subsidies conditional upon a guarantee by the applicant to pay the money back should the EAGGF consider the applicant as not eligible. These doubts were justified, as the Commission in a decision addressed to France refused to recognise the subsidies made to the applicant as chargeable to the EAGGF. The Court pointed out that 'the decision relates only to financial relations between the Commission and the French Republic'.[369] The Court found that the fact that the decision prompted the national authority to recover the money from the applicant 'was not a direct consequence of the contested decision itself but derived from the fact that the SIDO [the national authority] had made the definitive grant of the subsidies conditional upon their finally being charged to the EAGGF'.[370] The decision therefore did not directly affect the applicant's legal position.[371] The Court arrived at a similar conclusion in *Coillte*.[372] In this case the Commission in a decision addressed to Ireland declared certain expenditure incurred by the national authority as not eligible under the EAGGF. The CFI repeated its dictum that 'such a decision relates only to financial relations between the Commission and the Member State concerned'.[373] The CFI explained in more detail the reasons why such decisions do not concern third parties. The CFI found that 'a decision on the expenditure incurred by Member States under the EAGGF has a declaratory rather than a constitutive function, since the direct effects to which those traders are subject derive from the decisions adopted by the national intervention authorities in the exercise of their own powers'.[374] The Commission, so the CFI, had no power to require the national authorities to take specific measures, in particular it could not ask the national authorities to recover the sums from the recipients. The Member States only have to 'refund to the EAGGF the sums cor-

---

[368] Joined Cases 89 and 91/86 *CNTA v Commission* [1987] ECR 3005.

[369] Ibid., para. 9.

[370] Ibid., para. 13.

[371] Ibid., para. 14. See also Case T-54/96 *Oleifici Italiana and another v Commission* [1998] ECR II-3377, paras. 56–59.

[372] Case T-244/00 *Coillte Teoranta v Commission* [2001] ECR II-1275.

[373] Ibid., para. 41.

[374] Ibid., para. 44.

responding to the expenditure excluded from Community financing'.[375] Therefore, if the national authorities decided to have the funds reimbursed by the recipients, it would be 'the direct consequence, not of the contested decision, but of the action which would be taken for that purpose by those authorities'.[376] In any event, the national authorities might decide not to claim the money back and bear the financial burden themselves.

Similar issues arise in European Regional Development Fund (ERDF) cases. In *SLIM Sicilia*[377] the Commission had initially granted in 1984 financial assistance under the ERDF for the project for methanation of the city of Syracuse, Italy. The grant had to be finally concluded by September 1995 unless the project was suspended for judicial reasons. In 2000 the Commission rejected the request for an extension by the Italian government and reduced the assistance to the amount already paid to Italy. The CFI pointed out that the Commission decision had effects for the applicant's legal position only if the applicant had to repay the difference between what he received and what the Commission had actually paid to the Italian State.[378] Such an obligation could however be derived neither from the decision itself nor from any provision of Community law.[379] The CFI stated that the national authorities had discretion for the reimbursement of the difference. The Court did not consider as decisive that the public authorities had expressed their intention in the concession contract that the applicant should bear the financial consequences of any Commission decisions affecting the assistance. The CFI seemed to have attached great weight to the autonomous decision by the Italian authorities to pay the applicant the outstanding amount without awaiting the Commission decision as to the extension they had requested. That decision, argued the CFI, 'comes between the contested decision and the applicant's legal situation'.[380] Similarly, in *Regione Siciliana I*[381] the CFI argued that the applicant was not directly concerned by the Commission's decision to close the assistance relating to a project for the Messina Palermo Motorway. Even though the decision, which was addressed to Italy, meant that financial assistance would no longer be granted and that certain amounts even had to be repaid by Italy, the CFI argued that the financial assistance was granted to the

---

375 Ibid., para. 45.
376 Ibid., para. 47.
377 Case T-105/01 *SLIM Sicilia v Commission* [2002] ECR II-2697.
378 Ibid., para. 50.
379 Ibid., para. 51.
380 Ibid., para. 53.
381 Case T-341/02 *Regione Siciliana v Commission* [2004] ECR II-2877. The ruling was upheld on appeal in Case C-417/04 P *Regione Siciliana v Commission* [2006] ECR I-3881.

Italian Republic and nothing prevented Italy from paying out of its own funds the portion of Community financing withdrawn by the Commission. Moreover, the Commission decision did not oblige Italy to recover the sums withdrawn from the beneficiaries.

The CFI attempted a more liberal approach in *Regione Siciliana II*.[382] In this case the Commission had initially granted Italy in 1987 ERDF assistance of almost €50 million for the third part of construction work on a dam across the Gibbesi. In 2002 the Commission cancelled the aid granted and requested from the Italian authorities that the advance of €39 million made by the Commission be repaid, as the project did not seem to be capable of becoming operational and its intended use had been considerably altered.[383] The CFI found that the applicant which had carried out the project was directly concerned by the Commission's decision. The CFI argued that the decision affected the applicant's legal position by having the 'direct and immediate effect of changing the applicant's financial situation by depriving the applicant of the balance of the assistance [. . .] remaining to be paid by the Commission'.[384] The money would now not be paid to Italy, which in turn could not pass it on to the applicant. The CFI stated that the applicant's legal situation was also affected in respect of its duty to repay the sums already advanced. The CFI held that 'the effect of the contested decision is directly to change the applicant's legal status from that of unarguably being a creditor in respect of those sums to that of debtor, at least potentially'.[385] The CFI made it clear that the theoretical possibility that the Italian authorities would not request the repayment and would pay the remainder of the assistance was not relevant, as such a national decision would have to be adopted 'precisely in order to counter the automatic effects of the contested decisions'.[386] The CFI distinguished this case from the ruling in *Coillte* by arguing that in the latter case the Commission's decision 'did not automatically and mechanically cause the withholding of a balance still owed to the beneficiary'[387] and that 'only the adoption of a national decision subsequent to the Commission's contested decision could obligate the beneficiary to repay

---

[382] Case T-60/03 *Regione Siciliana v Commission* [2005] ECR II-4139.

[383] The project was designed to ensure a reliable water supply for an industrial centre which was to be built in Licata and for the irrigation of agricultural land. The destined use of the dam water was changed when it became clear the industrial centre would not materialise. Moreover, at the time the Commission adopted its decision the temporary reservoirs of the dam had not been built and the aqueduct had not been completed, even though it constituted an integral part of the project.

[384] Ibid., para. 53.

[385] Ibid., para. 43.

[386] Ibid., para. 60.

[387] Ibid., para. 61.

the advances already received'.[388] This ruling was clearly at odds with the Court's ruling in *Regione Siciliana I*[389] and on appeal the CFI's judgment was consequently set aside.[390]

The rulings in the EAGGF and ERDF cases should be contrasted with the decision of the Court in *Dreyfus*.[391] In first instance, the CFI[392] found that the refusal of the Commission to approve a contract concluded by the applicant with Exportkhleb, a Russian company authorised by the Russian Federation to conclude contracts for the purchase of wheat, did not affect the commercial validity of the contract and was therefore not of direct concern to the applicant. The Commission's refusal only affected its legal relations with VEB, the Russian Federation's financial agent, to whom the decision was addressed, insofar as it meant that Community funding was not made available for the contract. The Court[393] on appeal overturned the CFI's judgment by holding that it was 'purely theoretical'[394] that Exportkhleb would perform the contract in the form rejected by the Commission and thereby forgo Community funding. Therefore, 'although the contested decision was addressed to the VEB, as financial agent of the Russian Federation, it directly affected the appellant's situation.'[395] In contrast, in *Greenpeace*[396] the Commission had apparently taken a decision to continue to grant Spain financial assistance under the European Regional Development Fund for two power plants in the Canary Islands. The Court found that it was the decision to build the two power stations in question which was liable to affect the environmental rights arising under Directive 85/337 that the appellants, certain environmental associations and individuals, sought to invoke. The Court consequently held that 'the contested decision, which concerns the Community financing of those power stations, can affect those rights only indirectly'.[397] In contrast to *Dreyfus*, and the rulings in *Bock* and *Piraiki-Patraiki*, the Court must have assumed that it was not just 'purely theoretical' that the Spanish companies would have carried out the project even in the absence of Community funding, which given the amount of Community funding involved is rather doubtful.

---

388 Ibid., para. 61.
389 C-417/04 P *Regione Siciliana v Commission* [2006] ECR I-3881.
390 Case C-15/06 P *Regione Siciliana v Commission* [2007] ECR I-2591.
391 Case C-386/96 P *Dreyfus v Commission* [1998] ECR I-2309.
392 Case T-485/93 *Dreyfus v Commission* [1996] ECR II-1101.
393 Case C-386/96 P *Dreyfus v Commission* [1998] ECR I-2309.
394 Ibid., para. 52.
395 Ibid., para. 54.
396 Case C-321/95P *Greenpeace Council and Others v Commission* [1998] ECR I-1651.
397 Ibid., para. 31. See also Case C-486/01 P *Front National v European Parliament* [2004] ECR I-6289, para. 40.

Directives

In *Gibraltar*[398] the Court did not address the issue, but AG Lenz stated that the directive under review had indeed left a certain amount of discretion to the Member States. However, he argued that for certain provisions in the directive such discretion existed only in theory, as Member States would not use that discretion. As the directive directly deprived the applicant of certain undefined advantages, this would be sufficient to hold that the directive was of direct concern. In contrast, the CFI in *Salamander* categorically denied the possibility of direct concern of directives. The CFI required that for an individual to be directly concerned 'the measure must directly affect his legal situation and leave no discretion to the addressees of that measure who are entrusted with the task of implementing it, such implementation being purely automatic and resulting from the Community rules alone without the application of other intermediate rules'.[399] The CFI pointed out that a directive could not impose obligations on individuals and could therefore not be relied upon by individuals against other individuals. Consequently, 'a directive which, as in the present case, requires Member States to impose obligations on economic operators is not of itself, before the adoption of the national transposition measures and independently of them, such as to affect directly the legal situation of those economic operators [. . .]'.[400] The CFI also made it clear that the obligation imposed by the Court in *Inter-Environnement Wallonie*[401] to refrain, during the period laid down for transposition of the directive, from taking any measures which may seriously compromise the aims of that directive, only applies to Member States and could not be extended to individuals. Similarly, the CFI in *Japan Tobacco*[402] rejected the claim that Article 7 of Directive 2001/37[403] was of direct concern to the applicants. Even though Article 7 did not leave any discretion to the Member States as to whether or not to act in order to achieve the result prescribed therein, the CFI emphasised

---

[398] Case C-298/89 *Government of Gibraltar v Council* [1993] ECR I-3605.

[399] Joined Cases T-172/98 and T-175/98 to 177/98 *Salamander AG and Others v European Parliament and Council* [2000] ECR II-2487, para. 52.

[400] Ibid., para. 54. See also Opinion of AG Colomer in Case C-23/00P *Council v Boehringer* [2002] ECR I-1873, at para. 53. See Case T-45/02 DOW *AgroSciences BV and Another v European Parliament and Council* [2003] ECR II-1973, in which the CFI denied direct concern of an amendment to a Directive which merely provided for further action to be taken by the EP and the Council.

[401] Case C-129/96 *Inter-Environnement Wallonie v Région Wallonne* [1997] ECR I-7411.

[402] See Case T-223/01 *Japan Tobacco Inc and JT International SA v European Parliament and Council* [2002] ECR II-3259.

[403] [2001] OJ L 194/26.

that 'it does not follow that an automatic and immediate change is thereby brought about to the applicants' legal position or existing rights'.[404]

Rationale of direct concern

It can be seen from the above discussion that the case law on direct concern is not without its ambiguities. First, one could argue that direct concern requires that the Community act produce a direct impact on the legal position of the applicant. This was the conclusion drawn by the CFI in *DSTV* where it considered it necessary for an act to be of direct concern that 'that measure must directly affect the legal situation of the person concerned and its implementation must be purely automatic and result from Community rules alone without the application of other intermediate rules'.[405] This explains in particular the CFI's ruling in *Salamander*, where it was argued that a directive cannot directly concern an individual, as it cannot impose obligations on individuals. Direct concern was seemingly denied on the basis that a directive could not affect the legal position of individuals. In contrast, other cases seem to indicate that direct concern even exists where the Community act does not affect the legal position of an individual, but where such an impact is forseeable, in *Bock* because of an express declaration by the Member State in issue, in *Piraiki-Patraiki* due to the circumstances of the case. Obviously, on this basis directives could be of direct concern where it is forseeable as to how their provisions will be implemented.

Second, even though a substantial number of cases are decided on the basis of discretion as the relevant criterion, it has been argued that instead of focusing on discretion 'what is really central to the notion of direct concern is the existence of a direct relationship of causality between the Community decision and the damage suffered by the applicant'.[406] Indeed, discretion as the test for direct concern might not be satisfactory in all instances.[407] It is doubtful in the first place whether an adequate definition of discretion can be found. Moreover, in certain cases the Court rejected direct concern despite the fact that the Member State in issue had no

---

[404] Case T-223/01 *Japan Tobacco Inc and JT International SA v European Parliament and Council* [2002] ECR II-3259, para. 50.

[405] Case T-69/99 *DSTV v Commission* [2000] ECR II-4039, at para. 24. Compare with the definition of AG Verloren van Themaat in Case 11/82 *Piraiki-Patraiki v Commission* [1985] ECR 207 at p. 216, where he considers an EC measure of direct concern 'if, even though it requires the adoption of a further national implementing measure, it is possible to foresee with certainty or with a high degree of probability that the implementing measure will affect the applicant and the manner in which it will do so'.

[406] See A. Albors-Llorens, supra note 1, p. 73.

[407] Ibid., pp. 70–74.

discretion as to the application of the Community act. Furthermore, it is difficult to employ this test where acts are addressed not to Member States, but to individuals. On this understanding 'the *raison d'être* of this *locus standi* condition is to ensure that the prejudice sustained by the applicants derives directly from the Community decision'.[408]

Individual Concern

Article 230(4) requires private parties to be individually concerned[409] unless the act is addressed to them. Individual concern could be understood to operate only within the ambit of a decision in substance. Those to whom the act was formally addressed (formal addressees) would not have to demonstrate individual concern. However, those persons whose legal position was directly modified by the act (substantive addressees), but to whom the decision was not formally addressed, either because the decision was formally addressed to a third party or because the decision was adopted in the form of a regulation, would be affected by the decision just as the formal addressee and hence should be considered as individually concerned. On this understanding, individual concern operates as a functional substitute for determining the formal addressees of an action. This is how the Court seems to have understood individual concern in its seminal *Plaumann* formula.

The Court held that

> 'persons [. . .] may only claim to be individually concerned if that decision affects them by reason of certain attributes which are peculiar to them or by reason of circumstances in which they are differentiated from all other persons and by virtue of these factors distinguishes them individually *just as in the case of the person addressed.*'[410]

On this understanding, the notion of individual concern overlaps with the notion of decision in substance and has therefore only a restrictive field of application.[411] However, over time the Court considered private parties individually concerned even though the act was not a decision in substance. And indeed, the *Plaumann* formula provides a sufficiently flexible basis for such a more liberal interpretation. The Court has, however, resisted calls

---

408 Ibid., p. 73.

409 On individual concern, see the literature, supra note 2.

410 Case 25/62 *Plaumann v Commission* [1963] ECR 95, para. 9. Emphasis added.

411 Some authors have suggested that this was also a useful tool of protecting the developing body of EC laws against challenges: see A. Arnull (1995), supra note 2, p. 45; M. Hedemann-Robinson, supra note 2, p. 128.

for an even more generous interpretation of individual concern in its most recent decisions in *Unión de Pequeños* and *Jégo Quéré*.

This section will first explore the narrow interpretation of individual concern, the classical application of the *Plaumann* formula, before turning its attention to the cases in which the Court undertook a more liberal interpretation of individual concern. It will also discuss the question as to whether this approach spells the end for the relevance of the nature of the act. In the final part of this section, the limits of the liberal approach will be discussed.

Classical *Plaumann*

The classical application of the *Plaumann* formula showed the Court at its most restrictive in the interpretation of individual concern. This restrictive approach to individual concern can however be explained by linking individual concern with the nature of the act. Initially, it seems, the Court wanted to ensure that the scope of both concepts did not diverge.

It can be observed that the same reasons that lead the Court to consider an act that applies to an open class as being of general application will also be employed to deny individual concern. In *Plaumann* an importer of clementines challenged a Commission decision by which it refused to authorise Germany to apply its lower customs tariff of 10 per cent instead of the 13 per cent set out in the Common Customs Tariff. On the basis of the *Plaumann* formula the Court denied individual concern as 'the applicant is affected by the disputed Decision as an importer of clementines, that is to say, by reason of a commercial activity which may at any time be practised by any person and is not therefore such as to distinguish the applicant in relation to the contested Decision as in the case of the addressee.'[412] It did not matter that the group that was affected was easily identifiable, as it only consisted of 35 importers. It was also irrelevant that even though the act applied to an open class and therefore the membership of the group was constantly changing such change was likely to occur 'in practice only to a limited degree'.[413] AG Roemer expressly made the link between individual concern and the nature of the act when he argued that 'if however the legal effects of the decision are the same as in the case of a legislative measure against which individuals cannot bring an action, it cannot be admitted that there is any need for legal protection from the point of view of individual concern.'[414]

It is therefore not surprising that the reasoning the Court uses to deny individual concern to members of an open class is similar to that employed

---

412 Case 25/62 *Plaumann v Commission* [1963] ECR 95, para. 9.
413 Ibid., Opinion of AG Roemer, p. 116.
414 Ibid.

in cases where the Court establishes the general applicability of the act in the case of an open class. The criterion common to deny individual concern and to establish the general applicability of an act is that of 'objectively determined situations'. The Court has argued that 'the fact that the number and the identity of the persons affected can be ascertained does not mean that they are individually concerned' as long as the measure applies 'by virtue of an objective legal or factual situation defined by the measure in question'.[415] The measure is then considered as being 'addressed in general and abstract terms to indeterminate classes of persons and applies to objectively determined situations'[416] and the applicants are only concerned by the measure in their objective capacity in the sector. The Court then also considers as irrelevant in such a case 'the possibility of determining more or less precisely the number or even the identity of the persons'[417] to whom the act applies. This reasoning is identical to the reasoning used by the Court when defining the general applicability of an act and therefore its legislative nature.

This means that applicants cannot be individually concerned in case of an open class, even where the economic circumstances and/or the temporal limitation of the act make it unlikely that the class of those affected at the time the act is adopted will change later on.[418] In *Unicme*[419] the applicants, Italian importers of motor-cycles from Japan and their association UNICME, challenged Council Regulation 1692/77,[420] which limited the import of certain motor-cycles imported from Japan. From 1 January to 31 December 1977 the quantity of motor-cycles for which authorisation should be issued was fixed at 18,000. The Regulation entered into force on 29 July 1977. Even though the Regulation concerned an open class, it is readily apparent that a change in the membership of the persons affected was highly unlikely due to the temporal limitation of the act. The Court nevertheless found that 'the possibility of determining more or less precisely the number or even the identity of the persons to whom a measure applies by no means implies that it must be regarded as being of individual concern to them'.[421] This reasoning could easily have been used in the context of establishing the general applicability of the act.

---

415 Case C-213/91 *Abertal v Commission* [1993] ECR I-3177, at para. 17.

416 Ibid., at para. 19.

417 Case C-209/94P *Buralux v Council* [1996] ECR I-615, para. 24.

418 See also P. Craig and G. DeBúrca, supra note 1, p. 513.

419 Case 123/77 *Unicme v Council* [1978] ECR 845. See also Case C-213/91 *Abertal v Commission* [1993] ECR I-3177; Joined Cases C-232/91 and C-233/91 *Petridi v Commission* [1991] ECR I-5351; Case C-131/92 *Arnaud v Council* [1993] I-2573.

420 [1977] OJ L 188/11.

421 Case 123/77 *Unicme v Council* [1978] ECR 845, para. 16. See also Case T-82/06 *Apple Computer International v Commission*, order of 19 February 2008, at para. 52.

An objectively determined situation is, however, not limited to acts applying to an open class. In the same way as an act which affects a closed class does not necessarily have to be a decision in substance, not all individuals who find themselves within a closed class should expect to be considered as individually concerned. In *Compagnie*[422] the Court had to deal with transitional measures designed to govern the effects of the alterations of the amounts to be paid under the Common Agricultural Policy and which limited the application of the new rules to a certain date. The AG argued that the persons affected by the transitional provisions belonged to a closed class, as the provisions related to the past and concerned a limited category of ascertainable persons.[423] The Court implicitly accepted that the persons belonged to a closed class, but nevertheless reiterated its statement in *Zuckerfabrik Watenstedt*, namely that the number and identity of the persons were irrelevant as long as 'it is clear that this application depends on an objective legal or factual situation defined by the measure with reference to its purpose'.[424] The Court found that the date chosen by the Commission 'was necessary from an objective point of view'.[425] On that basis the Court denied individual concern without further ado.[426]

This can be contrasted with the ruling in *CAM*.[427] In this case the Council had adopted a regulation in 1967, which provided for the fixing and payment of export refunds on cereals, including barley. Such refunds could be fixed in advance on the day of the application for an export of such products. The refund would increase with a subsequent increase in prices for barley. When the Council therefore increased barley prices in 1974 with effect from 7 October 1974, the Commission, nevertheless, decided in a regulation that advance-fixing certificates for exports of barley dated before 7 October 1974 should not benefit from the increase in prices. The Court found that the applicants were concerned by the act as a closed class, as it applied to a fixed and known number of cereal exporters, and they were 'identified by reason of the individual course of action which they pursued or are regarded as having pursued during a particular period.'[428] The Court came therefore to the conclusion that 'such a measure, even if it

---

422 Case 64/69 *Compagnie Française Commerciale et Financière v Commission* [1970] ECR 221.

423 Opinion of AG Roemer, ibid, at pp. 217, 218, who argued that the act was a general act (*Allgemeinverfügung*) and therefore not of a legislative nature.

424 Case 64/69 *Compagnie Française Commerciale et Financière v Commission* [1970] ECR 221, at para. 11.

425 Ibid. para. 12.

426 Case 64/69 *Compagnie Française Commerciale et Financière v Commission* [1970] ECR 221, para. 17.

427 Case 100/74 *CAM v Commission* [1975] ECR 1393.

428 Ibid., para. 18.

is one of a number of provisions having a legislative function individually concerns the persons to whom it applies in that it affects their legal position because of a factual situation which differentiates them from all other persons and distinguishes them individually just as in the case of the person addressed.'[429] The Court's assessment of the act as legislative is in line with the case law on the nature of the act according to which acts that apply to a closed class can be of general application if they apply to objectively determined situations. What is surprising is that the Court was prepared to find the applicants individually concerned even though, in its view, the act did not constitute a decision in substance. *CAM* therefore foreshadows a more liberal approach in the interpretation of individual concern and indicates the Court's willingness to widen the scope of individual concern beyond that of decision in substance. However, it seems wrong to infer from *CAM* that belonging to a closed class is sufficient for individual concern. It should be noted that the Court did not consider the applicants as individually concerned merely because they belonged to a closed class, but because they could be 'identified by reason of the individual course of action which they pursued or are regarded as having pursued during a particular period'.[430]

This last point was confirmed in *Asteris*,[431] where the Court was also concerned with a closed class, namely traders who processed Greek tomatoes into tomato concentrate during the marketing year 1983/84. A regulation was adopted with retroactive effect to comply with a judgment by the Court that had declared void a previous regulation dealing with production aid to the traders in that year. In contrast to its AG, the Court found that the applicants were not individually concerned, as they were only concerned in their objective capacity as producers of tomato concentrate and 'as far as they are concerned, therefore, the regulation is a measure of general application which applies to objectively determined situations and entails legal effects for a category of persons considered generally and in the abstract'.[432] It is apparent also in this case that the Court used the same line of reasoning to establish the general applicability of the act and to deny individual concern.

Deutz und Geldermann[433] similarly demonstrates that belonging to a closed class is not sufficient to be considered individually concerned. The

---

[429] Ibid., para. 19. See also J. Usher, 'Individual concern in general legislation – 10 years on' (1994) *ELRev* 636–640, at pp. 637–8.

[430] Ibid., para. 18.

[431] Cases 97, 99, 193, 215/86 *Asteris v Commission* [1988] ECR 2181.

[432] Ibid., para. 15. See also Cases 103–109/78 *Beauport v Council and Commission* [1979] ECR 17.

[433] Case 26/86 *Deutz und Geldermann v Council* [1987] ECR 941.

Council adopted a regulation in 1985, which concerned the description and presentation of sparkling wines. The regulation prohibited, for the purposes of describing a quality sparkling wine, the use of any reference to a method of production containing a geographical name if the product in question would not qualify for the designation of origin. Deutz und Geldermann, German sparkling wine producers, were affected by this rule, as they had traditionally made reference on their sparkling wines to a production method, known as 'méthode champenoise'. Under the transitional provisions of the regulation, such a reference could only be made for another eight wine growing years. One could have assumed that the regulation concerned in its transitional provision a closed category. Those producers who had traditionally used such a reference could not be enlarged, as a new producer could not claim that the reference was 'traditional'. In order to determine whether the regulation was one in substance the Court employed the *Plaumann* formula and made an express reference to its *CAM* ruling. In contrast to *CAM*, the Court considered the fact as irrelevant that the measure concerned the producers as closed category. It held that 'the measure is still in substance a regulation, as it concerns the applicant in its objective capacity as a sparkling-wine producer which has traditionally used a particular method of production in just the same way as any other producer or trader in the same position'.[434]

AG Mischo in his Opinion argued that standing was granted in *CAM* and, as will be discussed below, in *Toepfer* on the basis that 'they had actually carried out before a given date a quite specific formality, such as requesting an import or export licence or advance fixing which only certain members of that category had carried out'.[435] As no such activity was carried out, the applicant could not have standing. This was confirmed by AG Lenz in *Codorniu*, where he pointed out with reference to *Deutz und Geldermann* that belonging to a closed category is not enough, as there must be a specific connection between the applicant's situation and the contested measure.[436]

Finally, in *Comafrica*,[437] the CFI was faced with a challenge to two Commission regulations which implemented the banana regime laid down in Council Regulation 404/93.[438] The applicants argued that Commission

---

434 Ibid., para. 12.
435 Opinion of AG Mischo, ibid., p. 948.
436 Opinion of AG Lenz in Case C-309/89 *Codorniu v Council* [1994] ECR I-1853 at para. 39. See also Case C-482/04 P *SNF v Commission*, order of 21 November 2005 (not published), at para. 39.
437 Case T-139/01 *Comafrica SpA and Another v Commission* [2005] ECR II-409.
438 [1993] OJ L47/1, as amended.

Regulation 896/2001[439] dealt with a closed class and therefore constituted a bundle of individual decisions, insofar as its Article 4(1) only applied to traditional operators with reference quantities for 1994 to 1996 'as taken into account in 1998'. They claimed that Regulation 1121/2001,[440] which was adopted on 7 June 2001, should also be considered as applying to a closed group, as it concerned only those operators who had submitted an application to the national authorities by 11 May 2001 at the latest. The CFI found that both regulations constituted acts of general application. The CFI held that even if the persons to whom Article 4(1) of Regulation 896/2001 applied were identifiable when the act was adopted, an assumption which the CFI refused to accept, 'its [Article 4(1) of Regulation 896/2001] legislative scope cannot be questioned given that [. . .] that provision refers only to objective situations of fact or law'.[441] The CFI accepted that Regulation 1121/2001 applied to a fixed and closed class of operators. All the same the CFI found that the act was of general application, as it 'was adopted in the light, not of the specific situation of traditional operators A/B, but of an objective factual situation, namely the fact that the sum of the reference quantities notified globally to the Commission by the Member States [. . .] was less than the available amount of the tariff quotas'.[442] In the same way, the CFI found that the measure concerned the applicants 'only in their objective capacity as traditional operators A/B, on the same basis as every other operator in that category'[443] and was therefore not of individual concern to them.

It is therefore difficult to assert that in case of a closed class the applicant would automatically have to be considered as individually concerned.[444] The reasoning of the Court in *Asteris* and *Comafrica* seems to represent the general principle that excludes individual concern, even if the act concerns only a closed class, where the measure applies to objectively determined situations, even though *CAM* indicates that in exceptional circumstances an individual can be considered to be individually concerned even in such a case.

On the other hand, it is clear from the case law that in those cases in which the Court came to the conclusion that the act constituted a decision in substance the Court invariably also found that the act was also

---

439 [2001] OJ L 126/6.

440 [2001] OJ L 153/12.

441 Case T-139/01 *Comafrica SpA and Another v Commission* [2005] ECR II-409, para. 95.

442 Ibid., para. 105.

443 Case T-139/01 *Comafrica SpA and Another v Commission* [2005] ECR II-409, para. 108.

444 A. Albors-Llorens, supra note 1, pp. 131–132.

of individual concern, where the applicant was one of the addressees of the decision. In *International Fruit*[445] the Court after having concluded that the legal act in issue had to be classified as a 'conglomeration of individual decisions taken by the Commission under the guise of a regulation',[446] also found that the decisions were of individual concern, as the legal position of each applicant was affected. The Court adopted a similar approach in *Weddel*.[447] After having identified the measure as a bundle of decisions taken in the guise of a regulation, the Court without further ado considered the applicant to be individually concerned. And in *Roquette*,[448] the Court, without discussing the nature of the measure, found that Article 9(4) of Regulation 1111/77 in combination with Annex II applied certain criteria 'to each of the undertakings in question who are the addressees'[449] of that measure and therefore directly and individually concerned.

The link between the nature of the act as a decision in substance and individual concern was not discussed in *Toepfer*,[450] but seems equally apparent. The applicant applied on 1 October 1963 for import licences for maize at a zero levy, which the German authorities had applied and notified on the basis of the existing rules for this day. The German authorities refused to grant the licences by adopting protective measures to prevent traders from taking advantage of the zero levy. As the levy resulted from the difference between the threshold price and the free-at-frontier price, the Commission attempted to rectify the situation by fixing on the same day a new free-at-frontier price, applicable from 2 October. In addition, on 3 October the Commission retroactively approved the protective measures taken by the German authorities until 4 October. The Court granted the applicant standing by holding that 'the only persons concerned by the said measures were importers who had applied for an import licence during the course of the day of 1 October 1963. The number and identity of these importers had already become fixed and ascertainable before 4 October, when the contested decision was made. The Commission was in a position to know that its decision affected the interests and the position of the said importers alone'.[451] Even though the Court in this case did not deal with the nature of

---

445 Cases 41–44/70 *International Fruit Company v Commission* [1971] ECR 411.
446 Ibid., para. 21.
447 Case C-354/87 *Weddel v Commission* [1990] ECR I-3847.
448 Case 138/79 *Roquette v Council* [1980] ECR 3333.
449 Ibid., para. 16.
450 Case 106, 107/63 *Toepfer v Commission* [1965] ECR 405.
451 Ibid., p. 411. See also Case 62/70 *Bock v Commission* [1971] ECR 897, at p. 908. For a more recent case, see Case C-125/06 P *Commission v Infront*, judgment of 13 March 2008, at paras. 71–72.

the act,[452] it is difficult to see how the act was not adopted on the basis of and with exclusive application to the situation of specific individuals and that it therefore constituted a decision in substance of individual concern to the applicant.

The traditional *Plaumann* approach is therefore not so much based on the distinction of open and closed class,[453] but should be perceived as a way of preventing individuals from challenging regulations in substance[454] thereby creating an 'almost insurmountable barrier'[455] to accessing the Community Courts under Article 230(4). Following this approach a private party is only individually concerned where it belongs to a closed class and has pursued a particular course of action creating a causal link between the measure and the situation of the applicant. In other words, a private party is considered to be individually concerned where the act has to be regarded as a decision in substance, as the act was adopted on the basis of and with exclusive application to the situation of specific individuals. It should also be noted that, contrary to what has been suggested,[456] it does not appear that the modification of an individual right is necessary to establish individual concern.[457] As a consequence of this restrictive interpretation only very few applicants have succeeded in showing that they were individually concerned on the basis that they belonged to a closed class.[458]

Extension of *Plaumann*

An act might not affect its addressees in the same way. This can be the case where certain persons have been granted specific rights to participate in the procedure that leads to the adoption of the act, procedural rights that might not be available to others. Similarly, the institution which adopts the act might be under an obligation to take account of the specific situation of certain persons, but not that of others within the same open class. In addition, those who benefit from the rules laid down in the act, because either rights

---

452 It is interesting to note that in *Toepfer* the Court disregarded the fact that the act applied, at least theoretically, to an open class and based its assessment on the fact that the class was in practice closed. See also A. Albors-Llorens, supra note 1, p. 48.

453 See Case T-482/93 *Weber v Commission* [1996] ECR II-609, at paras. 63–66; Case T-298/94 *Roquette Frères v Council* [1996] ECR II-1531, at para. 41; Case T-11/99 *Van Parys and Others v Commission* [1999] ECR II-2653, at para. 43. See also A. Arnull (2001), supra note 2, pp. 32–40.

454 See also C. Harding, supra note 2, at p. 355.

455 A. Barav, supra note 2, p. 191.

456 A. Albors-Llorens, supra note 1, p. 219.

457 See P. Nihoul, supra note 2, p. 180.

458 See Case 138/79 *Roquette v Council* [1980] ECR 3333; Case T-243/01 *Sony v Commission* [2003] ECR II-4189. See also Joined Cases T-218/03 to T-240/03 *Boyle v Commission* [2006] ECR II-1699, at paras. 48 and 49 and the appeal ruling in Joined Cases C-373/06 P, C-379/06 P and C-382/06 P *Flaherty and Others v Commission*, judgment of 17 April 2008, at para. 41.

or other benefits are conferred on them, can be set apart from those whose rights are negatively affected by the act. Even where the act does not affect any rights, its effects might be different. This might be particularly relevant, where the act influences the competitive relationship between the economic operators by benefiting some and disadvantaging others. Finally, those who fall within the scope of application of the act at the time the act is adopted can be distinguished from those that will fall within its scope in the future and are only potentially affected. This is particularly relevant where an activity is prohibited or restricted. Those who are (legally) carrying out the activity at the time of its restriction or prohibition might have made investments in reliance on the existing legal situation to continue. Those who are not yet active in the market can take account of the changed circumstances.

The Court in *Zuckerfabrik Watenstedt* categorically refused to accept that the fact that persons occupy such a special position within an open class is of relevance in determining the nature of the act. It held that 'the fact that a legal provision may have different practical effects on the different persons to whom it applies in no way contradicts its nature as a regulation provided that the situation to which it refers is objectively determined.'[459]

The same cannot be said for individual concern. Where an act applies in the same fashion to all members of an open class, then they cannot be regarded as individually concerned under the *Plaumann* formula. However, where the effects of the measure vary according to the situation in which the persons affected find themselves, then individual concern might be possible. The *Plaumann* formula takes account of distinguishing factors of those concerned by an act. Persons are individually concerned where they are distinguished individually 'by reason of certain attributes which are peculiar to them or by reason of circumstances in which they are differentiated from all other persons'.

And indeed, over time a split has emerged between the assessment of the nature of the act and individual concern. The Court has admitted that an act which is not a decision in substance can, nevertheless, be of individual concern to some persons. Four areas will be discussed below in which the Community Courts have applied the *Plaumann* formula in a more liberal fashion.[460] The first area comprises cases in which the individual enjoys procedural rights in the adoption of an act. In the second category the individual enjoys a specific

---

[459] Case 6/68 *Zuckerfabrik Watenstedt v Council* [1968] ECR 409, p. 415.

[460] See also Case 294/83 *Les Verts v Parliament* [1986] ECR 1339, at paras. 32–37, in which the Court considered the applicant individually concerned by a funding decision of the EP, which discriminated against political groupings not already represented in Parliament. The ruling seems to have been influenced by a concern for equality in parliamentary elections and by the fact that the applicant would be denied an effective remedy before the elections to the European Parliament.

substantive protection of its legal position. The third and fourth concern respectively cases in which the Court has found that the act affected the individual by virtue of its specific economic effects or by its specific effects on rights. In all these areas the Court has recognised individual concern to exist in certain circumstances and has thereby considerably widened the scope of the *Plaumann* formula beyond its classical application.

Administrative proceedings at EC level It could be argued that the participation of private parties in the procedure that leads to the adoption of a Community act should be considered as distinguishing them individually in the meaning of the *Plaumann* formula. The Community Courts have never accepted such a wide proposition, but have recognised that certain individuals, which are in a special procedural position, should be regarded as being individually concerned.[461] They have held that 'the fact that a person participates, in one way or another, in the process leading to the adoption of a Community act does not distinguish him individually in relation to the act in question unless the relevant Community legislation has laid down specific procedural guarantees for such a person'.[462] A person can therefore be individually concerned where 'Community law has made provision for a special procedure prior to the adoption of the contested act, in which those individuals may participate and submit their observations'.[463]

On the other hand, in *Greenpeace*, the AG rejected standing where the applicant participates in a procedure for environmental impact assessment, which is national in character, is governed by EC and national rules and is a matter for national authorities.[464] Also the CFI has rejected the argument that an exchange of letters with the Commission would constitute such a procedure, where there was no special procedure provided for.[465]

---

[461] See A. Arnull (1995), supra note 2, p. 34 and A. Arnull (2001), supra note 2, pp. 40–43; A. Ward, supra note 1, pp. 301–305.

[462] Case T-339/00 *Bactria v Commission* [2002] ECR II-2287, para. 51. Emphasis added. See also Joined Cases T-481/93 and T-484/93 *Exporteurs in Levende Varkens and Others v Commission* [1995] ECR II-2941, at para. 59; Case T-585/93 *Greenpeace and Others v Commission* [1995] ECR II-2205, at para. 56; Case T-12/96 *Area Cova and Others v Council and Commission* [1999] ECR II-2301, at para. 59; Case T-60/96 *Merck and Others v Commission* [1997] ECR II-849; Joined Cases T-38/99 to T-50/99 *Sociedade Agrícola dos Arinhos and Others v Commission* [2001] ECR II-585, at para. 46; Case T-47/00 *Rica Foods v Commission* [2002] ECR II-113, at para. 55; Case T-291/04 R *Enviro Tech Europe Ltd and Another v Commission* [2005] ECR II-475, at para. 67.

[463] Opinion of AG Cosmas in Case C-321/95P *Greenpeace v Commission* [1998] ECR I-1651, para. 79.

[464] Ibid., Opinion of AG Cosmas, at para. 96.

[465] Case T-585/93 *Greenpeace and Others v Commission* [1995] ECR II-2205 at para. 56. See also Cases T-38/99 to T-50/99 *Sociedade Agricola and Others v Commission* [2001] ECR II-585, at para. 46.

Also where individuals have participated in the adoption of a legislative act, although such participation is not provided for, as in the case of Article 37 EC, the Court has denied standing.[466] Where there is neither a statutory requirement to hear the applicant nor a general obligation to do so before the adoption of a measure, the CFI has equally denied standing.[467] This could mean that standing might be granted, where there was a general obligation to hear the applicant before the adoption of the measure, even though there was no statutory duty to do so.[468]

It is widely agreed, however, that in those areas of EC law where the EC institutions, mainly the Commission, apply EC law in accordance with a procedure which is laid down by Community legislation, the Court seems to apply a more generous interpretation of the *Plaumann* formula, in particular to those for whom Community law has provided certain procedural rights.[469] For this reason the case law in the areas of anti-dumping, competition and state aid law is more liberal than in areas where the EC institutions exercise more legislative activity. Procedural guarantees are, however, also provided in other areas of Community law, with the effect that persons that benefit from such guarantees are considered to have standing.[470]

COMPETITION Regulation 17/62[471] provided in Article 3(2)(b)[472] that natural or legal persons who claimed a legitimate interest could lodge a complaint with the Commission alleging a violation of Articles 81 and 82. Moreover, interested parties had the right to submit their observations under Article 19(3) where the Commission intended to give negative clearance[473] or to grant an exemption under Article 81(3).[474] The Community

---

466 Case T-99/94 *Asocarne v Council* [1994] ECR II-871 at para. 40.

467 Joined Cases T-481/93 and 484/93 *Exporteurs in Levende Varkens and Others v Commission* [1995] ECR II-2941 at paras. 55–58.

468 Case C-269/90 *Hauptzollamt München-Mitte v Technische Universität München* [1991] ECR I-5469.

469 P. Craig (1994), supra note 2, p. 527; T.C. Hartley, supra note 1, pp. 358–362; A. Arnull (1995), supra note 2, p. 30; S. Enchelmaier, supra note 2, p. 179.

470 See Case T-70/99 *Alpharma Inc v Council* [2002] ECR II-3495; Case T-13/99 *Pfizer Animal Health SA v Council* [2002] ECR II-3305; Case T-31/07 R *Du Pont de Nemours and Others v Commission*, order of 19 July 2007, at para. 112.

471 [1962] OJ L 13/204, as amended. Regulation 17/62 has been replaced by Regulation 1/2003, [2003] OJ L1/1, which applies from 1 May 2004.

472 Now Article 7(2) of Regulation 1/2003.

473 Article 2 of Regulation 17/62 stated that the Commission would certify on the basis of the facts in its possession that there were not grounds under Article 81(1) or 82 of the EC Treaty for action on its part in respect of an agreement, decision or practice.

474 The system of notification has been abandoned under Regulation 1/2003, as Article 81(3) is now considered to be applicable directly by national authorities and national courts, see Article 5 of Regulation 1/2003.

Courts have considered these procedural guarantees as relevant for the question of individual concern.

In *Metro I*,[475] the applicant, a self-service wholesaler of electronic products, had lodged a complaint with the Commission, in which it alleged that SABA, a producer of such products, was in breach of Article 81 by refusing to sell to Metro or to appoint it as wholesaler in its distribution system. The Commission adopted a decision in which it gave SABA negative clearance for certain features of its selective distribution system and granted it exemption for the remaining parts of the system. It was obvious that the decision applied to an open class, namely all wholesalers who wanted to sell SABA products but did not fulfil the requirements of participating in the distribution system.[476] Nevertheless, the Court found that Metro was individually concerned by that decision. The Court argued that 'it is in the interests of satisfactory administration of justice and of the proper application of Articles [81] and [82] that natural persons who are entitled, pursuant to Article 3(2)(b) of Regulation No 17, to request the Commission to find an infringement of Articles [81] and [82] should be able, if their request is not complied with wholly or in part, to institute proceedings in order to protect their legitimate interests.'[477] In *Metro II*[478] the Commission had granted an individual exemption under Article 81(3) to SABA's modified selective distribution system. Also in this case the decision applied to an open class. As AG Verloren Van Themaat pointed out, an individual exemption, which declared Article 81(1), which creates individual rights, inapplicable, deprived individuals concerned by the distribution system of those rights.[479] All the same, even though it had not made a complaint under Article 3(2)(b) of Regulation 17/62 the Court found that Metro, who challenged that decision, was individually concerned due to the fact that it had been refused access to SABA's distribution system and that it had made observations during the administrative procedure, to which it was entitled under Article 19(3) of Regulation 17/62 on the basis of its legitimate interest in the matter.

In *Metropole*[480] the CFI went one step further and held that a person which could rely on the procedural guarantees provided for in the

---

475 Case 26/76 *Metro v Commission* [1977] ECR 1875.

476 See Opinion of AG Reischl, ibid., p. 1922. See also P. Craig (1994), supra note 2, p. 518.

477 Case 26/76 *Metro v Commission* [1977] ECR 1875, para. 13. See also Case 210/81 *Demo-Studio Schmidt v Commission* [1983] ECR 3045, at paras. 14–15.

478 Case 75/84 *Metro v Commission* [1986] ECR 3021.

479 Ibid., Opinion of AG Verloren Van Themaat, p. 3055.

480 Joined Cases T-528/93, T-542/93, T-543/93 and T-546/93 *Metropole télévision SA and Others v Commission* [1996] ECR II-649.

Community rules governing competition procedures was individually concerned regardless of whether it had availed itself of these rights. In a decision the Commission had granted an individual exemption to EBU/Eurovision System, a trade association of radio and television organizations. Antena 3, one of the applicants who challenged the decision, was considered to be an interested third party under Article 19(3) of Regulation 17/62. On this basis Antena 3 was regarded as being individually concerned regardless of the fact that it had not made use of its procedural rights under Article 19(3) and had not made written or oral observations during the administrative procedure for the adoption of the decision.[481]

It seems clear that in the above cases the decision of the Commission to grant an individual exemption would have to be classified as being of general application, as the open class affected by the decision is 'a category viewed in the abstract'.[482] This did not prevent the Court from finding the applicants individually concerned on the basis of their specific procedural position. All the same, acts that granted negative clearance or an individual exemption under Regulation 17/62 were adopted in the form of decisions. This might be the reason why the Community Courts in these cases rarely discuss the nature of the act and focus instead on direct and individual concern.[483] AG Roemer in *Plaumann* argued that any other approach 'would involve attributing to the authors of the Treaty an intention to narrow down the right of action to an excessive degree'.[484] The same reasoning can, however, not be applied in the area of anti-dumping, where measures have to be adopted by way of regulation.

ANTI-DUMPING[485] Regulation 384/96[486] allows the Community to impose anti-dumping duties on third country products which are dumped on the Community market causing injury to Community industry. The procedure is normally started with a complaint.[487] Where it considers it justified,[488] the

---

[481] Ibid., para. 62. However, see Case T-87/92 *BVBA Kruidvat v Commission* [1996] ECR II-1931, paras. 69 and 70.

[482] Opinion of AG Reischl in Case 26/76 *Metro v Commission* [1977] ECR 1875, p. 1922.

[483] This does, of course, not mean that the nature of such acts is that of a decision. In the light of the findings above, it should be emphasised that the form of an act is not decisive of its nature.

[484] Opinion of AG Roemer in Case 25/62 *Plaumann v Commission* [1963] ECR 95, p. 113.

[485] See See R. Greaves, supra note 2; A. Arnull, 'Challenging EC Anti-dumping Regulations' (1992) 13 *ECLRev* 73–81; M. Nettesheim, supra note 2; T.C. Hartley, supra note 1, pp. 359–361.

[486] [1996] OJ L 56/1, as amended (the 'basic regulation').

[487] Under Article 5(6) of the basic regulation an investigation can be initiated without a complaint, however only in special circumstances.

[488] On the grounds for rejecting the initiation of an investigation, see Article 5(4) and (7).

Commission will initiate an investigation by publishing a notice to that end in the *Official Journal*. This allows interested parties to submit their views and to be heard during the investigation.[489] The Commission will then either terminate the investigation[490] or impose provisional anti-dumping duties,[491] which will then have to be confirmed by the Council imposing definitive anti-dumping duties.[492] The anti-dumping duties are fixed based on investigations of the production prices,[493] export prices[494] and exceptionally the import prices[495] of individually identified undertakings.

The difficulty in those cases with regard to Article 230(4) EC lies in the fact that the anti-dumping duty is adopted in the form of a regulation.[496] However, the Court has made it clear that direct and individual concern are the decisive factors to establish standing of applicants, even though anti-dumping regulations are regulations in substance.[497]

The Community Courts consider producers and exporters as individually concerned, where they were identified in the measures[498] or were concerned by the preliminary investigation.[499] Part of the reasoning is that there is no alternative remedy in a national court, as the respective Member State imposes the anti-dumping duty on the importer.[500]

---

489 See Articles 5(10) and 6(5) of the basic regulation.

490 See Articles 8 and 9 of the basic regulation.

491 See Article 7(1) of the basic regulation.

492 Article 9(4) of the basic regulation.

493 See Article 2(A) of the basic regulation.

494 Article 2(8) of the basic regulation.

495 Article 2(9) of the basic regulation.

496 See Article 14(1) of the basic regulation.

497 See Case 264/82 *Timex v Council and Commission* [1985] ECR 849 at para. 12. On the nature of anti-dumping regulations as regulations in substance, see also Joined Cases 239 and 275/82 *Allied Corporation and Others v Commission* [1984] ECR 1005, at para. 11; Case 264/82 *Timex v Council and Commission* [1985] ECR 849, at para. 12; Case C-156/87 *Gestetner Holdings v Commission and Council* [1990] ECR I-781, at para. 17; Case C-358/89 *Extramet v Council* [1991] ECR 2501, at para. 13. For a detailed discussion on the nature of anti-dumping regulations, see A. Türk, supra note 283, pp. 136–139.

498 This consideration has also been relevant in the sanctions cases. In Case T-306/01 *Yusuf and Al Barakaat International Foundation* [2005] ECR II-2533, at para. 186, the CFI found that despite the general application of the regulation the applicants were individually concerned, because they were expressly named in Annex I of Council Regulation 881/2002, [2002] OJ L 139/9. See also Case T-228/02 *Organisation des Modjahedines du people d'Iran v Council* [2006] ECR II-4665, at para. 98; Case T-47/03 *Sison v Council*, judgment of 11 July 2007, at para. 146; Case T-253/04 *Kongra-Gel and others v Council*, judgment of 3 April 2008, at para. 77.

499 See Case 279/86 *Sermes v Commission* [1987] ECR 3109, at para. 15; Joined Cases C-133/87 and C-150/87 *Nashua Corporation and Others v Commission* [1990] ECR I-719, at para. 14; Case C-156/87 *Gestetner Holdings v Council and Commission* [1990] ECR I781, at para. 17; Case T-597/97 *Euromin v Council* [2000] ECR II-2419, at para. 45.

500 See AG Jacobs in Case C-358/89 *Extramet v Commission* [1991] ECR I-2501 at para. 17.

In the case of complainants the Court granted standing in *Timex*[501] on the ground that the anti-dumping measure was 'based on the applicant's own situation'.[502] The Court arrived at this conclusion not merely on the basis that Timex participated in the proceedings leading to the adoption of the measure, but by the part it played in the anti-dumping proceeding and its position on the market in issue. In *Fediol*,[503] which concerned an anti-subsidy case, the Court granted standing to a complainant to protect the procedural guarantees provided for it in the basic regulation.

On the other hand, importers are treated less favourably. Importers are only considered to have standing where their resale prices are taken into account for the construction of the export prices,[504] but also where they are associated with the exporters on whose products anti-dumping duties were imposed.[505] Independent importers, which are not related to an exporter, are only granted standing in exceptional circumstances, such as where the anti-dumping measure has a serious impact on the business of the applicant.[506] The main reason for this more restrictive approach is apparently that importers could bring an action in national courts against the anti-dumping duty.

In *British Shoe Corporation*[507] the CFI therefore rejected the argument that standing against an anti-dumping measure was granted by the Community Courts merely on the basis of participation in the administrative procedure.[508] The CFI argued that:

> although participation by an undertaking in an anti-dumping proceeding may be taken into account amongst other factors, in order to establish whether that undertaking is individually concerned by the regulation introducing anti-dumping duties adopted at the conclusion of that proceeding, if there are no other factors giving rise to a particular situation which distinguishes that undertaking from all other traders, with respect to the measure in question, such participation does not, of itself give rise to a right enabling the undertaking to bring a direct action against that regulation.[509]

---

501 Case 264/82 *Timex v Council and Commission* [1985] ECR 849. See also Case C-76/01 *Eurocoton v Council* [2003] ECR I-10091, at paras. 73 and 85.

502 Case 264/82 *Timex v Council and Commission* [1985] ECR 849, para. 15.

503 Case 191/82 *Fediol v Commission* [1983] ECR 2913, at paras. 28–30.

504 Joined Cases C-133/87 and C-150/87 *Nashua Corporation and Others v Commission* [1990] ECR I-719, at para. 15; Case C-156/87 *Gestetner Holdings v Council and Commission* [1990] ECR I781, at para. 18; Case T-7/99 *Medici v Council* [2000] ECR II-2671, at para. 65.

505 See Joined Cases 277/85 and 300/85 *Canon v Council* [1988] ECR 5731, at para. 8; Case T-598/97 *British Shoe Corporation Footwear Supplies Ltd and Others v Council* [2002] ECR II-1155, at para. 47.

506 See Case C-358/89 *Extramet Industrie v Council* [1991] ECR I-2501, at para. 17.

507 Case T-598/97 *British Shoe Corporation Footwear Supplies Ltd and Others v Council* [2002] ECR II-1155.

508 Ibid., para. 60.

509 Ibid., para. 61.

However, even though in anti-dumping cases, in contrast to those in competition law, procedural guarantees provided in a Community act would not suffice to grant standing to those persons who can rely on these guarantees, they constitute an important, if not sufficient, element to establish individual concern. Consequently, the case law on individual concern in these cases is more liberal and the persons who can rely on procedural guarantees enjoy a specific legal position.

STATE AID[510] Articles 87 to 89 EC try to ensure that in each Member State common rules are applied with regard to subsidies given to undertakings, in order to prevent the common market from being distorted. Also in these cases the Commission will undertake an investigation and will address a decision to the Member State concerned. The procedure laid down in Article 88 EC has two stages. Article 88(3) EC requires that any Member State granting new aid, that is aid granted for the first time or aid altering existing aid, shall notify the Commission. Where it considers the aid to be compatible with the common market, the Commission will inform the Member State accordingly. Where the Commission considers the aid not compatible or where it reviews existing aid, the second stage in the procedure laid down in Article 88(2) EC will have to be followed. The Commission will invite the 'parties concerned' to submit their comments. The Court defined those parties as 'the persons, undertakings or associations whose interests might be affected by the grant of the aid, in particular competing undertakings and trade associations'.[511] The Commission will then take a decision and will address it to the Member State granting the aid.

The Member State and the undertaking which is refused the aid will have standing. The beneficiaries of aid schemes have *locus standi*, but only where they are the actual beneficiaries of the aid in question. In *Italy and Sardegna v Commission*, the Court held that a company could not contest 'a Commission decision prohibiting a sectoral aid scheme if it is concerned by that decision solely by virtue of belonging to the sector in question and being a potential beneficiary of the scheme'.[512]

---

[510] See J.A. Winter, 'The Rights of Complainants in State Aid Cases: Judicial Review of Commission Decisions Adopted under Article 88 (ex 93) EC' (1999) 36 *CMLRev* 521–568.

[511] Case 323/82 *Intermills v Commission* [1984] ECR 3809 at para. 16. See also Case C-78/03P *Commission v Aktionsgemeinschaft Recht und Eigentum* [2005] ECR I-10737, at para. 36; Case T-395/04 *Air One v Commission* [2006] ECR II-1343, at para. 36; Case T-167/04 *Asklepios Kliniken v Commission*, judgment of 11 July 2007, at para. 49; Case T-30/03 *SID v Commission* [2007] ECR II-34, at para. 31, in which the CFI held that the applicant was not affected in its competitive position.

[512] Case C-15/98 and C-105/99 *Italy and Sardegna v Commission* [2000] ECR I-8855, at para. 33. See, however, Case T-9/98 *Mitteldeutsche Erdoel-Raffinerie GmbH v Commission* [2001] ECR II-3367.

As in competition and anti-dumping cases, participation by third parties in state aid proceedings was initially considered to be an important factor in assessing individual concern. In *Cofaz*,[513] the Court had to determine the standing of French fertiliser companies against a decision by which the Commission terminated the procedure under Article 88(2) against the tariff structure for natural gas prices in the Netherlands, after the tariff had been modified. Such a decision, even though it was addressed to the Netherlands, affected the legal position of producers of ammonia and of nitrate fertilisers and was therefore of general application. All the same, the applicants who had brought the complaint and had participated in the procedure sought to have the decision annulled. With reference to competition and anti-dumping cases, the Court found that

> the same conclusions apply to undertakings which have played a comparable role in the procedure referred to in Article 93 EEC [now Article 88 EC] provided, however, that their position on the market is significantly affected by the aid which is the subject of the contested decision. Article 93(2) [now Article 88(2) EC] recognises in general terms that the undertakings concerned are entitled to submit their comments to the Commission but does not provide any further details.[514]

More recently, the Court has downgraded the importance of procedural participation. The Court has pointed out that while procedural participation is a relevant factor for assessing individual concern, such participation is not a necessary condition for individual concern, as other factors could be presented.[515] On the other hand, individual concern will be denied if the position of the applicant on the market is not substantially affected by the aid.[516] Even though various factors can be presented to establish the seriousness of the impact of the aid, the mere fact that the aid has an impact on the competitive relationship is not sufficient for individual concern.[517]

Active participation in the procedure seems to still be, however, an important factor in establishing the standing of an association responsible for protecting the collective interests of undertakings. The Court

---

513 Case 169/84 *Cofaz and Others v Commission* [1986] ECR 391.

514 Ibid, at para. 25. See also Case C-106/98P *Comité d'Entreprise and Others v Commission* [2000] ECR I-3659; Case T-210/02 *British Aggregates Association v Commission* [2006] ECR II-2789, at para. 62.

515 See Case C-260/05 P *Sniace v Commission* [2007] ECR I-10005, at paras. 56 and 57.

516 Ibid., para. 60.

517 Case C-525/04 P *Spain v Lenzing* [2007] ECR I-9947, at paras. 31–38. See also Case T-210/02 *British Aggregates Association v Commission* [2006] ECR II-2789, at paras. 50 and 51; Case C-78/03P *Commission v Aktionsgemeinschaft Recht und Eigentum* [2005] ECR I-10737, at para. 72; Case T-117/04 *Vereniging Werkgroep and Others v Commission* [2006] ECR II-3861, at para. 53.

considers such an association individually concerned by a final decision of the Commission on state aid either 'where the undertakings in question are also entitled to do so individually'[518] or 'where it is able to rely on a particular interest in acting, especially because its negotiating position is affected by the measure which it seeks to have annulled'.[519] In *Van der Kooy*,[520] the applicants challenged a decision in which the Commission declared the preferential tariff charged to glasshouse growers for natural gas in the Netherlands as incompatible with the common market. Landbouwschap, which acted as the growers' representative in the tariff negotiations, had to be considered as being individually concerned, in particular due to the role it had assumed in the negotiations with the Dutch authorities and its active participation in the procedure.[521] However, the Court made it clear in *Comité d'Entreprise*[522] that the mere status of negotiator was not sufficient in that respect.

The procedural guarantees awarded to certain parties in state aid proceedings are particularly relevant, where the Commission decides under Article 88(3) EC not to open an investigation under Article 88(2). In this case third parties cannot benefit from the procedural guarantees under Article 88(2) EC. Consequently, where the Commission adopts a decision in which it considers the aid to be compatible with the common market without proceeding to the second stage under Article 88(2) EC, third parties which are to be regarded as 'parties concerned' have standing to challenge that decision, but only to protect their procedural guarantees under Article 88(2).[523] On the other hand, where third parties want to challenge such a decision on the merits, they need to comply with the same

---

[518] Case T-95/03 *Asociación de Estaciones de Servicio de Madrid and Federación Catalana de Estaciones de Servicio v Commission* [2006] ECR II-4739, para. 42. See also Case 282/85 *DEFI* v *Commission* [1986] ECR 2469, para. 16; Case C-6/92 *Federmineraria and Others* v *Commission* [1993] ECR I-6357, para. 17; Case T-55/99 *CETM v Commission* [2000] ECR II-3207, para. 23.

[519] Case T-95/03 *Asociación de Estaciones de Servicio de Madrid and Federación Catalana de Estaciones de Servicio v Commission* [2006] ECR II-4739, para. 42. See also Case C-313/90 *CIRFS and Others v Commission* [1993] ECR I-1125, paras. 29 and 30; Case T-380/94 *AIUFFASS and AKT* v *Commission* [1996] ECR II-2169, para. 50; Case T-55/99 *CETM v Commission* [2000] ECR II-3207, para. 23.

[520] Joined Cases 67, 68 and 70/85 *Van der Kooy and Others v Commission* [1988] ECR 219.

[521] Ibid., paras. 21–24. See also Case C-313/90 *CIRFS and Others v Commission* [1993] ECR I-1125, paras. 28 and 30; Case T-55/99 *CETM v Commission* [2000] ECR II-3207, para. 23.

[522] Case C-106/98P *Comité d'Entreprise and Others v Commission* [2000] ECR I-3659, para. 51.

[523] Case C-198/91 *Cook v Commission* [1993] ECR I-2487. See Case T-27/02 *Kronofrance v Commission* [2004] ECR II-4177, at para. 34; Case C-78/03P *Commission v Aktionsgemeinschaft Recht und Eigentum* [2005] ECR I-10737, at para. 35; Case T-395/04 *Air One v Commission* [2006] ECR II-1343, at paras. 30 and 31.

standing requirements as are applicable to challenge decisions adopted under Article 88(2).[524]

OTHER AREAS OF COMMUNITY PROCEDURES Procedural guarantees are also provided in other areas of Community law, with the effect that those who benefit from such guarantees could be considered to have standing.[525] In *Alpharma*,[526] the Council adopted Regulation 2821/98,[527] which provided in Article 1 that *bacitracin* zinc, an antibiotic used as a growth promoter for livestock and also in the treatment of certain infections in human medicine, should be deleted from Annex B to Council Directive 70/524,[528] as amended by Council Directive 96/51[529] with the result that it could not be used as an additive in feedingstuffs. Alpharma, the only manufacturer and the largest supplier of *bacitracin* zinc in the EEA at the time the regulation was adopted, challenged the act. The CFI first analysed the nature of the Regulation and came to the conclusion that it applied 'not only to all the existing or potential manufacturers of that product but also to other traders, such as livestock farmers and producers and distributors of feedingstuffs'.[530] Consequently, it had to be considered as being of general application. However, in line with the anti-dumping cases it found that 'the fact that the contested regulation is of general application does not preclude it from being of direct and individual concern to certain natural and legal persons.'[531] With the introduction of new rules by Directive 96/51, which substantially amended Directive 70/524, Alpharma had to apply for a new authorisation for *bacitracin* zinc. When Alpharma made its application in June 1998 under Article 9g(2) and (4) of Directive 70/425, as amended by Directive 96/51, it was entitled to submit in accordance with the procedure laid down in Article 4 of the Directive a scientific dossier for the re-evaluation of the additive. The CFI found that the procedure in Article 4 provided Alpharma with procedural guarantees. When it adopted Regulation 2821/98 the Council, at least temporarily, terminated the procedure under which Alpharma enjoyed these procedural guarantees.

---

[524] Case C-78/03P *Commission v Aktionsgemeinschaft Recht und Eigentum* [2005] ECR I-10737, at para. 37; Case T-395/04 *Air One v Commission* [2006] ECR II-1343, at para. 32; Case T-210/02 *British Aggregates Association v Commission* [2006] ECR II-2789, at para. 53.

[525] See Case T-70/99 *Alpharma Inc v Council* [2002] ECR II-3495; Case T-13/99 *Pfizer Animal Health SA v Council* [2002] ECR II-3305; Case T-31/07 R *Du Pont de Nemours and Others v Commission*, order of 19 July 2007, at para. 112.

[526] Case T-70/99 *Alpharma v Council* [2002] ECR II-3495.

[527] [1998] OJ L 351/4.

[528] [1970] OJ Special Edition (III), p. 840.

[529] [1996] OJ L 235/39.

[530] Case T-70/99 *Alpharma v Council* [2002] ECR II-3495, para. 75.

[531] Ibid., para. 76.

In *BI Vetmedica*,[532] the applicant, a pharmaceutical company in the EU, applied in accordance with Article 7 of 2377/90[533] to the Commission in July 1994 for the establishment of maximum residue limits for *clenbuterol*. In July 1996 the Commission adopted Regulation 1312/96,[534] in which it established provisional maximum residue limits for *clenbuterol*, but exclusively for the therapeutic purposes authorised under Directive 96/22,[535] which otherwise prohibits the use of *beta-agonists*. The CFI had no difficulty in finding that Regulation 1312/96 was in substance a regulation, as its 'provisions apply to objectively determined situations and produce legal effects with respect to categories of persons envisaged in general and abstract terms, namely the pharmaceutical undertakings which produce *clenbuterol* and those who prescribe and use that substance'.[536] However, in the view of the CFI this did not preclude the possibility that 'a provision which, as a result of its nature and scope, is general in character may be of individual concern to a natural or legal person'.[537] The CFI found that the applicant was individually concerned, as the Regulation was adopted following a formal request by the applicant to fix maximum residue levels for clenbuterol. In this respect the CFI relied on the fact that Regulation 2377/90 expressly provided for the participation of the applicant in the procedure for establishing maximum residue limits.[538]

SUMMARY The above cases demonstrate that where an act applies to an open class, and therefore to objectively determined situations, the fact that some within that class benefit from procedural rights is of relevance for the assessment as to whether they are individually concerned, either on its own or in combination with other factors. Even though the case law of the Community Courts is not entirely coherent on this point,[539] a finding of individual concern in these cases is independent from the determination of the nature of the act.

---

532 Joined Cases T-125/96 *Boehringer Ingelheim Vetmedica GmbH and Other v Council* and T-152/96 *Boehringer Ingelheim Vetmedica GmbH and Other v Commission* [1999] ECR II-3427.

533 [1990] OJ L 224/1.

534 [1996] OJ L 170/8.

535 [1996] OJ L 125/3.

536 Joined Cases T-125/96 *Boehringer Ingelheim Vetmedica GmbH and Other v Council* and T-152/96 *Boehringer Ingelheim Vetmedica GmbH and Other v Commission* [1999] ECR II-3427, para. 162.

537 Ibid., para. 163.

538 Ibid., para. 165. See also Case T-120/96 *Lilly Industries v Commission* [1998] ECR II-2571, at para. 63.

539 See Case T-70/99 *Alpharma v Council* [2002] ECR II-3495, at para. 76.

Specific substantive protection under EC law Where it is granted authority to adopt a specific act, a Community institution might be obliged by a higher-ranking legal norm to take account of the situation of persons in specific situations. It can be argued that persons who benefit from such a substantive protection can be distinguished from others within an act that applies to an open class and hence to objectively determined situations. And indeed, even though such an act would have to be regarded as regulation in substance, the Community Courts have shown greater willingness to grant standing where the applicants can demonstrate that their interests are particularly protected by legal provisions which the institution that adopted the contested measure had to take into account.[540]

In *Greek Canners*[541] the Court had no difficulties in holding that the contested regulation was legislative in nature. It found that 'it is clear that the contested measure is a regulation which fixes the coefficients to be applied throughout the Community to all producers of tomato concentrates in order to take account of the dry extract content and the different forms of packing. Such a regulation is exclusively legislative in nature . . .'[542] The Court did, however, not take any notice of Article 103 of the Greek Act of Accession, which required the EC institutions to take into account the specific circumstances in that country. AG Slynn found that the applicants belonged to an open class. He did, however, not attach any importance to Article 103 of the Greek Act of Accession either.

In *Piraiki-Patraiki*,[543] in September 1981 France requested authorisation under Article 130(1) of the Act of Accession of Greece to take protective measures as regards the importation into France of cotton yarn from Greece. The Commission by Decision 81/988[544] of 30 October 1981 granted the authorisation, but limited it to 300 tons for the rest of 1981 and 650 tons for January 1982. Article 3 of that Decision provided that the decision did not apply to consignments of cotton yarn dispatched from Greece before its notification. The Court interpreted Article 130(3) of the Act of Accession of Greece as requiring the Commission to take into account any adverse effect the authorisation might have on the undertakings concerned and in particular on contracts they might have already concluded. As a result applicants who came within that protection were considered to be individually concerned provided that they had already entered into contracts, the execution of which would be wholly or partially prevented

---

540 See S. Enchelmaier, supra note 2, pp. 185–186.

541 Case 250/81 *Greek Canners v Commission* [1982] ECR 3535.

542 Ibid., para. 11.

543 Case 11/82 *Piraiki-Patraiki and Others v Commission* [1985] ECR 207.

544 [1981] OJ L 362/33.

by the decision authorising the protective measure.[545] Even 'without going into the legal nature of the decision',[546] the Court seemed to have been of the opinion that the decision applied to an open class. The applicants had argued that they belonged to a class that, for economic reasons, could not be enlarged from the adoption of the act (30 October 1981) until the end of the validity of the authorisation (end of January 1982) and was therefore closed. The Court rejected this argument.[547] The special situation in which the applicants found themselves was therefore not based on the fact that they belonged to a closed class, but that they enjoyed special protection under Article 130(3) of the Greek Act of Accession. The Court later confirmed the legislative nature of the decision in *Piraiki-Patraiki* by holding that the Court in that case 'had to consider whether, despite the fact that the legislative nature of the contested provision *was beyond doubt*, it was none the less of invididual concern'.[548] The ruling in *Piraiki-Patraiki* can therefore be seen as an extension of the strict *Plaumann* test to situations where legislative rules require the institution adopting the decision at issue to take into account, specifically, the interests of certain persons provided that they have already entered into contracts, the execution of which will be wholly or partially prevented by the decision authorising the protective measure.

Similarly, in *Sofrimport*[549] the Court found that the applicant was in a specifically protected legal situation, of which the Commission had to take account. On 12 April 1988 the Commission adopted Regulation 962/88[550] suspending the issue of import licences for dessert apples from Chile from 15 to 22 April which came into force on the following day. Under Article 1(2) of Regulation 962/88 applications for import licences pending on 18 April were to be rejected. The Commission made an exception for goods in transit provided they had been issued with import licences. By Regulation 984/88[551] of 14 April 1988 which came into force on 15 April 1988, the

---

[545] See also Case T-196/03 *EffCI v European Parliament and Council* [2004] ECR II-4263, at para. 53. For cases where these conditions were considered not to have been met, see Case C-451/98 *Antillean Rice Mills NV v Council* [2001] ECR I-8949; Case C-452/98 *Nederlands Antillen v Council* [2001] ECR I-8973; Case T-47/00 *Rica Foods v Commission* [2002] ECR II-113 and Case C-96/01P *Galileo v Council* [2002] ECR I-4025, at para. 44. For the specific conditions that need to be met, see Joined Cases T-94/00, T-110/00 and T-159/00 *Rica Foods and Others v Commission* [2002] ECR II-4677, at paras. 53–81.

[546] Case 11/82 *Piraiki-Patraiki and Others v Commission* [1985] ECR 207, para. 5.

[547] Ibid., paras. 13 and 14.

[548] Case C-96/01 P *Galileo Company and Other v Council* [2002] ECR I-4025, para. 34. Emphasis added.

[549] Case C-152/88 *Sofrimport v Commission* [1990] ECR I-2477.

[550] [1988] OJ L 95/10.

[551] [1988] OJ L 98/37.

Commission prolonged the period of suspension from 18 to 29 April. By Regulation 1040/88[552] of 20 April 1988, the Commission fixed the quantities of imports of dessert apples, amongst others from Chile, for the period ending on 31 August 1988, and provided that the issue of import licences for dessert apples was suspended where the quantities in respect of which import licences were applied for exceeded those quantities. In respect of Chile, quantities in import licences applied for exceeded the allocated reference quantity and therefore the issue of import licences continued to be suspended until the end of August 1988. On 31 March 1988 the applicant had shipped from San Antonio a cargo of 89,514 cartons of dessert apples from Chile. Prior to the arrival, on 20 April 1988, of the vessel transporting that cargo at the port of Marseille, it lodged an application on 12 April 1988 with the French authorities for import licences for its cargo. On 18 April 1988 the authority refused to issue the licences on the ground that following the entry into force of Regulation 962/88 it could no longer grant the application.

The Court found that the applicant was individually concerned, as it was specifically protected under Article 3(3) of Council Regulation 2707/72,[553] on which the contested Commission Regulations were based. The Court interpreted that provision as requiring the Commission, when adopting protective measures under that regulation, to take account of the special position of products in transit to the Community, as in the case of the applicant. The Court, therefore, found that 'those importers [whose goods were in transit] thus constitute a restricted group which is sufficiently well defined in relation to any other importer of Chilean apples and cannot be extended after the suspensory measures in question take effect'.[554] As AG Tesauro explained, the suspension adopted on 12 April concerned an open category, namely those who had already lodged applications and those who were to lodge them. The AG expressly rejected the argument that importers whose goods were in transit at the time of the suspension could be considered as individually concerned, as 'they too are affected by the regulation because they are importers and lodged applications for a licence'.[555] The argument for individual concern stems, therefore, from the fact, as in *Piraiki-Patraiki*, that a legislative provision, which the Commission had to consider, specifically protected the interests of the applicants.[556]

---

[552] [1988] OJ L 102/23.

[553] [1972] OJ English Special Edition (28–30 December), p. 3.

[554] Case C-152/89 *Sofrimport v Commission* [1990] ECR I-2477 at para. 11.

[555] Opinion of AG Tesauro in Case C-152/89 *Sofrimport v Commission* [1990] ECR I-2477 at para. 6.

[556] As A. Albors-Llorens, supra note 1, at pp. 148–9 and 151, has pointed out, the fact that the Court did not deny standing despite the legislative nature of the act, showed a considerable relaxation of the standing rules.

The CFI took this approach further in *Antillean Rice*.[557] On a complaint from France and Italy the Commission in February 1993 adopted Decision 93/127[558] introducing safeguard measures, which consisted of imposing a minimum price for imports into the EC of rice originating in the Netherlands Antilles. This decision was based on Article 109 of the OCT (Overseas Countries and Territories) Decision.[559] As this provision was substantially the same as Article 130(3) of the Act of Accession of Greece relevant in *Piraiki-Patraiki,* the CFI found that it obliged the Commission to inquire into the negative effects which its decision might have on the economy of the OCT. Even though Article 109, in contrast to *Sofrimport*, did not expressly refer to goods in transit, the CFI held that 'the specific interest which undertakings have in protecting their goods in transit against the effects of a safeguard measure'[560] had to be protected by the Commission. The fact that the Commission decision did not apply to one Member State, as in *Piraiki-Patraiki*, but to all Member States was considered as irrelevant by the CFI, as the relevant factor was the protection enjoyed by the applicants. The CFI, in contrast to the rulings in *Piraiki-Patraiki* and *Sofrimport*, discussed the legal nature of the act and found that:

> although the measures contested are 'decisions' addressed to the Member States, they are legislative by nature inasmuch as they apply to all the traders concerned, taken as whole. It has consistently been held that the fact that the identities of the traders to whom such measures apply was known to the Commission at the time they were adopted is not sufficient to call into question their legislative nature, as long as it is established that such application takes effect by virtue of an objective legal or factual situation defined by the measure in question in relation to its purpose.[561]

The judgment clearly shows that the concept of individual concern and the nature of the act are not identical, since 'the fact that the contested

---

557 Joined Cases T-480/93 and T-483/93 *Antillean Rice Mills and Others v Commission* [1995] ECR II-2305 upheld on appeal by the ECJ in Case C-390/95P *Antillean Rice Mills and Others v Commission* [1999] ECR I-769 at paras. 25–30. For the specific conditions that need to be met, see Joined Cases T-94/00, T-110/00 and T-159/00 *Rica Foods and Others v Commission* [2002] ECR II-4677, at paras. 53–81.

558 [1993] OJ L 50/27.

559 Council Decision 91/482, [1991] OJ L 263/1.

560 Joined Cases T-480/93 and T-483/93 *Antillean Rice Mills and Others v Commission* [1995] ECR II-2305, para. 76. Compare with Case C-142/00P *Commission v Nederlandse Antillen* [2003] ECR I-3483, where the Court on appeal found the Netherlandse Antillen not to be individually concerned and overturned the judgment of the CFI in Joined Cases T-32/98 and T-41/98 *Netherlands Antilles v Commission* [2000] ECR II-201. Similarly, see Case T-37/04 *Região autónoma dos Açores v Council*, judgment of 1 July 2008, at para. 55.

561 Joined Cases T-480/93 and T-483/93 *Antillean Rice Mills and Others v Commission* [1995] ECR II-2305, at para. 65.

measures are legislative by nature does not prevent them from being of individual concern to some of the traders concerned'.[562]

It follows from the above cases that even where an act applies to an open class, and therefore to objectively determined situations, the fact that some within that class benefit from a substantive protection clause is of relevance for the assessment as to whether they are individually concerned.

Specific economic effects In Zuckerfabrik Watenstedt the Court found that 'the fact that a legal provision may have different practical effects on the different persons to whom it applies in no way contradicts its nature as a regulation provided that the situation to which it refers is objectively determined.'[563] For the same reasons the Court would usually also deny that applicants are individually concerned, where the economic effects of the act concern them more than other addressees, as they are affected by the act merely in their objective capacity.[564] The Court held that 'the mere fact that the applicants are in an allegedly disadvantageous competitive position cannot therefore constitute specific circumstances of such a kind as to make them individually concerned by the contested regulation even though they are in a factual situation different from the situations defined objectively by that regulation.'[565]

However, *Extramet*[566] provides an example where the Court demonstrated that the economic effects of an act can, exceptionally, lead to individual concern without changing the nature of the act as regulation. The Court held that 'regulations imposing anti-dumping duties are in fact, as regards their nature and their scope, of a legislative character, inasmuch as they apply to all traders concerned, taken as a whole'.[567] However, the Court made it clear that these measures 'without losing their character as regulations'[568] could be of individual concern. The Court considered the applicant individually concerned as it was the largest importer of the

---

[562] Ibid., para. 66. See also Case C-451/98 *Antillean Rice Mills NV v Council* [2001] ECR I-8949, para. 46; Case C-452/98 *Nederlands Antillen v Council* [2001] ECR I-8973, para. 55 and Case T-47/00 *Rica Foods v Commission* [2002] ECR II-113, para. 36.

[563] Case 6/68 *Zuckerfabrik Watenstedt v Council* [1968] ECR 409, p. 415; see also Case 101/76 *KSH v Council and Commission* [1977] ECR 797 at para. 24; Case T-472/93 *Campo Ebro v Council* [1995] ECR II-421, at para. 36.

[564] See Case C-209/94P *Buralux and Others v Council* [1996] ECR I-615, at paras. 28 and 29.

[565] Case T-472/93 *Campo Ebro v Council* [1995] ECR II-421, at para. 35. See also Joined Cases 10/68 and 18/68 *Eridania and Others v Commission* [1969] ECR 117, at para. 7; Case T-196/03 *EffCI v European Parliament and Council* [2004] ECR II-4263, at para. 47.

[566] Case C-358/89 *Extramet v Council* [1991] ECR 2501.

[567] Ibid., para. 13.

[568] Ibid., para. 14.

product in question and at the same time the end-user of the product. Moreover, the applicant's business depended to a very large extent on imports and was seriously affected by the adopted measure, because of the limited number of manufacturers of the product and the difficulties it encountered in obtaining supplies from the sole EC producer, which was its main competitor. In essence, the Court found here individual concern because of the serious effects on the economic situation of the applicant.

However, the ruling in *Extramet* has proved to be of a rather exceptional character. It is not sufficient for an undertaking to rely on economic difficulties alone without establishing that the act has serious consequences for its activities.[569] As *Buralux*[570] shows, it might be difficult to satisfy the Community Courts on that account. In this case, the Court had to deal with an appeal from the CFI. The three appellant undertakings together carried out the collection, shipment and dumping of household waste originating in Germany and exportation to France. For that purpose in 1990 they had concluded renewable five-year contracts with public bodies in Germany. In 1992, France *de facto* prohibited the importation of household waste for dumping purposes. In 1993, the Council adopted Regulation 259/93,[571] which allowed the Member States to prohibit shipments of waste. The CFI considered that the applicants were only affected in their objective capacity and therefore not individually concerned.[572] On appeal the Court rejected the argument that the appellants should be given standing as they were the only operators transporting waste from Germany to France and they were seriously affected by the regulation. The Court found that 'a circumstance of that kind is not sufficient to differentiate the appellants from any other operator in the light of the contested provision, which deals generally with waste shipments between Member States without distinction.'[573] It is noteworthy that AG Lenz in his Opinion accepted the appellants' argument and considered the *Extramet* ruling as being applicable.[574]

Similarly, in *Fédération* the CFI rejected the applicants' argument that as their competitive position was affected by the act in question they were individually concerned. The CFI held that 'even if the contested provision had had a considerable impact on the competitive position of the applicants or of their members, that fact was not such as to distinguish them

---

569 Case C-96/01 *Galileo v Council* [2002] ECR I-4025, at para. 55.
570 Case C-209/94P *Buralux and Others v Council* [1996] ECR I-615.
571 [1993] OJ L 30/1.
572 See Case T-475/93 *Buralux and Others v Council*, order of 17 May 1994 (not published).
573 Case C-209/94P *Buralux and Others v Council* [1996] ECR I-615, para. 29.
574 Ibid., Opinion of AG Lenz, at paras. 32 and 33.

from all other operators', as they were concerned only 'in their objective status as economic operators in that market'.[575]

AG Cosmas in *Greenpeace* explained the Court's ruling in *Buralux* and found that 'the Court was seeking to exclude cases in which an increasingly broad interpretation and application of the procedural provisions of the fourth paragraph of Article [230] of the Treaty would lead to recognition of a right of action by individuals against rules of Community law and not against individual decisions. In other words, in *Buralux*, the Court wished to safeguard the legislative nature of the regulation'.[576] Consequently, the legislative nature seems to influence the Court's assessment of individual concern. However, even though, exceptionally, economic difficulties of a serious nature, as established in *Extramet*, can lead the Community Courts to find that a person is individually concerned despite the legislative nature of the act. In such a case, the assessment of the nature of the act and individual concern obviously follows different criteria.

Specific effects on rights Another more liberal approach to the interpretation of the *Plaumann* formula due to the divergence between the nature of the act and individual concern can be observed in *Codorniu*.[577] In 1989, the Council amended Regulation 3309/85[578] laying down general rules for the description and presentation of sparkling wines. The amendment, introduced by Regulation 2045/89,[579] provided that the term 'crémant' could only be used by quality sparkling wines made in France and Luxembourg. For a transitional period of five wine growing years, the regulation allowed the use of the term for other quality sparkling wines which had traditionally used the term. Codorniu, a Spanish producer of quality sparkling wines, had held the trade mark 'Gran Cremant de Codorniu' since 1924 for one of its sparkling wines. At the time it was the main Community producer of quality sparkling wines bearing the designation 'crémant'. In a similar case, *Deutz und Geldermann*, the Court had found the action to be inadmissible, as the regulation in issue was of general application and the applicants were only concerned in their objective capacity as producers of sparkling wines. The Court in *Codorniu* found that the contested regulation was 'by nature and by virtue of its sphere of application, of a legislative nature in that it

---

575 Case T-268/99 *FNAB and Others v Council* [2000] ECR II-2893, at para. 49. This judgment was upheld on appeal, in Case C-345/00P [2001] ECR I-3811.

576 Opinion of AG Cosmas in Case C-321/95P *Greenpeace v Commission* [1998] ECR I-1651, at para. 92.

577 Case C-309/89 *Codorniu v Council* [1994] ECR I-1853. See J.A. Usher, supra note 429; S. Enchelmaier, supra note 2, pp. 188–191.

578 [1985] OJ L 320/9.

579 [1989] OJ L 202/12.

applies to the traders concerned in general'.[580] As AG Lenz explained, the prohibition in issue affected 'not only those who (traditionally) used the term "crémant" when the provision was adopted but also potential users, that is to say, traders who, if the rule had not been introduced, might later have joined the circle of such traders'.[581] However, in an alignment with its approach in anti-dumping cases the Court emphasised that the legislative nature of the act 'does not prevent it from being of individual and direct concern to some of them'.[582] The Court did then find the applicant individually concerned. Codorniu distinguished itself sufficiently from other traders, as the contested amendment would prevent it from using its graphic trade mark that it had held since 1924.[583] *Codorniu* demonstrates that where an act affects the specific rights[584] of an individual, which is consequently individually concerned by it, that act can nevertheless be of a legislative nature.[585]

Summary It can be observed that an act which applies to an open class can contain certain addressees who occupy a special position within that class due to the procedural guarantees or substantive protection they enjoy or due to the impact of the act on their rights or economic situation. It cannot be concluded from the case law of the Community Courts that the existence of special addressees is capable of altering the assessment of the nature of the act, which is still determined by whether the act applies to an objectively determined situation with respect to all addressees, and not just those in a special situation. This seems to have also been accepted by the CFI, which initially followed the hybridity theory, which the Court so firmly rejected in *Moksel*.[586] Consequently, where an act applies to an open class it applies to an objectively determined situation regardless of whether it is comprised of special addressees.

---

580 Case C-309/89 *Codorniu v Council* [1994] ECR I-1853, para. 19.

581 Ibid., Opinion of AG Lenz, para. 20.

582 Ibid. para. 19.

583 The Court has recently explained that *Codorniu* could only be invoked where the applicants 'were prevented from exercising an exclusive right comparable to that in the case giving rise to that judgment', see Case C-96/01P *Galileo v Council* [2002] ECR I-4025, para. 51; Case C-258/02 P *Bactria v Commission* [2003] ECR I-15105, at paras. 50–51; Case T-213/02 *SNF SA v Commission* [2004] ECR II-3047, at paras. 64–71; Case T-196/03 *EffCI v European Parliament and Council* [2004] ECR II-4263, at para. 57; Case T-291/04 R *Enviro Tech Europe Ltd and Another v Commission* [2005] ECR II-475, at para. 70. See also Case C-351/99P *Eridania and Others v Council* [2001] ECR I-5007, paras. 61 and 62, where the Court refers to specific rights rather than exclusive rights.

584 See also A. Arnull (2001), supra note 2, pp. 40–43.

585 See also Case T-37/04 R *The Autonomous Region of the Azores v Council* [2004] ECR II-2153, where the CFI considered the impact on the applicant's legal powers as relevant for a finding of individual concern despite the general applicability of the contested act.

586 See A. Arnull (2001), supra note 2, pp. 20–21.

On the other hand, the case law of the Community Courts provides ample evidence that an act, even if it applies to an open class, and therefore to objectively determined situations, can be of individual concern to those addressees who find themselves in a special position. Procedural guarantees, either on their own or in combination with other factors, substantive protection and the special impact on rights or the economic situation of an addressee are factors that can distinguish these addressees sufficiently in the meaning of the *Plaumann* formula to establish individual concern.

This shows that the criteria applied for determining the nature of an act and those relevant for assessing individual concern overlap, but are not identical. The reason for that finding can be found in the fact that an assessment as to the nature of an act examines whether the act in issue applies to an objectively defined situation in relation to all its addressees, whereas individual concern is assessed in relation to each addressee's specific situation. Even though the criteria used for individual concern and for the determination of the nature of an act are not identical, it should be noted that the finding that an act is of general application is of relevance for the assessment as to whether an individual is individually concerned. It can be noticed that the Community Courts consider individuals only in exceptional circumstances to be individually concerned by an act of general application. This restrictive approach, which can be justified on the ground that Article 230(4) does in principle not allow a challenge to a regulation, is designed 'to safeguard the legislative nature of the regulation'.[587]

Individual concern for associations

The Court is increasingly concerned with challenges of EC acts by associations.[588] The Court has accepted the right of such associations to bring an action under Article 230(4) in two types of cases.

The first case concerns a situation 'where the association, by bringing its action, has substituted itself for one or more of the members whom it represents, on the condition that those members were themselves in a position to bring an admissible action'.[589] In this case, the association acts as representative of its members.

In the second case, the Court has accepted a genuine right, that is, not based on the rights of its members, to bring an action by an association,

[587] Opinion of AG Cosmas in Case C-321/95P *Greenpeace v Commission* [1998] ECR I-1651, at para. 92.

[588] O. De Schutter, 'Public Interest Litigation Before the European Court of Justice' (2006) *MJ* 9–34; D. Obradovic, 'EC rules on public participation in environmental decision-making operating at the European and national levels' (2007) *ELRev* 839–859.

[589] Joined Cases T-481/93 and 484/93 *Exporteurs in Levende Varkens and Others v Commission* [1995] ECR II-2941 at para. 64.

where 'the association has a particular interest in acting, especially because its negotiating position is affected by the measure which it seeks to have annulled'.[590] This arises where the association plays an active part in the procedure that leads to the adoption of the contested measure.[591] The mere exchange of correspondence is, however, not sufficient.

Limits to the further extension of individual concern

More recently, AG Jacobs in *Unión de Pequeños*[592] and the CFI in *Jégo Quéré*[593] have argued that the current interpretation of individual concern was insufficient to provide individuals with an effective remedy to challenge Community acts of general application and have presented their own, albeit differing, tests for a new interpretation of individual concern. The Court's rejection of a more liberal interpetation of the concept of individual concern in favour of private litigants has encountered fierce criticism in academic literature.[594]

The CFI in *UPA*[595] rejected a challenge by an association representing the interests of small Spanish agricultural businesses against Council Regulation 1638/98 which considerably modified the existing market in olive oil by reducing and finally abolishing aid to growers. The CFI was not prepared to modify the existing *Plaumann* test in the case of measures of general application. The CFI referred the applicant to seek redress on the basis of national remedies in the national court, which could then ask the Court to rule on the validity of the Regulation under Article 234. Where a national remedy did not exist, the Member State might be under an obligation to provide one. The length of the Article 234 preliminary rulings procedure could not lead to a different conclusion, as the CFI felt bound by the restrictive wording of Article 230(4).

On appeal, AG Jacobs[596] argued that the restrictive *Plaumann* test for the interpretation of individual concern denied private parties an effective remedy against Community acts of general application. He opined that

---

590 Ibid, at para. 64. See also Case C-368/05 P *Polyelectrolyte Producers Group v Council and Commission* [2006] ECR I-130*, at para. 59.

591 Joined Cases 67, 68 and 70/85 *Van der Kooy and Others v Commission* [1989] ECR 219 at paras. 20–24 and Case C-313/90 *CIRFS and Others v Commission* [1993] ECR I-1125.

592 Case C-50/00P *Unión de Pequeños Agricultores v Council* [2002] ECR I-6677.

593 Case T-177/01 *Jégo Quéré v Commission* [2002] ECR II-2365.

594 A. Albors-Llorens, supra note 2; J.M. Cortés Martin, supra note 2; F. Ragolle, supra note 2 ; C. Koch, supra note 2 ; P. Craig (2006), supra note 2, pp. 335–344, A. Ward, supra note 1, p. 331. For a more balanced analysis, see J. Usher (2003), supra note 2; S. Enchelmaier, supra note 2.

595 Case T-173/98 *Unión de Pequeños Agricultores v Council* [1999] ECR II-3357.

596 Opinion of AG Jacobs in Case 50/00P *Unión de Pequeños Agricultores v Council* [2002] ECR I-6677.

the assumption that the preliminary rulings procedure provided full and effective judicial protection against general measures was incorrect. He rejected the suggestion that standing be granted where an effective remedy in national court was not available or to require Member States to provide such a remedy. As, in his view, the *Plaumann* test was not the only possible interpretation of individual concern in Article 230(4), he suggested as a new test that 'a person is to be regarded as individually concerned by a Community measure where, by reason of his particular circumstances, the measure has, or is liable to have, a substantial adverse effect on his interests.'[597]

In his quest for a new approach to individual concern, AG Jacobs received support from the first chamber of the CFI in *Jégo Quéré*.[598] In this case the applicant challenged a Commission Regulation,[599] which imposed a minimum mesh size for fishing vessels in certain geographical areas to aid the recovery of the stock of hake. The CFI found that under the existing *Plaumann* test the applicant could not be considered as individually concerned. The CFI argued, however, that Article 230(4) had to be interpreted in the light of Articles 6 and 13 ECHR and Article 47 of the Charter of Fundamental Rights, which guarantee an effective remedy. As it did not consider the preliminary rulings procedure under Article 234 and the action for compensation under Article 288(2) as guaranteeing individuals an effective remedy against Community acts of general application, the CFI held that 'a natural or legal person is to be regarded as individually concerned by a Community measure of general application that concerns him directly if the measure in question affects his legal position, in a manner which is both definite and immediate, by restricting his rights or by imposing obligations on him'.[600] The CFI made it clear that 'the number and position of other persons who are likewise affected by the measure, or who may be so, are of no relevance in that regard'.[601]

The Court of Justice on appeal in *Unión de Pequeños*[602] and *Jégo Quéré*[603] firmly rejected any further liberalisation of the existing interpretation of individual concern under Article 230(4). The Court acknowledged that an applicant had to be provided with an effective remedy, which, however, did not mean that such a remedy had to be provided by the Community

597 Ibid., para. 60.
598 Case T-177/01 *Jégo Quéré v Commission* [2002] ECR II-2365.
599 Commission Regulation 1162/2001, [2001] OJ L 159/4.
600 Case T-177/01 *Jégo Quéré v Commission* [2002] ECR II-2365, para. 51.
601 Ibid., para. 51.
602 Case 50/00 P *Unión de Pequeños Agricultores v Council* [2002] ECR I-6677.
603 Case C-263/02 P *Commission v Jégo Quéré* [2004] ECR I-3425.

Courts alone.[604] Where an applicant did not satisfy the *Plaumann* test, the Member States had 'to establish a system of legal remedies and procedures which ensure respect for the right to effective judicial protection'.[605] Such a remedy would allow the individual to bring an action in the national court, which could refer the question on the validity of the EC act to the Court of Justice under Article 234. The Court felt unable to exceed what it perceived to be the clear meaning of Article 230(4). It was for the Member States alone 'to reform the system currently in force'[606] by amending that provision.

Conclusion

It has been shown that the characterisation of legal acts as being of general application, and therefore legislation in substance, seemed initially, and in accordance with the strict wording of Article 230(4), to have led to deny standing to private parties where they challenged an act of general application.[607] The test of 'objectively determined situation' was applied by the Court not only when considering the nature of the act, but also to assess whether the applicant was individually concerned. Therefore, also the traditional *Plaumann* approach is not based on the distinction of open and closed class,[608] but should be perceived as a way of preventing individuals from challenging regulations in substance[609] thereby creating an 'almost insurmountable barrier'[610] to accessing the Community Courts under Article 230(4). On the basis of this test and similar to the test employed for determining decisions, a private party is therefore only individually concerned where it belongs to a closed class and has pursued a particular course of action creating a causal link between the measure

---

[604] In Case C-167/02 P *Rothley and Others v European Parliament* [2004] ECR I-3149, the Court pointed out that effective judicial protection is available against subsequent measures which enforce the act, the challenge of which was declared inadmissible.

[605] Case C-50/00P *Unión de Pequeños Agricultores v Council* [2002] ECR I-6677, para. 41. See also Case C-368/05 P *Polyelectrolyte Producers Group v Council and Commission* [2006] ECR I-130*, at para. 68, in which the Court also considered EEA courts bound to provide an effective remedy.

[606] Case C-50/00P *Unión de Pequeños Agricultores v Council* [2002] ECR I-6677, para. 45.

[607] Some authors have suggested that this was also a useful tool of protecting the developing body of EC laws against challenges: see A. Arnull (1995), supra note 2, p. 45; M. Hedemann-Robinson, supra note 2, p. 128; A. Ward, supra note 1, p. 2.

[608] See Case T-482/93 *Weber v Commission* [1996] ECR II-609, at paras. 63–66; Case T-298/94 *Roquette Frères v Council* [1996] ECR II-1531, at para. 41; Case T-11/99 *Van Parys and Others v Commission* [1999] ECR II-2653, at para. 43. See also A. Arnull (2001), supra note 2, pp. 32–40.

[609] See also C. Harding, supra note 2, at p. 355.

[610] A. Barav, supra note 2, p. 191.

and the situation of the applicant. Contrary to what has been suggested,[611] it does not appear that the modification of an individual right is necessary to establish individual concern.[612]

However, over time a split has emerged between the assessment of the nature of the act and individual concern. This means that in some cases the Court has admitted that an act which is of general application can be of individual concern to some applicants. Addressees of an act can find themselves in a specific situation, and are therefore to be considered as individually concerned, either due to procedural or substantive guarantees they enjoy under provisions of Community law or because of the special impact of the measure on their rights or on their economic circumstances.

The hybridity theory, in accordance with which an act can be of general application to some, but of individual application to those special addressees, is an attempt to reconcile the wording of Article 230(4) with a more liberal approach on individual concern.[613] This approach, even though it was firmly rejected in *Moksel*, has lingered on in judgments of the CFI[614] and has recently been reverted to by the Court of Justice itself in *Unión de Pequeños*.[615] However attractive the hybridity theory might be, from a logical point of view it is not convincing that one and the same provision should have a different nature varying as to whom it applies to.[616] The CFI in *Antillean Rice* seemed to share this view when it held that:

> in the context of an action for annulment, the Court of Justice has consistently held that a measure which is legislative by nature and by virtue of its sphere of application, in that it applies to the traders concerned in general, may be of individual concern to some of them [. . .]. Even though such a measure may be regarded as a decision with regard to the applicants in question when determining the admissibility of the action for annulment, its legislative nature does not thereby cease to exist, since its intrinsic nature and sphere of application are not modified by that assessment.[617]

Consequently, it is submitted that the criteria relevant for the nature of an act overlap to a large extent with those applicable to individual concern, but are not identical. This does not mean that the nature of

---

611 A. Albors-Llorens, supra note 1, p. 219.

612 See P. Nihoul, supra note 2, p. 180.

613 A. Arnull (1995), supra note 2, p. 24.

614 See A. Arnull (2001), supra note 2, pp. 20–21. See e.g. Case T-196/03 *EffCI v European Parliament and Council* [2004] ECR II-4263, at para. 38.

615 Case C-50/00P *Unión de Pequeños Agricultores v Council* [2002] ECR I-6677, at para. 36.

616 See also M. Nettesheim, supra note 2, at p. 228.

617 Joined Cases T-480/93 and T-483/93 *Antillean Rice Mills and Others v Commission* [1995] ECR II-2305, para. 185.

an act is without relevance to the question of individual concern. The Community Courts have made it clear that individual concern will only be granted in exceptional circumstances where an applicant challenges an act of general application. This means that a presumption still exists that a challenge against an act of general application is inadmissible,[618] even though in specific cases that presumption can be overcome. In *Unión de Pequeños* the Court, in contrast to AG Jacobs, made it clear that Article 234 provides an adequate remedy to challenge regulations indirectly through a national court.[619] The possibility of such an indirect challenge also makes the suggestion unlikely that the Court has been reluctant to accord standing under Article 230(4) where it had to deal with discretionary norms, in particular in the sphere of the Common Agricultural Policy (CAP) in contrast to quasi-judicial determinations, where the Court has granted standing under Article 230(4) more liberally.[620] The argument wrongly implies that the Court can avoid dealing with the review of the validity of such discretionary norms by rejecting them under Article 230(4).[621] Moreover, also quasi-judicial determinations, where the Court has been more liberal in respect of standing under Article 230(4), involve a measure of discretion on the part of the Community institution, which has to balance what are often conflicting objectives, thereby reducing the degree of review exercised by the Community Courts.[622] It seems to be more plausible to suggest that in these cases the measures constituted the application of Community law by EC institutions, in contrast to measures adopted under the CAP, which are to be applied by the national authorities, and therefore could not be reviewed indirectly through proceedings in a national court.

---

618 See A. Ward, supra note 1, pp. 292–297 and pp. 331–332; A. Arnull (2001), supra note 2, pp. 22 and 51.

619 See Case C-50/00P *Unión de Pequeños Agricultores v Council* [2002] ECR I-6677, paras. 40 and 41; Case T-45/02 *DOW Agro Sciences BV and Another v European Parliament and Council* [2003] ECR II-1973, at para. 50; Case C-263/02P *Commission v Jégo Quéré* [2004] ECR I-3425, at paras. 30–32 and 35. On the issue of Article 234 as adequate alternative remedy, see AG Jacobs's Opinions in C-358/89 *Extramet Industrie v Council* [1991] ECR I-2501 and in Case 50/00P *Unión de Pequeños Agricultores v Council* [2002] ECR I-6677. See also C. Harding, supra note 2, pp. 357 *et seq.*; P. Craig (1994), supra note 2, pp. 528 *et seq.*; P. Nihoul, supra note 2, pp. 188 *et seq.*; J. Usher, supra note 429, p. 640; A. Arnull (1995), supra note 2, pp. 40 *et seq.*; A. Albors-Llorens, supra note 1, pp. 177 *et seq.*; A. Ward, supra note 1, chapter 7; A. Arnull (2001), supra note 2, pp. 48 *et seq.*; J. Usher, supra note 2.

620 P. Craig (1994), supra note 2, pp. 524–527; P. Craig and G. DeBúrca, supra note 1, p. 518; T.C. Hartley, supra note 1, pp. 349–362.

621 This is not called in question by the suggestion that not all these cases 'will find their way back to Luxembourg under the preliminary rulings procedure'. See A. Arnull (2001), supra note 2, p. 51.

622 For anti-dumping proceedings, see M. Nettesheim, supra note 2, pp. 232–234.

5. LEGAL INTEREST

In addition to the requirements of direct and individual concern, the Community Courts also require for an action to be admissible that the natural or legal person has an interest in seeing the contested measure annulled.[623] Such interest must be 'vested and present [. . .] and is evaluated as at the date on which the action is brought'.[624] This is not the case where a Commission decision approves, unconditionally and without time-limit, a state aid measure for the benefit of the applicant.[625]

6. TIME-LIMIT IN ARTICLE 230(5)

Article 230(5) EC stipulates that annulment proceedings have to be instituted within 'two months of the publication of the measure, or of its notification to the plaintiff, or, in the absence thereof, of the day on which it came to the knowledge of the latter, as the case may be'.

Notification, Publication and Knowledge

It is clear from the wording of Article 230(5) that the applicant's knowledge of the measure is only relevant where the act has neither been notified[626] nor published. In *Alitalia v Commission*, the Court held that 'the criterion of the day on which a measure came to the knowledge of an applicant, as the starting point for the period prescribed for instituting proceedings, is subsidiary to the criteria of publication or notification of the measure'.[627] The Court has defined notification as 'the operation by which the author of a decision of individual relevance communicates the latter to the addressees and thus puts them in a position to take cognizance of it'.[628]

---

623 See Joined Cases T-480/93 and T-483/93 *Antillean Rice Mills and Others v Commission* [1995] ECR II-2305, at para. 59; Case T-102/96 *Gencor v Commission* [1999] ECR II-753, at para. 40; Case T-212/00 *Nuove Industrie Molisane v Commission* [2002] ECR II-347, at para. 33; Case T-141/03 *Sniace v Commission* [2005] ECR II-1197, at para. 25; Case T-177/04 *easyJet v Commission* [2006] ECR II-1931, at para. 40; T-228/02 *Organisation des Modjahedines du people d'Iran v Council* [2006] ECR II-4665, at para. 35; Case T-474/04 *Pergan v Commission*, judgment of 12 October 2007, at paras. 39–42. See also A. Arnull (2001), supra note 2, pp. 45–48.

624 Case T-141/03 *Sniace v Commission* [2005] ECR II-1197, para. 25.

625 Ibid, paras 27–38.

626 For notification by DHL delivery, see Case T-14/06 *K-Swiss v OHIM* [2006] ECR II-106*.

627 Case T-296/97 *Alitalia v Commission* [2000] ECR II-3871, at para. 61. See also Case T-17/02 *Olsen v Commission* [2005] ECR II-2031, para. 73.

628 Case T-17/02 *Olsen v Commission* [2005] ECR II-2031, para. 74.

Where the act is neither published nor notified, 'it is for the party who has knowledge of an act concerning him to request the full text thereof within a reasonable period. Subject to that proviso, the period for bringing an action can begin to run only from the moment at which the third party concerned acquires precise knowledge of the content and grounds of the act in question, in such a way as to enable him to exercise his right of action'.[629] The Court added that 'the term "precise knowledge" does not mean knowledge of every aspect of the decision but of its essential contents'.[630]

Calculation of the Time-limit

The rules for the calculation of the time-limit in Article 230(5) can be found in Articles 80 and 81 of the Rules of Procedure of the Court[631] and Articles 101 and 102 of the Rules of Procedure of the CFI.[632] Both sets of rules are drafted in similar terms.

The rules distinguish between acts that have been notified to the applicant and those which have been published. Where an act has been notified to the applicant, Article 80(1)(a) of the Court's Rules[633] states that the time-limit of two months is to be calculated from the moment at which the notification occurs. The day on which the notification occurs is, however, not included. The exclusion of the day on which the notification occurs from the calculation of the time-limit on the ground is designed 'to ensure that parties are able to make full use of the periods allowed'.[634] Therefore 'regardless of the hour of the day when the measure in question is notified, time does not begin to run until the end of the day of notification'.[635] This means that the time-limit for a decision which was notified at 2pm on Tuesday, 4 July 2006, does not start running before the end of 4 July 2006.

The time-limit of two months ends in accordance with Article 80(1)(b)[636] 'at the end of the day which, in the month indicated by the time-limit, bears the same number as the day from which time was set running, that is to

[629] Ibid., para. 73. See also Case C-403/05 *European Parliament v Commission* [2007] ECR I-9045, at para. 28.

[630] Joined Cases T-485/93, T-491/93, T-494/93 and T-61/98 *Dreyfus and Others v Commission* [2000] ECR II-3659, para. 49.

[631] [1991] OJ L 176/7, as last amended on 8 July 2008, [2008] OJ L 200/18.

[632] [1991] OJ L 136/1, as last amended on 12 June 2008, [2008] OJ L 179/12.

[633] Article 101(1)(a) of the CFI Rules.

[634] See Case 152/85 *Misset v Council* [1987] ECR 223, para. 7. See also Case C-406/01 *Germany v European Parliament and Council* [2002] ECR I-4561, para. 14.

[635] Ibid.

[636] Article 101(1)(b) of the CFI Rules.

say the day of notification'.[637] This means that the time-limit for a decision which was notified at 2pm on Tuesday, 4 July 2006, ends at midnight on Monday, 4 September 2006. Article 80(1)(d)[638] makes it clear that the time period of two months also includes official holidays,[639] Sundays and Saturdays. Equally, judicial holidays do not suspend the time-limit.[640]

Where the act against which the challenge is brought was published,[641] Article 81(1) of the Court's Rules provides that the two-month period calculated in accordance with Article 80(1)(a) of the Court's Rules starts 'from the end of the 14th day after publication thereof in the *Official Journal of the European Union*'. Also in this case the day on which the measure was published will not be included in the period of 14 days. The applicant has therefore in addition to the normal period of two months an additional 14 full days. Hence, if a measure is published on Tuesday, 4 July 2006, the period for calculating the two months does not start before the end of Tuesday, 18 July 2006. The end of the two-month time-limit is therefore Monday, 18 September 2006.

Article 81(2)[642] of the Court's Rules stipulates that the time-limits discussed above 'shall be extended on account of distance by a single period of 10 days.' This rule applies regardless of whether the measure has been notified or published. Therefore, the time-limit of a measure which was notified at 2pm on Tuesday, 4 July 2006, ends at the end of Thursday, 14 September 2006. The time-limit for a measure which was published on Tuesday, 4 July 2006 ends at the end of Thursday, 28 September 2006.

Where the end of the time-limit falls on an official holiday, Sunday or Saturday, Article 80(2)(1)[643] stipulates that the time-limit is extended until the end of the first following working day. The Community Courts have made it clear that Article 80(2)(1) is applicable only where the entire prescribed period, including the extension on account of distance, ends on a Saturday or a Sunday or an official holiday.[644] Article 80(2)(1) does

---

637 See Case 152/85 *Misset v Council* [1987] ECR 223, para. 8. See also Case C-406/01 *Germany v European Parliament and Council* [2002] ECR I-4561, para. 14.

638 Article 101(1)(d).

639 What counts as official holiday is determined by the Decision on Official Holidays, which is annexed to the Court's Rules of Procedures and also applies to the CFI's Rules in accordance with Article 101(2)(2). Note that the official holidays referred to in the Decision are those observed at the place where the Court of Justice has its seat, that is Luxembourg.

640 See Article 80(1)(e) of the Court's Rules and Article 101(1)(e) of the CFI's Rules.

641 The period of 14 days is added in all cases where the act has been published, even if publication is not mandatory or is not the institution's consistent practice, see Case T-264/03 *Schmoldt and others v Commission* [2004] ECR II-1515, at paras. 55–61.

642 Article 102(2) of the CFI's Rules.

643 Article 101(2)(1) of the CFI's Rules.

644 Case C-122/90 *Emsland-Stärke v Commission*, order of 15 May 1991 (not published), para. 9. For a similar application of Article 101(2) of the CFI's Rules, see Case T-85/97

therefore not apply to intermediate steps in calculating the time-limit, such as the end of the 14 days period under Article 81(1) or the end of the two-month period in Article 80(1)(b). However, this interpretation is not convincing insofar as it also includes the period in Article 80(1)(b). The reference in Article 80(2)(1) to 'the period' can only be understood as referring to the one in Article 80(1), which it immediately follows. Moreover, Article 81(2), which contains the 10 days extension on account of distance, does not refer to Article 80(2)(1).

Extension of the Time-limit

The time-limit under Article 230(5) applies as 'a matter of public policy and is not subject to the discretion of the parties or the Court, since it was established in order to ensure that legal positions are clear and certain and to avoid any discrimination or arbitrary treatment in the administration of justice'.[645]

However, a modest modification of that strict approach can be found in Article 37(6) of the Court's Rules.[646] The time-limit under Article 230(5), as calculated above, is interrupted where the applicant has lodged the necessary documents in accordance with Articles 37(1)–(5). Where the applicant has lodged a copy of the signed original of a pleading by fax or other technical means of communication available to the Court (for example, e-mail), that date is taken into account for the purpose of complying with the time-limit in Article 230(5) if the signed original of the pleading is lodged no later than 10 days thereafter.[647] The Court has rejected the argument that the 10 days start to run from the end of the time-limit even where the faxed copy was lodged before.[648]

Another limited possibility to avoid the strictness of the time-limit in Article 230(5) is Article 45(2) of the Statute of the Court.

Effect of Exceeding the Time-limit

The time-limit applies to all applicants (privileged or not) and all reviewable acts. In *AssiDomän*, the Court found that 'a decision which has not

---

Horeca-Wallonie v Commission [1997] ECR II-2113, paras. 25 and 26; Case T-126/00 *Confindustria and Others v Commission* [2001] ECR II-85, para. 18; Joined Cases T-142/01 and T-283/01 *OPTUC v Commission* [2004] ECR II-329, para. 40.

645 Case T-2/06 *Yusef v Council*, order of 31 May 2006 (not published), para. 11.

646 A similar rule can be found in Article 43(6) of the CFI's Rules.

647 Article 37(6)(2) of the Court's Rules makes it clear that Article 81(2) of the Court's Rules does not apply in this context.

648 Case T-2/06 *Yusef v Council*, order of 31 May 2006 (not published), para. 13.

been challenged by the addressee within the time-limit laid down in Article 173 of the EC Treaty [now 230] becomes definitive as against him'.[649] This means the decision is considered as valid with regard to this person (or Member State), even though the Court might have annulled the decision with regard to other persons. However, a decision can not only become definitive as against its addressee, but also against a third party, where that third party could undoubtedly have challenged that decision.[650] In *Nachi Europe GmbH*, the Court extended this approach to anti-dumping regulations by holding that a regulation could become definitive against an individual 'in regard to whom it must be considered to be an individual decision and who could undoubtedly have sought its annulment under Article 230 EC'.[651] Given the notoriously uncertain standing of natural persons under Article 230(4) this development is worrying, as it will be difficult to say when a person could 'undoubtedly' have challenged an act.

A Community act which has become definitive can no longer be challenged under Article 230. Neither can its invalidity be raised indirectly on the basis of Article 241 EC,[652] in a preliminary reference under Article 234 EC,[653] in proceedings brought by the Commission against a Member State under Article 226 EC[654] and Article 88(2) EC,[655] and even in an action for damages under Article 288(2) EC, where the action in damages would lead to the same financial end as an action under Article 230 EC.[656]

---

[649] Case C-310/97P *Commission v AssiDomän and Others* [1999] ECR I-5363 at para 57. See also Case T-186/98 *Inpesca v Commission* [2001] ECR II-557, at para. 40.

[650] See Case C-188/92 *TWD Textilwerke Deggendorf v Germany* [1994] ECR I-833.

[651] Case C-239/99 *Nachi Europe GmbH v Hauptzollamt Krefeld* [2001] ECR I-1197, at para. 37. This approach seems also to apply to Member States who could have challenged an act, but did not do so within the time-limit provided for in Article 230(5), see Opinion of AG Mischo in Case C-241/01 *National Farmers' Union v Secrétariat général du gouvernement* [2002] ECR I-9079.

[652] See Case C-183/91 *Commission v Greece* [1993] ECR I-3131 at para 10; Case T-299/04 *Abdelghani Selmani v Council and Commission* [2005] ECR II-20, at para. 76.

[653] See Case C-188/92 *TWD Textilwerke Deggendorf v Germany* [1994] ECR I-833 at para. 13, where a private party failed to challenge an act under Article 230(4), and Case C-241/01 *National Farmers' Union v Secrétariat général du gouvernement* [2002] ECR I-9079, at para. 36, where a Member State (France) failed to challenge an act under Article 230(2). See also Case C-239/99 *Nachi Europe GmbH v Hauptzollamt Krefeld* [2001] ECR I-1197, at para. 37, and Case C-232/05 *Commission v France* [2006] ECR I-10071, at paras. 59–60.

[654] See Case C-53/05 *Commission v Portugal* [2006] ECR I-6215, at para. 30.

[655] Case C-404/97 *Commission v Portugal* [2000] ECR I-4897.

[656] See Case 175/84 *Krohn v Commission* [1986] ECR 753 at para. 33.

7. GROUNDS OF REVIEW

Article 230(2)[657] provides that the Court shall review acts of EC institutions 'on grounds of lack of competence, infringement of an essential procedural requirement, infringement of this Treaty or of any rule of law relating to its application, or misuse of powers'.[658] The legality of an act is assessed on the basis of the elements of fact and of law existing at the time when the measure was adopted.[659]

As the four grounds of review, which will be discussed in detail below, overlap to a considerable degree, the Court has not tried to distinguish them.[660] In any event, a wide interpretation of the rule of law, as mentioned in Article 230(2), covers all other grounds. Even though these grounds of review allow a comprehensive review of the legality of the act in question, the differing degree of intensity with which the Community Courts have carried out their review demonstrates how they perceive their role *vis-à-vis* the other institutions.

Lack of Competence

The Community legal system is based on the principle of attribution of powers. The principle laid down in Article 5 marks the demarcation between the competences of the Community and its Member States. This means that the Community's law-making powers are limited. At the same time, the EC Treaty contains a wide range of competences, including the general provision in Article 308. Moreover, the Court has interpreted these provisions broadly[661] and with the doctrine of implied powers[662] has given them added scope. Instances where the Court found that the Community lacked competence to act are therefore rare.[663]

The second aspect of the principle of attributed powers can be found in Article 7(1), which states that 'each institution shall act within the limits of the powers conferred upon it by this Treaty'. Article 7(1) acts as corollary to Article 5 and thereby marks the delineation of competences between the

---

657 The same grounds of review are available in an action for annulment in the third pillar under Article 35(6) TEU against a framework decision or decision.

658 For a general overview, see T.C. Hartley, supra note 1, chapter 15.

659 See Case T-73/98 *Société Chimique Prayon-Rupel SA v Commission* [2001] ECR II-867, para. 49.

660 See T.C. Hartley, supra note 1, p. 398.

661 See ibid., p. 105.

662 See Cases 281, 283 to 285, 287/85 *Germany v Commission* [1987] ECR 3203.

663 But see Opinion 2/94 ECHR [1996] ECR I-1759; Case C-376/98 *Germany v European Parliament and Council* [2000] ECR I-2247.

institutions. An EC institution can therefore not rely on a general lawmaking power, but can act only insofar as powers have been attributed to it.[664] Consequently, the Court would annul an act where an institution arrogates a power which belongs to another institution. This situation can clearly be subsumed within the ground of lack of competence, as can be seen from *France v Commission*.[665] In this case the Court found that the Commission lacked competence under Article 300 (ex 228) ECT to conclude an international agreement on behalf of the Community with the USA regarding the application of their competition laws, as this power was vested in the Council. The same is true where the Council adopts an act for which another institution was competent.

The Court would also declare a Community act invalid if the institution chooses an incorrect legal basis. This is the case where the institution's choice of legal basis affects its voting rules or the rights of other institutions in the procedure for its adoption. In *Commission v Council (Tariff Preferences)*[666] the Court annulled a Council Regulation applying general tariff preferences for developing countries on the ground that Article 133 (ex 113) ECT provided the correct legal basis for the act. Even though the Council's choice of Article 308 (ex 235) ECT in addition to Article 133 ECT also provided for the adoption of the act by the Council, both provisions differ with regard to the voting rules applicable in Council. Article 308 ECT requires unanimity whereas under Article 133 ECT qualified majority suffices for the adoption of an act. Consequently, the Court found that 'the choice of the legal basis could thus affect the determination of the content of the contested regulations'.[667] In contrast, in *Commission v Council*[668] the fact that the Council based its decision to conclude the International Convention on the Harmonised Commodity Description and Coding System on Articles 26 (ex 28), 133 (ex 113) and 308 (ex 235) ECT instead of Articles 26 (ex 28) and 133 (ex 113) ECT alone did not mean that the Court annulled the decision, given that at the material time both Article 26 (ex 28) and Article 308 ECT provided for unanimity.

Disputes where an institution is dissatisfied with the choice of legal basis on the ground that it provides fewer rights for it to participate in the adoption of the act have mainly arisen between the Council and the European

---

664 See Joined Cases 188 to 190/80 *France, Italy and United Kingdom v Commission* [1982] ECR 2545, para. 6.

665 Case C-327/91 *France v Commission* [1994] ECR I-3641.

666 Case 45/86 *Commission v Council* [1987] ECR 1493.

667 Ibid., para. 12. See also Case C-259/90 *European Parliament v Council* [1992] ECR I-4193.

668 Case 165/87 *Commission v Council* [1988] ECR 5545.

Parliament. As Article 308 ECT is subsidiary to other legal bases in the ECT, the Court will annul an act based on this provision where the correct legal basis contains greater participation rights for the EP.[669] Difficulties arise where more than one legal basis seems to be appropriate. The position of the Court can be summarised as follows. Where the act relates principally to one field of action and has only incidental effects on another area, a single legal basis has to be chosen.[670] Where the measure covers two policy areas which are equally important then the measure has to be based on both of the provisions from which the competence derives.[671] The latter is however not possible where both provisions provide for different participation rights of the European Parliament. In this case the legal basis which constitutes the centre of gravity has to be chosen.[672]

It is not always clear whether the annulment of acts which were adopted on an incorrect legal basis rests on the ground of lack of competence or infringement of an essential procedural requirement. In *European Parliament v Council (student residence rights)*[673] the Court seemed to have relied on the former, whereas in *European Parliament v Council (protection of forests)*,[674] the latter was chosen. It has been argued that the annulment should be based on the latter as the institution had the power to adopt the act in these cases.[675] This argument is not convincing. Such cases are characterised by the fact that the institution had chosen for the adoption of its act a legal basis which it was not competent to rely on. An infringement of an essential procedural requirement presupposes that the institution chose the correct legal basis, but violates the procedural rights provided in that provision for other institutions.

Where the Community has a competence to act, but the institution chooses the wrong legal basis, the Court subjects the choice of legal basis to strict review. In these cases the Court has consistently held that 'in the context of the organization of the powers of the Community the choice of

---

669 See Case C-22/96 *European Parliament v Council* [1998] ECR I-3231.

670 See Case C-70/88 *European Parliament v Council* [1991] ECR I-4529, para. 17; Case C-271/94 *European Parliament v Council* [1996] ECR I-1689, paras. 32–37; Case C-42/97 *European Parliament v Council* [1999] ECR I-869, para. 61.

671 Case 165/87 *Commission v Council* [1988] ECR 5545, paras. 6–13.

672 See Case C-300/89 *Commission v Council* [1991] ECR I-2867, paras. 17–21; Joined Cases C-164 and C-165/97 *European Parliament v Council* [1999] ECR I-1139, paras. 15–20. An act which contains two components, neither of which is incidental to the other, one falling within the CFSP and the other within Community development co-operation policy, will be annulled for breach of Article 47 TEU where it is exclusively based on Title V of the EU Treaty, see Case C-91/05 *Commission v Council*, judgment of 20 May 2008.

673 Case C-295/90 *European Parliament v Council* [1992] ECR I-4193, paras. 12 and 20.

674 See Joined Cases C-164 and C-165/97 *European Parliament v Council* [1999] ECR I-1139, para. 20.

675 T.C. Hartley, supra note 1, p. 399.

legal basis for a measure may not depend simply on an institution's conviction as to the objective pursued but must be based on objective factors which are amenable to judicial review'.[676]

Lack of competence as ground for annulment could also be relied on where the act contravenes the principle of subsidiarity,[677] which is laid down in Article 5(2) ECT.[678] The principle only applies in areas which do not fall within the exclusive competence of the Community.[679] It requires the Community to take action only if and to the extent that the Member States cannot sufficiently achieve the Community's objectives and that the Community by reasons of scale or effects of the proposed action can achieve those objectives better. Further details on the application of the principle of subsidiarity are set out in a Protocol which has been added by the Amsterdam Treaty.[680] Despite the difficulties as to the justiciability of the principle of subsidiarity,[681] the Court seems to be willing to review Community acts as to their compliance with the principle.[682] All the same, the Court seems to be reluctant to interfere with the need for Community action once it has established that a legal basis for such action exists[683] and the institution has given adequate reasons for compliance with the principle.[684]

The competence to adopt legal acts is however not limited to instances where the EC Treaty provides the legal basis for the institution to act. Article 202 3rd indent ECT gives the Council the right to authorise the Commission[685] to implement legal acts adopted by the Council.[686] In

---

676 Case C-300/89 *Commission v Council* [1991] ECR I-2867, para. 10.

677 See P. Craig and G. DeBúrca, supra note 1, pp. 100–105; A. Estella, *The EU Principle of Subsidiarity and its Critique* (OUP, 2002).

678 See P. Craig and G. DeBúrca, supra note 1, p. 539.

679 For the differing views as to the meaning of this requirement, see A.G. Toth, 'A Legal Analysis of Subsidiarity', in D. O'Keeffe and P.M. Twomey (eds.), *Legal Issues of the Maastricht Treaty* (Chancery, 1994); J. Steiner, 'Subsidiarity under the Maastricht Treaty', in D. O'Keeffe and P.M. Twomey (eds.), ibid.

680 Protocol on the Application of the Principles of Subsidiarity and Proportionality.

681 See P. Craig and G. DeBúrca, supra note 1, p. 105.

682 Case C-84/94 *United Kingdom v Council* [1996] ECR I-5755, at para. 55; Case C-377/98 *Netherlands v European Parliament and Council* [2001] ECR I-7079, at paras. 30–32; Case C-103/01 *Commission v Germany* [2003] ECR I-5369, at para. 47; Case C-491/01 *BAT and Imperial Tobacco* [2002] ECR I-11453, at paras. 180–183; Case C-154/04 *Alliance for Natural Health* [2005] ECR I-6451, at paras. 104–107. See however Case T-253/02 *Ayadi v Council* [2006] ECR II-2139, para. 110.

683 See C-154/04 *Alliance for Natural Health* [2005] ECR I-6451, at paras. 101–108.

684 Case C-233/94 *Germany v Council* [1997] ECR I-2405, at para. 28; C-377/98 *Netherlands v European Parliament and Council* [2001] ECR I-7079, at para. 33.

685 In exceptional cases implementing powers can also be delegated to the Council.

686 The Court has made it clear that Article 202 EC refers 'both to measures adopted by the Council alone and to measures adopted by the Council together with the Parliament under the co-decision procedure to measures adopted by the Council alone', see Case C-378/00 *Commission v European Parliament and Council* [2003] ECR I-937, para. 40. The

addition to the delegation of powers under the comitology system,[687] the Court has also allowed the conferral of, albeit limited, powers to agencies, even though they are not referred to in Article 202 3rd indent.[688]

For the conferral of implementing powers under Article 202 3rd indent ECT the ECJ requires that the 'basic elements of the matter to be dealt with'[689] have to be contained in the basic act.[690] The notion of 'basic elements' has been interpreted generously in favour of the legislative authority conferring implementing powers. This is in particular true for the Common Agricultural Policy, where the Court found that the Council could 'confer on the Commission wide powers of discretion and action'[691] through a 'provision drafted in general terms'.[692] In practice, the legislative authority has made use of the possibility of wide conferrals, delegating even matters of determining aspects central to the exercise of fundamental rights.[693] It should, however, be noted that in subject areas other than agricultural policy, the ECJ defined the requirements for the precision of the delegating norm more narrowly.[694]

Given the wide interpretation of implementation allowing the Council to confer considerable power to the Commission and to phrase the

same interpretation was already reached for a similar provision in Case C-259/95 *Parliament v Council* [1997] ECR I-5303, at para. 26.

[687] See C. Joerges and E. Vos (eds.), *EU Committees: Social Regulation, Law and Politics* (Hart, 1999); M. Andenas, A. Türk (eds.), *Delegated Legislation and the Role of Committees in the EC* (Kluwer, 2000); C. Bergström, *Comitology, Delegation of Powers in the European Union and the Committee System* (OUP, 2005); P. Craig (2006), supra note 2, chapter 4; T. Christiansen und T. Larsson, *The Role of the Committees in the Policy Process of the European Union* (Edward Elgar Publishing, 2007).

[688] Cases 9 and 10/56 *Meroni v High Authority* [1957/58] ECR 133. For a discussion as to whether the Meroni doctrine can be applied to the EC Treaty, see K. Lenaerts, 'Regulating the Regulatory Process "Delegation of Powers" in the European Community' (1993) *ELRev* 22, at p. 41; R. Dehousse, 'Misfits: EU Law and the Transformation of European Governance', in: C. Joerges and R. Dehousse, *Good Governance in Europe's Integrated Market* (OUP, 2002), p. 221. For a more general discussion on agencies, see P. Craig (2006), supra note 2, chapter 5.

[689] Case 25/70 *Einfuhrstelle v Köster* [1970] ECR 1161, para. 6. See also Case C-240/90 *Germany v Commission* [1992] ECR I-5383, at para. 36; Case C-104/97 P *Atlanta and Others v Council and Commission* [1999] ECR I-6983, at para. 76; Joined Cases T-64/01 and T-65/01 *Afrikanische Frucht-Compagnie GmbH and another v Council and Commission* [2004] ECR II-521, para. 119. See also Case C-66/04 *United Kingdom v European Parliament and Council* [2005] ECR I-10553, at para. 50.

[690] For a discussion of the case-law, see A. Türk, 'The role of the European Court of Justice in the area of comitology', in T. Christiansen und T. Larsson, supra note 687, pp. 227–248.

[691] Case 23/75 *Rey Soda* [1975] ECR 1279, para. 11.

[692] Case C-240/90 *Germany v Commission* [1992] ECR I-5383, para. 41.

[693] Ibid.

[694] See Case 291/86 *Central-Import Münster* [1988] ECR 3679, at p. 3706; Case 22/88 *Vreugdenhil* [1989] ECR 2049, at p. 2076; Joined Cases C-154/04 and C-155/04 *Alliance for Natural Health and others* [2005] ECR I-6451, at para. 90.

enabling provision in general terms, it should not be surprising that the Court has also interpreted the limits of the powers conferred on the Commission widely. This was made clear by the Court in *Rey Soda*, where the Court held that '[w]hen the Council has thus conferred extensive power on the Commission the limits of this power must be judged with regard to the basic general objectives of the organization of the market and less in terms of the literal meaning of the enabling word'.[695] A literal interpretation seems all the more difficult where the Court allows for the enabling provision to be drafted in general terms. It seems, however, that such a wide interpretation of the Commission's implementing power is limited to the agricultural sector, for the Court held in *Vreugdenhil*[696] that 'such a wide interpretation of the Commission's powers can be accepted only in the specific framework of the rules on agricultural markets. It cannot be relied upon in support of provisions adopted by the Commission on the basis of its implementing powers in agricultural matters where the purpose of the provision in question lies outside that sphere.'[697] Where enabling provisions in the agricultural markets confer on the Commission general powers, the Court determines the limits of these powers with regard to 'the basic general objectives of the organization of the market and less in terms of the literal meaning of the enabling word'.[698]

The limits of the implementing powers of the Commission are also set by the provisions of the basic regulation. The Court held that the implementing measure could not derogate 'from the provisions of the basic regulation to which it is subordinate'.[699] The implementing measure can derogate from the basic act only if the basic act expressly confers the power to do so.[700] However, as the Court decided in *Eridania*,[701] these derogations have to be related to the general system of the basic act and may not 'jeopardize the essential elements embodied in that regulation'.[702] In *European Parliament v Commission*[703] the Court found that the Commission was allowed to provide for the inclusion of genetically modified micro-organisms (GMMOs) in organic products, as such inclusion could not be considered 'as contrary

---

695 Case 23/75 *Rey Soda* [1975] ECR 1279, para. 14. See also Case 22/88 *Vreugdenhil* [1989] ECR 2049, para. 16.

696 Case 22/88 *Vreugdenhil* [1989] ECR 2049.

697 Ibid., para. 17.

698 Case 23/75 *Rey Soda* [1975] ECR 1279, para. 14. See also Case 61/86 *United Kingdom v Commission* [1988] ECR 431.

699 Case 38/70 *Tradax* [1971] ECR 145, para. 10.

700 Case 100/74 *C.A.M. v Commission* [1975] ECR 1393.

701 Case 230/78 *Eridania* [1979] ECR 2749.

702 Ibid., para. 8.

703 Case C-156/93 *Parliament v Commission* [1995] ECR I-2019.

to the provisions of the basic regulation'.[704] In contrast, the Court applied a more restrictive approach in *European Parliament v Council*.[705] The Court held that 'an implementing directive such as the contested directive, adopted without consultation of the Parliament, must respect the provisions enacted in the basic directive'.[706] The Court stated that while it pursued the aim of improving agricultural production through the use of plant protection products, the basic directive also required respect for the environment in general, and of groundwater in particular, as an essential precondition for the authorisation of such products. The Court found that 'by not taking account of the effects which plant protection products may have on all groundwater, the contested [implementing] directive failed to observe one of the essential elements of the matter expressly laid down by the basic directive.'[707]

Outside the agricultural area, the Community Courts seem to take a stricter line as to the scope of the Commission's implementing powers. In *Netherlands v Commission*[708] the Court had to assess whether Commission Directive 1999/51/EC[709] could validly have been adopted on the basis of Article 2a of Council Directive 76/769.[710] Article 2a provided that amendments required to adapt the Annexes of the Directive to technical progress should be adopted in accordance with a comitology procedure. The Commission, by amending point 24 of Annex I of Directive 76/769, simply prolonged the derogations granted to Austria and Sweden in the Act of Accession in order to allow them to maintain stricter rules on the use of cadmium than were provided for under point 24 of Annex I of Directive 76/769. The Court came to the conclusion that such a derogation was not an adaptation to technical progress and that therefore the Commission could not adopt the measure on the basis of Article 2a of Directive 76/769.[711]

It has to be admitted, though, that it is not always easy to determine the correct scope of an authorisation granted in the basic act. This is

---

704 Ibid., para. 24.

705 Case C-303/94 *European Parliament v Council* [1996] ECR I-2943.

706 Ibid., para. 23. See also Case C-239/01 *Germany v Commission* [2003] ECR I-10333, para. 58.

707 Case C-303/94 *European Parliament v Council* [1996] ECR I-2943, para. 31.

708 Case C-314/99 *Netherlands v Commission* [2002] ECR I-5521.

709 OJ [1999] 142/22.

710 OJ [1996] L 262/201, as amended.

711 For a similar example see Case C-93/00 *European Parliament v Council* [2001] ECR I-10119, where the Court found that the Council could not prolong the voluntary system on the labelling of beef on the basis of Article 19 of Council Directive 820/97. See also Joined Cases T-74/00 etc *Artegodan and Others v Commission* [2002] ECR II-4945 and Case T-147/00 *Les Laboratoires Servier v Commission* [2003] ECR II-85. For an instructive example of the Court's approach, see also Joined Cases C-14/06 and C-295/06 *European Parliament and Denmark v Commission*, judgment of 1 April 2008.

demonstrated by the interpretation of Article 6(1) of Council Regulation 2377/90 laying down a Community procedure for the establishment of maximum residue limits (MRLs) of veterinary medicinal products in foodstuffs of animal origin.[712] Similar problems to determine the competences of the Commission in the implementation of basic acts arose with regard to the interpretation of Article 3(1) of Council Regulation 2081/92 on the protection of geographical indications and designations of origin for agricultural products and foodstuffs.[713]

Infringement of an Essential Procedural Requirement

Procedural requirements can be provided in the EC Treaty itself, and also in secondary legislation. In addition, the Court has developed such procedural requirements on the basis of general principles of law, which are binding on the institutions, even in the absence of statutory provisions. However, only the violation of essential procedural rules leads to the annulment of the act.[714]

Procedural rights are all the more important where the institution has discretion or a power of appraisal. As the Court pointed out in *Technische Universität München*[715] 'where the Community institutions have such a power of appraisal, respect for the rights guaranteed by the Community legal order in administrative procedures is of even more fundamental importance. Those guarantees include, in particular, the duty of the competent institution to examine carefully and impartially all the relevant aspects of the individual case, the right of the person concerned to make his views known and to have an adequately reasoned decision. Only in this way can the Court verify whether the factual and legal elements upon which the exercise of the power of appraisal depends were present'.[716]

---

[712] OJ [1990] L 224/1, as amended. Joined Cases T-125/96 and T-152/96 *Boehringer v Council and Commission* [1999] ECR II-3427, in which the CFI annulled a Commission measure for lack of competence. This judgment was overturned by the Court of Justice in Case C-32/00 P *Boehringer v Council and Commission* [2002] ECR I-1917 (see also the Opinion of AG Colomer). See also Case T-112/97 *Monsanto v Commission* [1999] ECR II-1277 which was overturned on appeal by the Court of Justice in Case C-248/99 P *Monsanto v Commission* [2002] ECR I-1 which preferred a wider interpretation of Article 6 of Regulation 2377/90.

[713] OJ [1992] L 208/1, as amended. See Joined Cases C-289/96, C-293/96 and C-299/96 *Denmark, Germany and France v Commission* [1999] ECR I-1541.

[714] On what constitutes an 'essential' procedural requirement, see T.C. Hartley, supra note 1, pp. 399–401.

[715] Case C-269/90 *Technische Universität München v Hauptzollamt München Mitte* [1991] ECR I-5469.

[716] Ibid., para. 14.

Duty to give reasons

The duty to give reasons under Article 253 ECT[717] applies to all legally binding acts adopted by the Community institutions. Due to its wide scope covering as it does legislative and administrative acts, the provision constitutes an effective tool in the review of these legal acts. It is therefore not surprising that the Community Courts have identified as one of the rationales for the duty to give reasons that it gives an opportunity 'to the court of exercising its supervisory function'.[718] The strict[719] review of whether the institution concerned has complied with the requirement to give reasons, which the Court has to raise as a matter of public policy of its own motion,[720] assumes an even greater importance where the substantive review of the measure is reduced due to the discretion the institution enjoys.[721] In these cases the Community Courts seem to employ the duty to give reasons as substitute for substantive review.[722]

However, Article 253 ECT pursues additional objectives. The Community Courts have pointed out that the provision also enables those concerned by an act to defend their rights.[723] And interested parties can take note of the reasoning of the institution which adopted the act and adjust their future behaviour accordingly.[724] Two further functions are frequently mentioned: first, the duty to give reasons imposes some self-control on the authority adopting the act[725] and second, it allows the European Parliament to exercise its political scrutiny role more effectively.[726]

The content of the duty to give reasons is influenced by these rationales[727] and the Community Courts have held that the statement of reasons 'must disclose in a clear and unequivocal fashion the reasoning followed by the institution which adopted the measure in question in such a way as to enable the persons concerned to ascertain the reasons for the measure and to enable the competent Community Court to exercise its power of review'.[728]

---

717 Case C-143/95P *Commission v Socurte* [1997] ECR I-1.

718 Case 24/62 *Germany v Commission* [1963] ECR 63, 69.

719 See D. Chalmers, C. Hadjiemmanuil, G. Monti, A. Tomkins, *European Union Law* (CUP, 2006), p. 447.

720 Case T-102/03 *CIS v Commission* [2005] ECR II-2357, at para. 46.

721 See Case C-269/90 *Technische Universität München* [1991] ECR I-5469, at para. 14.

722 See M. Shapiro, 'The Giving Reasons Requirement' (1992) *University Chicago Legal Forum* 179, p. 182.

723 Ibid.

724 Ibid.

725 See P. Craig and G. DeBúrca, supra note 1, p. 541. For a more sober assessment of this rationale, see T.C. Hartley, supra note 1, p. 128.

726 See T.C. Hartley, supra note 1, p. 124.

727 Ibid., p. 125.

728 Case T-102/03 *CIS v Commission* [2005] ECR II-2357, para. 47. See also Case T-245/03 R *FNSEA and Others v Commission* [2004] ECR II-271, para. 48; C-304/01 *Spain v*

This means that the institution which adopted the act has to state the legal basis for the act.[729] It also has to set out the factual and legal considerations which underpin its measure. On the other hand, '[i]t is not necessary for the reasoning to go into all the relevant facts and points of law, since the question whether the statement of reasons meets the requirements of Article [253] must be assessed with regard not only to its wording but also to its context and to all the legal rules governing the matter in question'.[730]

The extent of the reasoning often depends on the particular circumstances of the case. It is therefore not possible to set out the specific requirements which are applicable in all cases. The Community Courts have argued that 'the requirements to be satisfied by the statement of reasons depend on the circumstances of each case, in particular the content of the measure in question, the nature of the reasons given and the interest which the addressees of the measure, or other parties to whom it is of direct and individual concern, may have in obtaining explanations'.[731]

It is however clear that 'the extent of the requirement laid down by Article [253] of the Treaty to state the reasons on which measures are based, depends on the nature of the measure in question.'[732] Where the act is of general application it would be excessive 'to require a specific statement of reasons for each of the technical choices made by the institution.'[733] Instead it is sufficient that the preamble to an act of general application is 'confined to indicating the general situation which led to its adoption, on the one hand, and the general objectives which it intended to achieve on the other.'[734] In contrast, acts of individual application often have to contain

---

Commission [2004] ECR I-7655, para. 50.

[729] See Case 45/86 *Commission v Council* [1987] ECR 1493. Breach of this requirement will however not in all cases lead to the annulment of the act, see T.C. Hartley, supra note 1, pp. 400–401.

[730] Case T-317/02 *FICF and Others v Commission* [2004] ECR II-4325, para. 129. See also Case C-257/01 *Commission v Council* [2005] ECR I-345, para. 53. On the relevance of this dialogue function, see M. Shapiro, supra note 722, pp. 203–204.

[731] Case T-317/02 *FICF and Others v Commission* [2004] ECR II-4325, para. 129. See also Case C-76/01 P *Eurocoton and Others v Council* [2003] ECR I-10091, para. 88.

[732] Case 5/67 *Beus* [1968] ECR 83, p. 95. See also Case T-213/00 *CMA DGM and others v Commission* [2003] ECR II-913, para. 80; Case T-251/00 *Lagardère and Canal+ v Commission* [2002] ECR II-4825, para. 155; Joined Cases T-44/01, T-119/01 and T-126/01 *Vieira and others v Commission* [2003] ECR II-1209, para. 193; Case C-304/01 *Spain v Commission* [2004] ECR I-7655, para. 51; Case T-245/03 R *FNSEA and others v Commission* [2004] ECR II-271, para. 48. See also T.C. Hartley, supra note 1, p. 125.

[733] Case C-122/94 *Commission v Council* [1996] ECR I-881, para. 29. See also Case C-110/97 *Netherlands v Council* [2001] ECR I-8763, para. 166; Case T-189/00 R *'Invest' Import and Export and Invest Commerce v Commission* [2000] ECR II-2993, para. 43; Case C-304/01 *Spain v Commission* [2004] ECR I-7655, para. 51.

[734] Case 5/67 *Beus* [1968] ECR 83, p. 95. See also Case T-13/99 *Pfizer Animal Health v Council* [2002] ECR II-3305, para. 510; Case T-70/99 *Alpharma v Council* [2002] ECR II-3495,

greater detail of reasoning.[735] This is in particular the case for measures imposing fines[736] or disciplinary measures.[737]

It is, however, doubtful that the nature of the act can always be the decisive criterion determining the extent of the duty to provide reasons under Article 253 ECT. The case law of the Community Courts[738] seems to suggest that the reasoning in an anti-dumping act is 'assimilated more to the statement of reasons for an individual act, since it must include more than just a general statement about the overall situation.'[739] It is submitted that the rationale for this approach in anti-dumping cases results from the more general considerations that underlie the duty to provide reasons. The Court has pointed out that the duty to give reasons is, in particular, necessary to enable individuals to assess the possibility of a successful challenge. Only where the individual is in possession of all the relevant factual and legal arguments can the requirement of effective legal protection for individuals be satisfied. Consequently, an act of general application which takes account, or should have taken account, of the specific situation of individuals which are directly and individually concerned[740] by the act requires a more in-depth reasoning in order to make the motivation which relates specifically to their situation apparent for these individuals.[741] It also follows from its general nature that such a rationale is not limited to

para. 394; Case C-304/01 *Spain v Commission* [2004] ECR I-7655, para. 51; Case C-184/02 *Spain and Finland v European Parliament and Council* [2004] ECR I-7789, para. 79; Case C-342/03 *Spain v Council* [2005] ECR 1975, para. 55.

[735] See Case 24/62 *Commission v Germany* [1963] ECR 63; Case T-102/03 *CIS v Commission* [2005] ECR II-2357; Case T-251/00 *Lagardère v Commission* [2002] ECR II-4825, paras. 155–158.

[736] See Case T-245/03R *FNSEA and Others v Commission* [2004] ECR II-271, para. 49.

[737] See Case T-11/03 *Afari v European Central Bank* [2004] ECR II-267, para. 38.

[738] See Case 53/83 *Allied Corporation v Council* [1985] ECR 1621, at paras. 17–19. See also Case C-76/00 P *Petrotub and Republica v Council and Commission* [2003] ECR I-79, at paras. 79–91, in which the Court on appeal considered the statement of reasons in the anti-dumping regulation in issue as insufficient.

[739] J. Schwarze, *European Administrative Law* (Sweet & Maxwell, 1992), p. 1414.

[740] See the following recent cases, in which the Court makes the link between the duty to give reasons and direct and individual concern: Case T-74/00 *Verband der freien Rohrwerke and others v Commission* [2003] ECR II-2275, at para. 185; C-76/00 P *Petrotub and Republica v Council and Commission* [2003] ECR I-79, at para. 88; Case C-42/01 *Portugal v Commission* [2004] ECR I-6079, at para. 66; Joined Cases T-116/01 and T-118/01 *P&O European Ferries (Vizcaya) and another v Commission* [2003] ECR II-2957, at para. 170; Case T-317/02 *FICF and others v Commission* [2004] ECR II-4325, at para. 129.

[741] See C-76/00 P *Petrotub and Republica v Council and Commission* [2003] ECR I-79, where the Court at para. 87 emphasised the link between the statement of reasons and the position of the applicants by holding that '[s]uch a peremptory statement [. . .] does not contain any explanatory element of such a kind as to enlighten the parties concerned [. . .] as to the reasons which led the Council to consider that the prices charged in connection with those sales made using compensation had not been affected by the relationship'.

the field of anti-dumping, but applies in all areas where the Community institutions adopt acts of general application which are of direct and individual concern to individuals.[742]

Finally, it should be pointed out that the institution cannot remedy a defective statement of reasons subsequently in the judicial proceedings, save in exceptional circumstances.[743] The Community Courts have made it clear that 'the statement of reasons must in principle be notified to the person concerned at the same time as the decision adversely affecting him and that a failure to state the reasons cannot be remedied by the fact that the person concerned learns the reasons for the decision during the proceedings before the Court'.[744]

Rights of defence

The rights of defence constitute essential procedural requirements. The most important of these rights are the right to be heard and access to documents.[745] Community law has established statutory rules which deal with the participation of individuals in administrative proceedings carried out by Community institutions. These statutory rights have, however, to be seen in the light of the case law of the Community Courts, which have recognised the right to a hearing as a general principle of law[746] or even a 'fundamental principle of community law',[747] which 'cannot be excluded or restricted by any legislative provision.'[748] Consequently, the right to a fair

---

[742] But see Case T-13/99 *Pfizer Animal Health v Council* [2002] ECR II-3305, para. 510 and Case T-70/99 *Alpharma v Council* [2002] ECR II-3495, para. 394 in which the CFI allowed for a more general statement of reasons due to the general application of the act in issue despite the fact that the applicant was directly and individually concerned.

[743] See Case T-37/89 *Hanning v European Parliament* [1990] ECR II-463, at paras. 41–44.

[744] Case 195/80 *Michel v European Parliament* [1981] ECR 2861, para. 22. See also Case T-16/91 RV *Rendo and Others v Commission* [1996] ECR II-1827, para. 45; Case T-613/97 *UFEX and Others v Commission* [2006] ECR II-4055, para. 67; Joined Cases T-46/98 and T-151/98 *CEMR v Commission* [2000] ECR II-167, para. 47; Case C-233/00 *Commission v France* [2003] ECR I-6625, para. 90; Case C-189/02 P etc. *Dansk Rørindustri and Others v Commission* [2005] ECR I-5425, para. 463.

[745] See K. Lenaerts and J. Vanhamme, 'Procedural Rights of Private Parties in the Community Administrative Process' (1997) *CMLRev* 531; H.P. Nehl, *Principles of Administrative Procedure in EC Law* (OUP, 1999), pp. 70–99; P. Craig (2006), supra note 2, chapters 10 and 11; T. Tridimas, *The General Principles of EC Law* (OUP, 2nd edn., 2006), chapter 8; I. Rabinowitz, *The Fundamental Right to be Heard in the Administrative Procedures of the European Union* (PhD thesis, University of London, 2008). The rights of defence also include a limited right of legal professional privilege (see Case 155/79 *AM&S* [1982] ECR 1575, at paras. 23–26, Case T-30/90 *Hilti* [1990] ECR II-163, at para. 18 and most recently Joined Cases T-125/03 and T-253/03 *Akzo and Akcros*, judgment of 17 September 2007) and a limited right against self-incrimination (see Case 227/88 *Hoechst AG v Commission* [1989] ECR 2859).

[746] This was first established in Case 32/62 *Alvis v Council* [1963] ECR 49, at p. 55.

[747] Case 85/76 *Hoffmann-La Roche v Commission* [1979] ECR 461, para. 9.

[748] Case T-260/94 *Air Inter v Commission* [1997] ECR II-997, para. 60.

hearing is enforced 'where there is no specific legislation and also where legislation exists which does not itself take account of that principle.'[749]

It is clear that the right to a fair hearing, as a general principle of Community law, applies in proceedings 'initiated against a person which are liable to culminate in a measure adversely affecting that person.'[750] The right to be heard was first recognised in disciplinary procedures against Community civil servants. In *Alvis*[751] the Court made it clear that the rule that civil servants must have 'the opportunity of replying to allegations before any disciplinary decision is taken concerning them [. . .] must be followed by Community institutions'.[752] The right to be heard has however found its most profound formation in the area of competition law.[753] In *Hoffmann-La Roche*[754] the Court held that 'the undertakings concerned must have been afforded the opportunity to make known their views on the truth and relevance of the facts and circumstances alleged on the documents used by the Commission to support its claim that there has been an infringement of Article 86 [now 82] of the Treaty'.[755] The right to a fair hearing also requires the Commission to allow the parties to inspect all the information in its files.[756] The Commission can therefore not limit itself to providing the evidence which it considers relevant for the case. However, it is clear from the case law that the right stretches no further than the parties under investigation whether initiated *ex officio* by the Commission or on application by the parties themselves. In *Kish Glass*[757] the CFI found that the right to a fair hearing only applied to 'those in respect of whom the Commission carries out its investigation'.[758] Complainants,[759] trade unions[760] and other interested third parties[761] therefore do not come within the scope of the right.

---

[749] Ibid. See also Case C-32/95P *Commission v Lisrestal and Others* [1996] ECR I-5373, at para. 30.

[750] Case C-135/92 *Fiscano v Commission* [1994] ECR I-2885, para. 39.

[751] Case 32/62 *Alvis v Council* [1963] ECR 49.

[752] Ibid., p. 59.

[753] F. Bignami, 'Three Generations of Participation Rights before the European Commission' (2004) 68 *Law and Contemporary Problems* 61–83, p. 63.

[754] Case 85/76 *Hoffmann-La Roche v Commission* [1979] ECR 461.

[755] Ibid., para. 11.

[756] Case T-7/89 *Hercules Chemicals v Commission* [1991] ECR II-1711, at paras. 53 and 54; Case T-65/89 *BPB Industries and British Gypsum v Commission* [1993] ECR II-389; Joined Cases C-238, 244–245, 247, 250, 252 and 254/99 P *Limburgse Vinyl Maatschappij v Commission* [2002] ECR I-8375.

[757] Case T-65/96 *Kish Glass v Commission* [2001] ECR II-3261.

[758] Ibid., para. 32.

[759] Ibid., para. 33.

[760] Case T-96/92 *CCE v Commission* [1995] ECR II-1213.

[761] Case 209/78 *Sarl v Commission* [1980] ECR 3125; Case 43/85 *ANCIDES v Commission* [1987] ECR 3131; Case T-290/94 *Kayserberg v Commission* [1997] ECR 2137.

That the Community Courts reserve the right to a hearing, at least in its widest form, to those natural or legal persons under investigation by Community institutions, is also clear from their approach in state aid cases. This means that the full right to a hearing is only guaranteed for the Member State whose grant of aid is under investigation. The Court has made it clear that 'the procedure for reviewing State aid [. . .] is [. . .] a procedure initiated in respect of the Member State responsible, in light of its obligations, for granting the aid.'[762] In contrast, other interested parties have the more limited rights contained in the EC Treaty and secondary legislation.[763] Their role is therefore limited to provide 'information required for the guidance of the Commission with regard to its future action'.[764] The Court has emphasised in particular that 'no special role is reserved for the recipient of aid',[765] as 'the procedure for reviewing State aid is not a procedure initiated against the recipient or recipients of aid entailing rights on which it or they could rely which are as extensive as the rights of defence as such'.[766] A similarly limited right exists for public undertakings where the Commission investigates state monopolies under Article 86 ECT.[767]

In contrast to state aid cases, however, the Court has made it clear in *Lisrestal*[768] that the right to a fair hearing applies in structural fund cases not only to the Member State, but also to beneficiaries in proceedings in which the Commission considers a reduction in the assistance initially granted to the beneficiary. The Court argued that in such a case 'the decision at issue was "initiated against" the respondents'[769] and that 'despite the central role played by the Member State concerned in the system established by Regulation No 2950/83, the respondents were directly implicated in the investigation which led to the decision'.[770]

---

[762] Joined Cases C-74/00P and C-75/00P *Falck and Acciairie di Bolzano v Commission* [2002] ECR I-7869, para. 81.

[763] Case T-198/01 *Technische Glaswerke v Commission* [2004] ECR II-2717, at para. 194.

[764] Joined Cases C-74/00P and C-75/00P *Falck and Acciairie di Bolzano v Commission* [2002] ECR I-7869, para. 80.

[765] Joined Cases C-74/00P and C-75/00P *Falck and Acciairie di Bolzano v Commission* [2002] ECR I-7869, para. 83. See also Case T-198/01 *Technische Glaswerke v Commission* [2004] ECR II-2717, at para. 195.

[766] Joined Cases C-74/00P and C-75/00P *Falck and Acciairie di Bolzano v Commission* [2002] ECR I-7869, para. 83.

[767] Case T-266/97 *Vlaamse Televisie Maatschappij v Commission* [1999] ECR II-2329, at para. 37. On the limited content of the right to be heard by public undertakings, see also Case T-260/94 *Air Inter v Commission* [1997] ECR II-997, paras. 64–72.

[768] Case C-32/95P *Commission v Lisrestal* [1996] ECR I-5373.

[769] Ibid., para. 24. See also Case C-462/98P *Mediocurso v Commission* [2000] ECR I-7183, para. 36.

[770] Case C-32/95P *Commission v Lisrestal* [1996] ECR I-5373, para. 24.

The right to a hearing is also recognised in the customs area, where the Court has made it clear that the rights of defence assume an even greater importance where the substantive review of the Community Courts is reduced due to the Commission's power of appraisal. In *Technische Universität München*[771] the national authority referred to the Commission a case on whether an imported scientific instrument could benefit from an exemption of customs duties under Regulation 1798/75.[772] After consultation of an expert group, the Commission rejected the request on the ground that an instrument of equivalent scientific value was manufactured in the EC, without having heard the importing institution. The Court pointed out that the Commission had a power of appraisal, as the administrative procedure involved complex technical evaluations. However, the Court emphasised that where the Commission had such power of appraisal 'respect for the rights guaranteed by the Community legal order in administrative procedures is of even more fundamental importance'.[773] The Court made it clear that these guarantees included, amongst others, 'the right of the person to make his views known'[774] even where the applicable statutory provision did not provide such an opportunity.

In *France Aviation*[775] the CFI applied the *Technische Universität München* ruling to a case in which the importer applied for repayment of a customs duty under Article 13 of Regulation 1430/79.[776] With reference to the judgment in *Technische Universität München* the CFI found that the Commission's power of appraisal had as a consequence that 'respect for the right to be heard must be guaranteed in procedures for the repayment of customs duty'.[777] The Court held that where the Commission wanted to reject the application on the ground of 'obvious negligence' contrary to the national authority's position, it had 'a duty to arrange for the applicant to be heard by the French authorities'.[778] In *Eyckeler & Malt*[779] the CFI went even further by holding that before it could reject the application for a

---

771 Case C-269/90 *Technische Universität München v Hauptzollamt München Mitte* [1991] ECR I-5469.

772 [1979] OJ L 318/32.

773 Case C-269/90 *Technische Universität München v Hauptzollamt München Mitte* [1991] ECR I-5469, para. 14.

774 Ibid., para. 14.

775 Case T-246/95 *France Aviation v Commission* [1995] ECR II-2841.

776 [1979] OJ L 175/1, as amended by Council Regulation 3069/86 [1986] OJ L 286/1.

777 Case T-246/95 *France Aviation v Commission* [1995] ECR II-2841, para. 34. This stands in contrast to earlier decisions by the Court, see Case 294/81 *Control Data v Commission* [1983] ECR 911 and Joined Cases C-121/91 and C-122/91 *CT Control (Rotterdam) and JCT Benelux v Commission* [1993] ECR I-3873.

778 Case T-246/95 *France Aviation v Commission* [1995] ECR II-2841, para. 36.

779 Case T-42/96 *Eyckeler & Malt v Commission* [1998] ECR II-401.

remission of customs duties on the basis of 'obvious negligence' on the part of the applicant, contrary to the favourable assessment of the applicant's case by the national authorities, the Commission had to 'provide access to all non-confidential official documents concerning the contested decision, if requested to do so'[780] and had to allow the applicant 'to put its case and effectively make its views known on the relevant circumstances relied on against it as the basis for the contested decision'.[781] It should be noted that the CFI based the application of the right to a fair hearing on its general formula that the right applied 'in all proceedings which are initiated against a person and are liable to culminate in a measure adversely affecting that person'.[782] The power of appraisal that formed the basis of the rulings in *Technische Universität München* and *France Aviation* merely served to reinforce that right. In its recent case-law,[783] the CFI has extended the right to a fair hearing to all aspects of remission or repayment cases.[784]

However, the 'initiated against' formula is not employed in all areas of Community law. The Community Courts seem to be prepared to give the principle a wider scope of application in cases dealing with requests by individuals or Member States[785] and trademark proceedings.[786]

---

780 Ibid., para. 81. Where the Commission bases its decision solely on the file submitted by the national authority, the applicant's access to the file during the administrative procedure before the national authority is sufficient, see Case T-250/99 *Hyper v Commission* [2002] ECR II-3141, at para. 55. Similarly, the Commission does not have on its own initiative to grant access to all the documents which may have some connection with the case, see Case T-329/00 *Bonn Fleisch v Commission* [2003] ECR II-287, at para. 46.

781 Case T-42/96 *Eyckeler & Malt v Commission* [1998] ECR II-401, para. 86. This requirement was not satisfied, as the Commission discussed the case with the applicant's lawyer before the application for remission instead of providing the applicant with an opportunity to comment on the Commission's provisional decision. However, this does not mean that the Commission has to grant the applicant an oral hearing, see Joined Cases T-134/03 and T-135/03 *Common Market Fertilizers v Commission* [2005] ECR II-3923, at para. 108.

782 Case T-42/96 *Eyckeler & Malt v Commission* [1998] ECR II-401, para. 76. See also Case T-50/96 *Primex and others v Commission* [1998] ECR II-3773, para. 59; Joined Cases T-186/97 etc. *Kaufring and others v Commission* [2001] ECR II-1337, para. 151; Case T-290/97 *Mehibas Dordtselaan v Commission* [2000] ECR II-15, para. 46.

783 See Case T-290/97 *Mehibas Dordtselaan v Commission* [2000] ECR II-15; Case T-250/99 *Hyper v Commission* [2002] ECR II-3141 and Case T-329/00 *Bonn Fleisch v Commission* [2003] ECR II-287.

784 In addition to the lack of deception and obvious negligence, the remission or repayment of import duties also presupposes the existence of a special situation.

785 Case T-82/01 *VOF Josanne and others v Commission* [2003] ECR II-2013. On the other hand, see Case T-109/94 *Windpark Groothusen v Commission* [1995] ECR II-3007; Case C-3/00 *Denmark v Commission* [2003] ECR I-2643; Case T-366/03 *Land Oberösterreich v Commission* [2005] ECR II-4005, at paras. 37–47.

786 Case T-289/02 *Telepharmacy Solutions v OHIM* [2004] ECR II-2851, para. 21. See also Case T-122/99 *Procter & Gamble v OHIM* [2000] ECR II-265, para. 42; Case T-34/00 *Eurocool Logistik v OHIM* [2002] ECR II-683, para. 21; Case T-79/00 *Rewe Zentral v OHIM* [2002] ECR II-705, para. 14. The right to a fair hearing is also recognised for the party opposing

It is clear that the right to a fair hearing, as a general principle of Community law, applies in proceedings that lead to the adoption of an act of individual application. It is less clear under what circumstances or even whether a right to a hearing exists where the proceedings lead to the adoption of an act of general application. The Court has acknowledged the right to a hearing in anti-dumping proceedings. It held in *Al-Jubail* that the requirements of a right to a fair hearing must be respected also 'in investigative proceedings prior to the adoption of anti-dumping regulations which, despite their general scope, may directly and individually affect the undertakings concerned and entail adverse consequences for them.'[787] The Community Courts seem to exclude a right to a hearing only where the act in issue 'is part of the legislative process resulting in the adoption of a measure of general application'[788] unless it is of direct and individual concern to the applicant.[789]

Where the institution concerned infringes the rights of defence, the question arises as to whether such a breach will automatically lead to the annulment of the act.[790] On the one hand, the efficiency of administrative action would be impeded if the institution could not have taken a different decision, if the institution did not rely on the document in issue, if the result could have been reached by other evidence on which the person concerned was heard or where the persons concerned could voice their views in the judicial proceedings. In other words, where the breach was not causal for the specific content of the decision or did not undermine the efficiency of the defence, it is doubtful whether it should lead to the annulment of the act. On the other hand, the rights of defence constitute an essential procedural requirement and therefore a breach should lead to the annulment of the act. This also has the advantage that the institution concerned takes the rights seriously.

The Community Courts have made it clear that infringements of the rights of defence by the institution which adopted the act cannot be

---

the registration of a trademark, see Case T-273/02 *Krüger v OHIM* [2005] ECR II-1271, at para. 65.

[787] Case C-49/88 *Al-Jubail and Other v Council* [1991] ECR I-3187, para. 15. However, see Case T-13/99 *Pfizer Animal Health v Council* [2002] ECR II-3305 and Case T-70/99 *Alpharma v Council* [2002] ECR II-3495 where the CFI denied a right to a hearing in case of an implementing act of general application, even though it was of direct and individual concern to the applicant.

[788] Case C-3/00 *Denmark v Commission* [2003] ECR I-2643, para. 39. See also Case T-521/93 *Atlanta and Others v Council and Commission* [1996] ECR II-1707, at para. 70.

[789] See Case T-306/01 *Yusuf and Another v Council and Commission* [2005] ECR II-3533; Case C-104/97 P *Atlanta and Others v Council and Commission* [1999] ECR I-6983, at para. 36.

[790] See also P. Craig (2006), supra note 2, pp. 372–373.

subsequently cured in the judicial proceedings. The Community Courts have justified this approach by pointing out that the court 'carries out the review solely in relation to the pleas raised and which cannot therefore be a substitute for a thorough investigation of the case in the course of the administrative procedure'.[791]

It is less clear whether the non-disclosure of a document on which the Commission has not relied will lead to the annulment of an act. In *Eyckeler*[792] the CFI argued that 'in order for the right to be heard to be exercised effectively the Commission must provide access to all non-confidential official documents concerning the contested decision, if requested to do so',[793] as the document, though not relevant for the institution concerned, might be of interest to the person concerned. This means that where the institution refuses access to such a document, the rights of defence are infringed and the act needs to be annulled. On the other hand, in *Hyper*[794] the CFI rejected an infringement of the rights of defence on the ground that the Commission had not relied on the document in issue.[795] Similarly, in *Technische Glaswerke Ilmenau*[796] the CFI pointed out that the act could not be annulled where the institution reached the decision on the basis of other documents on which the person concerned was able to comment.[797] Similarly, an act will not be annulled where the institution fails to provide a relevant document, but the persons concerned obtain the evidence by other means provided they have enough time to make their views known.[798]

Consequently, the infringement of the rights of defence will lead to the annulment of the act only if it is established that, 'had it not been for such an irregularity, the outcome of the procedure might have been different'.[799] It should be observed however that the Community Courts apply different degrees of scrutiny as to the possibility of a different outcome. On the one hand, in *France Aviation*[800] the Court stated that it was 'not empowered to take the place of the competent administrative authority or to anticipate

---

791 Case T-30/91 *Solvay v Commission* [1995] ECR II-1775, para. 98. See also Case C-51/92 P *Hercules v Commission* [1999] ECR I-4235, at para. 78; Case T-42/96 *Eyckeler & Malt v Commission* [1998] ECR II-401, para. 81; Case T-50/96 *Primex v Commission* [1998] ECR II-3773, para. 64.

792 Case T-42/96 *Eyckeler & Malt v Commission* [1998] ECR II-401.

793 Ibid., para. 81. See also Case T-50/96 *Primex v Commission* [1998] ECR II-3773, para. 64; Joined Cases T-186/97 etc. *Kaufring and Others v Commission* [2001] ECR II-1337, para. 186.

794 Case T-205/99 *Hyper v Commission* [2002] ECR II-3141.

795 Ibid., para. 60.

796 Case T-198/01 *Technische Glaswerke Ilmenau v Commission* [2004] ECR II-2717.

797 Ibid., para. 209.

798 Case T-35/01 *Shanghai Teraoka Electronic v Council* [2001] ECR II-3661, at para. 330.

799 Ibid., para. 201.

800 Case T-346/94 *France Aviation v Commission* [1995] II-2841.

the result which it will reach following a fresh administrative procedure'.[801] On the other hand, in other cases the Community Courts have taken it upon themselves to assess the (ir)relevance of the documents for the outcome of the case.[802] In *Hercules*[803] the Court made it clear that in order for the person concerned to show that the outcome of the procedure may have been different, '[t]he undertaking concerned does not have to show that, if it had had access to the replies provided by the other producers to the statement of objections, the Commission decision would have been different in content, but only that it would have been able to use those documents for its defence'.[804]

Other essential procedural requirements

The breach of participation rights of the institutions which form part of the law-making process can constitute an infringement of an essential procedural requirement. It can be inferred from *United Kingdom v Council*[805] that, where a Commission proposal is required for the adoption of an act, such a proposal would constitute an essential procedural requirement. In *Roquette*[806] the Court found that the consultation of the EP under Article 37 (ex 43) ECT, which provides for the consultation procedure, was an essential procedural requirement. As the Council had adopted the act without having obtained the opinion of the EP, the Court annulled the regulation. The Court will however not annul an act where 'the essential procedural requirement of Parliamentary consultation was not complied with because of the Parliament's failure to discharge its obligation to cooperate sincerely with the Council.'[807] The Court has also pointed out that 'the duty to consult the European Parliament in the course of the legislative procedure, in the cases provided for by the Treaty, includes a requirement that the Parliament be reconsulted on each occasion when the text finally adopted, viewed as a whole, departs substantially from the text on which the Parliament has already been

---

801 Ibid., para. 39. See also Case T-11/03 *Afari v ECB* [2004] ECR II-267, para. 90; Case T-102/00 *Vlaams fonds v Commission* [2003] ECR II-2433, para. 85.

802 See Case C-288/96 *Germany v Commission* [2000] ECR I-8237, para. 105; Case T-5/02 *Tetra Laval v Commission* [2002] ECR II-4381, para. 102 *et seq*.; Case T-217/01 *Forum des migrants v Commission* [2003] ECR II-1563, para. 61.

803 Case C-51/92 P *Hercules v Commission* [1999] ECR I-4235.

804 Ibid., para. 81. See also Case C-194/99 P *Thyssen v Commission* [2003] ECR I-10821, para. 31; Case T-198/01 *Technische Glaswerke Ilmenau v Commission* [2004] ECR II-2717, para. 203.

805 Case 68/86 *United Kingdom v Council* [1988] ECR 855, at para. 32.

806 Case 138/79 *Roquette v Council* [1980] ECR 3333.

807 Case C-65/93 *European Parliament v Council* [1995] ECR I-643, para. 28.

consulted'.[808] Such reconsultation is however not necessary where the amendments are insubstantial or essentially correspond to the wish of the Parliament itself.[809] Similarly, the assent of an institution required for the adoption of an act would constitute an essential procedural requirement.[810]

Essential procedural requirements can not only be found in the EC Treaty or EC legislation, but also in the Rules of Procedure of the institutions. In *BASF*[811] the Court pointed out that Article 12 of the Commission's Rules of Procedure, which required that acts adopted by the Commission had to be authenticated, constituted an essential procedural requirement.[812] The Court stated that this requirement was not 'a mere formality for archival purposes',[813] as the Commission had claimed, but 'is intended to guarantee legal certainty by ensuring that the text adopted by the college of Commissioners becomes fixed in the languages which are binding.'[814] Authentication therefore allowed verifying that 'the texts notified or published correspond precisely to the text adopted by the college and so with the intention of the author.'[815] In *ICI*[816] the Court added that authentication had to precede notification.[817] Moreover, the Court found that the mere failure to authenticate an act constituted the infringement of an essential procedural requirement, which the Court had to raise of its own motion. Consequently, the breach of the requirement to authenticate the act would lead to its annulment without there being any need to demonstrate that the act caused harm to the person relying on it.[818] Similarly, in *UK v Council*[819] the Court held that breach of Article 6(1) of the Council's Rules of Procedure, which required unanimity for the adoption of an act by written procedure, constituted an infringement of an essential procedural requirement.

---

808 Case C-65/90 *European Parliament v Council* [1992] ECR I-4593, para. 16. See also Case C-388/92 *European Parliament v Council* [1994] ECR I-2067, para. 10; Case C-417/93 *European Parliament v Council* [1995] ECR I-1185, para. 17; Case C-21/94 *European Parliament v Council* [1995] ECR I-1827, para. 18.

809 Case 41/69 *ACF Chemiefarma v Commission* [1970] ECR 661, at para. 178; Case 817/79 *Buyl and Others v Commission* [1982] ECR 245, at para. 23; Case C-331/88 *ex parte FEDESA* [1990] ECR I-4023, at para. 39; Case C-417/93 *European Parliament v Council* [1995] ECR I-1185, paras. 19, 21, 23 and 26.

810 Case 119/81 *Klöckner-Werke v Commission* [1982] ECR 2617, at para. 6.

811 Case C-137/92 P *Commission v BASF and Others* [1994] ECR I-2555.

812 Ibid., para. 75.

813 Ibid., para. 75.

814 Ibid., para. 75.

815 Ibid., para. 75.

816 Case C-286/95 P *Commission v ICI* [2000] ECR I-2341 upholding the judgment of the CFI in Case T-37/91 *ICI v Commission* [1995] ECR II-1901.

817 Case C-286/95 P *Commission v ICI* [2000] ECR I-2341, para. 62.

818 Ibid., paras. 42 and 52.

819 Case 68/86 *United Kingdom v Council* [1988] ECR 855, at para. 49.

Infringement of the Treaty or of any Rule Relating to its Application

Article 230(2) includes as a ground of review 'the infringement of this Treaty or of any rule of law relating to its application'. This is the most comprehensive ground of review and overlaps with the other three grounds.[820] The Treaty as rule whose infringement leads to the annulment of the act comprises all constitutive Treaties.[821] Consequently, the provisions of the EC Treaty with all its amending and supplementing Treaties are included. This ground also encompasses the provisions of Accession Treaties. The phrase 'any rule relating to its application' has been interpreted widely by the Community Courts and embraces all rules of Community law which are not covered by the Treaties.[822]

Most obviously Community acts are rules of Community law. Consequently, it constitutes an infringement of such a rule if an implementing act infringes the basic act which provides its legal basis, but also if it violates any other basic act. However, in some cases a Community act is based on an implementing measure of the Council which also adopted the basic act. In *Zuckerfabrik Franken*,[823] it was up to the Council to adopt the general rules[824] for the implementation of the basic act, whilst the adoption of the detailed rules[825] for its implementation was the responsibility of the Commission. The Court ruled that this 'must be understood as meaning that, in the exercise of its powers, the Commission is authorized to adopt all the measures which are necessary or appropriate for the implementation of the basic legislation, provided that they are not contrary to such legislation or to the implementing legislation adopted by the Council'.[826]

The rules of Community law also comprise international agreements and international law as well as unwritten general principles of law which the Community Courts have developed over time.[827] Both types of rules provide insights as to how the Community Courts review Community acts. The Community Courts have not accepted the premise that all international agreements can serve as rules of review. Difficulties arise here as

---

[820] See also T.C. Hartley, supra note 1, pp. 402–403.
[821] Ibid., p. 402.
[822] Ibid., p. 402.
[823] Case 121/83 *Zuckerfabrik Franken* [1984] ECR 2039.
[824] OJ [1977] L 156/4.
[825] OJ [1978] L 231/5.
[826] Case 121/83 *Zuckerfabrik Franken* [1984] ECR 2039, para. 13. See also Cases 6, 7/88 *France and Spain v Commission* [1989] ECR 3639 and Case 264/86 *France v Commission* [1988] ECR 973, para. 21.
[827] On the other hand, it has been argued that subsidiary conventions and acts of the representatives of the Member States are excluded, see T.C. Hartley, supra note 1, p. 403.

to the conditions that such agreements need to meet in order to serve as rules of review. General principles, on the other hand, are often invoked by litigants, but rarely with success. This is mainly because the Community Courts apply varying degrees of intensity in their application. Both are therefore discussed in more detail below.

International agreements and international law

International agreements which are binding on the Community also fall within this ground of review.[828] However, in contrast to other grounds of review, the Community Courts seem to require that international agreements as grounds of review of Community acts be directly effective. In *International Fruit*[829] the Court was asked in a preliminary reference under Article 234 ECT to review the validity of certain Commission regulations against provisions of the GATT. The Court imposed two conditions for such review. First, the Court found that the incompatibility of a Community act with a provision of international law could only affect its validity where the Community was bound by that provision. Second, the Court held that 'before invalidity can be relied upon before a national court, that provision of international law must also be capable of conferring rights on citizens of the Community which they can invoke before the courts.'[830] The Court then proceeded to examine the two conditions and found that the first condition was met, but not the second. In *Germany v Council* (bananas) the Court confirmed that this approach would also be taken in direct actions under Article 230 ECT.[831] The Court, however, made two exceptions to that rule and noted that 'it is only if the Community intended to implement a particular obligation entered into within the framework of GATT, or if the Community act expressly refers to specific provisions of GATT, that the court can review the lawfulness of the Community act in question from the point of view of the GATT'.[832] And in *Portugal v Council* (textiles)[833] the Court made it clear that the same principles applied also in relation to WTO rules. The Court did however not refer to direct effect but simply stated that 'having regard to their nature and structure, the WTO agreements are not in principle among the rules in the light of which the

---

828 See P. Eeckhout, *External Relations of the European Union – Legal and Constitutional Foundations* (OUP, 2004), pp. 246–252.

829 Joined Cases 21 to 24/72 *International Fruit* [1972] ECR 1219.

830 Ibid., para. 8. See also Case 9/73 *Schlüter* [1973] ECR 1135, para. 27.

831 Case C-280/93 *Germany v Council* [1994] ECR I-4973, para. 109.

832 Ibid., para. 111. See also Case C-69/89 *Nakajima v Council* [1991] ECR I-2069, para. 31.

833 Case C-149/96 *Portugal v Council* [1999] ECR I-8395.

Court is to review the legality of measures adopted by the Community institutions.'[834]

On the basis of these rulings it is clear that international agreements which are binding on the Community and are directly effective are amongst the rules against which the validity of Community acts can be assessed. The Community Courts have considered as directly effective Article 2(1) of the Youndé Convention,[835] Article 21 of the free trade agreement with Portugal,[836] the fourth Lomé Convention[837] and the Co-operation agreement with the former Republic of Yugoslavia.[838] Community acts which are not in compliance with these agreements are therefore invalid.

Most recently in *Netherlands v EP and Council* (biotechnology inventions),[839] the Court seemed to have moved away from the requirement that only directly effective agreements can serve as rules against which Community acts can be reviewed. The Court reiterated its approach in *Portugal v Council* and found that the lawfulness of Directive 98/44 EC on the legal protection of biotechnological inventions[840] could not be reviewed in light of the WTO agreement.[841] The same, the Court argued, could not be said in relation to the Convention on biological diversity.[842] Controversially, the Court argued that even if the Convention 'contains provisions which do not have direct effect, in the sense that they do not create rights which individuals can rely on directly before the courts, that fact does not preclude review by the courts of compliance with the obligations incumbent of the Community as a party to that agreement.'[843] This

---

834 Ibid., para. 47. In Case C-377/98 *Netherlands v European Parliament and Council* [2001] ECR I-7079, at para. 52, the Court found that the validity of EC acts can also not be assessed in light of the TRIPs and TBT (Technical Barriers to Trade) agreements; see also Joined Cases C-300/98 and C-392/98 *Parfums Christian Dior and Others* [2000] ECR I-11307, para. 44, and Case C-89/99 *Schieving-Nijstad and Others v Groenveld* [2001] ECR I-5851, at para. 53. In Case T-18/99 *Cordis v Commission* [2001] ECR II-913, the CFI also rejected WTO panel reports as grounds against which EC acts could be reviewed.

835 [1964] JO, p. 1430. See Case 87/75 *Bresciani* [1976] ECR 129, at paras. 23–25.

836 [1972] OJ Spec. English Edn. L 301/165. See Case 104/81 *Kupferberg* [1982] ECR 3641, at para. 27. However, see Case 270/80 *Polydor* [1982] ECR 329, at paras. 15–18, in which the Court denied that Articles 14(2) and 23 of the agreement had direct effect.

837 [1991] OJ L 229/1. See Case C-469/93 *Chiquita Italia* [1995] ECR I-4533, at para. 35.

838 [1983] OJ L 41/1. See Case C-162/96 *Racke* [1998] ECR I-3655, at paras. 34–36.

839 Case C-377/98 *Netherlands v European Parliament and Council* [2001] ECR I-7079.

840 [1998] OJ L 213/13.

841 Case C-377/98 *Netherlands v European Parliament and Council* [2001] ECR I-7079, para. 52.

842 Approved by the European Community by Council Decision 93/626/EEC, [1993] OJ L 309/1.

843 Case C-377/98 *Netherlands v European Parliament and Council* [2001] ECR I-7079, para. 54. Cf Case C-308/06 *Intertanko and others*, judgment of 3 June 2008, at paras. 42 *et seq.*

approach stands in stark contrast with the Court's earlier rulings in relation to GATT and WTO, discussed above. It is not clear from the ruling under which conditions an agreement can serve as a basis for the review of Community acts, if its direct effect is no longer a prerequisite.

Finally, in *Racke*[844] the Court held that Community acts can not only be reviewed against directly effective international agreements, but also rules of customary international law. The Court argued that the Community was required to comply with those rules 'when adopting a regulation suspending the trade concession granted by, or by virtue of, an agreement which it has concluded with a non-member country'.[845]

General principles of law

Given the paucity of provisions in the original Treaties, the Court of Justice has established general principles of Community law by resorting to a creative method of 'evaluative comparison'[846] of the laws of the Member States to fill gaps in Community law.[847] While general principles derived from the rule of law also serve to provide a guide to the interpretation of Community law, including the Treaties themselves, and to establish the non-contractual liability of the Community under Articles 235 and 288(2), they also constitute grounds of the review of Community law, whether they are based on the Treaty itself or are implementing acts.[848] Such general principles are of constitutional status in that they bind Community institutions[849] in the exercise of their legislative and administrative competences. The following discussion will focus on the principles of legal certainty and legitimate expectations, the principle of proportionality, the principle of equality and the protection of fundamental rights.

Legal certainty and legitimate expectations As general principles of Community law, legal certainty and the protection of legitimate expectations form part of its constitutional and administrative law, in that they

---

844 Case C-162/96 *Racke v Hauptzollamt Mainz* [1998] ECR I-3655.

845 Ibid., para. 45.

846 J. Schwarze, supra note 739, p. 72.

847 For a general discussion of general principles, see J. Schwarze, supra note 739; J. Usher, *General Principles of EC Law* (Longman, 1998); U. Bernitz and J. Nergelius, *General Principles of European Community Law* (Kluwer, 2000); T. Tridimas, supra note 745.

848 On the functions of such general principles, see T. Tridimas, supra note 745, pp. 29–35.

849 General principles of Community law also have to be observed by the Member States, see T. Tridimas, supra note 745, pp. 36–47. On the application of general principles against individuals, see T. Tridimas, supra note 745, pp. 47–50.

apply to legislative acts as much as administrative acts.[850] The principle of legal certainty provides an important assertion of the rule of law that 'those subject to the law must know what the law is so as to plan their action accordingly'.[851] The Community Courts employ the formulation that legal certainty requires that 'legal rules be clear and precise, and aims to ensure that situations and legal relationships governed by Community law remain forseeable'.[852] Even though it operates foremost as an objective principle[853] and interpretative tool, the principle of legal certainty can also be invoked in judicial review proceedings, in particular in cases where litigants plead the infringement of the principle of non-retroactivity of rules.

The principle of the protection of legitimate expectations is closely linked to that of legal certainty, as it provides those subject to the law to rely on Community measures or the conduct of its officials. In this respect the principle of the protection of legitimate expectations 'appears to be an expression, taking the form of a subjective right, of legal certainty'.[854] The principle requires some action or inaction by the Community institutions on which a legitimate expectation can be based. Such behaviour can consist of legal acts adopted by Community institutions or their conduct. In addition, the Community Courts often require a subjective element and a causal link.

Legitimate expectations are strongest where they are based on vested rights which result from administrative acts conferring rights or benefits. Consequently, the revocation of lawful acts, in particular where they create rights, is in principle prohibited, as the interest of the individual in the legality of the act prevails over the public interest.[855] On the other hand, the retroactive revocation of unlawful acts is 'permissible provided that the withdrawal occurs within a reasonable time and provided that the institution from which it emanates has had sufficient regard to how far the applicant might have been led to rely on the lawfulness of the measure.'[856] In this

---

[850] See generally, J. Schwarze, supra note 739, chapter 6; S. Schonberg, *Legitimate Expectations in Administrative Law* (OUP, 2000); T. Tridimas, supra note 745, chapter 6; P. Craig, supra note 2, chapter 16.

[851] T. Tridimas, supra note 745, p. 242.

[852] Case C-199/03 *Ireland v Commission* [2005] ECR I-8027, para. 69.

[853] J. Schwarze, supra note 739, p. 948.

[854] J. Schwarze, supra note 739, p. 946. See also C-177/99 *Ampafrance* [2000] ECR I-7013, at para. 67, where the Court regarded the principle of legitimate expectations as 'corollary of the principle of legal certainty'.

[855] See Joined Cases 7/56, 3–7/57 *Algera and Others v Common Assembly* [1957–1958] ECR 39. See also Case 159/82 *Verli-Wallace v Commission* [1983] ECR 2711, para. 8; Case T-123/89 *Chomel v Commission* [1990] ECR II-131, para. 34; Case T-197/99 *Gooch v Commission* [2000] ECR II-1247, para. 52; Case T-251/00 *Lagardère and Canal+ v Commission* [2002] ECR II-4825, para. 139.

[856] Case T-251/00 *Lagardère and Canal+ v Commission* [2002] ECR II-4825, para. 140. See also Case 14/81 *Alpha Steel v Commission* [1982] ECR 749, p. 764. See also Case 15/85

case the legitimate expectations of the person relying on the act have to be balanced against a legitimate public interest in the legality of Community law.

However, legislative acts can also provide a basis for legitimate expectations.[857] This is the case where Community legislation contains a protection clause, which requires specific interests of individuals to be taken into account.[858] Similarly, the Court held in *Mulder* that where a milk producer 'has been encouraged by a Community measure to suspend marketing for a limited period in the general interest and against payment of a premium he may legitimately expect not to be subject, upon the expiry of his undertaking, to restrictions which specifically affect him precisely because he availed himself of the possibilities offered by the Community provisions'.[859] And in *Commission v Council*,[860] the Court found that the Council by laying down in a decision certain procedures for adjusting staff salaries had created a legitimate expectation that the Council would abide by these criteria.

Those subject to Community law rely on its continuance to plan their affairs and therefore have the expectation that the law will not be changed. On the other hand, the law-maker must be free to adapt to changing conditions or policy considerations. The case law has therefore been concerned with striking the appropriate balance between the expectation of the existing law being maintained and the need to change it. The need to protect the legitimate expectation in the law being maintained is greatest where it concerns the expectation that events concluded in the past will not be modified. Therefore, actual retroactivity, which can be said to exist 'where a rule is to be introduced by the legislature in respect of events which have already been concluded',[861] is in principle prohibited, as 'the principle of legal certainty precludes a Community act from taking effect as from a date prior to its publication'.[862]

Consorzio Cooperative d'Abruzzo v Commission [1987] ECR 1005; Case C-24/89 *Cargill v Commission* [1991] ECR I-2987; Case C-365/89 *Cargill v Produktschap voor Margarine, Vetten en Oliën* [1991] ECR I-3045; Case C-90/95P *De Compte v Parliament* [1997] ECR I-1999; Case T-197/99 *Gooch v Commission* [2000] ECR II-1247, para. 53.

857 See J. Schwarze, supra note 739, pp. 1136–1138; T. Tridimas, supra note 745, pp. 273–280.

858 Case C-152/88 *Sofrimport v Commission* [1990] ECR I-2477. See also Case T-94/00, T-110/00 and T-159/00 *Rica Foods and others v Commission* [2002] ECR II-4677, para. 222.

859 See Case 120/86 *Mulder* [1988] ECR 2321, para. 24.

860 Case 81/72 *Commission v Council* [1973] ECR 575.

861 J. Schwarze, supra note 739, p. 1120.

862 Case C-110/97 *Netherlands v Council* [2001] ECR I-8763, para. 151. See also Case 98/78 *Racke v Hauptzollamt Mainz* [1979] ECR 69, para. 20; Case T-7/99 *Medici Grimm v Council* [2000] ECR II-2671, para. 90.

Retroactive rules[863] will only be allowed where the public interest[864] overrides the private interest in the maintenance of the existing legal situation.[865]

The protection of the expectation in the maintenance of the law is more limited in a case of apparent retroactivity, which can be defined as the 'applicability of legislative acts to events which originated in the past but which have yet to be definitively concluded'.[866] Such an application of the law is in principle permissible, as 'according to a generally accepted principle, the laws amending a legislative provision apply, unless otherwise provided, to the future consequences of situations which arose under the former law.'[867] However, this rule has to be balanced against the general principle of the protection of legitimate expectations. Such expectations arise in particular where the individual has undertaken certain obligations *vis-à-vis* the public authorities. The Court has emphasised, however, that legitimate expectations cannot be invoked if the change in the law was foreseeable, as in this case the expectations are not worthy of protection.[868] As in the case of actual retroactivity, the Court balances the legitimate expectations of those concerned with the public interest.[869]

The protection of expectations in the maintenance of rules is weakest where the rules do not apply retroactively, where, in the case of apparent retroactivity, concrete commitments worthy of protection have not been entered into, and where no specific assurances by the authorities have been made. The Court has consistently held that 'since the Community institutions enjoy a margin of discretion in the choice of the means intended to implement their policy, operators cannot claim to have a legitimate expectation that an existing situation which is capable of being altered by

---

[863] The reason for the retroactivity of the rule must be clearly stated in the legal instrument, see Case 1/84R *Ilford v Commission* [1984] ECR 423, para. 19; Joined Cases C-260/91 and C-261/91 *Diversinte and Iberlacta* [1993] ECR I-1885.

[864] For the public interests recognised by the Court, see T. Tridimas, supra note 745, pp. 256–266.

[865] See T. Tridimas, supra note 745, p. 256.

[866] J. Schwarze, supra note 739, p. 1121. See also P. Craig (2006), supra note 2, pp. 610–614.

[867] Case 1/73 *Westzucker GmbH v Einfuhr- und Vorratsstelle für Zucker* [1973] ECR 723, p. 729. See also Case C-60/98 *Butterfly Music* [1999] ECR I-3939, para. 25; Case T-49/00 *Iposea v Commission* [2001] ECR II-163, para. 30; Joined Cases T-64/01 and T-65/01 *Afrikanische Frucht-Compagnie and another v Council* [2004] ECR II-521, para. 90.

[868] Case 78/77 *Lührs* [1978] ECR 169, para. 6; Case C-350/88 *Delacre and others v Commission* [1990] ECR I-395, para. 37; Case 265/85 *Van den Bergh en Jurgen v Commission* [1987] ECR 1155, para. 44.

[869] See Case 74/74 *CNTA v Commission* [1975] ECR 533, para. 44; Case 84/78 *Tomadini* [1979] ECR 1801, para. 20.

decisions taken by those institutions within the limits of their discretionary powers will be maintained'.[870]

The basis for legitimate expectations can, however, also be the conduct of Community institutions. The Community Courts have acknowledged that an individual can rely on the principle 'where the Community authorities, by giving him precise assurances, have caused him to entertain legitimate expectations'.[871] In *Branco*[872] the CFI has specified the conditions that need to be met in this respect. The CFI stated that '[f]irst, precise, unconditional and consistent assurances originating from authorised and reliable sources must have been given to the person concerned by Community authorities. Second, those assurances must be such as to give rise to a legitimate expectation on the part of the person to whom they are addressed. Third the assurances given must comply with the applicable rules'.[873]

Principle of equality The principle of equality has a long tradition[874] and is now recognised in all Member States as a political prerequisite in democratic states and as a judicial instrument to review administrative acts and, where constitutionally provided, also acts adopted by the legislative authority. Its legal function is to ensure not only formal but also substantive equality by preventing public authorities from engaging in arbitrary action and thereby imposing a justification for differential treatment.[875] In this sense the principle of equality[876] is also firmly established in Community law.[877] The principle binds the MS when they act within the scope of Community Law.[878] The principle of equality also constitutes a ground for review of acts adopted by EC institutions.[879] The occasional references in the EC Treaty[880] have been treated by the Court as 'merely a

---

[870] Case 245/81 *Edeka Zentrale* [1982] ECR 2745, para. 27. See also Case 52/81 *Faust v Commission* [1982] ECR 3745, para. 27; Joined Cases T-64/01 and T-65/01 *Afrikanische Frucht-Compagnie and another v Council and Commission* [2004] ECR II-521, para. 83; Case C-342/03 *Spain v Council* [2005] ECR I-1975, para. 49.

[871] Case T-283/02 *EnBW v Commission* [2005] ECR II-913, para. 89.

[872] Case T-347/03 *Branco v Commission* [2005] ECR II-2555.

[873] Ibid., para. 102.

[874] See J. Schwarze, supra note 739, pp. 545 *et seq.* See also T. Tridimas, supra note 745, pp. 59–60.

[875] See J. Schwarze, supra note 739, p. 551; T. Tridimas, supra note 745, p. 61. P. Craig (2006), supra note 2, p. 545, distinguishes between equality of results and equality of opportunity.

[876] Also referred to as non-discrimination. See T. Tridimas, supra note 745, p. 64.

[877] See J. Schwarze, supra note 739, chapter 4; P. Craig (2006), supra note 2, chapter 15; T. Tridimas, supra note 745, chapter 2.

[878] P. Craig (2006), supra note 2, pp. 546–578; T. Tridimas, supra note 745, p. 74.

[879] P. Craig (2006), supra note 2, pp. 578–585; T. Tridimas, supra note 745, 60.

[880] See in particular Article 34(2) ECT.

specific enunciation of the general principle of equality which is one of the fundamental principles of Community law'.[881] The principle of equal treatment requires that 'comparable situations must not be treated differently and that different situations must not be treated in the same way unless such treatment is objectively justified'.[882]

Even though the principle of equality as a general principle of law comprehensively applies to all Community acts,[883] the intensity of review of the measure seems to vary according to the nature of the act. It has been stated that in the application of the principle of equality the intensity of review of the measure is more reduced for acts adopted by the Community legislator.[884] When assessing basic acts of general application, in particular in the agricultural area, as to their compatibility with the principle of equality the Court indeed reduces the intensity of its review in light of the discretion that the institution adopting the act enjoys.[885] However, the Court does not restrict its marginal review to basic acts, but extends its more limited review to implementing acts of general application as well.[886] In the field of agriculture the Community Courts explain their deferential approach to acts of general application usually with the argument 'that the Community legislature has in relation to the common agricultural policy a discretionary power which corresponds to the political responsibilities given to it by Articles 40 and 43 [now 34 and 37] of the Treaty'.[887] It has been argued elsewhere that such a rationale ignores the fact that acts of general application can be adopted in different procedures.[888] Even if one regards the difference in the agricultural sector between basic acts adopted in the consultation procedure and implementing acts adopted by the Commission as marginal, the difference becomes more marked in areas where the co-decision procedure

---

[881] See Joined Cases 117/76 and 16/77 *Albert Ruckdeschel & Co. and Others v Hauptzollament Hamburg St. Annen* [1977] ECR 1753, para. 7. See also J. Schwarze, supra note 739, pp. 562 and 627.

[882] Case C-154/04 *Alliance for Natural Health* [2005] ECR I-6451, para. 115. See also J. Schwarze, supra note 739, pp. 564–574.

[883] J. Schwarze, supra note 739, p. 644.

[884] T. Tridimas, supra note 745, p. 86.

[885] See Case C-280/93 *Germany v Council* [1994] ECR I-4973, at paras. 47 and 66–75; Case C-100/99 *Italy v Council and Commission* [2001] ECR I-5217, at para. 36. See also T. Tridimas, supra note 745, at pp. 84–88.

[886] Case 6/71 *Rheinmühlen Düsseldorf v Einfuhr- und Vorratsstelle für Getreide und Futtermittel* [1971] ECR 823, at para. 14; Case 43/72 *Merkur v Commission* [1973] ECR 1055, paras. 22 and 23; Case T-19/01 *Chiquita Brands and others v Commission* [2005] ECR II-315, at para. 214; Joined Cases T-64/01 and T-65/01 *Afrikanische Frucht-Compagnie and another v Council and Commission*, [2004] ECR II-521, at para. 101; Joined Cases T-94/01, T-152/01 and T-286/01 *Hirsch and others v ECB* [2003] ECR II-27, at para. 51.

[887] Joined Cases T-64/01 and T-65/01 *Afrikanische Frucht-Compagnie and another v Council and Commission* [2004] ECR II-521, at para. 101.

[888] A. Türk, supra note 283, p. 180.

applies. Indiscriminate deference to all acts of general application therefore disregards that such acts involve the Community institutions, and in particular the EP, to a greater or lesser degree and that they might therefore be of varying legitimacy. In other cases the Community Courts argue that significant discretion for the Community institutions is justified when 'the evaluation of a complex economic situation' is in issue. However, acts of individual application can also involve the assessment of complex economic situations. And indeed in some cases the Community Courts have accorded discretion when the Community institutions adopted acts of individual application.[889]

The relevance of acts of general application is more convincing when the Court states that such acts do not have 'to take account of every difference that may exist in the organisation of economic units subject to the action of the High Authority for fear of fettering that action and rendering it ineffective'.[890] This is, as AG Jacobs has put it, 'inherent in the nature of legislation'.[891] Due to the generality of its application, the consequences of an act can impose greater burdens on some than on others. However, as the Court has pointed out 'in a common organisation of markets with no system of national quotas all Community producers, regardless of the Member States in which they are based, must together, in an egalitarian manner, bear the consequences of the decisions which the Community institutions are led to adopt, in the exercise of their powers, in order to respond to the risk of an imbalance which may arise in the market between production and market outlets'.[892]

Principle of proportionality In Community law the principle of proportionality has become an integral part of the general principles of Community

---

[889] See Joined Cases T-67/00, T-68/00, T-71/00 and T-78/00 *JFE Engineering and others v Commission* [2004] ECR II-2501, at para. 572; Case T-67/01 *JCB Service v Commission* [2004] ECR II-49, at para. 187; Joined Cases T-236/01 etc. *Tokai Carbon and others v Commission* [2004] ECR II-1181, at para. 309; Cases T-71/03 etc. *Tokai Carbon and others v Commission* [2005] ECR II-10*, at para. 371.

[890] Joined Cases 17 and 20/61 *Klöckner-Werke AG and Others v High Authority* [1962] ECR 325, at p. 340. See also Case 179/84 *Bozzetti v Invermizzi* [1985] ECR 2301, para. 34; Case C-311/90 *Hierl v Hauptzollamt Regensburg* [1992] ECR I-2061, para. 19; Case C-56/94 *SCAC v ASIPO* [1995] ECR I-1769, para. 28; Joined Cases C-248 and C-249/95 *Sam Schiffahrt and Stapf v Germany* [1997] ECR I-4475, para. 37. See also T. Tridimas, supra note 745, at pp. 90–91.

[891] Opinion of AG Jacobs in Joined Cases C-13 to C-16/92 *Driessen and Others* [1993] ECR I-4751, p. 4780.

[892] Case C-27/90 *SITPA v Oniflhor* [1991] ECR I-133, para. 20. See also Joined Cases C-133, C-300 and C-362/93 *Crispoltoni v Tabacchi and Others* [1994] ECR I-4863, at para. 51; Case 250/84 *Eridania v Cassa Conguaglio Zucchero* [1986] ECR 117, para. 32.

law.[893] As an instrument of market integration[894] it limits the action of Member States within the scope of application of Community law and subjects national authorities to justify the acts they adopt.[895] In the present context of greater importance is its function in the review of Community acts. The principle of proportionality is a valuable tool to protect Member States and individuals against excessive Community acts.[896] The precise content of the principle is disputed, as the Court of Justice uses sometimes a two-stage and at other times a three stage-test.[897] The principle requires that the measure is suitable or appropriate, that is likely, to achieve the aim in issue. The second stage would consist of assessing whether the measure is necessary, that is whether less restrictive means could have been used to achieve the aim. The third stage, often treated without distinction to the second stage in the case law,[898] would then enquire whether the measure is excessive, that is whether the means employed go beyond the aim to be achieved.

Even though it can be invoked against basic acts and implementing acts alike,[899] the principle of proportionality varies in the intensity of its application and is employed by the Community Courts as a flexible instrument when reviewing Community acts.[900] It has been suggested that when assessing the proportionality of Community acts the Community Courts make a distinction between basic acts, where a marginal form of review is applied, and implementing acts, as 'the Court is more willing to review the discretion of the administration rather than to question the policy choices made by the Community legislature'.[901] A detailed analysis of the case

---

[893] See generally, J. Schwarze, supra note 739, chapter 5; N. Emiliou, *The Principle of Proportionality in Euroepan Law* (Kluwer, 1996); E. Ellis (ed.) *The Principle of Proportionality* (Hart, 1999); P. Craig (2006), supra note 2, chapters 17 and 18; T. Tridimas, supra note 745, chapters 3–5.

[894] T. Tridimas, supra note 745, p. 138. As Tridimas has pointed out, the market-integration function of the principle does not exclude that it also serve to protect fundamental rights, see ibid. at p. 138.

[895] See F.G. Jacobs 'Recent Developments in the Principle of Proportionality in European Community Law', in E. Ellis (ed.), supra note 893, pp. 1–21, at pp. 8 *et seq.*; P. Craig (2006), supra note 2, chapter 18; T. Tridimas, supra note 745, chapter 5.

[896] See P. Craig (2006), supra note 2, chapter 17; T. Tridimas, supra note 745, chapter 3.

[897] W. Van Gerven, 'The Effect of Proportionality on the Actions of Member States of the European Community: National Viewpoints from Continental Europe', in E. Ellis, supra note 893, pp. 37–63, identifies a two-stage and a three-stage test, at pp. 37/38 and 60. T. Tridimas, 'Proportionality in European Community Law: Searching for the Appropriate Standard of Scrutiny' in E. Ellis (ed.), supra note 893, pp. 65–84, argues for a two stage test at p. 68. See also P. Craig and G. DeBúrca, supra note 1, at p. 545.

[898] T. Tridimas, supra note 897, p. 68.

[899] On its constitutional status, see J. Schwarze, supra note 739, pp. 717–719.

[900] See P. Craig & G. DeBúrca, supra note 1, pp. 546–549.

[901] T. Tridimas, supra note 745, p. 156. See also F.G. Jacobs, supra note 895, p. 20.

law[902] supports the view that in relation to basic acts of general application the Court applies a more limited review, which finds its expression in the formula that 'the lawfulness of a measure [. . .] can be affected only if the measure is manifestly inappropriate, having regard to the objective which the competent institution is seeking to pursue'.[903] However, the picture is less clear for implementing acts of general application. It has been argued that 'an implementing Commission measure may require more intensive scrutiny'.[904] It is submitted that the most recent case-law only partially supports this view. Implementing acts of individual application seem to be subject to more intensive scrutiny.[905] In contrast, the Community Courts seem to favour a more marginal review for implementing acts of general application.[906] The underlying uncertainty as to which acts should benefit from more marginal review stems from the unclear rationale for according discretion to the institution. Also in relation to the application of the principle of proportionality the Community Courts justify the reduced intensity of judicial review with the 'political responsibilities'[907] of the institutions and the reluctance to re-evaluate the assessment of 'complex economic

---

902 For a detailed analysis of the case law, see T. Tridimas, supra note 745, at pp. 142–173. See also J. Schwarze, supra note 739, pp. 726–773; G. DeBúrca, 'The Principle of Proportionality and its Application in EC Law' (1993) 13 *YEL* 105; F.G. Jacobs, supra note 895, pp. 3–8. See also Case T-43/98 *Emesa Sugar v Council* [2001] ECR I-3519, at para. 119; Case C-11/00 *Commission v ECB* [2003] ECR I-7147, at para. 157; Case C-491/01 *BAT and Imperial Tobacco* [2002] ECR I-11453, at para. 123; Joined Cases C-184/02 and C-223/02 *Spain and Finland v EP and Council* [2004] ECR I-7789, para. 56; Case C-347/03 *Regione autonoma Friuli-Venezia Guilia and ERSA* [2005] ECR I-3785, at para. 131.

903 Case C-347/03 *Regione autonoma Friuli-Venezia Guilia and ERSA* [2005] ECR I-3785, at para. 131.

904 F.G. Jacobs, supra note 895, p. 20. Similarly, T. Tridimas, supra note 745, p. 156.

905 See Case C-349/97 *Spain v Commission* [2003] ECR I-3851, at paras. 226 and 271; Case T-72/98 *Astilleros Zamacona v Commission* [2000] ECR II-1683, at para. 89; Case T-55/99 *CETM v Commission* [2000] ECR II-3207, at para. 163; Case T-59/99 *Ventouris v Commission* [2003] ECR II-5257, at para. 219; Case T-141/99 *Vela and Tecnagrind v Commission* [2002] ECR II-4547, at para. 396; Case C-177/99 *Ampafrance and Sanofi* [2000] ECR I-7013, at para. 42; Joined Cases T-44/01, T-1991/01 and T-126/01 *Eduardo Vieira and others v Commission* [2003] ECR II-1209, at paras. 136–154.

906 See Case C-110/97 *Netherlands v Council* [2001] ECR I-8763, at para. 126; Case T-13/99 *Pfizer Animal Health* [2002] ECR II-3305, at para. 412; Case C-179/00 *Weidacher* [2002] ECR I-501, at para. 26; Case C-180/00 *Netherlands v Commission* [2005] ECR I-6603, at para. 104; Joined Cases T-332/00 and T-350/00 *Rica Foods and Free Trade Foods v Commission* [2002] ECR II-4755, at para. 155; Case T-19/01 *Chiquita Brands and others v Commission* [2005] ECR II-315, at para. 228. Exceptionally, cases exist in which the Court applies a stricter review, see Case C-210/00 *Käserei Champignon Hofmeister* [2002] ECR I-6453, at paras. 59 et seq.

907 Case T-13/99 *Pfizer Animal Health* [2002] ECR II-3305, at para. 412; Case T-19/01 *Chiquita Brands and others v Commission* [2005] ECR II-315, at para. 228; Case C-491/01 *BAT and Imperial Tobacco* [2002] ECR I-11453, at para. 123; Case C-347/03 *Regione autonoma Friuli-Venezia Guilia and ERSA* [2005] ECR I-3785, at para. 131.

situations'[908] or 'choices of a political, economic and social nature'.[909] These justifications for all acts of general application are unconvincing for the same reasons put forward above in relation to the application of the principle of equality, as they do not take account of the difference in the procedure for the adoption of Community acts.[910] Moreover, also in cases of individual application, the Community institutions have political responsibility, must make choices and conduct complex assessments. This might also be the reason why in some instances the Court pursues a more marginal review in relation to acts of individual application.[911]

Protection of fundamental rights The emergence of a fundamental-rights jurisprudence in the case law of the Court resulted from the Court's desire to maintain supremacy and autonomy of the Community legal order in the face of resistance by national courts to abandon their role in the protection of fundamental rights.[912] The Court therefore refused, on the one hand, to review Community acts against fundamental rights of national provenance,[913] but on the other hand proclaimed that 'respect for fundamental rights forms an integral part of the general principles of law protected by the Court of Justice'.[914] In the absence of any reference to fundamental rights in the Rome Treaty[915] the Court had to depend on external sources to build a system of Community fundamental rights while at the same time preserving the autonomy of the Community legal order. The Court has therefore emphasised that it draws inspiration from the common constitutional traditions of the Member States and from guidelines supplied by international treaties for the protection of human rights on which the Member States have collaborated or to which they are

---

908 Case T-180/00 *Astipesca v Commission* [2002] ECR II-3985, at para. 79; Case T-125/01 *Marti Peix v Commission* [2003] ECR II-865, at para. 123.

909 Joined Cases T-332/00 and T-350/00 *Rica Foods and Free Trade Foods v Commission* [2002] ECR II-4755, at para. 155.

910 See A. Türk supra note 283, pp. 182.

911 See the following cases, where the manifestly inappropriate test is applied: Case T-9/98 *Mitteldeutsche Erdöl-Raffinerie v Commission* [2001] ECR II-3367, at para. 114; Case T-333/99 *X v ECB* [2001] ECR II-3021, at para. 224; Case T-180/00 *Astipesca v Commission* [2002] ECR II-3985, at para. 79; Case T-125/01 *Marti Peix v Commission* [2003] ECR II-865, at para. 123.

912 See T. Tridimas, supra note 745, pp. 300–304; P. Craig and G. DeBúrca, supra note 1, p. 381–383; T.C. Hartley, supra note 1, pp. 133–134.

913 See Case 11/70 *Internationale Handelsgesellschaft v Einfuhr- und Vorratsstelle für Getreide und Futtermittel* [1970] ECR 1125, at para. 3; Case 44/79 *Hauer v Land Rheinland-Pfalz* [1979] ECR 3727, para. 14.

914 Case 11/70 *Internationale Handelsgesellschaft v Einfuhr- und Vorratsstelle für Getreide und Futtermittel* [1970] ECR 1125, para. 4. See also Case 44/79 *Hauer v Land Rheinland-Pfalz* [1979] ECR 3727, para. 15.

915 For the reasons, see T. Tridimas, supra note 745, p. 300.

signatories, with special significance given to the ECHR.[916] As they provide only inspiration, these external sources have to be adapted to the objectives of the Community legal order. Consequently, the identification of a right as fundamental, while being influenced by external sources, is the result of the Court's own creative effort.[917]

However, fundamental rights are not absolute and are subject to limitations in the public interest.[918] The way the Court strikes the balance depends, on the one hand, on the weight the Court attaches to the fundamental right in issue. It can be observed that the Court's case law distinguishes between economic rights and civil and political liberties.[919] In respect to the former the Court seems to set a less restrictive standard. The Court has accepted in relation to the right to property and the freedom to pursue a trade or profession that 'restrictions may be imposed on the exercise of those rights, [. . .] provided that those restrictions in fact correspond to objectives of general interest pursued by the Community and do not constitute, with regard to the aim pursued, a disproportionate and intolerable interference, impairing the very substance of those rights'.[920] In relation to civil and political liberties, the Court appears to take a stricter stand and imposes higher justifications for their interference. In *Connolly v Commission*,[921] the Court interpreted Article 17(2) of the Staff Regulations, which requires civil servants to seek prior permission

---

[916] See Joined Cases C-20/00 and C-64/00 *Booker Aquaculture and Another v The Scottish Ministers* [2003] ECR I-7411, para. 65; Case 44/79 *Hauer v Land Rheinland-Pfalz* [1979] ECR 3727, para. 15. This approach is now reflected in Article 6(2) TEU. The 'solemnly proclaimed', but not yet binding, Charter of Fundamental Rights of 2000 might prove increasingly important as external source of inspiration. Under the Lisbon Treaty Article 6 TEU (Lisbon) provides that the Union shall recognise the rights, freedoms and principles set out in the Charter, as amended in December 2007, which shall have the same legal value as the Treaties. A breach of fundamental rights protected under the Charter should therefore be construed as an infringement of Article 6(1) TEU (Lisbon), which constitutes a ground of review under Article 263(2) TFEU. For an extensive discussion of the Charter, see P. Craig (2006), supra note 2, chapter 14.

[917] The Court's approach should therefore not be perceived in terms of minimum or maximum protection, see T. Tridimas, supra note 745, p. 312, and J.H.H. Weiler, *The Constitution of Europe* (CUP, 1999), pp. 107 *et seq.*

[918] Case 4/73 *Nold KG v Commission* [1974] ECR 491, para. 14. See also T. Tridimas, supra note 745, p. 311.

[919] See the distinction by T. Tridimas, supra note 745, at pp. 307–308.

[920] Joined Cases C-20/00 and C-64/00 *Booker Aquaculture and Another v The Scottish Ministers* [2003] ECR I-7411, para. 68. See also Case C-491/01 *BAT and Imperial Tobacco* [2002] ECR I-11453, at para. 149. Case C-280/93 *Germany v Council* [1994] ECR I-4973, at para. 78. Case T-113/96 *Dubois v Council and Commission* [1998] ECR II-125, para. 74. Case C-177/90 *Kühn v Landwirtschaftskammer Weser-Ems* [1992] ECR I-35, para. 16. Case C-248/95 and C-249/95 *SAM Schiffahrt and Stapf v Germany* [1997] ECR I-4475, para. 72. Case 44/79 *Hauer v Land Rheinland-Pfalz* [1979] ECR I-3727, para. 23.

[921] Case C-274/99P *Connolly v Commission* [2001] ECR I-1611.

before publishing materials, restrictively in the light of the importance of the freedom of expression.[922] On the other hand, the Court has to take account of the political responsibility of the Community institutions to pursue the Community's objectives, which represent the public interest. Moreover, as the EC institutions, in the exercise of this responsibility, are also bound by the obligation to protect fundamental rights,[923] their actions often reflect in themselves a balance between the Community interest and fundamental rights[924] and/or between conflicting fundamental rights.[925]

It has also been noted in relation to the review of Community acts for breach of fundamental rights that 'there has been a greater degree of success in challenging individual administrative acts of the Commission or other EC actors, but that the Court has remained deferential in its review of EU legislation'.[926] And indeed a more relaxed scrutiny is in evidence when the Court reviews acts of general application, be they basic acts[927] or implementing acts,[928] while a more searching approach is applied in case of acts of individual application.[929] Such a restricted review is convincing when it is based on the consideration that acts of general application cannot, by their nature, determine every possible situation, in which the various rights and interests in issue need to be balanced. Such acts must rather seek to provide 'the mechanisms allowing those different rights and interests to be balanced'.[930] It is then in the application of these general acts in individual

---

922 Ibid., at para. 53. See also Case C-340/00P *Cwik v Commission* [2001] ECR I-10269, at paras. 17 and 18.

923 See Case C-104/97P *Atlanta AG and Others v Council and Commission* [1999] ECR I-6983, para. 42. This obligation seems to flow now directly from Article 6(2) TEU.

924 See Case 44/79 *Hauer v Land Rheinland-Pfalz* [1979] ECR I-3727.

925 See Case C-101/01 *Bodil Lindqvist* [2003] ECR I-12971, at para. 82.

926 P. Craig and G. DeBúrca, supra note 1, p. 390.

927 See Case C-280/93 *Germany v Council* [1994] ECR I-4973, at paras. 77–87; Case C-186/96 *Demand* [1998] ECR I-8529, at paras. 40–42; Joined Cases C-20/00 and C-64/00 *Booker Aquaculture and Hydro Seafood* [2003] ECR I-7411, at para. 64–86; Case C-101/01 *Lindqvist* [2003] ECR I-12971, at paras. 82–84; Case C-491/01 *BAT and Imperial Tobacco* [2002] ECR I-11453, at paras. 149–153; Case C-347/03 *Regione autonoma Friuli-Venezia Guilia and ERSA* [2005] ECR I-3785, at paras. 119–134; Joined Cases C-154/04 and C-155/04 *Alliance for Natural Health and others* [2005] ECR I-6451, at paras. 120–130.

928 Joined Case T-79/96, T-260/97 and T-117/98 *Camar and Tico v Commission and Council* [2000] ECR II-2193, at para. 138; Joined Cases C-37/02 and C-38/02 *Di Lenardo Adriano and Dilexport* [2004] ECR I-6911, at paras. 82–88; Case C-295/03 P *Alessandrini and others v Commission* [2005] ECR I-5673, at paras. 85–91.

929 Case T-112/98 *Mannesmannröhren-Werke v Commission* [2001] ECR II-729, at paras. 60–79; Case C-274/99 P *Connolly v Commission* [2001] ECR I-1611, at paras. 37–62; Joined Cases T-67/00, T-68/00, T-71/00 and T-78/00 *JFE Engineering and others v Commission* [2004] ECR II-49, at paras. 178 *et seq.*; Case C-340/00 P *Commission v Cwik* [2001] ECR I-10269, at paras. 17–28.

930 Case C-101/01 *Lindqvist* [2003] ECR I-12971, at para. 82.

cases that the EC or national institution has to show that in applying these mechanisms it adequately balanced the concrete and individualised rights and interests in issue.[931]

Misuse of Power

The concept of misuse of powers has functional equivalents in many, if not all, national administrative systems of the European Union, but has found its most prominent expression in French administrative law, where it is known as *détournement de pouvoir*.[932] The latter applies where an administrative authority uses its powers for ends other than those granted by law.[933] This ground of French administrative law therefore requires an examination of the motives which led the administrative authority to adopt the contested act.[934] Under the ECSC Treaty, misuse of powers was of particular importance to private parties, as it was the only ground of review which allowed them to challenge acts of general application.[935] However, despite its frequent invocation in cases before the Community Courts, misuse of powers, similar to its French counterpart, occupies only a residuary position in Community law as a ground of review in comparison with other grounds.[936]

The Community Courts consider a measure vitiated by misuse of powers, 'if it appears, on the basis of objective, relevant and consistent evidence, to have been taken with the exclusive or main purpose of achieving an end other than that stated or evading a procedure specifically prescribed by the Treaty'.[937] Even though misuse of powers is mostly invoked against administrative measures,[938] it can also be used to review legislative acts.[939]

---

[931] Ibid., para. 85.

[932] See L.N. Brown and J.S. Bell, *French Administrative Law* (Clarendon Press Oxford, 4th edn., 1993), pp. 229–235.

[933] Ibid., p. 230.

[934] Ibid., p. 230.

[935] This might also explain the more expansive use of the concept under Article 33 ECSC. See T.C. Hartley, supra note 1, p. 404, at fn. 34.

[936] On the relevance of *détournement de pouvoir* in French administrative law, see L.N. Brown and J.S. Bell, supra note 932, pp. 234–235.

[937] Case T-415/03 *Cofradía v Council* [2005] ECR II-4355, para. 79. See also Case T-47/01 *Co-Frutta v Commission* [2003] ECR II-4441, para. 72; Case C-121/01 P *O'Hannrachain v European Parliament* [2003] ECR I-5539, para. 46; Case C-210/03 *Swedish Match* [2004] ECR I-11893, para. 75; Case C-342/03 *Spain v Council* [2005] ECR I-1975, para. 64.

[938] The definition of misuse by the Community Courts therefore frequently refers to acts adopted by the 'administrative authority', see Case T-87/05 *EDP v Commission* [2005] ECR II-3745.

[939] See Case C-491/01 *BAT and Imperial Tobacco* [2002] ECR I-11453, paras. 189–192; Case C-210/03 *Swedish Match* [2004] ECR I-11893, paras. 75–78.

As it relates to the purpose for which the power granted was used, misuse of powers requires an inquiry as to the motives of the author of the act and is therefore subjective.[940] This subjective element distinguishes misuse of powers in theory from the principle of proportionality, which is based on objective grounds.[941] In cases of proportionality, the institution pursues a proper objective with inappropriate means, whereas in cases of misuse of powers the institution pursues an improper objective.

Misuse of powers presupposes that the aim is not covered by the power on which the institution relies. Therefore, in many cases the Community Courts will have to inquire as to which aims can be legitimately pursued by the provision relied on by the institution. This means that the institution does not have to act in bad faith.[942] The institution will have misused its powers even if it assumed that the aim it pursued was covered by the provision it relied on. Misuse of powers will, however, only exist where the institution exclusively, or at least mainly, pursues an improper aim. In *EDP* the CFI stated that '[w]here more than one aim is pursued, even if the grounds of a decision include, in addition to proper grounds, an improper one, that would not make the decision invalid for misuse of powers, since if does not nullify the main aim'.[943]

Misuse of powers can also be invoked where the institution took the measure with the aim of 'evading a procedure specifically prescribed by the Treaty for dealing with the circumstances of the case'.[944] The Community Courts consider such a misuse of procedure as just another form of misuse of powers.[945] In *Frydendahl Pedersen*[946] the Commission had requested Denmark to withdraw its request for the application of Article 13 of Council Regulation 1430/79[947] for the repayment of import duties for which the applicant, a Danish company, had applied. The Commission admitted that the reason for this request was to avoid the expiration of the prescribed period of four months for dealing with the

---

[940] See T.C. Hartley, supra note 1, p. 404.

[941] Ibid., p. 404 and P. Craig and G. DeBúrca, supra note 1, p. 568.

[942] T.C. Hartley, supra note 1, p. 404.

[943] Case T-87/05 *EDP v Commission* [2005] ECR II-3745, para. 87. See also Case 1/54 *France v High Authority* [1954] ECR 1, p. 16; Case 2/54 *Italy v High Authority* [1954] ECR 37, 54; Case 8/55 *Fédération Charbonnière de Belgique v High Authority* [1956] ECR 292, p. 301; Case 2/57 *Compagnie des Hauts Fourneaux de Chasse v High Authority* [1958] ECR 199, p. 208; Case T-266/97 *VTM v Commission* [1999] ECR II-2329, para. 131; Case T-364/03 *Medici Grimm v Council* [2006] ECR II-79, para. 96.

[944] Case C-342/03 *Spain v Council* [2005] ECR I-1975, para. 64.

[945] Case 15/57 *Compagnie des Hauts Fourneaux de Chasse v High Authority* [1958] ECR 211, at p. 231; Case T-109/97 *Molkerei Großbraunshain and Another v Commission* [1998] ECR II-3533, para. 62; Case T-166/99 *de Dios and Others v Council* [2001] ECR II-645, para. 48.

[946] Case 148/87 *Frydendahl Pedersen v Commission* [1988] ECR 4993.

[947] [1979] OJ L 175/1.

request, as in this case the national authority had to grant the application. The Court found that the procedure was vitiated by misuse of powers, as the Commission's request was less concerned with requesting additional information from the Danish authorities, but that 'the real purpose of the practice complained of was to avoid the consequences provided for in Article 7 of Regulation 1575/80 should no decision be taken within the prescribed period'. In *Molkerei Großbraunshain and Bene Nahrungsmittel*[948] the CFI seems to suggest that such misuse occurs where the institution chooses a procedure in order to deprive individuals of their participation rights which another procedure might have granted. The CFI found however that the applicants had produced no evidence 'to show that the Commission [. . .] chose the "shortened" legislative procedure precisely in order to deal with the particular situation and evade the "ordinary" procedure giving the applicants procedural rights'.[949] A misuse of procedure can also occur where the legislative authority chooses a legal basis for an end other than that for which the legal basis provides the power to adopt legislative acts.[950] Consequently the legislative authority must not choose other articles of the Treaty in order to circumvent the prohibition in Article 152(4)(1) ECT, which excludes the harmonisation of national rules designed to protect and improve human health.[951] This ground seems, however, residuary to the objective ground of review of the legal basis chosen by the institution.[952]

The most difficult aspect of this ground of review is providing evidence sufficient to convince the Community Courts of its existence. The requirement of 'objective, relevant and consistent evidence' is often difficult to satisfy. Apart from cases where the institution displays its motives in open court,[953] the incriminating evidence is often not readily accessible for the applicant. The ruling of the Court in *Ufex*[954] provides therefore some relief for litigants. The applicants had asked the CFI in first instance to order a letter which the applicants claimed provided evidence for their claim that the Commission had misused its powers. The CFI rejected the request on the ground that the letter had not been produced and that its very existence

---

[948] Case T-109/97 *Molkerei Großbraunshain and Bene Nahrungsmittel v Commission* [1998] ECR II-3533.

[949] Ibid., para. 63. See also Case T-166/99 *de Dios and Others v Council* [2001] ECR II-645, para. 50.

[950] See Case C-84/94 *United Kingdom v Council* [1996] ECR I-5755, para. 70.

[951] Case C-210/03 *Swedish Match and Others* [2004] ECR I-11893, para. 76; Case C-491/01 *BAT and Imperial Tobacco* [2002] ECR I-11453, para. 190.

[952] See Case C-376/98 *Germany v Parliament and Council* [2000] ECR I-2247.

[953] See Case 148/87 *Frydendahl Pedersen v Commission* [1988] ECR 4993, para. 11.

[954] Case C-119/97 P *Ufex and Others v Commission* [1999] ECR I-1341.

was unconfirmed. On appeal the Court found the rejection of the request unjustified given that the letter 'was apparently material to the outcome of the case'[955] and that the appellants 'had stated the author, the addressee and the date of the letter they wished to be produced'.[956] In the absence of a 'smoking gun' the applicants often have to rely on circumstantial evidence,[957] often without success.[958]

The following cases provide rare examples of successful claims of misuse of power. In *Giuffrida*,[959] the Court annulled a Council decision appointing one of its civil servants, Mr Martino, to a higher grade on the ground that the competition for the post was a misuse of powers. The Council had already admitted in a note that the sole purpose of the competition was to appoint Mr Martino, who had already performed the duties attached to the post. Moreover, the terms of admission to the competition corresponded exactly to the duties performed by Mr. Martino. The Court held that competition for a post should have as its purpose to select the best-qualified person and not to give the post to someone who had been selected in advance by the institution.

In *C v Council*,[960] the CFI found that the Council had misused its powers by retiring the applicant, an official of the General Secretariat of the Council, on the ground of total permanent invalidity. The CFI noted a series of circumstantial factors which underpinned its ruling. The setting up of an Invalidity Committee was initially deemed premature, as a change of post was thought best to deal with the applicant's absenteeism. Only when the applicant refused to apply for a vacant post, was the Invalidity Committee established. Moreover, the medical file before the Committee and forwarded to the applicant's doctor merely consisted of blood analyses and smear tests, all of which were normal. Furthermore, the Council admitted that the applicant's problems could be solved through various mechanisms of which the establishment of the Invalidity Committee was only one. Lastly, the Council refused to provide the applicant with information of the specific provision in the Staff Regulations and the medical reasons for setting up the Invalidity Committee. What is more, the Council stated that the decision to refer the applicant to the Committee was not only based on her absences, but also on her staff reports, her allegedly

---

955 Ibid., para. 110.

956 Ibid., para. 111.

957 See T.C. Hartley, supra note 1, p. 404.

958 See Case C-121/01 P *O'Hannrachain v European Parliament* [2003] ECR I-5539, paras. 46 *et seq*.

959 Case 105/75 *Giuffrida v Council* [1976] ECR 1395.

960 Case T-84/98 *C v Council* [2000] ECR II-497. See also Cases 18 and 35/65 *Gutmann v Commission* [1966] ECR 103.

bad relations with some colleagues and her reluctance to engage with the Committee.

In *Giannini*[961] the CFI had annulled in its judgment of 19 March 1997[962] a Commission Decision appointing Mr X as Head of Unit even though he had, in contrast to the applicant, no experience in the textiles or in the footwear sector, one of the requirements set out in the vacancy notice. Following that ruling, the Commission replaced the earlier vacancy notice with a new one, which no longer required experience in the sector concerned, but gave instead preference to candidates with experience in international negotiations and in the management of a unit. The CFI found that the measures taken by the Commission in compliance with the earlier judgment constituted a misuse of powers. The CFI identified three factors in its ruling to show that the Commission had misused its power. First, the Commission had replaced the original notice and therefore eliminated the original applicants even though the CFI had not required such action to be taken. Second, the new notice contained two additional conditions which corresponded precisely to the qualifications of Mr X. Third, the Commission re-appointed Mr X despite strong competition.

Intensity of Review

The discussion of the grounds of review in the previous sections has already shown that the Community Courts exercise their task of judicial review with varying degrees of intensity. The intensity of assessment can vary not only between different grounds of review, different fields of EC policy, between EC legislation and its application, but also in its temporal dimension. Competence review is more intense when the Community's institutional balance is at stake than when the Court delimits the competence of the Community *vis-à-vis* its Member States, including any assessment of subsidiarity. This is true, even though the Community Courts have recently undertaken to scrutinise EC legislation in greater depth when assessing whether the Community was competent to act. It can also be observed that the conferral of powers under the CAP has been allowed to be more extensive than in other areas. Procedural requirements are also enforced with a differing degree of intensity depending on whether the act in issue is considered as legislative or administrative in nature. While the rights of defence do not apply to legislative acts, the duty to give reasons demands

---

[961] Joined Cases T-282/97 and T-57/98 *Giannini v Commission* [1999] ECR II-151. The CFI's ruling was upheld on appeal by the court in Case C-153/99 P *Commission v Giannini* [2000] ECR I-2891.

[962] Case T-21/96 *Giannini v Commission* [1997] ECR II-211.

less detail in the case of EC legislation than when an administrative act is adopted. Similarly, in the application of general principles of law the Community Courts apply the manifestly inappropriate test to legislative acts while a harder look is taken at administrative acts.

It has also been observed that the Community Courts reduce the intensity of their review to the application of manifest error, misuse of powers, or clear excess of discretion, where the Community institutions are considered to enjoy discretion.[963] Firstly, many provisions of the EC Treaty provide for the adoption of Community legislation, in which various, sometimes conflicting, objectives and interests have to be reconciled, as in the case of the CAP. The Court has shown great reluctance to interfere with the choices made by the Community legislator. This can be seen in the *Banana* case.[964] In 1993, the Council adopted a regulation which established a common organisation of the market in bananas.[965] The objective of the regulation was to ensure that bananas produced in the EC and in the ACP States provide an adequate income for the producers and fair prices for consumers without undermining imports of bananas from other third countries' suppliers. The regime protected the import of ACP bananas and restricted the import of third country bananas. Germany challenged the regulation on various grounds, in particular that the regulation did not ensure fair prices for consumers, one of the objectives of Article 33(1)(e). The Court rejected that argument. It pointed out that:

> in pursuing the objectives of the common agricultural policy the Community institutions must secure the permanent harmonisation made necessary by any conflicts between those objectives taken individually and, where necessary, give any one of them temporary priority in order to satisfy the demands of the economic factors or conditions in view of which their decisions are made [...]. The Court has also held that, in matters concerning the common agricultural policy, the Community legislature has a broad discretion which corresponds to the political responsibilities imposed on it by Articles 40 and 43 [now 34 and 37].[966]

Second, in the adoption of administrative measures EC institutions might be entrusted with the application of vague and general provisions[967] and/or provisions which give them genuine discretion as to whether to act at

---

[963] P. Craig (2006), supra note 2, chapter 13.

[964] Case C-280/93 *Germany v Council* [1994] ECR I-4973.

[965] Council Regulation (EEC) No 404/93 of 13 February 1993 on the common organisation of the market in bananas, OJ [1993] L 47, p. 1.

[966] Case C-280/93 *Germany v Council* [1994] ECR I-4973 at para 47.

[967] These provisions usually relate to the conditions for administrative action. P. Craig, supra note 2, at p. 433, terms this type jurisdictional discretion. It might perhaps be more accurate in these cases to speak of a margin of appreciation.

all.[968] In particular the exercise of broadly-drafted conditions for administrative action might make it necessary to make complex evaluations of economic and scientific matters. This gives the institution a certain freedom of evaluation as to whether the conditions set out in Community law are met. The Community Courts have therefore held that 'when examining the lawfulness of the exercise of such freedom the courts cannot substitute their own evaluation of the matter for that of the competent authority, but must restrict themselves to examining whether the evaluation of the competent authority contains a patent error or constitutes a misuse of power.'[969] While maintaining the language of manifest error, the Community Courts have more recently tightened the margin of appreciation which the Community institutions, in particular the Commission, have in establishing and evaluating the relevant facts.[970] In particular in the area of competition law and risk regulation a more searching review is applied.[971] A more detailed review by the CFI of complex economic and scientific matters raises, however, difficult questions of the role of judicial review in Community law.[972]

More recently, the appropriate standard of review of Council Regulations imposing sanctions, such as the freezing of funds and other resources, against persons suspected of supporting terrorism has been in issue. In *Kadi*,[973] the CFI had to decide on a challenge brought against Council Regulation 881/2002[974] which listed the applicant in Annex I as a person whose funds had to be frozen. The regulation gave effect to Council Common Position 2002/402/CFSP[975] which was based in turn on various resolutions of the Security Council of the United Nations.[976] The CFI examined the

968 Where the conditions for administrative action are met, such provisions provide that the institution 'may' act, see Article 87(3). P. Craig (2006), supra note 2, at p. 433, terms this classical discretion.

969 Case 78/74 *Deuka v Einfuhr- und Vorratsstelle Getreide* [1975] ECR 421 at para 9. For a discussion of the early case law, see T.C. Hartley, supra note 1, pp. 409–412; P. Craig (2006), supra note 2, pp. 439–446.

970 See the discussion of the more recent case-law by P. Craig (2006), supra note 2, p. 446–464.

971 See Case T-342/99 *Airtours v Commission* [2002] ECR II-2585; Case T-5/02 *Tetra Laval v Commission* [2002] ECR II-4381, upheld on appeal in Case C-12/03 P *Commission v Tetra Laval* [2005] ECR I-987. See also D. Bailey, 'Standard of Proof in EC Merger Proceedings: A Common Law Perspective' (2003) *CMLRev* 845; B. Versterdorf, 'Certain Reflections on Recent Judgments Reviewing Commission Merger Control Decisions', in M. Hoskins and W. Robinson (eds.), *A True European, Essays for Judge David Edward* (Hart, 2003), chapter 10.

972 For a discussion of the issues, see P. Craig (2006), supra note 2, pp. 464–481.

973 Case T-315/01 *Kadi v Council and Commission* [2005] ECR II-3649. The appeal in Case C-402/05 is pending.

974 [2002] OJ L 139/9.

975 [2002] OJ L 139/4.

976 See Resolutions 1267(1999), 1333(2000) and 1390(2002).

competence of the Community on its own motion and subjected the choice of legal basis by the Council to strict review. The CFI found, however, that Articles 60, 301 and 308 EC did indeed constitute the correct legal basis for the imposition of sanctions on persons suspected of terrorism. The CFI pursued a more cautious approach in respect of the claim that the contested regulation breached the applicant's fundamental rights. Even though it emphasised the rule of law principle demanding review of Community acts, the CFI made it clear that 'the resolutions of the Security Council at issue fall, in principle, outside the ambit of the Court's judicial review and that the Court has no authority to call in question, even indirectly, their lawfulness in the light of Community law'.[977] The CFI did, however, find that it was 'empowered to check, indirectly, the lawfulness of the resolutions of the Security Council in question with regard to *jus cogens*, understood as a body of higher rules of public international law binding on all subjects of international law, including the bodies of the United Nations, and from which no derogation is possible'.[978] The assessment of the applicant's claim as to a breach of his property rights and the principle of proportionality in light of *jus cogens* led to a much reduced intensity. The CFI argued that exceptions to the freezing of funds as regards basic expenses did not amount to inhuman or degrading treatment and that there was also no arbitrary deprivation of the right to property.[979] Similarly, the CFI rejected the applicant's claim that his right to a fair hearing was infringed. The CFI found that due to the lack of discretion on the part of the Council in implementing the Security Council resolutions in issue, the Council was not under an obligation to hear the applicant.[980] The CFI also held that the lack of a hearing before the Sanctions Committee, a subsidiary body of the Security Council, in connection with the inclusion in the list of persons whose funds must be frozen was not such as to infringe his right to be heard. The CFI noted that no right to be heard before the Sanctions Committee existed and that the mechanism for the re-examination of individual cases set up by the Sanctions Committee was dependent on the willingness of the national government, which the applicant could petition for this purpose, to submit a request for delisting by the Sanctions Committee. Moreover, the CFI expressly acknowledged that 'any opportunity for the applicant effectively to make known his views on the correctness and relevance of the facts in consideration of which his funds have been frozen and on the evidence adduced against him appears

---

[977] Case T-315/01 *Kadi v Council and Commission* [2005] ECR II-3649, para. 225.
[978] Ibid., para. 226.
[979] Ibid., paras. 237–252.
[980] Ibid., paras. 255–260.

to be definitively excluded.'[981] All the same, the CFI denied a breach of the right to a fair hearing. Finally, as to the applicant's claim that his right to an effective remedy was breached, the CFI admitted that to the extent that the CFI could not, subject to *jus cogens* considerations, review the Security Council resolution 'there is no judicial remedy available to the applicant, the Security Council not having thought it advisable to establish an independent international court responsible for ruling, in law and on the facts, in actions brought against individual decisions taken by the Sanctions Committee'.[982] All the same, the CFI held that 'any such lacuna in the judicial protection available to the applicant is not in itself contrary to *jus cogens*'.[983]

On appeal, AG Maduro in his Opinion[984] vividly disagreed with the timid approach to judicial review by the CFI. While he argued that Articles 60 and 301 EC were sufficient as legal basis for the adoption of the contested regulation, his main criticism was directed against the exclusion of judicial review. AG Maduro noted that 'although the Court takes great care to respect the obligations that are incumbent on the Community by virtue of international law, it seeks, first and foremost, to preserve the constitutional framework created by the Treaty'.[985] He rejected that Article 307 EC or the specific subject-matter of the case could exempt the contested regulation from judicial review.[986] AG Maduro pointed out that 'the claim that a measure is necessary for the maintenance of international peace and security cannot operate so as to silence the general principles of Community law and deprive individuals of their fundamental rights'.[987] He found that '[o]n the contrary, when the risks to public security are believed to be extraordinarily high, the pressure is particularly strong to take measures that disregard individual rights, especially in respect of individuals who have little or no access to the political process. Therefore, in those instances, the courts should fufil their duty to uphold the rule of law with increased vigilance'.[988] AG Maduro therefore found that the CFI's judgment erred in law and should be set aside. Moreover, he requested the Court to give final judgment in the case. When assessing the appellant's breach of fundamental rights, he also refused the argument that the

---

981 Ibid., para. 273.
982 Ibid., para. 285.
983 Ibid., para. 286.
984 Case C-402/05 P *Kadi v Council and Commission*, Opinion of AG Maduro of 16 January 2008.
985 Ibid., para. 24.
986 Ibid., paras. 29–32 (on Article 307) and paras. 33–35 (on maintenance of international peace and security as 'political question').
987 Ibid., para. 34.
988 Ibid., para. 35.

Court should apply a more reduced approach to judicial review. While he acknowledged that the Court should recognise the authority of bodies, such as the Security Council, 'that are established under a different legal order than its own and that are sometime better placed to weigh those fundamental interests',[989] he insisted that 'the Court cannot, in deference to the views of those institutions, turn its back on the fundamental values that lie at the basis of the Community legal order and which it has the duty to protect'.[990] Consequently, he argued that:

> the weight to be given to the different interests which are always to be balanced in the application of the fundamental rights at issue may be different as a consequence of the specific needs arising from the prevention of international terrorism. But this is to be assessed in a normal exercise of judcial review by this Court. The present circumstances may result in a different balance being struck among the values involved in the protection of fundamental rights but the standard of protection afforded by them ought not to change.[991]

The AG stated that the delisting mechanism of the Sanctions Committee could not provide a substitute for the appellant being heard by the Council. The absence of a hearing and the lack of judicial review by an independent tribunal at the level of the United Nations, led the AG to conclude that the appellant's claim was well founded.

It is in particular the complete absence of any judicial review mechanism at the level of the United Nations which makes the arguments against a reduced form of judicial review by the Community Courts in sanctions cases so compelling. A reduction in judicial review by the Community Courts, along the lines of the European Court of Human Rights in its *Bosphorus* ruling,[992] can only be entertained if the United Nations establishes an independent tribunal in which actions against UN Security Council resolutions imposing sactions on individual can be brought.[993]

8. EFFECTS OF ILLEGALITY

Articles 231 and 233 determine the consequences of a ruling of illegality. While Article 231(1) states that the Court will declare an illegal act void,

---

989 Ibid., para. 44.

990 Ibid., para. 44.

991 Ibid., para. 46.

992 *Bosphorus Hava Yollari Turizm v Ticaret Anonim Sirketi (Bosphorus Airways) v Ireland*, ECHR (2005) No. 45036/98.

993 See also Case C-402/05 P *Kadi v Council and Commission*, Opinion of AG Maduro of 16 January 2008, at para. 54.

Article 231(2) allows the Court to limit the effects of such a ruling. On the other hand, Article 233 requires the institution whose act has been declared void to take the necessary measures to comply with the Court's judgment.

Article 231

Article 231(1) stipulates that 'if the action is well founded, the Court of Justice shall declare the act concerned to be void'.[994] The Community Courts can also grant partial annulment, however, only if the annulled part can be severed from the rest of the act.[995] The requirement of severability is not satisfied where, viewed from an objective perspective, the partial annulment of an act would have the effect of altering its substance.[996]

The judgment which annuls an act 'takes effect *ex tunc* and thus has the effect of retroactively eliminating the annulled measure from the legal system'.[997] The retroactive effect of the annulment affects not just the parties to the dispute, but has effect *erga omnes*.[998] The declaration of annulment therefore produces legal consequences for Community institutions and Member States which adopted legal acts to implement or apply the act which has been declared void. Consequently, those acts which are based on the annulled act become unlawful. Similarly, grants that have been made or payments that have been collected on the basis of the annulled act also become unlawful. And unwelcome consequences can also arise for private parties who have relied on the validity of the annulled act.

To avoid the consequences that flow from the annulment of an act, Article 231(2) therefore allows the Court to limit the effects of nullity. The provision stipulates that 'in the case of a regulation, however, the Court of Justice shall, if it considers this necessary, state which of the effects of

---

994 See P. Craig (2006), supra note 2, pp. 756–758; T.C. Hartley, supra note 1, pp. 414–416.

995 Case C-36/04 *Spain v Council* [2006] ECR I-2981, at para 12; Case C-540/03 *EP v Council* [2006] ECR I-5769, at para 27.

996 Case C-36/04 *Spain v Council* [2006] ECR I-2981, at paras 13–14; Case C-244/03 *France v EP and Council* [2005] ECR I-4021, at paras 13–14; Case T-31/07 R *Du Pont de Nemours (France) and Others v Commission*, order of 19 July 2007, at para. 119.

997 Case T-171/99 *Corus v Commission* [2001] ECR II-2967, para. 50. See also Joined Cases 97/86, 99/86, 193/86 and 215/86 *Asteris and Others v Commission* [1988] ECR 2181, para. 30; Joined Cases T-481/93 and T-484/93 *Exporteurs and Others v Commission* [1995] ECR II-2941, para. 46.

998 See Case C-310/97 P *Commission v AssiDomän and Others* [1999] ECR I-5363, para. 54.

the regulation which it has declared void shall be considered as definitive'. Despite its wording, the Court has used Article 231(2) not only to limit the effects of the annulment of an act to regulations, but has equally invoked Article 231(2) in the case of decisions[999] and directives.[1000] The main ground on which the Court considers the limitation to be justified is that of legal certainty, but the Court on occasion also invokes other justifications, such as the continuity of Community policy.[1001]

In *UK v Commission*,[1002] the Court annulled a Commission decision which provided certain grants for European projects seeking to overcome social exclusion, on ground of lack of competence. However, as most of the relevant payments had already been made, the Court decided for reasons of legal certainty that the annulment 'should not affect the validity of payments made or undertakings given under the contracts in issue'.[1003] Similar considerations of legal certainty apply in the case of invalidity rulings under Article 234, in which the Court applies Article 231(2) by analogy.[1004] On this basis, the Court was prepared to limit the temporal effects of the invalidity of a Community measure where 'overriding considerations of legal certainty involving all the interests, public as well as private, at stake in the cases concerned precluded the calling in to question of the charging or payment of sums of money effected on the basis of that measure in respect of the period prior to the date of the judgment'.[1005]

The Court is inclined to limit the effects of nullity where the Commission has already taken implementing measures on the basis of the act which is then later declared void. In *EP v Council*[1006] the Court annulled a Council Decision on a Community contribution for telematic interchange of data between administrations in the Community on the ground that it was adopted on the wrong legal basis. As the Commission had already adopted several measures to implement the Council Decision the Court was prepared to maintain the effect of those implementing acts 'in order

---

999 See Case C-106/96 *UK v Commission* [1998] ECR I-2729, at para. 41; Case C-22/96 *EP v Council* [1998] ECR I-3231, at para. 42.

1000 See Case C-314/99 *Netherlands v Commission* [2002] ECR I-5521, at para. 31; Case C-21/94 *EP v Council* [1995] ECR I-1827, at para. 31; Case C-295/90 *EP v Council* [1992] ECR I-4193.

1001 See Case C-21/94 *European Parliament v Council* [1995] ECR I-1827, para. 31; Case C-22/96 *EP v Council* [1998] ECR I-3231, para. 41.

1002 Case C-106/96 *UK v Commission* [1998] ECR I-2729.

1003 Ibid., para. 41.

1004 Case 4/79 *Providence agricole de la Champagne* [1980] ECR 2823, para. 45; Case 41/84 *Pinna* [1986] ECR 1, para. 28.

1005 Case C-228/99 *Silos* [2001] ECR I-8401, para. 36.

1006 Case C-22/96 *EP v Council* [1998] ECR I-3231.

to avoid discontinuity in the measures commenced, and for important reasons of legal certainty'.[1007] The Court rejected, however, the application of Article 231(2) to other effects of the decision, as 'neither the Council nor the Commission has explained the difficulties which annulment of the contested decision would entail in that regard'.[1008] In the *LIFE* case,[1009] the Court found Article 11(2) of Regulation 1655/2000[1010] unlawful, as the requirement to use the regulatory procedure for the adoption of implementing acts was not adequately reasoned. The Court was however prepared '[i]n the interest of legal certainty' to declare that implementing measures already adopted under the Regulation were not affected and that the effects of the contested provision were 'to be fully maintained until the European Parliament and the Council adopt new provisions concerning the committee procedure to which the measures for the implementation of that regulation are subject'.[1011] And in another case,[1012] the Court found that Regulation 304/2003 concerning the import and export of dangerous chemicals[1013] was unlawful, as Article 175 ECT alone was not sufficient as legal basis. Since the Commission had already adopted, in the implementation of the Regulation, a number of Community import decisions on certain chemical products and substances, the Court was prepared to maintain the effects of the Regulation 'to avoid any legal uncertainty regarding the rules applicable to trade in those products following annulment of the contested regulation'.[1014]

The Court applies similar considerations when the Member States have already taken decisions in application of the contested act. In the *Beef labelling* case[1015] the Court found a Council regulation providing for the general rules for a compulsory beef labelling system[1016] unlawful as the Council had chosen an inadequate legal basis for the adoption of the regulation. And even though the regulation had been replaced in the interim by another act, the Court stated that the annulment of the regulation 'could create a legal lacuna'[1017] and therefore declared that 'the effects of those

---

1007 Ibid., para. 41.

1008 Ibid., para. 41.

1009 Case C-378/00 *Commission v European Parliament and Council* [2003] ECR I-937.

1010 [2000] OJ L 192/1.

1011 Case C-378/00 *Commission v European Parliament and Council* [2003] ECR I-937, para. 76.

1012 Case C-178/03 *Commission v European Parliament and Council* [2006] ECR I-107.

1013 [2003] OJ L 63/1.

1014 Case C-178/03 *Commission v European Parliament and Council* [2006] ECR I-107, para. 65.

1015 Case C-93/00 *European Parliament v Council* [2001] ECR I-10119.

1016 Council Regulation 2772/1999, [1999] OJ L 334/1.

1017 Case C-93/00 *European Parliament v Council* [2001] ECR I-10119, para. 48.

provisions in the contested regulation pursuant to which the Member States may have adopted decisions which could be affected by the annulment are to be regarded as definitive'.[1018]

The Court is prepared to maintain the effects of an unlawful act where the act was designed to grant individuals rights or benefits. In *Commission v Council*[1019] the Court found that the Council was bound by an earlier undertaking to use an agreed formula for the calculation of future increases of staff salaries and that the Council decision which later fixed the salary scales contrary to that formula was unlawful. However, to avoid staff being left without any increase in salaries, the Court declared that 'to avoid discontinuity in the system of remuneration [. . .] the articles declared void shall continue to have effect until the Council passes a new regulation in consequence of the present judgment'.[1020] In *European Parliament v Council*[1021] the Court annulled Decision 93/323,[1022] which approved an agreement between the Community and the USA on government procurement, and Decision 93/324,[1023] which extended the benefits of the Community's public procurement procedures laid down in Directive 90/531[1024] to the USA. Given the type of service provisions covered by the decisions, the Court found that the decisions could not be based on Article 133 ECT alone. However, the Court noted that if the decisions were simply annulled, 'this would be liable adversely to affect the exercise of the rights arising under them'.[1025] Consequently, the Court preserved the effects of the annulled decisions.

The Court was also prepared to limit the effects of nullity of regulations on the protection of Community forests against respectively atmospheric pollution and fire, where 'annulment might be seriously detrimental to the progress of action undertaken in the Member States, with the support of the Community, for protection of the environment'.[1026]

The above cases show that the Court does not automatically grant a limitation of the effects of nullity, but needs to be persuaded that sufficient

---

1018 Ibid., para. 48.

1019 Case 81/72 *Commission v Council* [1973] ECR 575.

1020 Ibid., para. 15.

1021 Case C-360/93 *European Parliament v Council* [1996] ECR I-1195. See also Case C-295/90 *European Parliament v Council* [1992] ECR I-4193.

1022 [1993] OJ L 125/1.

1023 [1993] OJ L 125/54.

1024 [1990] OJ L 297/1.

1025 Case C-360/93 *European Parliament v Council* [1996] ECR I-1195, para. 33. Cf. Case C-239/01 *Germany v Commission* [2003] ECR I-10333, para. 78. See also Joined Cases C-14/06 and C-295/06 *European Parliament and Denmark v Commission*, judgment of 1 April 2008.

1026 Joined Cases C-164/97 and C-165/97 *EP v Council* [1999] ECR I-1139, para. 22.

justification for such an action exists and would grant a limitation only to the extent that it is necessary in the light of that justification. Therefore in some cases the Court only maintains certain effects of the annulled act, but might reject requests for more far-reaching limitations on the effects of nullity. As can also be seen from the above cases, the Court usually maintains the effects of an annulled act until it is replaced by a new act. In *European Parliament v Council*,[1027] the EP requested that the Court impose a time-limit on the Council within which the new act must be adopted. The Court found that it did not have jurisdiction to give such an order, but insisted that 'the Council is under a duty to put an end within a reasonable period to the infringement it has committed'.[1028] Even though four years passed before the act was finally replaced, the Court allowed the Commission to bring an action under Article 226 ECT against Austria for failure to comply with the annulled Directive. The Court stated that 'even if such a time-lapse between the annulling judgment and the adoption of the new Directive 1999/62 may, at first sight, seem long, that fact cannot prevent the Commission, in the discharge of its duties as guardian of the Treaty, from resorting to the procedure under Article 169 [now 226], which may lead to proceedings before the Court to establish a failure to fulfil obligations under the annulled directive which, by virtue of the judgment in [. . .],[1029] and for the reasons set out therein, was to continue to take effect despite being annulled'.[1030] Even though this position is quite formalistic, it is entirely logical. Where the Court preserves the effects of an annulled act until a new act is adopted, this act continues to have legal effects, and must be observed, until such time as the new act is adopted.[1031]

Article 233

Article 233 concerns the obligation of the institution that has adopted the act declared invalid.[1032] The provision stipulates that 'the institution or institutions whose act has been declared void [. . .] shall be required to take the necessary measures to comply with the judgment of the Court of Justice'.

1027 Case C-21/94 *European Parliament v Council* [1995] ECR I-1827.

1028 Ibid., para. 33.

1029 See Case C-21/94 *Parliament v Council* [1995] ECR I-1827.

1030 Case C-205/98 *Commission v Austria* [2000] ECR I-7367, para. 43.

1031 A different question is, of course, at what point the non-adoption of an act becomes abusive.

1032 See P. Craig (2006), supra note 2, pp. 758–761; T.C. Hartley, supra note 1, pp. 416–417.

The obligation to comply with the judgment declaring the act void exists, even where the institution has lodged an appeal against that judgment, as the appeal does not have any suspensory effect (see Article 242). In *Hautem*[1033] the European Investment Bank refused to comply with an earlier judgment of the CFI on the ground that it wanted to await the outcome of its appeal in the Court of Justice. The Court found this *de facto* stay of execution contrary to Article 233, as it was 'for the Court of Justice alone to prescribe, pursuant to Article 243 EC, any interim measures which it may consider to be necessary; that is a prerogative which the EIB cannot arrogate to itself'.[1034]

Even though it is under a strict obligation to comply with the judgment, the institution concerned is left with some discretion as to the manner in which such compliance is to be effected. The Community Courts have always insisted that it was for the institution whose act has been declared void to take the necessary measures, and that it was not for the Court to give the institution instructions.[1035] The CFI therefore rejected the applicant's request 'to grant it remission of the anti-dumping duties imposed on it'.[1036] The CFI also found it outside its power 'to rule on the quality of the applicant's tender compared with those of its competitors in the tendering procedure at issue or to order the Commission to award the applicant the contract'.[1037] Similarly, the CFI refused 'to order the Member State concerned to reimburse any aid unlawfully granted to the applicants by the Fiuli-Venezia Giulia Region'.[1038] And in *Graphischer Maschinenbau v Commission*, the CFI considered as inadmissible the applicant's request 'that the Court should order the Commission to declare the planned aid compatible in its entirety with the common market'.[1039] A Community institution has therefore certain discretion as to how to comply with a judgment annulling its act.[1040]

[1033] Case T-11/00 *Hautem v European Investment Bank* [2000] ECR II-1295.

[1034] Ibid., para. 40.

[1035] See Joined Cases T-298/97 etc. *Alzetta and Others v Commission* [2000] ECR II-2319, para. 42; Case T-145/98 *ADT v Commission* [2000] ECR II-2627, para. 84; Case T-126/99 *Graphischer Maschinenbau v Commission* [2002] ECR II-2427, para. 17; Case C-153/99 P *Commission v Giannini* [2000] ECR I-2891, para. 14; Case T-104/02 *Gondrand Frères v Commission* [2004] ECR II-3211, para. 20; Case T-372/02 *Internationaler Hilfsfonds v Commission* [2003] ECR II-4389, para. 48; Case T-28/03 *Holcim v Commission* [2005] ECR II-1357, para. 39; Case T-216/05 *Mebrom v Commission* [2007] ECR II-1507, at para. 56.

[1036] Case T-104/02 *Gondrand Freres v Commission* [2004] ECR II-3211, para. 20.

[1037] Case T-145/98 *ADT v Commission* [2000] ECR II-2627, para. 86.

[1038] Joined Cases T-298/97 etc. *Alzetta and Others v Commission* [2000] ECR II-2319, para. 43.

[1039] Case T-126/99 *Graphischer Maschinenbau v Commission* [2002] ECR II-2427, para. 17.

[1040] See Case T-196/01 *Thessalonikis v Commission* [2003] ECR II-3987, para. 226; Case T-241/00 *Le Canne v Commission* [2002] ECR II-1251, para. 62.

On the other hand, even though they cannot order the institution whose act has been declared void to take a particular course of action, the Community Courts in certain instances give guidance to the institution as to how to implement their judgments. In *Hirsch v European Central Bank*,[1041] the CFI elaborated on the obligations incumbent on the European Central Bank (ECB) following from its ruling of having declared void Article 19 of the ECB's Conditions of Employment on the ground that the provision infringed the principle of equal treatment, as well as the decisions to refuse an education allowance which were adopted on the basis of that provision. The CFI held that 'it is for the ECB to give due effect to this judgment by modifying the scheme of education allowances under Article 19 of the Conditions of Employment, in the light of the grounds of this judgment, so that they accord with the principle of equal treatment, and by reviewing, under the scheme as so modified, the applicant's requests for the grant of an education allowance in respect of their children'.[1042]

Notwithstanding the discretion left to the institution concerned, the Community Courts have developed a number of obligations incumbent on the institution whose act has been declared void. In order to comply adequately with these obligations, the institution concerned is required 'to have regard not only to the operative part of the judgment but also of the grounds which led to the judgment and constitute its essential basis, in so far as they are necessary to determine the exact meaning of what is stated in the operative part. It is those grounds which, on the one hand, identify the precise provision held to be illegal and, on the other, indicate the specific reasons which underlie the finding of illegality contained in the operative part and which the institution concerned must take into account when replacing the annulled measure'.[1043]

The most obvious obligation on the institution is not to enforce the act declared void.[1044] However, the obligations of the institution go further and include 'the removal of the effects of the illegal conduct found in the judgment annulling the act, and the institution is thus required to take

---

[1041] Joined Cases T-94/01, T-152/01 and T-286/01 *Hirsch and Others v European Central Bank* [2003] ECR II-27.

[1042] Ibid., para. 73. For a more elaborate explanation of the Commission's obligation, see also Case T-310/01 *Schneider Electric v Commission* [2002] ECR II-4071, para. 465.

[1043] Joined Cases 97/86, 99/86, 193/86 and 215/86 *Asteris and Others v Commission* [1988] ECR 2181, para. 27. See also Case T-154/98 *Asia Motor France and Others v Commission* [2000] ECR II-1703, para. 101; Case C-458/98 P *Industrie des Poudres Sphériques v Council* [2000] ECR I-8147, para. 81; Case T-206/99 *Métropole Télévision v Commission* [2001] ECR II-1057, para. 35; Case C-41/00 P *Interporc v Commission* [2003] ECR I-2125, para. 29; Case T-89/00 *Europe Chemi-Con v Council* [2002] ECR II-3651, para. 32.

[1044] T.C. Hartley, supra note 1, p. 416.

adequate steps to restore the applicant to its original position'.[1045] The CFI in *Corus*[1046] stated that amongst the necessary steps to be taken, 'in case of a judgment annulling or reducing the fine imposed on an undertaking for infringement of the Treaty competition rules, is the Commission's obligation to repay all or part of the fine paid by the undertaking in question, in so far as that payment must be described as a sum unduly paid following the annulment decision.'[1047] The CFI made it clear in this judgment that this obligation 'applies not only to the principal amount of the fine overpaid but also to default interest on that amount'.[1048] The CFI justified the requirement to pay interest on the ground that over time the principal amount is reduced in value and that the Commission would be otherwise unjustly enriched.[1049] In contrast, the CFI in *Holcim*[1050] found that those considerations did not apply to bank guarantee charges in cases where the individual provided the Commission with a bank guarantee instead of paying the fine.[1051] The obligation to repay unduly paid sums also arises in other cases. In *Astipesca*[1052] the CFI found that the Commission would have been obliged in case a timely challenge had been brought against its decision to suspend aid 'to pay the applicant the part of the aid unpaid on the date of that decision, with interest for late payment'.[1053] And in *François v Commission*,[1054] the CFI held that the Commission was under an obligation in staff cases to repay lost income as a result of disciplinary measures which were later annulled.[1055]

The removal of the illegal effects of the judgment and the restoration of the applicant to its original position even includes the obligation 'to make good the damage which has resulted from the unlawful act, subject to

---

1045 Case T-211/02 *Tideland Signal v Commission* [2002] ECR II-3781, para. 44. See also Case 22/70 *Commission v Council* [1971] ECR 263, paras. 59 and 60; Joined Cases T-480/93 and T-483/93 *Antillean Rice Mills and Others v Commission* [1995] ECR 795, paras. 59 and 60; Joined Cases T-481/93 and T-484/93 *Exporteurs in Levende Varkens and Others v Commission* [1995] ECR II-2941, para. 47; Case T-48/00 *Corus UK v Commission* [2004] ECR II-2325, para. 222.

1046 Case T-171/99 *Corus UK v Commission* [2001] ECR II-2967.

1047 Ibid., para. 52. See also Case T-48/00 *Corus UK v Commission* [2004] ECR II-2325, para. 223.

1048 Case T-171/99 *Corus UK v Commission* [2001] ECR II-2967, para. 53. On the calculation of the interest, see paras. 60–65.

1049 See Case T-171/99 *Corus UK v Commission* [2001] ECR II-2967, at paras. 54–56.

1050 Case T-28/03 *Holcim (Deutschland) v Commission* [2005] ECR II-1357.

1051 Ibid., at para. 127.

1052 Case T-180/00 *Astipesca v Commission* [2002] ECR II-3985.

1053 Ibid., para. 142.

1054 Case T-307/01 *François v Commission* [2004] ECR II-823.

1055 Ibid., para. 109. In the light of the cases discussed above, the obligation to repay lost income would also include interest.

fulfilment of the conditions laid down in the second paragraph of Article 288 EC'.[1056]

In certain cases the obligation under Article 233 includes the review of decisions which the institution has already taken. In *SNUPAT*[1057] the Court held that its earlier ruling,[1058] in which it had rejected the applicant's interpretation that group scrap should qualify as 'own resources' and therefore be exempt from the equalisation levy on ferrous scrap, should have prompted the Commission to review the exemptions it had granted to two other companies. The Court pointed out that the earlier judgment 'must therefore have led the High Authority to re-examine its previous position and to consider whether the disputed exemptions could be retained [. . .]'.[1059] In *Asteris*[1060] the Court had annulled Commission Regulation 1615/83[1061] fixing the coefficients to be applied to the production aid for tomato concentrates for the 1983/84 marketing year to the extent to which the coefficients laid down by the regulation discriminated between producers in Greece and those in other Member States.[1062] In order to comply with the judgment the Commission adopted Regulation 381/86,[1063] which provided for additional aid for Greek producers, but was limited to the marketing year 1983/84. The Court held that Article 233 ECT required the Commission not only to eliminate the illegality in the measure intended to replace the annulled act, but it was also 'under an obligation to ensure that new legislation adopted following the judgment annulling the previous measure and governing the marketing years subsequent to that judgment contains no provisions having the same effect as the provisions held to be illegal'.[1064] The Court pointed out, however, that the finding of illegality took effect from the date on which the annulled measure entered into force. Consequently, the Commission was under an obligation 'to eliminate from the regulations already adopted when the annulling judgment was delivered and governing marketing years after 1983/84 any provisions with the same effect as the provision held to be

---

1056 Case T-220/97 *Ecroyd Holdings v Commission* [1999] ECR II-1677, para. 56.
1057 Joined Cases 42 and 49/59 *SNUPAT v High Authority* [1961] ECR 53.
1058 Joined Cases 32 and 33/58 *SNUPAT v High Authority* [1959] ECR 127.
1059 Joined Cases 42 and 49/59 *SNUPAT v High Authority* [1961] ECR 53, p. 79.
1060 Joined Cases 97, 193, 99 and 215/86 *Asteris and Others v Commission* [1988] ECR 2181.
1061 [1983] OJ L159/48.
1062 See Case 192/83 *Greece v Commission* [1985] ECR 2791.
1063 [1986] OJ L 44/10.
1064 Joined Cases 97, 99, 193 and 215/86 *Asteris and Others v Commission* [1988] ECR 2181, para. 29.

illegal',[1065] but did not have do so for the regulations adopted before the 1983/84 marketing year.[1066]

In the light of these judgments, the CFI found in *AssiDomän*[1067] that Article 233 required the Commission to review decisions which the latter had addressed to the applicants for breach of Article 81 in light of the *Wood Pulp* ruling of the Court.[1068] As discussed above,[1069] the Commission had adopted a decision addressed to several companies for breach of Article 81 and imposed fines on those companies. When the decision was annulled by the Court on application by some companies, those companies who had not brought an action against the decision requested the Commission to review the decisions and fines addressed to them. The CFI justified its decision by arguing with reference to the ruling in *Asteris* that 'the measures that the institution must adopt may, in exceptional cases, extend beyond the specific context of the dispute which resulted in the judgment of annulment in order to eradicate the effects of the illegalities found in that judgment'.[1070] In light of the *SNUPAT* ruling and the principle of legality the CFI found that Article 233 ECT required the Commission 'to consider, pursuant to a request made within a reasonable period, whether it needs to take measures in relation not only to the successful parties but also to the addressees of that act who did not bring an action for annulment'.[1071]

On appeal the Court[1072] overturned the CFI's judgment. The Court pointed out that the scope of Article 233 was limited in two respects. First, the scope of the annulment which the judgment pronounces 'may not go further than that sought by the applicant'.[1073] Second, even though an annulment has authority *erga omnes*, it 'cannot entail annulment of an act not challenged before the Community judicature but alleged to be vitiated by the same illegality'.[1074] Consequently, even though Article 233 ECT 'requires the institution concerned to ensure that any act intended to replace the annulled act is not affected by the same irregularities as those identified in the judgment annulling the original act, that article [. . .] does not mean that the Commission must, at the request of interested parties, re-examine identical or similar decisions allegedly affected by the same

---

1065 Ibid., para. 30.
1066 Ibid., para. 31.
1067 Case T-227/95 *AssiDomän and Others v Commission* [1997] ECR II-1185.
1068 Joined Cases C-89/85 etc. *Ahlström Osakeyhtiö and Others v Commission* [1993] ECR I-1307.
1069 See supra, section 2.
1070 Case T-227/95 *AssiDomän and Others v Commission* [1997] ECR II-1185, para. 69.
1071 Ibid., para. 72.
1072 Case C-310/97P *Commission v AssiDomän and Others* [1999] ECR I-5363.
1073 Ibid., para. 52.
1074 Ibid., para. 54.

irregularity, addressed to addressees other than the applicant'.[1075] This statement, however, throws in doubt the rulings in *SNUPAT* and *Asteris*. In *SNUPAT*, the decisions addressed to the other two companies granting the unlawful exemptions were affected by the same irregularity as the one identified in the Court's earlier ruling. The Court in *AssiDomän* found that *SNUPAT* differed in that, firstly, the applicant in the latter case had 'systematically used the means of redress open to it'[1076] and, secondly, 'the exemptions granted to the two other producers were directly prejudicial to Snupat'.[1077] These distinctions do not seem convincing, as, firstly, despite its litigious activities, SNUPAT had never challenged the decisions granting the exemptions to the other two companies and, secondly, the annulment of the fines imposed on the parties in the *Wood Pulp* case created a competitive disadvantage for the applicants in *AssiDomän*. Similarly problematic is the Court's claim that the judgment in *Asteris* was not applicable, as that case 'concerned the annulment of consecutive regulations so that the annulment of an earlier regulation necessarily obliged the enacting institution to take account of the judgment of the Court of Justice when drawing up the regulations subsequent to the annulled regulation'.[1078] It should be noted that the Court in *Asteris* inferred an obligation to rectify the illegalities in these subsequent regulations, even though they had not been, and in case of private parties could not have been, challenged under Article 230. It follows that the ruling in *AssiDomän* should be limited to cases in which the addressee of an act chose not to challenge the measure. It is therefore submitted that the core holding of the ruling can be found in para. 63 of the judgment where the Court stated that '[w]here a number of similar individual decisions imposing fines have been adopted pursuant to a common procedure and only some addressees have taken legal action against the decisions concerning them and obtained their annulment, the principle of legal certainty [. . .] therefore precludes any necessity for the institution which adopted the decisions to re-examine, at the request of other addressees, in the light of the grounds of the annulling judgment, the legality of the unchallenged decisions and to determine, on the basis of that examination, whether the fines paid must be refunded'.[1079]

More recently, the CFI found in *Dunnett and Others*[1080] that the decision of the European Investment Bank to abolish the system of special

---

1075 Ibid., para. 56.
1076 Ibid., para. 67.
1077 Ibid., para. 68.
1078 Ibid., para. 70.
1079 Ibid., para. 63.
1080 Case T-192/99 *Dunnett and Others v European Investment Bank* [2001] ECR II-313.

conversion rates was unlawful on the ground that the Bank failed to hold *bona fide* consultations with staff representatives before adopting the decision. The CFI therefore annulled the applicants' salary statements for January 1999 which the EIB had drawn up on the basis of the unlawful decision. The CFI found that the obligation of the EIB under Article 233 ECT consisted not only in replacing the annulled salary statements for January 1999, but the Bank was also obliged 'to take into account the unlawfulness of the applicants' salary statements for the months following January 1999 in so far as the same unlawful decision was applied to them'.[1081]

The institution is also under an obligation to avoid the illegalities found in the act declared void. This is in particular relevant when the institution chooses to replace the annulled act with a new act. In this case the institution is required 'to ensure that any act intended to replace the annulled act is not affected by the same irregularities as those identified in the judgment annulling the original act'.[1082] Where the illegalities are of a procedural nature, the institution does not have to start the procedure replacing the act declared void from the beginning, but can recommence it at the time before the illegality occurred.[1083] In *Industrie des Poudres Sphériques*[1084] the Court found that the earlier annulment of an anti-dumping Regulation adopted by the Council occurred in the course of the investigation and therefore left the initiation of the anti-dumping proceeding unaffected.[1085] In this case the Commission was entitled to continue the proceeding and could choose a different reference period from the one selected in the annulled decision.[1086] And in *LVM v Commission*[1087] the Court held that the Commission had not infringed its obligation under Article 233 ECT when the Commission adopted a new decision which simply confirmed its initial decision to penalise certain infringements of Article 81 ECT which had been annulled earlier on the sole ground that the Commission had failed to authenticate its initial decision contrary to Article 12(1) of its Rules of Procedure.[1088] The Commission was also not obliged to conduct a new hearing, as 'the questions of law which may arise in

---

1081 Ibid., para. 109.

1082 Case C-41/00 P *Interporc v Commission* [2003] ECR I-2125, para. 30. See also Joined Cases C-238/99 P *LVM and Others v Commission* [2002] ECR I-8375, para. 48; Joined Cases C-199/01 P and C-200/01 P *IPK-München v Commission* [2004] ECR I-4627, para. 83.

1083 Case C-458/98 P *Industrie des Poudres Sphériques v Council* [2000] ECR I-8147, para. 82.

1084 Case C-458/98 P *Industrie des Poudres Sphériques v Council* [2000] ECR I-8147.

1085 Ibid., paras. 83 and 84.

1086 Ibid., para. 96.

1087 Joined Cases C-238/99 P etc. *LVM and Others v Commission* [2002] ECR I-8375.

1088 Ibid., para. 451. For the illegality of the initial decision, see the earlier ruling of the Court in Case C-137/92 P *Commission v BASF and Others* [1994] ECR I-2555, at para. 77.

the context of the application of Article 176 [now Article 233] of the Treaty, such as those relating to the passage of time, the possibility of resuming proceedings, the access to the file required on resumption of the proceedings, the intervention of the Hearing Officer and the Advisory Committee and the possible implications of Article 20 of Regulation No 17, do not render a new hearing necessary since they do not alter the substance of the objections, being at most amenable to subsequent judicial review'.[1089]

Where the Court has annulled an act on substantive grounds, the institution is entitled, when adopting a new act replacing the illegal act, to substitute the old (illegal) grounds for its decision with new ones. In *Interporc*[1090] the Court found that after the Commission's decision refusing the applicant access to certain information on public interest grounds had been annulled, the 'Secretary-General was entitled to undertake a full review of the applications for access and, therefore, could rely, in the contested decisions, on grounds other than those on which he based the [annulled] decision of 29 May 1996, notably the authorship rule'.[1091] The illegality of a measure can also result from the fact that the act which constituted its legal basis was found to be unlawful. In *Hirsch*,[1092] the CFI annulled the refusal by the ECB to grant the applicants their respective education allowances on the ground that the legal basis for those decisions, Article 19 of the Conditions of Employment, was unlawful. Unusually, the CFI made it clear that Article 233 required the institution to modify the scheme of education allowances under Article 19 of the Conditions of Employment to accord with the principle of equality. In addition, the institution had to give effect to this judgment 'by reviewing, under the scheme as so modified, the applicant's requests for the grant of an education allowance in respect of their children'.[1093] The ECB was still left with some discretion as to how it wanted to reform the scheme as long as it complied with the principle of equality. However, as *Commission v Giannini*[1094] shows, the institution must act in good faith. In this case the CFI had annulled in its judgment of 19 March 1997[1095] a Commission Decision appointing Mr X as Head of Unit even though he had, in contrast to the applicant, no experience in the textiles or in the footwear sector, one of the requirements set out in

---

1089 Ibid., para. 93.

1090 Case C-41/00 P *Interporc v Commission* [2003] ECR I-2125.

1091 Ibid., para. 31 upholding the CFI's ruling in Case T-92/98 *Interporc v Commission* [1999] ECR II-3521, at para. 56.

1092 Joined Cases T-94/01, T-152/01 and T-286/01 *Hirsch and Others v European Central Bank* [2003] ECR II-27.

1093 Ibid., para. 73.

1094 Case C-153/99 P *Commission v Giannini* [2000] ECR I-2891.

1095 Case T-21/96 *Giannini v Commission* [1997] ECR II-211.

the vacancy notice. In response to the ruling the Commission replaced the earlier vacancy notice with a new one, which no longer required experience in the sector concerned, but gave instead preference to candidates with experience in international negotiations and in the management of a unit. Following the notice the Commission re-appointed Mr X, a decision which was duly annulled by the CFI.[1096] On appeal the Court admitted that 'it is for the Commission, after considering the interests of the service with regard to each post to be filled, to adopt the appropriate measures, which may include initiating a fresh recruitment procedure based on a vacancy notice which has, if necessary, been amended'.[1097] The Court upheld, however, the ruling of the CFI, which considered the measures taken by the Commission contrary to Article 233 and an abuse of powers based on 'the evidence of a number of facts [. . .] which it considered to be objective, relevant and consistent in showing that the measures had been adopted in order to achieve a purpose other than that of complying in good faith with the judgment of 19 March 1997'.[1098]

The requirement to avoid the illegalities found in the act declared void is not only relevant where the institution intends to replace the annulled act, but also concerns the adoption of future acts. In *AKZO*[1099] the Court pointed out that the annulment of a Commission Decision to forward certain documents of a confidential nature to a company, ECS, which brought a complaint against the applicant would have had the consequence of 'preventing a repetition by the Commission of the practice complained of'.[1100] Interestingly, the Court seems to suggest that also the complainant would be bound by the annulment in that it would render 'unlawful the use by ECS of any documents improperly communicated to it'.[1101]

9. REFORM

The system of judicial review was not central to the constitutional reform project. All the same the Convention on the Future of Europe could not

---

[1096] Joined Cases T-282/97 and T-57/98 *Giannini v Commission* [1999] ECR II-151.

[1097] Case C-153/99 P *Commission v Giannini* [2000] ECR I-2891, para. 14.

[1098] Ibid., para. 15. The appraisal of facts cannot be reviewed by the Court on appeal, see ibid., para. 16.

[1099] Case 53/85 *AKZO v Commission* [1996] ECR 1965.

[1100] Ibid., para. 21. See also Case 207/86 *Apesco v Commission* [1988] ECR 21, para. 16; Case T-46/92 *Scottish Football Association v Commission* [1994] ECR II-1039, para. 14; Case T-509/93 *Glencore Grain v Commission* [2000] ECR II-3697, para. 31; Case T-256/97 *BEUC v Commission* [1999] ECR II-169, para. 18.

[1101] Ibid., para. 21.

ignore the issue of judicial review entirely, in particular the Court's position in *UPA* that any reform of Article 230(4) had to be undertaken by the appropriate political forum. The Convention set up, rather belatedly, a Discussion Circle on the Court of Justice to deal with matters related to the Court, including those on judicial review. With the Discussion Circle divided over the issue of reform in Article 230(4),[1102] only a modest liberalisation of the standing for private parties was agreed on in Article III-365(4) of the Constitutional Treaty.[1103] On the other hand, the collapse of the pillar structure in the Constitutional Treaty brought about an extension of the jurisdiction of the Court. While measures under the CFSP remained immune from challenge, the limitations on judicial review of acts which previously fell within the third pillar were lifted. The Lisbon Treaty has incorporated many of the amendments relating to judicial review of the now abandoned Constitutional Treaty. This section will assess the effects those amendments would have on the action for annulment by discussing the relevant provisions in the Lisbon Treaty.

Reviewable Acts

Article 263(1) TFEU, which contains the action for annulment, does not alter the notion of reviewable act. At the same time, the reforms undertaken in the Lisbon Treaty widen the scope of acts which can be reviewed under Article 263(1) TFEU. First, the collapse of the pillar structure in the Lisbon Treaty brings within the ambit of that provision also acts adopted in the Area of Freedom, Security and Justice,[1104] which contains the provisions which are currently part of the third pillar of the EU Treaty.[1105] On the other hand, the Lisbon Treaty still only grants the Court[1106] limited jurisdiction to review Union acts adopted under the CFSP. While the Court's

---

[1102] On the various proposals advanced within the group, see Final Report of the Discussion Circle on the Court of Justice under 'on question (d) of the framework' (CONV 636/03).

[1103] For a discussion of Article III-365(4) Constitutional Treaty, see J. Usher, supra note 2; C. Koch, supra note 2; P. Craig (2006), supra note 2, pp. 344–347.

[1104] Title V of Part Three of the TFEU. See, however, Title VII of the Protocol of Transitional Provisions. For a transitional period of five years the powers of the Court of Justice remain those provided under the existing Title VI of the TEU in relation to acts of the Union adopted in the field of police co-operation and judicial co-operation in criminal matters which have been adopted before the Treaty of Lisbon (see Article 10(1) of the Protocol). The limitation does not apply to amendments of such acts (see Article 10(2) of the Protocol). Special provisions apply to the UK (see Article 10(4) and (5) of the Protocol).

[1105] The limitation of the Court's jurisdiction in Article 276 TFEU concerns only the review of national police or national security measures.

[1106] According to Article 19(1) TEU (Lisbon) the Court of Justice of the European Union consists of the Court of Justice, the General Court and specialised courts.

jurisdiction in relation to provisions of the CFSP and acts adopted on the basis of those provisions is generally excluded,[1107] Article 275 TFEU grants the Court jurisdiction in actions brought under Article 263(4) TFEU to review 'the legality of decisions providing for restrictive measures against natural or legal persons adopted by the Council on the basis of Chapter 2 of Title V of the Treaty on European Union.' Secondly, Article 263(1) TFEU includes also acts of the European Council amongst the measures which can be reviewed by the Court. This is all the more important as the Lisbon Treaty considerably increases the decision-making powers of the European Council. Thirdly, the amended version of Article 263(1) TFEU provides the Court with jurisdiction to review the legality of acts of 'bodies, offices or agencies of the Union intended to produce legal effects vis-à-vis third parties'. However, Article 263(5) TFEU specifies that the acts which set up agencies and other Union bodies may lay down specific conditions and arrangements in relation to actions brought by private parties against acts of such bodies 'intended to produce legal effects in relation to them'.

The Lisbon Treaty also makes an attempt to reinforce the principle of subsidiarity by granting national parliaments scrutiny rights in the Protocol on the Application of the Principles of Subsidiarity and Proportionality. Article 8 of the Protocol also provides for a mechanism of judicial review by granting the Court jurisdiction in actions against a legislative act for infringement of the principle of subsidiarity. In accordance with Article 8(1) of the Protocol such actions can be brought by Member States, or notified by them in accordance with their legal order on behalf of their national Parliament or a chamber thereof. However, the action under Article 8(1) of the Protocol must be lodged in accordance with the rules laid down in Article 263 TFEU. Subject to a similar proviso, the Committee of the Regions is also entitled to bring such an action under Article 8(2) of the Protocol.

Locus Standi

The TFEU also makes some changes to the provisions dealing with *locus standi* under Article 263 TFEU. First, Article 263(3) TFEU enhances the status of the Committee of the Regions to that of a semi-privileged applicant. It is, however, not clear why the Economic and Social Committee has been excluded from this position.

[1107] See Article 275(1) TFEU and also Article 24(1)(2) TEU (Lisbon). According to Article 275(2) TFEU the Court can, however, monitor compliance with Article 40 TEU (Lisbon), which stipulates that the implementation of the CFSP shall not affect procedures and competences granted to the institutions in other areas.

Second, the position of non-privileged applicants under Article 263(4) TFEU is liberalised in accordance with the formula found in Article III-365(4) of the Constitutional Treaty.[1108] Article 263(4) TFEU reads:

> Any natural or legal person may, under the conditions laid down in the first and second paragraphs, institute proceedings against an act addressed to that person or which is of direct and individual concern to them, and against a regulatory act which is of direct concern to them and does not entail implementing measures.

According to this provision private parties can, as is currently the case, challenge acts addressed to them without any further standing requirements. An annulment action can be brought against other acts[1109] only under the restrictive conditions of direct and individual concern.[1110] An exception is, however, made for challenges against regulatory acts which do not entail implementing measures; in this case the requirement of individual concern is dispensed with and an applicant needs to show only direct concern.

The rationale for the relaxation of the standing requirements for challenges against regulatory acts which do not require implementing measures seems to lie in providing private parties with effective judicial protection in case indirect means of review are not available.[1111] Where an act, as in the case of Directives, requires implementing measures at national level, the applicant can, even though a direct challenge will generally founder on the requirement of direct concern, raise the invalidity

---

[1108] For a detailed discussion of this provision, see C. Koch, supra note 2.

[1109] It should be noted that in contrast to the text of Article 230(4) EC, Article 263(4) TFEU allows actions for annulment being brought not only against decisions in substance, but against any reviewable act thereby following the approach of the Community Courts.

[1110] While there can be little doubt that the interpretation of direct concern in Article 263(4) TFEU will follow the established approach under Article 230(4), some reflection on the continued relevance of the restrictive *Plaumann* formula might be appropriate. The very existence of a more relaxed approach against regulatory acts which do not entail implementing measures, which will be discussed in more detail infra, suggests that the drafters of Article 263(4) TFEU assumed the continuance of the restrictive approach to individual concern. On the other hand, the fact that the text Article of 263(4) TFEU no longer limits challenges to decisions in substance seems finally to break the link between the nature of the act and individual concern, which has already been weakened in the case law. In other words Article 263(4) TFEU removes the rationale of *Plaumann* as functional equivalent to a decision in substance and thereby opens the way to a more liberal interpretation of individual concern under Article 263(4) TFEU.

[1111] See also C. Koch, supra note 2, p. 519. See, however, Article Article 19(1)(2) TEU (Lisbon) which obliges Member States to provide 'remedies sufficient to ensure legal protection in the fields covered by Union law.'

of the act when challenging the implementing measures. On the other hand, if the act does not entail any implementing measures, as in the case of Regulations, private parties will generally find it hard to satisfy the requirement of individual concern, but at the same time might find it difficult to access national courts to raise the invalidity of the act. In this case direct access is granted to the Court provided the act is of direct concern to the applicant.

It is, however, not entirely clear how the term 'regulatory act' is to be interpreted.[1112] There does not seem to be any justification to limit the concept of regulatory acts to regulations, but to apply it to any act of general application irrespective of its form. On the other hand, the view that regulatory acts should include any legal act of general application[1113] is difficult to reconcile with the carefully crafted distinction between legislative and non-legislative acts. Article 289(3) TFEU introduces the category of legislative acts, which are defined as legal acts adopted by legislative procedure, which can either be the ordinary legislative procedure,[1114] laid down in Article 294 TFEU, or the special legislative procedure.[1115] Yet, the Lisbon Treaty, in contrast to the Constitutional Treaty, which provided a specific nomenclature for legislative acts, maintains the types of legal instruments currently in use. Regulations can therefore be adopted as legislative acts, but also as delegated acts under Article 290(3) TFEU or implementing acts under Article 291(4) TFEU. It is therefore decisive to know whether the concept of regulatory act in Article 263(4) TFEU is primarily concerned with the general application of the act or intends to distinguish regulatory acts from legislative acts. The term *regulatory act* in the English language version, or *actes réglementaires* in the French language version, or *Rechtsakte mit Verordnungscharakter* in the German language version seems to support the latter view, as in the national legal orders such terms are exclusively used to refer to non-legislative acts. It would therefore be a contradiction in terms to apply the concept of regulatory acts also to legislative acts. This interpretation is also supported by the genesis of Article III-365(4) of the Constitutional Treaty, which is identical to Article 263(4) TFEU.[1116] It is doubtful that the drafters of the Lisbon Treaty by maintaining the current nomenclature for legal

1112 For a detailed analysis, see ibid., pp. 520–521.

1113 So A. von Bogdandy and J. Bast, '*La loi européenne*: Promise and Pretence', in D. Curtin, A.E. Kellermann and S. Blockmans (eds.), *The EU Constitution: the best Way Forward?* (T.M.C. Asser Press, The Hague, 2006), pp. 171–181.

1114 Article 289(1) TFEU.

1115 Article 289(2) TFEU.

1116 See C. Koch, supra note 2, p. 520.

instruments wanted to change the meaning of regulatory act in Article 263(4) TFEU.[1117]

This interpretation leads undoubtedly to a reduction in judicial protection against legislative acts of general application. However, the obligation on Member States under Article 19(1)(2) TEU (Lisbon) to 'provide remedies sufficient to ensure legal protection in the fields covered by Union law' would provide private parties with access to national courts, in which they can raise the invalidity of the legislative act in issue.[1118] Moreover, it should be noted that also in the legal systems of the Member States direct challenges to legislative acts[1119] are the exception and even indirect means of review are not available in all Member States. All the same, a limitation of judicial protection can only be justified in relation to legislative acts adopted in the ordinary legislative procedure, as only those acts are functionally equivalent to national legislation.[1120] On the other hand, acts of general application adopted in the special legislative procedure in which either the Council or the European Parliament are merely consulted cannot occupy such a privileged position, as such acts are in substance and procedure indistinguishable from non-legislative acts of general application. Such acts should be subsumed within the notion of regulatory act under Article 263(4) TFEU.[1121]

Effects of Illegality

By taking account of the Court's case-law[1122] the wording of Article 264(2) TFEU makes it clear that the Court may limit the effects of the annulment of an act not only in case of a regulation, but of any other act which it has declared void.

The absence of paragraph 3 of Article 233 EC in Article 266 TFEU takes account of the fact that the Lisbon Treaty has elevated the ECB amongst the Union's institutions[1123] and as such the ECB whose act has been declared void is subject to the obligation under Article 266 TFEU.

1117 The explanation that the nomenclature of European Laws and European Framework Laws was abandoned due to their constitutional significance seems more plausible.

1118 On the validity review under Article 234, see Chapter 4.

1119 Legislative acts are here understood as acts adopted in the legislative procedure provided for in the Constitution or by constitutional principle in the Member States.

1120 See A. Türk, supra note 283, p. 228.

1121 So already for Article III-365(4) Constitutional Treaty, A. Türk, 'The Concept of the "Legislative" Act in the Constitutional Treaty' (2005) *German Law Journal* 1555–1570, at p. 1569.

1122 See supra, section 8.

1123 See Article 13(1) TEU (Lisbon).

Article 269 TFEU

Article 269 TFEU has been inserted by the Lisbon Treaty to allow the Court to review the legality of an act adopted by the European Council or the Council under Article 7 TEU (Lisbon). However, the Court's jurisdiction is considerably circumscribed. The Court can only review such an act at the request of the Member concerned by the determination of the European Council or of the Council and only in respect of the procedural stipulations contained in Article 7 TEU (Lisbon). The Court can therefore not assess the act on substantive grounds.

2 Failure to act

The action for failure to act under Article 232 EC contains many similarities to Article 230 EC.[1] This was recognised by the Court in *Chevalley*, where it held that Articles 230 and 232 'merely prescribe one and the same method of recourse'.[2] The applicant can bring proceedings under Article 232, where the institution instead of adopting an act fails to adopt such an act. This unity principle has led the Court to apply principles that have been developed under Article 230 to proceedings under Article 232. In line with Article 230, the Community Courts have emphasised that reviewable omissions, at least in Article 232(3), can only be those which produce legal effects. Similarly, the standing of non-privileged applicants under Article 232(3) has been brought in line with that under Article 230(4). Both proceedings display, however, differences as well. The most obvious difference between Article 230 and Article 232 is that the latter provides for a special procedure, whereby the applicant has to call upon the institution to take action. Only where the institution fails to comply with that request within two months is the applicant allowed to bring proceedings before the Court within another two months. Another difference is that Article 232 limits the grounds of review to the infringement of the EC Treaty. The similarities and differences between Articles 230 and 232 will be further explored in this chapter.

The relationship between Articles 230 and 232 can be seen in cases where the applicant asks an EC institution to repeal a previous act. The issue is, whether the applicant can only bring an action under Article 230 to have the act annulled or whether it could also bring an action under Article 232, where its request to have the act repealed has not been complied with. The Court took the position in *Eridania*[3] that an action under Article 232 would in this situation be inadmissible. In *Eridania*, the applicant brought an action under Article 230 against Commission decisions granting aid to its competitors. The Court considered the action as inadmissible, on the ground that the applicant was not individually and directly concerned by

---

1 See generally on Article 232, T.C. Hartley, *The Foundations of European Community Law* (OUP, 6th edn., 2007), chapter 13; P. Craig and G. DeBúrca, *EU Law – Text, Cases and Materials* (OUP, 4th edn., 2008), pp. 530–533.

2 Case 15/70 *Chevalley v Commission* [1970] ECR 975 at para. 6.

3 Joined Cases 10 and 18/68 *Eridania v Commission* [1969] ECR 459.

the decisions. The Court also rejected the alternative claim under Article 232 by holding that:

> to admit, as the applicants wish to do, that the parties concerned could ask the institution from which the measure came to revoke it and, in the event of the Commission's failing to act, refer such failure to the Court as an illegal omission to deal with the matter would amount to providing them with a method of recourse parallel to that of Article 173 [now Article 230], which would not be subject to the conditions laid down by the Treaty.[4]

With the entry into force of the Lisbon Treaty, Article 265 TFEU would replace Article 232 EC, but would bring about few changes.[5] The interpretation of Article 232 EC, which forms the focus of this chapter, would therefore be of continued relevance under the new regime. After presenting the parties to the proceedings under Article 232 in section 1, this chapter will discuss which failures to act can be reviewed in section 2. The special procedure under Article 232(2) will be dealt with in section 3 and standing to bring proceedings under Article 232 will be considered in section 4. Section 5 examines the grounds of review and section 6 sets out the form and effects of a judgment declaring a failure to act.

1. PARTIES TO THE PROCEEDINGS

Similar to Article 230, Article 232(1) also contains a list of privileged applicants which can bring an action for failure to act. These are the Member States and the EC institutions. In the *Transport* case, the Court rejected the argument raised by the Council that the European Parliament (EP) should not be included amongst the privileged applicants, by holding that Article 232(1) 'gives the same right of action to all the Community institutions. It is not possible to restrict the exercise of that right by one of them without adversely affecting its status as an institution under the Treaty, in particular Article 4(1) [now 7(1)]'.[6] The reference to what is now Article 7(1) makes it also likely that the Court of Auditors has to be considered as privileged applicant under Article 232(1). With the insertion of Article 232(4), the Maastricht Treaty has added the ECB as semi-privileged applicant.[7]

---

[4] Joined Cases 10 and 18/68 *Eridania v Commission* [1969] ECR 459, para 17.

[5] These changes will be discussed where relevant.

[6] See Case 13/83 *Parliament v Council* [1985] ECR 1513, para. 17.

[7] The Lisbon Treaty elevates the European Central Bank to the status of institution of the Union, which allows the European Central Bank to bring an action as privileged applicant under Article 265(1) TFEU. Consequently, what is now paragraph four of Article 232 has been deleted.

Article 232(3) also allows a natural or legal person to bring an action for failure to act. These applicants are, however, to be considered as non-privileged applicants, as they can bring such an action only where the defendant failed 'to address to that person any act other than a recommendation or an opinion'. The question of *locus standi* for non-privileged applicants will be discussed in more detail in section 4 below.

In accordance with Article 232(1), an action for failure to act can be brought against the European Parliament, the Council or the Commission.[8] The European Ombudsman is however not amongst the parties against whom an action can be brought under Article 232.[9]

2. REVIEWABLE FAILURES TO ACT

As discussed above,[10] the Court has defined reviewable acts under Article 230 as 'all measures adopted by the institutions, whatever their nature or form, which are intended to have legal effects'.[11] The unity principle would suggest that this definition should also be applied for Article 232 actions. In *Les Verts* the Court pointed out that 'the general scheme of the Treaty is to make a direct action available against "all measures adopted by the institutions . . . which are intended to have legal effects"'.[12] AG Mischo in the *Draft Budget* case[13] emphasised that this statement was not only applicable to actions for annulment, in which the legality of an act is under review, but also to those for failure to act, in which the 'legality of the non-adoption of such measures'[14] is in issue. Consequently, he argued that a reviewable omission under Article 232 resulted from the 'non-adoption . . . of an act or a measure, of whatever nature, form or description, which is capable of producing legal effects *vis-à-vis* third parties'.[15] Similarly, by referring to the close relationship between actions under Article 230 and

[8] The Lisbon Treaty adds in Article 265(1) TFEU the European Council and the European Central Bank as institutions against whom an action can be brought. In addition, bodies, offices and agencies of the Union will also be included as defendants in Article 265(1) TFEU.

[9] Case T-103/99 *ACSV v European Ombudsman and European Parliament* [2000] ECR II-4165, at para. 46. Under Article 265(1) TFEU the Ombudsman might be considered as a body or office of the Union and hence could theoretically become a defendant.

[10] See Chapter 1, pp. 12–40.

[11] Case 22/70 *Commission v Council* [1971] ECR 263 at para. 42.

[12] Case 294/83 *Les Verts v European Parliament* [1986] ECR 1339, para. 24.

[13] Case 377/87 *Parliament v Council* [1988] ECR 4017.

[14] Ibid., Opinion of AG Mischo, para. 28.

[15] Ibid., Opinion of AG Mischo, para. 30.

those under Article 232, AG Darmon in *Liberal Democrats*[16] considered the criterion of legal effects as decisive and argued that 'any omission by a Community institution to adopt a measure having legal effects, irrespective of its nature, constitutes a failure to act within the meaning of Article 175 [now Article 232]'.[17]

This interpretation of Article 232 enjoys the textual support of Article 232(3), which, like Article 230(1), excludes recommendations and opinions from the list of acts the non-adoption of which is reviewable. On the other hand, Article 232(1) refers to a failure 'to act', without the exclusion of recommendations and opinions. The difference in wording in Article 232(1) could indeed be taken to mean that this provision does not limit reviewable omissions to instances where the institution failed to adopt an act having legal effects.[18] The Court seemed to have at some stage supported the wider interpretation, when it held in the *Comitology* case[19] that 'the action for failure to act enables the European Parliament to induce the adoption of measures which cannot in all cases be the subject of an action for annulment'.[20] Similarly, the CFI in *Korkmaz*[21] understood the *Comitology* ruling as establishing a dichotomy between the wider interpretation in Article 232(1) of a failure to act and its narrower definition in Article 232(3). The CFI found that Article 232(3) 'only allows a natural or legal person to seek a finding that an institution has wrongly failed to address to him an act intended to produce binding legal effects capable of affecting his interests by bringing about a distinct change in his legal position'.[22]

It is, however, doubtful whether the Court in *Comitology* wanted to abandon the criterion of legal effects. Hartley[23] has argued that the reason why the Court opted for the wider interpretation should be understood in the context of the judgment, which was to deny standing to the European Parliament under Article 230. The more generous approach to Article 232 was therefore designed to 'sweeten the pill'.[24] It did not seem to be the Court's intention to promote an interpretation of Article 232(1) which

---

16 Case C-41/92 *Liberal Democrats v Parliament* [1993] ECR I-3153.

17 Ibid., Opinion of AG Darmon, para 29.

18 See T.C. Hartley, supra note 1, p. 375.

19 Case 302/87 *European Parliament v Council* [1988] ECR 5615.

20 Ibid., para. 16.

21 Case T-2/04 *Korkmaz and Others v Commission* [2006] ECR II-32.

22 Ibid., para. 63. See also Case 15/70 *Chevalley v Commission* [1970] ECR 975, para. 11; Joined Cases 83 and 84/84 *N.M. v Commission and Council* [1984] ECR 3571, para. 10; Case T-167/95 *Kuchlenz-Winter v Council* [1996] ECR II-1607, para. 20; Case T-103/99 *ACSV v Ombudsman and Parliament* [2000] ECR II-4165, para. 50.

23 T.C. Hartley, supra note 1, p. 376.

24 Ibid., p. 376.

would allow privileged applicants to bring an action for failure to adopt an act even though the non-adoption of the act did not produce any legal effects for these applicants. As AG Darmon pointed out in *Liberal Democrats* such an interpretation would be incompatible with 'the structure of the Community judicial system'[25] and also 'the coherence of legal remedies'.[26] The former raises the question as to why measures which are not reviewable under Article 230 should be reviewable under Article 232.[27] The latter highlights the problem that an action for failure to adopt a non-binding act could be countered by a refusal on the part of the institution to adopt such an act, a refusal which would not be reviewable under Article 230.[28] Finally, it is difficult to see how an institution can upset the institutional balance, which guides the Court's interpretation of the Treaty's system of judicial remedies, where its failure to act does not produce any binding legal effects.

The requirement of legal effects as a precondition for the admissibility of an action under Article 232 excludes the possibility of bringing an action under this provision where the individual claims that the Commission failed to adopt an opinion or recommendation. In *Chevalley v Commission*,[29] the Court held that the action under Article 232 was inadmissible, as the applicant requested the Commission to adopt an opinion within the meaning of Article 249. Similarly, in *ACSV v European Ombudsman and European Parliament*,[30] the CFI rejected an action under Article 232 for a declaration that the Ombudsman and the European Parliament failed to make a finding of maladministration on the part of the Commission. The CFI found that a report finding a case of maladministration submitted by the Ombudsman to the European Parliament could not be classified as having legally binding effects.[31]

On the other hand, in *Schlüsselverlag v Commission*,[32] the Court held that the Commission is required at the request of third-party undertakings to decide whether or not a concentration which has not been notified to it falls within the scope of the merger regulation.[33] Where the Commission

---

[25] Opinion of AG Darmon in Case C-41/92 *Liberal Democrats v Parliament* [1993] ECR I-3153 at para. 62.

[26] Ibid., para. 62.

[27] See A. Barav, 'Considerations sur la spécificité du recours en carence' (1975) *RTDE* 53, p. 59.

[28] See M. and D. Waelbroek, *Encyclopédie Dalloz*, 'Failure to act', No 26 and No. 27.

[29] Case 15/70 *Chevalley v Commission* [1970] ECR 975.

[30] Case T-103/99 *ACSV v European Ombudsman and European Parliament* [2000] ECR II-4165.

[31] Ibid., paras. 51 and 52.

[32] Case C-170/02 P *Schlüsselverlag and others v Commission* [2003] ECR I-9889.

[33] Ibid., at para. 28.

fails to provide a reasoned response to a complaint that it had failed to exercise its competence, an action can be brought under Article 232.[34] The Community Courts have adopted a similar position in respect of complaints against state aid. As discussed above, an undertaking can challenge a decision by the Commission under Article 88(3) ECT to secure its procedural rights as party concerned. In *Air One*[35] the CFI found that such an undertaking is also entitled 'to seek from the Court of First Instance a declaration as to any failure to act on the part of the Commission, given that the possibility remains open to the Commission to define its position on the complaint without initiating the formal investigation procedure'.[36] Such a definition of position would constitute a reviewable act and could be reviewed under Article 230.

While the requirement of legal effect as criterion for a reviewable omission under Article 232 has been firmly established, it has, however, to be examined carefully what constitutes legal effects for the purpose of bringing an action under Article 232. While it is clear that a failure to adopt an act which produces binding legal effects can constitute a reviewable omission under Article 232, it is also clear that in some cases the non-adoption of an act can produce legal effects, even though the act itself does not produce such effects. It is therefore submitted that the Court in the *Comitology* case merely highlighted a structural difference in the assessment of legal effects under both provisions, which can occur in some cases. This difference can be seen in the case of preparatory acts. As will be seen from the discussion below, while preparatory acts cannot be challenged under Article 230 their non-adoption can produce legal effects which can be invoked in an action under Article 232.

In the *Draft Budget* case[37] the EP had brought an action against the Council for failure to adopt the draft budget for 1988, which was the necessary precondition for the President of the EP to adopt the final budget. The judgment of the Court does not explicitly tackle the question as to the admissibility of the action.[38] The Court merely decided that the action was devoid of purpose, as the Council had adopted the requested draft after the action had been brought. A clearer explanation as to the admissibility of the action can be gleaned from the Opinion of AG Mischo. He argued that a failure to act 'may be constituted by the non-adoption by

34 Ibid., para. 29.

35 Case T-395/04 *Air One v Commission* [2006] ECR II-1343.

36 Ibid., para. 41.

37 Case 377/87 *Parliament v Council* [1988] ECR 4017.

38 The only implicit indication that the Court thought the action to be admissible can be found in the decision on costs, which had to be borne by the Council, see ibid., para. 12.

the Council or by the Commission of an act or a measure, of whatever nature, form or description, which is capable of producing legal effects *vis-à-vis* third parties'.[39] He came to the conclusion that the non-adoption of the draft budget produced legal effects for the European Parliament, as the European Parliament can exercise its budgetary powers only once the Council has adopted the draft budget.[40] AG Mischo suggested that '[j]ust as the Court must be able to verify whether an institution is encroaching upon the powers of the other institutions or of the Member States by adopting certain measures, it should also be empowered to do so where an institution's failure to act is liable to bring about the same result and hinder the exercise by the other institutions or the Member States of their respective powers'.[41] Consequently, it was not the legal effects of the draft budget, which as a preparatory act did not produce legal effects, but the legal effects of the non-adoption of the draft budget which were relevant for the purposes of Article 232 in the *Draft Budget* case.

The same issue arose in *Liberal Democrats v European Parliament.*[42] In this case the Liberal Democrats, a political party from the UK, brought an action under Article 232 against the EP for failure to adopt proposals for elections to the EP. The case concerned Article 190(3) ECT, which provides that the EP shall draw up proposals for elections to the EP by direct universal suffrage. On the basis of these proposals the Council shall then lay down the appropriate provisions, which it then recommends to the Member States for adoption. The proposals adopted by the EP are therefore preparatory measures. Without considering the admissibility of the action,[43] and therefore whether the omission was reviewable, the Court ruled that the action was devoid of purpose after the EP adopted the requested proposals. In his comprehensive opinion AG Darmon argued that 'any omission by a Community institution to adopt a measure having legal effects, irrespective of its nature, constitutes a failure to act within the meaning of Article 175 [now 232]'.[44] The AG, however, made it clear that if proceedings under Article 232 could be brought for failure to adopt a measure producing legal effects, 'it must also be possible to bring such proceedings against the institution which, at an earlier stage, fails to adopt a measure, the performance of which is a precondition to the action of the former', as '[s]uch a failure to act itself produces legal

39 Ibid., Opinion of AG Mischo, para. 30.
40 Ibid., para. 32.
41 Ibid., para. 36.
42 Case C-41/92 *Liberal Democrats v Parliament* [1993] ECR I-3153.
43 See ibid., para. 4.
44 Ibid., Opinion of AG Darmon, para. 29.

effects'.[45] He therefore suggested that 'where an institution fails to take a preparatory measure necessary for the adoption by another institution of a definitive measure producing legal effects, that failure itself produces legal effects inasmuch as it prevents the adoption of the definitive measure'.[46] Consequently, the failure of the EP to submit proposals to the Council under Article 190(4) produced legal effects for the Council, as it prevented the Council from adopting measures under that provision.[47] AG Darmon argued that this approach was also applicable under Article 232(3) and that an individual could bring an action under this provision where the non-adoption of an act produced legal effects in respect of an individual, 'even though such measure could not be contested under Article 173 [now 230] of the Treaty, particularly where the measure in question is preparatory in nature'.[48] The non-adoption of a measure has, however, only legal effects in respect of an individual where its legal position has been affected by such failure to act.[49] The failure by the EP to submit proposals to Council under Article 190(3) did not produce such legal effects in respect of the applicants as individuals, as there was no 'direct connecting link between the absence of Liberal Democrat representation in the Parliament and the failure to act'.[50]

The analysis of AG Darmon in *Liberal Democrats v European Parliament* shows that Article 232 can be invoked against the failure to adopt preparatory acts where their non-adoption produces legal effects. His Opinion also shows that far from creating a distinction between Article 232(1) and Article 232(3) the Court's dictum in *Comitology* merely referred to a general difference between Article 230 and Article 232 in so far as in Article 232 'we encounter once again the idea that, although the measure adopted does not create legal effects, its non-adoption may do so'.[51] The requirement of legal effects is therefore a precondition of an action under Article 232(1) and Article 232(3). This is also, it is submitted, the appropriate justification to consider an action by a private party against a failure of the Commission to initiate an action against a Member State under Article 226 as inadmissible.

Preparatory acts, which in themselves do not produce legal effects, but the non-adoption of which adversely affects the interests of others, can appear in various ways. In the legislative process, the Council can

45 Ibid., Opinion of AG Darmon, para. 37.
46 Ibid., Opinion of AG Darmon, para. 63.
47 Ibid., Opinion of AG Darmon, para. 67.
48 Ibid., Opinion of AG Darmon, para. 80.
49 Ibid., Opinion of AG Darmon, para. 82.
50 Ibid., Opinion of AG Darmon, para. 82.
51 Ibid., Opinion of AG Darmon, para. 81.

request a proposal from the Commission under Article 208 ECT. As the Council can only adopt a legal act if the Commission submits the proposal, the failure to submit the proposal would prevent the Council from exercising its legislative powers. Even though the proposal as such could not be subject to proceedings under Article 230, the failure by the Commission to present such a proposal adversely affects the position of the Council and therefore produces legal effects.[52] On the other hand the non-adoption of a Commission proposal does not produce any legal effects for individuals.[53] In *Korkmaz and others v Commission*[54] the CFI rejected an action against the Commission for failure to adopt a proposal to the Council for the suspension of financial aid granted to Turkey under Article 4 of Regulation 390/2001.[55] The CFI argued that such a proposal had legal effects, as it allowed the Council to take appropriate steps, but 'that effect does not appear to be liable to affect the applicants' interests by bringing about a distinct change in their legal position since, until such time as the Council has taken appropriate steps, that situation remains entirely as it was before the Commission made any proposal to it in that connection'.[56] Moreover, the CFI pointed out that the Commission has discretion as to whether to make such a proposal 'excluding the right, for an individual, to require the Commission to take a position in that connection'.[57]

Similarly, the opinion of the European Parliament in the consultation procedure constitutes a necessary prerequisite for the Council to adopt a legal act.[58] It is, however, doubtful whether Article 232 constitutes the adequate remedy, where the non-action can be overridden by the institution dependent on the measure.[59] In *European Parliament v Council*[60] the Court made it clear that an indefinite delay by the EP to provide its opinion was not possible, as the EP had a duty to co-operate, which in this case the EP had failed to observe. The Council was therefore entitled to adopt

---

[52] Opinion of AG Darmon in Case C-41/92 *Liberal Democrats v Parliament* [1993] ECR I-3153 at para 64.

[53] See Case T-184/04 *Sulvida v Commission* [2005] ECR II-85, para. 14. See also Case 90/78 *Granaria v Council and Commission* [1979] ECR 1081, paras. 12 *et seq.*; Case T-167/95 *Kuchlenz-Winter v Council* [1996] ECR II-1607, paras. 20 *et seq.*; Case T-175/96 *Berthu v Commission* [1997] ECR II-811, paras. 18 *et seq.*; Case T-198/99 *Buchbinder and Nöcker v Commission*, order of 1 December 1999 (not published), para. 11.

[54] Case T-2/04 *Korkmaz and others v Commission* [2006] ECR II-32.

[55] [2001] OJ L 58/2.

[56] Case T-2/04 *Korkmaz and others v Commission* [2006] ECR II-32, para. 49.

[57] Ibid., para. 50.

[58] See Case 138/79 *Roquette Frères v Council* [1980] ECR 3333.

[59] Cf. Opinion of AG Darmon in Case C-41/92 *Liberal Democrats v Parliament* [1993] ECR I-3153, paras. 35 and 36.

[60] Case C-65/93 *European Parliament v Council* [1995] ECR I-643.

the act without having received the opinion. A failure to act seems also to be excluded where the EC Treaty sets out the consequences which result from the non-action of an institution in the co-operation and co-decision procedures.[61]

The issue of whether the non-adoption of preparatory acts can give rise to proceedings under Article 232 can also arise in the comitology process. Under Article 202 3rd indent ECT the legislative authority, when conferring the power to implement a legislative act to the Commission, can require the Commission to follow one of the procedures set out in Council Decision 1999/468.[62] Under these procedures the Commission has to present a draft measure to a committee comprised of representatives of the Member States before it can adopt an implementing act. In the management procedure,[63] the Commission has to communicate the measures to the Council where the committee issues a negative opinion. When following the regulatory procedure,[64] the Commission has to submit a proposal to Council where its draft measures do not obtain a qualified majority in favour in the committee. These measures are preliminary steps in the procedure and are therefore not reviewable under Article 230. However, the non-adoption of these measures can produce legal effects. Where the Commission fails to submit draft measures to the committee, legal effects can arise for individuals, as this step is a necessary prerequisite for the adoption of an implementing act.[65] If the Commission fails to communicate its measures in the management procedure the Council is prevented from taking a different decision. Similarly, where the Commission does not submit a proposal to Council in the regulatory procedure, the Council is prevented from acting.

Disputes about the failure to adopt preliminary measures which can give rise to an action under Article 232 also occur in the area of competition law. Article 3(2) of Regulation 17[66] provided that natural or legal persons who claimed a legitimate interest could lodge a complaint with the Commission alleging a violation of Articles 81 and 82. Where the Commission decided not to pursue the investigation further, it would inform the complainant of its intention in accordance with Article 6 of

---

[61] See Article 252(2) second subparagraph and Article 251(2) second subpara (a).

[62] [1999] OJ L 184/23, as amended by Council Decision 2006/512, [2006] OJ L 200/11.

[63] See Article 4 of Council Decision 1999/468, as amended.

[64] See Article 5 of Council Decision 1999/468, as amended.

[65] See Case T-212/99 *Intervet International BV v Commission* [2002] ECR II-1445.

[66] [1962] OJ Sp. Ed., No. 204/82, p. 87. This regulation has now been replaced by Regulation 1/2003, [2003] OJ L1/1. The right to lodge a complaint for natural or legal persons is now contained in Article 7(2) of Regulation 1/2003.

Regulation 99/63.[67] The complainant was thus given the opportunity to respond before the Commission took the final decision to reject the complaint. The 'Article 6 letter' was therefore only a preparatory measure and could accordingly not be challenged under Article 230.[68] Only the final decision to reject the complaint could be challenged under Article 230.[69] Nevertheless, an action could be brought under Article 232, where the Commission failed to send the Article 6 letter, as the complainant was deprived of its right to make its views known and the omission therefore produced legal effects for the complainant.[70] Similarly, the applicant was held to be entitled to bring another action under Article 232, where the Commission failed to adopt a final decision after the applicant had made its views known.[71]

3. PROCEDURE: ARTICLE 232(2)

Article 232(2) provides for a special procedure that has to be completed before the case can be brought before the Court. The applicant has to call first on the institution to act. If within two months of that request, the institution has not defined its position, the applicant can bring the action before the Court within a further period of two months.

Formal Notice

Article 232(2) ECT makes it a prerequisite for the admissibility of the action for failure to act that the institution concerned has first been called upon to act.[72] This condition is considered as an essential procedural requirement 'the effects of which are, first, to cause the two-month period within which the institution is required to define its position to begin to run and,

---

[67] [1963–64] OJ Sp. Ed., p. 47. This regulation is no longer in force. The relevant provision is now contained in Article 7 of Regulation 773/2004, [2004] OJ L123/18.

[68] See Case T-64/89 *Automec v Commission* [1990] ECR II-367, para. 46; Case T-186/94 *Guérin Automobiles v Commission* [1995] ECR II-1753, upheld on appeal in Case C-282/95 P *Guérin Automobiles v Commission* [1997] ECR I-1503, para. 34.

[69] See Case 26/76 *Metro v Commission* [1977] ECR 1875, para. 13; Case 210/81 *Demo-Studio Schmidt v Commission* [1983] ECR 3045, para. 14; Case 298/83 *CICCE v Commission* [1985] ECR 1105, para. 18; Joined Cases 142 and 156/84 *BAT and Reynolds v Commission* [1987] ECR 4487, para. 12; Case T-64/89 *Automec v Commission* [1990] ECR II-367, para. 46; Case C-39/93 P *SFEI v Commission* [1994] ECR I-2681, para. 28; Case C-282/95 P *Guérin Automobiles v Commission* [1997] ECR I-1503, para. 36.

[70] Case T-28/90 *Asia Motor France and others v Commission* [1992] ECR II-2285, para. 29.

[71] Case C-282/95 P *Guérin Automobiles v Commission* [1997] ECR I-1503, para. 38.

[72] Case T-17/96 *TF1 v Commission* [1999] ECR II-1757, para. 41.

secondly, to delimit any action that might be brought should the institution fail to define its position'.[73] The formal notice therefore puts the institution to which it is addressed formally in default and also determines the scope of the subject matter of the action.[74] Where the Court comes to the conclusion that the action is well founded the defendant would then know what to do, in order to comply with its obligation under Article 233.

In *Nuovo Campsider* the Court stated that 'an action for failure to act must be preceded by formal notice calling upon the Commission to act and that the subject-matter of that notice must be set out in such a manner as to make clear what decision the Commission should have taken'.[75] This means that the applicant has to make it clear that the notice is a preliminary step, which will be followed by legal proceedings. The Court also insisted that the applicant has to prescribe in the request with sufficient clarity the action to be taken by the institution.[76] Similarly, the CFI found in *Makhteshim-Agan*[77] that 'the notice must be sufficiently clear and precise to enable the Commission to ascertain in specific terms the content of the decision which it is being asked to adopt and must make clear that its purpose is to compel the Commission to state its position'.[78]

Article 232(2) is therefore not satisfied where the notice only contains requests for telephone and fax numbers of officials and does not indicate that it has been sent in preparation for legal proceedings.[79] Similarly, it is unlikely that a notice will satisfy the requirement under Article 232(2) where the notifying party, even though it makes the purpose of its request sufficiently clear, expresses its readiness to provide further details, as this might indicate that it considers the possibility of further discussions with the Commission to take place.[80]

On the other hand, in *European Parliament v Council*[81] the Court held that the EP had satisfied the requirements in Article 232(2) in that 'after expressly referring to that provision the Parliament clearly stated in the

---

73 Ibid., para. 41.

74 T.C. Hartley, supra note 1, p. 382.

75 Case 25/85 *Nuovo Campsider v Commission* [1986] ECR 1531 at para. 8.

76 Ibid., para. 8.

77 Case T-34/05 R *Makhteshim-Agan and others v Commission* [2005] ECR II-1465.

78 Ibid., para. 57. See also Joined Cases 81/85 and 119/85 *Usinor v Commission* [1986] ECR 1777, para.15; Case T-17/96 *TF1 v Commission* [1999] ECR II-1757; Case C-249/99 P *Pescados Congelados Jogamar v Commission* [1999] ECR I-8333, para. 18.

79 Case C-249/99 P *Pescados Congelados Jogamar v Commission* [1999] ECR I-8333, para. 19.

80 Joined Cases 81/85 and 119/85 *Usinor v Commission* [1986] ECR 1777, para. 16. This case was decided under Article 35 ECSC, but the legal requirement of compelling the institution to act remains the same.

81 Case 13/83 *European Parliament v Council* [1985] ECR 1513.

letter from its President that it was calling upon the Council to act pursuant to Article 175 [now 232] and appended a list of actions which in its opinion ought to be undertaken by the Council to remedy its failure'.[82] Also in *TF1 v Commission*,[83] the CFI considered it sufficient that the applicant made a formal and explicit request to the Commission to act on the submissions set out in its earlier complaint, which contained a reference to an infringement of Article 81, even though the letter containing the formal notice did not.

Once the formal notice has been given, the person requesting action to be taken must not submit new considerations which could influence the assessment by the defendant, as in this case the obligation to act ceases to exist. In *Spain v Commission*[84] the Court found that due to the new submissions made by Spain after having given formal notice, the Commission was not in a position to decide on the Spanish request.

There is no time limit laid down in Article 232(2) for the request to be made. All the same the Court has established the requirement that the applicant has to observe 'a reasonable period'[85] for making the request. In *Netherlands v Commission*[86] the applicant brought an action under Article 35 ECSC[87] 18 months after it had been informed by the Commission that no action would be taken against France as requested by the applicant. The Court first stated that unlike Article 33 ECSC,[88] Article 35 ECSC did not provide for any specific time-period within which an interested party had to call on the Commission to compel it to take action. However, both Articles 33 and 35 ECSC had the common purpose that 'the requirements of legal certainty and of the continuity of Community action underlying the time-limits laid down for bringing proceedings under Article 33 [ECSC] must also be taken into account – having regard to the special difficulties which the silence of the competent authorities may involve for the interested parties – in the exercise of the rights conferred by Article 35 [ECSC]'.[89] The absence of any limitation in Article 35 ECSC would be contradictory to the short time-limit within which an action had to be brought under Article 33

---

82 Ibid., para. 24.

83 Case T-17/96 *TF1 v Commission* [1999] ECR II-1757, para. 42.

84 Case T-209/04 *Spain v Commission* [2005] ECR II-47, para. 43.

85 Case C-170/02P *Schlüsselverlag and Others v Commission* [2003] ECR I-9889, para. 36.

86 Case 59/70 *Netherlands v Commission* [1971] ECR 639.

87 Article 35 ECSC was the equivalent of Article 232 ECT, but showed some differences. If the Commission had not taken any action within two months after having been called upon, the applicant had one month to bring an action before the Court against the implied decision of refusal which was to be inferred from the silence of the Commission. Like Article 232 ECT Article 35 ECSC did not contain a time-limit for formally calling on the Commission to act.

88 Article 33 ECSC was the equivalent of Article 230.

89 Case 59/70 *Netherlands v Commission* [1971] ECR 639, para. 15.

ECSC. Moreover, once the formal request is made, Article 35 ECSC provided for time-limits within which the action must be brought. The Court concluded that it was 'implicit in the system of Articles 33 and 35 [ECSC] that the exercise of the right to raise the matter with the Commission may not be delayed indefinitely'.[90] The Court held that 'if the interested parties are thus bound to observe a reasonable time-limit where the Commission remains silent, this is so a fortiori once it is clear that the Commission has decided to take no action'.[91] The Court therefore considered that a period of 18 months could not be considered as reasonable.[92]

In *Schlüsselverlag and others v Commission*[93] the Court made it clear that the observance of a reasonable time-limit also applied to requests made under Article 232. Four months after the *Oberlandesgericht* Wien had approved a concentration between two newspaper companies, the appellant had lodged a complaint with the Commission. The Court pointed out that the undertakings concerned could bring an action against a Commission decision only within the two-month time-limit laid down in Article 230(5). The Court therefore concluded that 'the requirements of legal certainty and of continuity of Community action which are at the origin of all those provisions would be disregarded if the Commission could, pursuant to the second paragraph of Article 232 EC, be requested to make a determination, outside a reasonable period, on the compatibility with the common market of a concentration which was not notified to it'.[94] The Court held that during the period from the concentration being notified to the *Oberlandesgericht* until the approval by that court, the appellants were entitled to request the Commission to examine whether the transaction had a Community dimension. The Court found that the period of four months which had elapsed since the approval of the concentration by the *Oberlandesgericht* could not be regarded as reasonable. The Court pointed out that such a period equalled that afforded to the Commission to undertake an investigation of a notified transaction.

The imposition of a time-limit raises delicate questions. First, it is doubtful whether the requirement of a time-limit within which the matter has to be raised with the institution concerned is justifiable.[95] The parallelism with the strict time-limit in Article 230 seems to be misplaced, as Article 232 differs from Article 230 in that the latter does not contain

---

[90] Ibid., para. 18.
[91] Ibid., para. 19.
[92] Ibid., para. 22.
[93] Case C-170/02 P *Schlüsselverlag and others v Commission* [2003] ECR I-9889.
[94] Ibid., para. 36.
[95] See Opinion of AG Roemer in Case 59/70 *Netherlands v Commission* [1971] ECR 639, at p. 658.

any preliminary procedure.[96] Otherwise, the time-limits in Article 232 for bringing the action are equally strict as those in Article 230. Legal certainty as argument for a time-limit is at best a double-edged sword. On the one hand, legal certainty seems to refer to the necessity of protecting the interests of third parties in the continued inaction of the institution concerned.[97] It is doubtful whether the inaction of a Community institution can produce a legitimate expectation on the part of third parties. Moreover, a promise not to apply or enforce the law contrary to the applicable rules cannot be the basis of a legitimate expectation.[98] This is even more so for inaction on the part of the institution. In any event, any justified reliance[99] on the conduct of Community institutions can be taken into account when considering the temporal application of a legal act. What is more, unlike judgments on Article 230, which have retroactive effect, a judgment under Article 232 does not require the institution to adopt a retroactive act.[100]

On the other hand, it is not clear from the case-law what constitutes a reasonable period of time. The ruling in *Schlüsselverlag v Commission* seems to suggest that the time-limit depends on the specific legal context of the case.[101] The short time-limits in the merger regulation, which are designed to provide the parties to the concentration with legal certainty, were obviously of importance in this case. However, it seems doubtful whether those time-limits can serve as reasonable guidance. First, the time-limits in the merger regulation apply to the investigation by the Commission. Where the concentration has not been notified to the Commission, those time-limits do not apply. Moreover, parties to a concentration which should have notified their concentration to the Commission, but did not do so, do not enjoy any legal certainty as to the non-application of the EC merger regulation. If there is no time-limit on an *ex officio* investigation by the Commission, why should there be one for third parties to raise the matter

---

96 See also T.C. Hartley, supra note 1, pp. 383–384.

97 See the discussion in T.C. Hartley, supra note 1, p. 384, on the legal expectations in Case 59/70 *Netherlands v Commission* [1971] ECR 639.

98 See Joined Cases 303 and 312/81 *Klöckner v Commission* [1983] ECR 1507, at para. 34; Case 188/82 *Thyssen v Commission* [1983] ECR 3721, para. 11; Case C 162/84 *Vlachou v Court of Auditors* [1986] ECR 459, para. 6.

99 See Opinion of AG Roemer in Case 59/70 *Netherlands v Commission* [1971] ECR 639, at pp. 658–659.

100 See T.C. Hartley, supra note 1, p. 384.

101 See Case T-135/02 *Greencore v Commission*, judgment of 14 December 2005, para. 63, where the CFI held that 'the period of 22 months which passed between the payment of the principal sum without interest on 4 January 2000 and the request addressed to the Commission by registered letter of 1 November 2001 was reasonable and justified in the specific circumstances of the case'.

with the Commission? Moreover, the practical consequence of the ruling is that interested third parties will have to submit precautionary requests to the Commission without having had the time to study the concentration in more detail.

It is equally doubtful when the time-limit starts to run.[102] In *Netherlands v Commission* the Court pointed out that the time-limit applied where the Commission had decided to take no action,[103] but also where it remained silent.[104] In the former case it is clear to determine the beginning of the time-limit. However, the time-limit under Article 230(5) has to be observed, where the refusal to act constitutes a reviewable act. Apart from the problem in attaching legal consequences to silence on the part of an institution, it is not clear from which point in time the silence of an institution triggers the time-limit to run. The time-limit can also be triggered by the action of a third party. In *Schlüsselverlag v Commission* the time-limit started to run with the notification of the transaction in the *Oberlandesgericht*. The Court has made it clear however that the time limit does not start to run, where the institution gives the impression that it will take action.[105]

Definition of Position

After the request has been made the institution has two months within which it has to define its position. The institution defines its position, where it 'positively and unequivocally gives notice of its intention to act or not to act as required'.[106] The institution can therefore certainly define its position by complying with the request. It can, however, also define its position by taking a measure which does not correspond to the one requested and therefore does not satisfy the request.[107] In *Makhteshim-Agan and others v Commission*[108] the Court justified this approach on the ground that 'Article 232 refers to failure to act in the sense of failure to take a decision or to

---

[102] See also T.C. Hartley, supra note 1, pp. 384–385.

[103] In this case the time-limit under Article 230 starts to run, where the refusal to act constitutes a reviewable act. Only in the specific circumstances of Article 88 ECSC did the decision not to take action not constitute such a reviewable act, see T.C. Hartley, supra note 1, p. 383, fn. 42.

[104] See Case 59/70 *Netherlands v Commission* [1971] ECR 639, at para. 19.

[105] See Case C-107/91 *ENU v Commission* [1993] ECR I-599 at para 24.

[106] Opinion of AG Lenz in Case 13/83 *Parliament v Council* [1985] ECR 1513 at p. 1528.

[107] See Joined Cases C-15/91 and C-108/91 *Buckl and others v Commission* [1992] ECR I-6061, para. 15; Case T-276/03 *Le Canne v Commission* [2006] ECR II-10, para. 37.

[108] Case C-258/05 P(R) *Makhteshim-Agan and others v Commission*, judgment of 28 October 2005 (not published).

define a position, and not in the sense of the adoption of a measure different from that desired or considered necessary by the applicant'.[109]

The refusal to comply with the request should therefore constitute a definition of position. The position of the Court is however unclear on this point. In the *Comitology* case,[110] it found that 'a refusal to act, however explicit it may be, can be brought before the Court under Article 175 [now Article 232] since it does not put an end to the failure to act'.[111] On the other hand, in numerous other cases the Community Courts have considered the refusal to comply with a request as a definition of position.[112] Already in *Lütticke*,[113] the Court found that the Commission had defined its position when it rejected the applicant's complaint that Germany was in breach of Article 95 (now Article 90) and that it should commence proceedings against Germany. Similarly, in *Asia Motor France and others v Commission*,[114] the CFI found that the definitive rejection of the applicants' complaint constituted a definition of position. The CFI distinguished this case from the *Comitology* case on the ground that the Commission's definitive rejection of the complaint did not amount to a refusal to act. And in *Campailla v Commission*[115] the Court found that 'it follows from a constant case-law that a decision to reject a complaint constitutes the definition of a position'.[116] A refusal to comply with a request therefore constitutes the definition of a position. A refusal to act can, however, be challenged under Article 230, where the positive act requested from the institution could be challenged under Article 230. The different position of the Court in the *Comitology* case can be explained by the fact that the Parliament at the time did not have the possibility to challenge acts of the other institutions under Article 230. It might well be that where the applicant could not have challenged a measure under Article 230, a

---

109 Ibid., para. 14. See also Joined Cases 166 and 220/86 *Irish Cement Ltd v Commission* [1988] ECR 6473, para 17; Case C-44/00 P *Sodima v Commission* [2000] ECR I-11231, para. 83; Case T-26/01 *Fiocchi Munizioni v Commission* [2003] ECR II-3951, para 82; Case T-3/02 *Schlüsselverlag JS Moser and Others v Commission* [2002] ECR II-1473, at para 27; Case T-66/02 *Institouto N. Avgerinopoulou and others v Commission* [2004] ECR II-855, para. 34; Case T-89/05 *GAEC Salat v Commission* [2005] ECR II-16, para. 22.

110 Case 302/87 *Parliament v Council* [1988] ECR 5615.

111 Ibid., para. 17.

112 See Case T-66/02 *Institouto N. Avgerinopoulou and others v Commission* [2004] ECR II-855, para. 33; Case T-34/05 R *Makhteshim-Agan and others v Commission* [2005] ECR II-1465, para. 70.

113 Case 48/65 *Lütticke v Commission* [1965] ECR 19 at p. 27.

114 Case T-28/90 *Asia Motor France and others v Commission* [1992] ECR II-2285, at para. 37.

115 Case C-211/05 P *Campailla v Commission*, order of 8 December 2005 (not published).

116 Ibid., para. 17. Author's translation.

refusal to act will not be considered as the definition of a position within the meaning of Article 232.[117]

It is also clear from the case law that 'even an act which is not challengeable by an annulment action may constitute a definition of position terminating the failure to act if it is the prerequisite for the next step in a procedure which has, in principle, to culminate in a legal act that itself will be challengeable by an action for annulment'.[118] A Commission letter which initiated the first stage of an examination as to whether grants paid by a Member State were new or existing aid under Community state aid rules therefore constituted a definition of position.[119] Similarly, the formal submission of a draft decision by the Commission to a comitology committee for a decision not to include Endosulfan in Annex I of Directive 91/414[120] was considered to be a definition of position.[121] And in *Pharos v Commission*[122] the CFI found that the Commission's referral to the Council of a proposal for a regulation including somatosalm in Annex II of Regulation 2377/90[123] had to be considered as a definition of position. The Community Courts have been equally clear in their treatment of an 'Article 6' letter, which will be issued by the Commission following a complaint in competition matters.[124] Where the institution fails to take the next step in the procedure, be it another intermediate step or indeed the final decision, a fresh action for failure to act under Article 232 can be brought, since such an action would have a different object.[125]

The case-law of the Community Courts also contains some guidance as to when a measure does not constitute a definition of position. In *Parliament v Council*,[126] the European Parliament had requested the

---

[117] T.C. Hartley, supra note 1, p. 374.

[118] Joined Cases T-297/01 and T-298/01 *SIC v Commission* [2004] ECR II-743, para. 53. See also Case T-186/94 *Guérin Automobiles v Commission* [1995] ECR II-1753, para. 26, upheld on appeal in Case C-282/95 *Guérin Automobiles v Commission* [1997] ECR I-1503, para. 35; Case T-105/96 *Pharos v Commission* [1998] ECR II-285, para. 43; Case T-34/05 R *Makhteshim-Agan and others v Commission* [2005] ECR II-1465, para. 69.

[119] Ibid., para. 42.

[120] [1991] OJ L 230/1.

[121] Case T-34/05 R *Makhteshim-Agan and others v Commission* [2005] ECR II-1465, para. 69; upheld on appeal in C-258/05 P(R) *Makhteshim-Agan and others v Commission*, judgment of 28 October 2005 (not published), para. 15.

[122] Case T-105/96 *Pharos v Commission* [1998] ECR II-285, para. 44.

[123] [1990] OJ L 224/1.

[124] See Case 125/78 *GEMA v Commission* [1979] ECR 3173, para. 21 ; Case T-186/94 *Guérin Automobiles v Commission* [1995] ECR II-1753, para. 32, upheld on appeal in Case C-282/95 P *Guérin Automobiles v Commission* [1997] ECR I-1503, para. 30. For the contrary view, see Opinion of AG Tesauro in Case C-282/95 P *Guérin Automobiles v Commission* [1997] ECR I-1503, at paras. 29 *et seq.*

[125] See Case C-282/95 P *Guérin Automobiles v Commission* [1997] ECR I-1503, para. 38.

[126] Case 13/83 *Parliament v Council* [1985] ECR 1513.

Council to undertake a list of actions in the area of the common transport policy. The Council in its reply merely set out what action it had already taken. The Court found that 'the reply neither denied nor confirmed the alleged failure to act nor gave any indication of the Council's view as to the measures which, according to the Parliament, remained to be taken.'[127] Similarly, a letter by the Commission that the examination of an application is in progress could not constitute a definition of position.[128] And in *Asklepios Kliniken v Commission*[129] the CFI held that the laying down of abstract criteria for the basis of a decision in response to a specific complaint could not be considered as an adoption of a position.

Where the institution has defined its position, within the two-month period, the subject matter of Article 232 ceases to exist and any application brought to the Court under Article 232 would be considered as inadmissible. The Community Courts do, however, also not proceed to a decision where the requested act was adopted after the two-month time limit but before the adoption of the judgment.[130] The Community Courts would then consider the action as being 'devoid of purpose'[131] or that it was 'no longer necessary to give judgment'.[132] Such a finding can however have an impact on the decision on costs.[133]

The Court justified this approach in *European Parliament v Council*[134] with the argument that Article 232 was based on the presumption that,

---

[127] Ibid., para 25.

[128] Case T-212/99 *Intervet International v Commission* [2002] ECR II-1445, at para 61. See also Case T-95/96 *Gestevision Telecinco v Commission* [1998] ECR II-3407, para. 88; Joined Cases T-344/00 and T-345/00 *CEVA and Other v Commission* [2003] ECR II-229, at para. 80.

[129] Case T-167/04 *Asklepios Kliniken v Commission*, judgment of 11 July 2007, at para. 77.

[130] See Joined Cases C-15/91 and C-108/91 *Buckl and Others v Commission* [1992] ECR I-6061 at para. 15, Case 377/87 *Parliament v Council* [1988] ECR 4017 at para. 10 and Joined Cases C-302/99 P and C-308/99P *Commission and France v TF1* [2001] ECR I-5603, at para. 28. See also Case T-212/99 *Intervet International v Commission* [2002] ECR II-1445, at para. 67 and Joined Cases T-344/00 and T-345/00 *CEVA and Other v Commission* [2003] ECR II-229, at para 85; Case T-276/03 *Le Canne v Commission* [2006] ECR II-10, at para. 36.

[131] See Case T-28/90 *Asia Motor France and others v Commission* [1992] ECR II-2285, para. 35.

[132] Case C-41/92 *Liberal Democrats v Parliament* [1993] ECR I-3153 at para. 4.

[133] In some cases the defaulting institution had to bear the costs, see Case 377/87 *European Parliament v Council* [1988] ECR, at para. 12; Joined Cases T-297/01 and T-298/01 *SIC v Commission* [2004] ECR II-743, at paras. 61–63; Case T-451/04 *Mediocurso v Commission*, order of 28 March 2006 (not published), para. 30. In other cases each party had to bear their own costs, see Case C-41/92 *Liberal Democrats v Parliament* [1993] ECR I-3153 at para 5; Case T-291/01 *Dessauer Versorgungs- und Verkehrsgesellschaft and Others v Commission* [2002] ECR II-5033, at paras 13 to 18; Case T-66/02 *Institouto N. Avgerinopoulou and others v Commission* [2004] ECR II-855, at para. 36; Case T-276/03 *Le Canne v Commission* [2006] ECR II-10, para. 52.

[134] Case 377/87 *European Parliament v Council* [1988] ECR 4017.

where an EC institution had unlawfully failed to take action, applicants could obtain from the Court a declaration that the institution had failed to act contrary to the Treaty. Under Article 233 the effect of such a declaration was that that institution had to take the necessary measures to comply with the judgment. The Court therefore found that 'where the act whose absence constitutes the subject-matter of the proceedings was adopted after the action was brought but before judgment, a declaration to the effect that the initial failure to act is unlawful can no longer bring about the consequences prescribed by Article [233]'.[135] In this case the subject matter has ceased to exist. In this case AG Mischo noted that the rationale of Article 232 was less 'to issue a reprimand to the institution concerned',[136] but 'to prompt the institution concerned to take action'.[137] The AG argued that the parallel with Article 226 was less convincing than a comparison with Article 230 and that when an institution withdrew an allegedly unlawful act during the proceedings under Article 230 the Court would declare the action as devoid of purpose. Consequently, the AG opined, 'the purpose of proceedings for a failure to act disappears as soon as the measure called for has been adopted and the applicant has thus obtained satisfaction'.[138]

The CFI in *Mediocurso v Commission*[139] confirmed this argument by refusing to accept the view that despite a definition of position after the action under Article 232 had been brought the subject-matter of the action had not ceased to exist. The CFI pointed out that the action under Article 232 pursued objectives different from that of Article 226. In contrast to Article 226, the action for failure to act is not intended to produce a public condemnation of the EC institution's lack of action, but to force them to take action.[140] Where the requested acts have been adopted by the EC institution the action therefore loses its purpose.[141] The CFI found that the action under Article 232 was more akin to that in Article 230. In the same

[135] Ibid., para. 10. See also Case T-28/90 *Asia Motor France and others v Commission* [1992] ECR II-2285, para. 37; Joined Cases T-297/01 and T-298/01 *SIC v Commission* [2004] ECR II-743, para. 31; Case 66/02 *Institouto N. Avgerinopoulou* [2004] ECR II-855, para. 31; Case T-276/03 *Le Canne v Commission* [2006] ECR II-10, para. 36; Case T-451/04 *Mediocurso v Commission*, judgment of 28 March 2006 (not published), para. 19; Case T-34/05 R *Makhteshim-Agan and others v Commission* [2005] ECR II-1465, para. 67.

[136] Opinion of AG Mischo in Case 377/87 *European Parliament v Council* [1988] ECR 4017, para. 115.

[137] Ibid., Opinion of AG Mischo, para. 115. See also Opinion of AG Darmon in Case C-41/92 *Liberal Democrats v Parliament* [1993] ECR I-3153 at para. 9.

[138] Opinion of AG Mischo in Case 377/87 *European Parliament v Council* [1988] ECR 4017, para. 130.

[139] Case T-451/04 *Mediocurso v Commission*, judgment of 28 March 2006 (not published).

[140] Ibid., para. 25.

[141] Ibid., para. 25.

way as the withdrawal of an allegedly unlawful act removes the subject matter in an action under Article 230, the action under Article 232 ceases to exist where the defending institution adopts the requested acts.[142] The CFI similarly rejected the argument that an applicant had an interest in having the unlawfulness of the inaction established by the court as basis for an action under Article 288(2) by holding that the court could not make such a statement without exceeding its powers under Article 232.[143]

It should, firstly, be noted that the CFI's reasoning, and that of AG Mischo, is limited to situations where the institution adopts the measures requested by the applicant. It is, however, clear from the case law that, in a situation where an action under Article 232 has been brought but before judgment has been given, an institution can also define its position and thereby render the action devoid of purpose by adopting measures which do not satisfy the applicant.[144] Where the institution's position consists in a refusal which can be reviewed under Article 230, it does not seem to serve any apparent purpose to require the individual to bring another action, this time under Article 230, when the Court could proceed to judgment on the existing action under Article 232. Similarly, AG Tesauro highlighted in his Opinion in *Guérin automobiles v Commission*[145] the problems, in a case where an action has already been brought under Article 232, caused by the adoption of a preliminary act as a definition of position. He pointed out that the main disadvantage of such an approach consists in requiring the applicant 'to bring a series of actions for failure to act, to produce a useful result'.[146] AG Tesauro proposed that, where the Commission issues an 'Article 6 letter' after the applicant has brought its action under Article 232, the court should, instead of declaring the action devoid of purpose, require the Commission to reply to the comments made by the complainant within a reasonable time and where the Commission has not complied with the time-limit proceed to declare that it has failed to act.[147]

It is, secondly, submitted that the arguments presented by the CFI in *Mediocurso* are not entirely convincing. In Article 226 cases the Court argues that an interest in pursuing the action still subsists in situations where the Member State remedies the default after the action has been brought. The Court would argue that 'that interest may consist in

---

[142] Ibid., para. 26.

[143] Ibid., para. 27.

[144] See Case C-44/00 P *Sodima v Commission* [2000] ECR I-11231, para. 83; Case T-66/02 *Institouto N. Avgerinopoulou and others v Commission* [2004] ECR II-855, para. 34. Joined Cases C-302/99 P and C-308/99P *Commission v TF1* [2001] ECR I-5603, at paras. 7 and 28.

[145] Case C-282/95 *Guérin automobiles v Commission* [1997] ECR I-1503.

[146] Opinion of AG Tesauro, ibid., para. 33.

[147] Ibid., para. 34.

establishing the basis for a liability which a Member State may incur, by reason of its failure to fulfil its obligations, towards those to whom rights accrue as a result of that failure'.[148] It is not immediately apparent why this argument is not equally applicable in Article 232 cases.[149]

Thirdly, the CFI's argument that the position under Article 232 is similar to the situation where the withdrawal of an unlawful act, after an action under Article 230 has been initiated, terminates the proceedings under Article 230 is not convincing. It is true that the judgment of the CFI in *IMS Health v Commission*,[150] to which the CFI in *Mediocurso* refers,[151] states that the applicant had no interest in pursuing the action under Article 230 after the Commission had withdrawn the act in issue.[152] However, the CFI emphasised that 'la partie requérante peut conserver un intérêt à voir annuler un acte abrogé en cours d'instance si l'annulation de cet acte est susceptible, par elle-même, d'avoir des conséquences juridiques'.[153] And in *Gencor v Commission*[154] the CFI held that:

> the annulment of an act which has already been carried out or which, in the meantime, has been repealed from a given date is still capable of having legal consequences. The act could have produced legal effects during the period when it was in force and those effects are not necessarily eradicated by its repeal. An action for annulment is also admissible if it allows future repetition of the alleged illegality to be avoided. For those reasons, a judgment annulling an act is the basis upon which the institution concerned may be led to restore the applicant sufficiently to his original position or avoid the adoption of an identical act.[155]

Therefore, far from confirming the CFI's position in *Mediocurso*, the case law shows that an applicant can preserve its interest in a judgment under Article 230 even where the act has been withdrawn. Consequently, where the defending institution defines its position after an action under Article 232 has been brought, the action becomes devoid of purpose only if the applicant cannot show any interest in a judgment. Such an interest can

---

148 Case 240/86 *Commission v Greece* [1988] ECR 1835, para. 14. See also Case 103/84 *Commission v Italy* [1986] ECR 1759, para. 9; Case 154/85 *Commission v Italy* [1987] ECR 2717, para. 6.

149 It should be noted that the cases which the CFI cites in para. 25 of its judgment to support its claim that the action under Article 226 pursues different objectives than the one in Article 232 deal with an unrelated issue.

150 Case T-184/01 *IMS Health v Commission* [2005] ECR II-817.

151 Case T-451/04 *Mediocurso v Commission*, judgment of 28 March 2006 (not published), para. 26.

152 Case T-184/01 *IMS Health v Commission* [2005] ECR II-817, at para. 41.

153 Ibid., para. 38.

154 Case T-102/96 *Gencor v Commission*, judgment of 25 March 1999.

155 Ibid, para. 41. See also Case T-25/96 *Arbeitsgemeinschaft Deutscher Luftfahrt-Unternehmen and Hapag-Lloyd* [1997] ECR II-363, para. 16.

consist in the avoidance of future illegalities or in the establishment of the liability of the Community institution.

4. *LOCUS STANDI*

Article 232 distinguishes between three types of applicants. Article 232(1) gives the Member States and the Community institutions the right to bring an action against reviewable omissions without further conditions. In contrast to Article 230, where it is only a semi-privileged applicant, the Court of Auditors is considered as a privileged applicant under Article 232(1), because according to Article 7(1) it is one of the Community's institutions.[156] On the other hand, the CFI found in *Cantine Sociali Venete v European Ombudsman and European Parliament*[157] that the European Ombudsman could not be considered as an institution within the meaning of Article 232. Article 232(4) provides the ECB with the same right of action as provided for Community institutions, but limited to its field of competence. The ECB can therefore be considered as semi-privileged applicant.[158]

More severe restrictions are imposed on the third category of applicants in Article 232(3). Natural and legal persons can only bring an action against reviewable omissions if 'an institution of the Community has failed to address to that person any act other than a recommendation or an opinion'.[159] In addition, therefore, to the requirement that the non-adoption of an act must be a reviewable omission, which they share with privileged and semi-privileged applicants, non-privileged applicants must demonstrate that the act whose adoption they have requested must be addressed to them. The English language version suggests that only the non-adoption of an act which formally has to be addressed to the applicant can be challenged. This narrow interpretation is, however, not convincing. First, other language versions suggest a wider interpretation.[160] Secondly, such an interpretation would have the disadvantage of allowing the institution whose action was requested to deprive an applicant of a remedy.[161]

---

156 See Case 13/83 *European Parliament v Council* [1985] ECR 1513, para. 17.

157 Case T-103/99 *ACSV v European Ombudsman and European Parliament* [2000] ECR II-4165, at para. 46.

158 Under the Lisbon Treaty the ECB becomes a privileged applicant under Article 265(1) TFEU.

159 The Lisbon Treaty includes in Article 265(3) TFEU also bodies, offices or agencies of the Union as defendants against whom private parties can bring an action.

160 T.C. Hartley, supra note 1, p. 385.

161 See Opinion of AG Dutheillet de Lamothe in Case 15/71 *Mackprang v Commission* [1971] ECR 797.

Were the institution to refuse the adoption of an act which was of direct and individual concern to him, the applicant could bring an action under Article 230(4). On the other hand, if the institution did not act, the applicant could not bring an action under Article 232 unless he was the formal addressee of such an act.[162] Consequently, a harmonious interpretation of Articles 230(4) and 232(3) would suggest that Article 232(3) has to be interpreted as allowing non-privileged applicants to bring an action against the non-adoption of an act not only where it has to be addressed to them, but also where it is of direct and individual concern to them.

After giving some indications as to its preference for the wider interpretation of Article 232(3),[163] the Court in *ENU v Commission*[164] expressly accepted the view that an action could be brought under Article 232 where the requested act would have been of direct and individual concern to the applicant, even though the act had to be formally addressed to someone else. ENU, a company which produced uranium concentrates, encountered severe financial hardship due to problems of selling its production. It therefore requested the European Supply Agency under Article 57 EAEC Treaty to exercise its right of option on ENU's uranium production. Even though it indicated its willingness to help, the Agency did not take any action. Consequently, ENU requested the Commission to take action under Article 53 EAEC Treaty in respect of the Agency. The Commission argued that ENU lacked standing under Article 148 EAEC Treaty, which is similar to Article 232 ECT, as any act under Article 53 EAEC Treaty would have to be addressed to the Agency and not ENU. The Court found that the Commission's decision, had it been addressed to the Agency 'would have been of direct and individual concern to the applicant',[165] which could have challenged it under Article 146(2) EAEC Treaty, the equivalent of Article 230(4) ECT. The Court found that the applicant therefore also had to be given the possibility to bring an action for failure to adopt the requested decision under Article 148 EAEC Treaty. The Court argued that if such a possibility did not exist 'the right provided for in the second paragraph of Article 53 [EAEC] would be bereft of judicial protection'.[166]

This approach has also been applied under Article 232(3) ECT thereby bringing the rules on standing for private parties under Article 232(3)

---

[162] Ibid., Opinion of AG Dutheillet de Lamothe, p. 807–808.

[163] See Case 246/81 *Lord Bethell v Commission* [1982] ECR 2277, paras. 13, 15 and 16; Case 247/87 *Star Fruit v Commission* [1989] ECR 291, para. 13.

[164] Case C-107/91 *ENU v Commission* [1993] ECR I-599.

[165] Ibid., para. 17.

[166] Ibid., para. 18.

in line with those applicable under Article 230(4). In *T.Port*[167] the Court stated that 'just as the fourth paragraph of Article [230] allows individuals to bring an action for annulment against a measure of an institution not addressed to them provided that the measure is of direct and individual concern to them, the third paragraph of Article [232] must be interpreted as also entitling them to bring an action for failure to act against an institution which they claim has failed to adopt a measure which would have concerned them in the same way'.[168] The Court emphasised the link with Article 230 by arguing that '[t]he possibility for individuals to assert their rights should not depend upon whether the institution concerned has acted or failed to act.'[169] The Court therefore declared admissible an action under Article 232(3), where the Commission had failed to take any decision at the preliminary stage of the procedure for reviewing aid under Article 88(3) ECT.[170] On the other hand, the CFI in *Cantina sociale and others v Commission*[171] made it clear that 'individuals who have no standing to challenge the legality of a legislative measure likewise have no standing to bring an action before the Court for a declaration that a Community institution has failed to act after being called upon to adopt such a measure'.[172]

Where the applicant requests the Commission to take an action against a Member State under Article 226, the application will equally be rejected as such an act would not be of direct and individual concern to the applicant.[173] It has been held that the measures adopted by the Commission in the course of the procedure, such as the reasoned opinion or the bringing of the action before the Court, do not constitute acts which concern individuals directly.[174] In *GAEC Salat v Commission* the CFI rejected any

---

[167] Case C-68/95 *T. Port v Bundesanstalt für Landwirtschaft und Ernährung* [1996] ECR I-6065.

[168] Ibid., para. 59. See also Case T-95/96 *Gestevision Telecinco v Commission* [1998] ECR II-3407, para. 58; Case T-395/04 *Air One v Commission* [2006] ECR II-1343, para. 25; Case T-167/04 *Asklepios Kliniken v Commission*, judgment of 11 July 2007, para. 45.

[169] Case C-68/95 *T. Port v Bundesanstalt für Landwirtschaft und Ernährung* [1996] ECR I-6065, para. 59.

[170] See Case T-17/96 *TF1 v Commission* [1999] ECR II-1757, paras. 26–36; Case T-95/96 *Gestevision Telecinco v Commission* [1998] ECR II-3407, paras 57–70; Case T-395/04 *Air One v Commission* [2006] ECR II-1343, para. 26–41.

[171] Case T-166/98 *Cantina sociale and others v Commission* [2004] ECR II-3991.

[172] Ibid., para. 82, where the CFI declared inadmissible an action for failure to adopt a generally applicable regulation; see also Case 134/73 *Holtz v Council* [1975] ECR 1. Similarly, in Case T-184/04 *Sulvida v Commission* [2005] ECR II-85, para. 15, the CFI found inadmissible an action which was directed at the failure to adopt a Directive, the substance of which was of general application.

[173] Case 247/87 *Star Fruit v Commission* [1989] ECR 291.

[174] Case T-89/05 *GAEC Salat v Commission* [2005] ECR II-16, para. 2; Case T-426/05 *Nicolas Molliné v Commission*, order of 16 May 2006 (not published), para. 9. See also Case 83/84 *N.M. v Commission* [1984] ECR 3571, at para. 10.

comparisons between Article 226 and the procedural position of individuals under Regulation 17/62[175] and Article 86(3) ECT.[176]

5. GROUNDS OF REVIEW

Article 232 limits the grounds of review to instances where the defendant institution has failed to act 'in infringement of this Treaty'. The exclusion of other grounds of review which are set out in Article 230(2) results from the special nature of the action under Article 232.[177] An institution can only act where it is competent to do so. Where it lacks competence to act an institution cannot have failed to act.[178] Similarly, a failure to act cannot in itself infringe an essential procedural requirement. Also a misuse of powers, in the definition of the Community Courts, can only be achieved through action, not inaction.

In *European Parliament v Council*,[179] the Court had to determine when a failure to act by an institution had to be regarded as an infringement of the Treaty. The European Parliament had brought an action under Article 232 alleging that the Council had failed to introduce a common transport policy, in particular its framework, and to act on 16 proposals of the Commission relating to transport. The Council argued that Article 232 could only be used to challenge the failure to adopt a specific legal measure, but was 'an inappropriate instrument for resolving cases involving the introduction of a whole system of measures within the framework of a complex legislative process'.[180] The Court rejected the argument on the ground that the purpose of Article 232 would be frustrated if 'an applicant were not able to refer to the Court an institution's failure to adopt several decisions, or a series of decisions, where the adoption of such decisions is an obligation which the Treaty imposes on that institution'.[181] The Court made it clear, however, that the European Parliament had to specify with a degree of precision the measures which it claimed the Council had failed to adopt. Only such precision would allow the Council pursuant to Article 233 to comply with the Court's

---

175 Now replaced by Regulation 1/2003.

176 Case T-89/05 *GAEC Salat v Commission* [2005] ECR II-16, at paras. 26 and 27.

177 See T.C. Hartley, supra note 1, p. 413.

178 See Case 83/84 *N.M. v Commission and Council* [1984] ECR 3571, para. 10; Case T-166/98 *Cantina sociale di Dolianova and others v Commission* [2004] ECR II-3991, para. 81.

179 Case 13/83 *European Parliament v Council* [1985] ECR 1513.

180 Ibid., para. 29.

181 Ibid., para. 34.

judgment allowing that claim. The Court therefore concluded that the EP's claim could only be upheld 'in so far as the absence of a common transport policy with which the Council is charged is due to failure to take measures the scope of which can be sufficiently defined for them to be identified individually and adopted in compliance with the Court's judgment pursuant to Article [233]'.[182]

The Court emphasised from the outset that 'objective difficulties which, according to the Council, stand in the way of the necessary progress towards a common transport policy are irrelevant for the purposes of the present action'.[183] It is therefore of no avail for an institution to plead that it was too difficult to comply with its obligation. The Court accepted, however, that the Council had discretion in the matter. The Court noted that it was for the Council, within the framework of the Treaty, to specify the aims and means for implementing a common transport policy. Even though it had to adopt the necessary measures for the gradual introduction of such a policy, the Council could determine the substance of those measures. The Court pointed out that the EP failed to specify which measures the Council should adopt and in what sequence. The Court concluded that 'the absence of a common policy which the Treaty requires to be brought into being does not in itself necessarily constitute a failure to act sufficiently specific in nature to form the subject of an action under Article [232]'.[184] Given the discretion of the Council, the Court also rejected the proposition that the Council had failed to adopt specific Commission proposals relating to this area.

On the other hand, the Court found that Article 70(1)(a) and (b) imposed clearly defined obligations on the Council for the introduction of the freedom to provide services in relation to transport. The Court argued that 'in that respect the Council does not have the discretion on which it may rely in other areas of the common transport policy'.[185] The Court made it clear that the result to be achieved was determined by the Treaty provisions and that the Council had a certain measure of discretion only as to the means to be employed to reach that result. The Court therefore concluded that the Council had failed to adopt measures to ensure freedom to provide services in the sphere of international transport and to lay down the conditions under which non-resident carriers may operate transport services in a Member State. This also meant that the Council had an obligation to adopt Commission proposals relating to achieving freedom to provide services

---

182 Ibid., para. 37.
183 Ibid., para. 48.
184 Ibid., para. 53.
185 Ibid., para. 65.

in the transport sector, whereas no such obligation existed for proposals falling outside that category.[186]

It follows from the judgment that where the EC Treaty imposes on an institution a clearly defined obligation to achieve a specific result a failure to act can be challenged under Article 232. Such a specific obligations can result from the requirement in Article 233 ECT that an institution adopt the necessary measures to comply with a judgment of the Court of Justice.[187] Despite the wording of Article 232, which seems to limit failures to act to instances where the defendant institution was required to act under the Treaty, the Community Courts have, however, accepted that such an obligation can also arise from secondary legislation.[188] It has been argued that such obligations can also result from general principles of law as developed by the Court and international agreements.[189] Moreover, an obligation to act does, however, not only exist where the EC Treaty provides for the adoption of final acts, but also where it imposes a duty to adopt preparatory measures.[190]

The judgment in *European Parliament v Council*[191] seems to suggest that where the institution has discretionary powers, a failure to act cannot be challenged, as an obligation to act does not exist. On this basis the Court has consistently held that the Commission is under no obligation to initiate the procedure under Article 226 against a Member State.[192] The institution is, however, under an obligation to exercise its discretion properly.[193] This can mean that in some cases the discretion might give way to a specific obligation, as is demonstrated by the Court's

---

186 Ibid., para. 78.

187 See Joined Cases T-297/01 and T-298/01 *SIC v Commission* [2004] ECR II-743, at paras. 32 and 45. For a discussion of the obligation under Article 233, see above pp. 155–164.

188 See Case C-68/95 *T-Port v Bundesanstalt für Landwirtschaft und Ernährung* [1996] ECR I-6065, at para. 43, where the Court held that, depending on the circumstances, Article 30 of Regulation 404/93, [1993] OJ L 47/1, might require the Commission to adopt rules for cases of hardship. See also Case C-282/95 P *Guérin automobiles v Commission* [1997] ECR I-1503, at para. 36, where the Court held that under Regulation 17/62 the Commission had to adopt a final decision upon a complaint after completion of the notification procedure.

189 T.C. Hartley, supra note 1, at p. 413.

190 See Opinion of AG Mischo in Case 377/87 *Parliament v Council* [1988] ECR 4017, at paras. 40–48, in relation to the adoption of the draft budget by the Council; Opinion of AG Darmon in Case C-41/92 *Liberal Democrats v European Parliament* [1993] ECR I-3153, at para. 49, with regard to the obligation of the EP to adopt proposals under Article 190(4); Case T-28/90 *Asia Motor France and others v Commission* [1992] ECR II-2285, at para. 29, where the CFI ruled that the applicants were entitled to obtain from the Commission an Article 6 letter under Commission Regulation No 99/63/EEC.

191 Case 13/83 *European Parliament v Council* [1985] ECR 1513.

192 See Case 247/87 *Star Fruit v Commission* [1989] ECR 291 at para 11; Case T-571/93 *Lefebvre v Commission* [1995] ECR II-2379 at para. 60.

193 T.C. Hartley, supra note 1, p. 414.

ruling in *T-Port*.[194] Regulation 404/93[195] established a common market in bananas. In order to deal with disturbances as a result of the replacement of the various national arrangements by a common market, Article 30 of the Regulation provided the Commission with the power to take any transitional measures it deemed necessary. The Court found that the Commission had broad discretion when assessing whether such transitional measures were necessary. The Court emphasised, however, that the Commission was under an obligation to act 'if the difficulties associated with the transition from national arrangements to the common organization of the market so require'.[196] The Court found that such an obligation existed in particular when the transition infringed traders' fundamental rights. The Court therefore concluded that 'Article 30 of the Regulation authorizes and, depending on the circumstances, requires the Commission to lay down rules catering for cases of hardship'.[197]

Similarly, the Court has accepted that an obligation exists for the Commission to examine complaints in competition cases. Under Article 7(2) of Regulation 1/2003[198] natural or legal persons with a legitimate interest can bring a complaint alleging an infringement of Article 81 or 82. The Commission is not under an obligation to adopt a decision establishing the existence of an infringement of the competition rules or even to open an investigation.[199] The Commission is, however, required 'to examine carefully the factual and legal particulars brought to its notice by the complainant in order to decide whether they disclose conduct of such a kind as to distort competition in the common market and affect trade between Member States'.[200] Where it intends to reject the complaint, the Commission has to inform the complainant of its reasons and has to give the complainant

---

194 Case C-68/95 *T-Port v Bundesanstalt für Landwirtschaft und Ernährung* [1996] ECR I-6065.

195 [1993] OJ L 47/1.

196 Case C-68/95 *T-Port v Bundesanstalt für Landwirtschaft und Ernährung* [1996] ECR I-6065, para. 38.

197 Ibid., para. 43.

198 [2003] OJ L 1/1. See also Article 5 of Regulation 774/2004, [2004] OJ L 123/18.

199 See Case 125/78 *GEMA v Commission* [1979] ECR 3173, at para. 17; Case T-24/90 *Automec v Commission* [1992] ECR II-2223, para. 76. See also AG Tesauro in Case C-282/95 *Guérin automobiles v Commission* [1997] ECR I-1503, at paras. 10 and 46.

200 See Case T-24/90 *Automec v Commission* [1992] ECR II-2223, para. 79. See also Case 210/81 *Demo-Studio Schmidt v Commission* [1983] ECR 3045, at para. 19; Case 298/83 *CICCE v Commission* [1985] ECR 1105, para. 18; Joined Cases 142 and 156/84 *BAT and Reynolds v Commission* [1987] ECR 4487, para. 20. In Joined Case T-213/95 and 18/96 *SCK and FNK v Commission* [1997] ECR II-1739, at para. 55, the CFI found that under Regulation 17/62 the Commission had an obligation to proceed to a decision or a formal letter within a reasonable time on an application for clearance or individual exemption.

the opportunity to make its views known.[201] Where the applicant responds within a time-limit set by the Commission, 'the Commission is bound either to initiate a procedure against the subject of the complaint [. . .] or to adopt a definitive decision rejecting the complaint'.[202]

A similar approach is also taken in state aid cases. In *Gestevisión Telecinco v Commission*[203] the CFI held that '[s]ince it has exclusive jurisdiction to assess the compatibility of State aid with the common market, the Commission must, in the interests of sound administration and of the fundamental rules of the Treaty relating to State aid, conduct a diligent and impartial examination of a complaint alleging the existence of aid that is incompatible with the common market'.[204] The CFI found that where it has approved the initiation of an investigation into State aid, which formed the subject matter of the complaint, the Commission could not indefinitely prolong its preliminary investigation.[205] The Court pointed out that whether the Commission has acted within a reasonable period of time had to be assessed 'in relation to the particular circumstances of each case and, especially, its context, the various procedural stages to be followed by the Commission and the complexity of the case and its importance to the parties involved'.[206] The Court argued that the periods of 47 months for the first complaint and 26 months for the second complaint, from when it received the complaint to the time when formal notice was given, were 'so long that they should have been sufficient to enable the Commission to close the preliminary stage of investigation into the aid in question and thus be in a position to adopt a decision thereon [. . .], unless it could show exceptional circumstances justifying such periods'.[207] The CFI found the Commission's explanation for these delays insufficient and concluded that the delays were unreasonable.[208]

---

[201] See Article 7(2) of Regulation 773/2004. See also Case T-28/90 *Asia Motor France v Commission* [1992] ECR II-2285, at para. 29, where the CFI found that the applicants were entitled to obtain from the Commission a provisional communication under Article 6 of Commission Regulation No 99/63/EEC, [1963-64] OJ English Special Edition, p. 47.

[202] Case C-282/95 *Guérin automobiles v Commission* [1997] ECR I-1503, para. 36. See also Article 7(2) of Regulation 773/2004.

[203] Case T-95/96 *Gestevisión Telecinco v Commission* [1998] ECR II-3407.

[204] Ibid., para. 72. See also Case C-367/95 P *Commission v Sytraval et Brink's France* [1998] ECR I-1719, para. 62; Case T-395/04 *Air One v Commission* [2006] ECR II-1343, para. 61; Case T-167/04 *Asklepios Kliniken v Commission*, judgment of 11 July 2007, at para. 81.

[205] Case T-95/96 *Gestevisión Telecinco v Commission* [1998] ECR II-3407, para. 74.

[206] Ibid., para. 75. See also Case T-395/04 *Air One v Commission* [2006] ECR II-1343, para. 61.

[207] Case T-95/96 *Gestevisión Telecinco v Commission* [1998] ECR II-3407, para. 81.

[208] Ibid., at paras. 82–86. See also Case T-395/04 *Air One v Commission* [2006] ECR II-1343, at paras. 62–67, in which a period of six months was considered reasonable due to the complexity of the case and the fact that it contained a certain novelty, and Case T-167/04

And in *Schlüsselverlag and others v Commission*,[209] the Court had to rule on the Commission's submission that it was under no obligation to examine a complaint brought by the appellants, which were the owners of newspapers in Austria, alleging that the transaction between two other newspaper companies should have been notified under the Merger Regulation.[210] The Court rejected the Commission's point of view by pointing out that 'the Commission cannot refrain from taking account of complaints from undertakings which are not party to a concentration capable of having a Community dimension'.[211] The Court argued that it was likely that such a transaction between the complainants' competitors was likely to have an impact on their situation on the market concerned. Article 18 of the Merger Regulation therefore provided them with a right to be heard. Moreover, the Court found that the Commission could not argue that it was not required to take a decision on whether it was competent as supervising authority, as it was solely responsible under Article 21 of the Merger Regulation to take such decisions. Otherwise, third-party undertakings would not be able to take advantage of the procedural guarantees which Community legislation affords them. In addition, the Commission would forego a means to examine whether parties to a concentration ought to have notified their transaction. Finally, the complainants would be without a legal remedy against the refusal to entertain their complaint under Article 230. The Court therefore concluded that the Commission was obliged 'to undertake, in the interests of sound administration, a thorough and impartial examination of the complaints which are made to it'.[212] The Commission must examine 'whether the matter is within its competence and to draw the necessary conclusions'.[213]

6. FORM AND EFFECTS OF THE JUDGMENT

In accordance with Article 233, the Court will declare that the institution has failed to act, in infringement of the Treaty. It is not allowed to

---

Asklepios Kliniken v Commission, judgment of 11 July 2007, at paras. 82–91, in which a period of 12 months for a preliminary examination was considered reasonable.

[209] Case C-170/02 P *Schlüsselverlag and others v Commission* [2003] ECR I-9889.

[210] Council Regulation 4064/89 [1989] OJ L 395/1, as amended by Council Regulation 1310/97 [1997] OJ L 257/13.

[211] Case C-170/02 P *Schlüsselverlag and others v Commission* [2003] ECR I-9889, para. 27.

[212] Ibid., para. 29.

[213] Ibid., para. 29.

adopt the act instead of the institution. Article 233 requires the institution, however, to take the necessary steps to comply with the judgment. Although the institution is therefore under an obligation to take action, it retains the power to determine how to act, where such discretion is granted by the relevant provision.

3 Incidental review

The EC Treaty provides privileged applicants with effective remedies for direct action to challenge the legality of Community acts under Article 230 and to bring a failure to act to an end under Article 232. On the other hand, the opportunity for private parties to bring a direct action under Article 230 and Article 232 are considerably more limited in scope. Private parties therefore depend on indirect means of review. The EC Treaty bases the availability of direct and indirect remedies on the distinction between acts of general and individual application. As discussed above,[1] the plain text of Article 230(4) makes it clear that Community acts should only be open to a direct challenge by private parties, where they are of individual application. Acts of general application can only be reviewed indirectly. The Community Courts, which have broadly followed this approach in their case law, have defended the narrow application of Article 230(4) by referring unsuccessful applicants to the remedies available for an indirect challenge. The Court stated to that effect in *UPA* that:

> [b]y Article 173 [now 230] and Article 184 [now 241], on the one hand, and by Article 177 [now 234], on the other, the Treaty has established a complete system of legal remedies and procedures designed to ensure judicial review of the legality of acts of the institutions, and has entrusted such review to the Community Courts [. . .]. Under that system, where natural or legal persons cannot, by reason of the conditions for admissibility laid down in the fourth paragraph of Article 173 [now 230] of the Treaty, directly challenge Community measures of general application, they are able, depending on the case, either indirectly to plead the invalidity of such acts before the Community Courts under Article 184 [now 241] of the Treaty or to do so before the national courts and ask them [. . .] to make a reference to the Court of Justice for a preliminary ruling on validity.[2]

Given the restrictive rules on standing for private parties under Article 230(4) and Article 232(3), the remedies for an indirect challenge of Community acts assume considerable importance, not only practically because they often constitute the only means to contest Community acts,

[1] See supra pp. 45–48.
[2] Case C-50/00 *Unión de Pequeños Agricultores v Council* [2002] ECR I-6677, para. 40.

but also theoretically as they are meant to ensure a comprehensive system of review providing private parties with an effective remedy in accordance with Articles 6 and 13 of the ECHR and Article 47 of the Charter of Fundamental Rights.

The system of indirect remedies takes account of the allocation of implementing powers between the Community and its Member States. The Community legal system is based on the principle that the Member States are entrusted with the implementation and application of Community law. However, Article 202 3rd indent allows the legislative authority to delegate powers to the Commission, and in duly substantiated cases also the Council, for the implementation of EC legislation. Such implementation does not only include the adoption of acts of general application, but also those of individual application. Consequently, the EC Treaty provides in Article 241 for an indirect remedy where the main action is brought against an act adopted by a Community institution,[3] whereas Article 234 allows a national court to request the Court of Justice to review the validity of a Community act where the main action is brought against an act adopted by a national authority. Both remedies have, therefore, a similar purpose in that they allow Community acts to be reviewed indirectly. This common purpose often results in the application of common rules for both provisions. All the same, as both judicial avenues follow different procedures each remedy will be assessed separately in this chapter. This allows a more in-depth analysis of the alleged drawbacks of the indirect review under Article 234. This chapter will also discuss the changes which Articles 277 and 267 TFEU as respective successors to Articles 241 and 234 would bring about with the entry into force of the Lisbon Treaty.

1. PLEA OF ILLEGALITY

The plea of illegality under Article 241[4] constitutes a carefully crafted balance between the principle of legal certainty, which suggests that after the

[3] See Joined Cases 31 and 33/62 *Wöhrmann and Lütticke v Commission* [1962] ECR 501.

[4] See generally, G. Bebr, 'Judicial Remedy of Private Parties against Normative Acts of the European Communities: The Role of the Exception of Illegality' (1966) 4 *CMLRev* 7; A. Barav, 'The Exception of Illegality in Community Law: A Critical Analysis' (1974) 11 *CMLRev* 366; D. Sinaniotis, 'The Plea of Illegality in EC Law' (2001) *EPL* 103; M. Vogt, 'Indirect judicial protection in EC law – the case of the plea of illegality' (2006) *ELRev* 364–377; T.C. Hartley, *The Foundations of European Community Law* (OUP, 6th edn., 2007), chapter 14; P. Craig and G. DeBúrca, *EU Law – Text, Cases and Materials* (OUP, 4th edn., 2008), pp. 533–536.

expiry of the time limit for a direct challenge acts should become definitive in their effects, and the principle of legality, which advocates that unlawful acts should not be immune from challenge.[5] Article 241 EC provides that '[n]otwithstanding the expiry of the period laid down in the fifth paragraph of Article 230, any party may, in proceedings in which a regulation adopted jointly by the European Parliament and the Council, or a regulation of the Council, of the Commission, or of the ECB is at issue, plead the grounds specified in the second paragraph of Article 230 in order to invoke before the Court of Justice the inapplicability of that regulation.'

Nature and Scope of the Provision

It is clear from its wording that Article 241 'does not constitute an independent right of action',[6] but can only be invoked incidentally in other proceedings. However, it is not clear from the provision in which other proceedings Article 241 can be invoked. The Court held in *Wöhrmann and Lütticke v Commission*[7] that Article 241 could only be invoked 'in proceedings brought before the Court of Justice itself under some other provision of the Treaty'.[8] The Court emphasised that parties to proceedings in a national court could not invoke Article 241 in the Community Courts.[9] This would undermine the powers of the national court to request a preliminary ruling from the Court under Article 234.

Even though it provides a clear delimitation of jurisdiction between the Community Courts and the national courts, this ruling limits, at least for private parties, the application of Article 241 to those, exceptional, cases where a Community institution has been entrusted with the application of Community legislation. Otherwise, applicants need to challenge acts adopted by the national authorities in the application of Community legislation, and this is the usual scenario under Community law, in the national court and persuade that court to request the Court of Justice to rule on the validity of the Community legislation in issue.

---

5 See M. Vogt, supra note 4, pp. 365–370.

6 Case C-239/99 *Nachi Europe v Hauptzollamt Krefeld* [2001] ECR I-1197, para. 33. See also Case T-369/03 *Arizona Chemical and Others v Commission* [2005] ECR II-5839, para. 129; Case T-299/04 *Selmani v Council and Commission* [2005] ECR II-20*, para. 76; Case T-376/04 *Polyelectrolyte Producers Group v Council and Commission* [2005] ECR II-3007, para. 49; Case T-386/04 *Eridania and others v Commission* [2005] ECR II-2531, para. 51.

7 Joined Cases 31 and 33/62 *Wöhrmann and Lütticke v Commission* [1962] ECR 501.

8 Ibid., at p. 507.

9 Ibid., p. 507. See also Case C-239/99 *Nachi Europe v Hauptzollamt Krefeld* [2001] ECR I-1197, para. 34. See, however, the contrary view by J. Temple Lang, 'Actions for declarations that Community Regulations are invalid; the duties of national courts under Article 10 EC' (2003) *CMLRev* 102.

Article 241 is most often invoked in the Community Courts where an applicant challenges a Community act under Articles 230 and 236.[10] Its application has also been allowed in proceedings under Article 226.[11] Other proceedings, such as those under Article 232, Article 235 in combination with Article 288, and Article 238, are, however, conceivable as main actions in which Article 241 could be invoked.[12]

The dependence of the remedy under Article 241 on a main action has consequences for the admissibility of the indirect challenge under Article 241. The Community Courts have held that where the main action is inadmissible, the indirect challenge is therefore also inadmissible.[13] Similarly, the Community Courts require that the regulation challenged under Article 241 must be 'applicable, directly or indirectly, to the issue with which the action is concerned and there must be a direct legal connection between the contested individual decision and the general measure in question'.[14] A direct link between the act challenged in the main action and the act indirectly challenged under Article 241 exists where the general act constitutes the legal basis for the act in issue in the main action.[15] In *Kik v OHIM*[16] the CFI allowed the applicant to invoke Article 241 against Article 115(3) of Regulation 40/94,[17] which requires an applicant for a Community trade mark to indicate one of the five official languages of the Office for Harmonisation in the Internal Market for specific proceedings, in her main action against the decision of OHIM to reject her application on the ground that she had not indicated one of the five official languages as second language. However, a direct link can exist even where the general

---

[10] Case 20/71 *Sabbatini v Parliament* [1072] ECR 345.

[11] Case 116/82 *Commission v Germany* [1986] ECR 2519.

[12] T.C. Hartley, supra note 4, p. 390. In Case C-91/05 *Commission v Council*, judgment of 20 May 2008, at paras. 29–34, the Court held that Article 241 could also be invoked against a measure adopted under the second pillar for an infringement of Article 47 TEU.

[13] See Case C-64/ 93 *Donatab v Commission* [1993] ECR I-3595 at para. 20; Case T-369/03 *Arizona Chemical and Others v Commission* [2005] ECR II-5839, para. 129; Case T-299/04 *Selmani v Council and Commission* [2005] ECR II-20*, para. 77; Case T-376/04 *Polyelectrolyte Producers Group v Council and Commission* [2005] ECR II-3007, para. 49; Case T-386/04 *Eridania and Others v Commission* [2005] ECR II-2531, para. 51.

[14] Joined Cases T-93/00 and T-46/01 *Alessandrini and Others v Commission* [2003] ECR II-1635, para. 77. See also Case 32/65 *Italy v Council* [1966] ECR 389, p. 409; Case T-120/99 *Kik v OHIM* [2001] ECR II-2235, para. 24; Case F-19/05 *Sanchez Ferriz v Commission*, judgment of 28 June 2006, para. 57.

[15] See AG Slynn in Case 181/85 *France v Commission* [1987] ECR 689, at p. 703. See also Case T-251/02 *E v Commission* [2004] ECR II-1643, para. 122.

[16] Case T-120/99 *Kik v OHIM* [2001] ECR II-2235, at paras. 24 and 25; upheld on appeal in Case C-361/01 P *Kik v OHIM* [2003] ECR I-8283, para. 76.

[17] [1994] OJ L 11/1.

measure challenged under Article 241 does not constitute the legal basis of the act in issue in the main action.[18]

On the other hand, the Community Courts will declare Article 241 inadmissible where no legal connection exists between the general act and the act in issue in the main action. In *Italy v Commission* the Court found that Regulation 17/62[19] and Regulation 153/62[20] were not 'sufficiently related' to Regulation 19/65,[21] which formed the subject of the main action, 'to have any repercussions on its legality'.[22] In *Alessandrini and Others v Commission*[23] the CFI found that a causal link between the damage caused to the applicants and Regulation 2362/98[24] for the purpose of an action for compensation would not have been sufficient to establish a direct legal link in the context of an indirect challenge under Article 241.

Acts Subject to Challenge

Article 241 limits the acts subject to a challenge under this provision to regulations adopted jointly by the European Parliament and the Council, of the Council, of the Commission or of the ECB. The application of Article 241 poses no problems where the challenge is directed against acts which are regulations in form and substance and are adopted by the above-named institutions.[25]

The Community Courts have however expanded the scope of this provision by giving the term regulation a wide interpretation.[26] In *Simmenthal* the Court found that Article 241 'must include acts of the institutions which, although they are not in the form of a regulation, nevertheless produce similar effects and on those grounds may not be challenged

---

18 See Joined Cases C-189/02 P etc. *Dansk Rørindustri and Others v Commission* [2005] ECR I-5425, at paras. 214 and 237.

19 [1959–62] OJ English Special Edition p. 87.

20 [1962] OJ No 139.

21 [1965–66] OJ English Special Edition, p. 35.

22 Case 32/65 *Italy v Council* [1966] ECR 389, p. 409. See also Case F-19/05 *Sanchez Ferriz v Commission*, judgment of 28 June 2006, para. 58.

23 Joined Cases T-93/00 and T-46/01 *Alessandrini and Others v Commission* [2003] ECR II-1635, at para. 79, upheld on appeal in Case C-295/03 P *Alessandrini and Others v Commission* [2005] ECR I-5673, para. 69.

24 [1998] OJ L 293/32.

25 See Case 20/71 *Sabbatini v European Parliament* [1972] ECR 345; Case T-120/99 *Kik v OHIM* [2001] ECR II-2235. See also Case T-43/02 *Jungbunzlauer v Commission* [2006] ECR II-3435, paras. 69 *et seq.*, and Case T-279/02 *Degussa v Commission* [2006] ECR II-897, at paras. 66 *et seq.*, in which the CFI examined challenges under Article 241 against Article 15(2) of Regulation 17/62.

26 For the various legal instruments which can be the subject of an indirect challenge under Article 241 EC, see M. Vogt, supra note 4, pp. 370–377.

under Article 173 [now Article 230] by natural or legal persons other than Community institutions and Member States.'[27] The form of the act is therefore not relevant. Consequently, challenges under Article 241 can be considered against acts of general application[28] in diverse forms, such as 'notices of invitation to tender',[29] 'Staff Rules'[30] or 'evaluation guides'.[31] Similarly, there does not appear to be any reason why Directives should not be amongst the acts which can be challenged under Article 241.[32] The Community Courts have even accepted challenges under Article 241 to certain internal measures laid down by Community institutions. In *Libéros v Commission*[33] the Court found that 'internal measures adopted by the administration [. . .] may not be regarded as rules of law which the administration is always bound to observe, they nevertheless form rules of practice from which the administration may not depart without giving the reasons which led it to do so, which must be compatible with the principle of equal treatment. Consequently, the officials and other staff concerned may invoke their illegality in support of an action against the individual decision taken on the basis of the measures'.[34] In *Dansk Rørindustri v Commission*[35] the Court held that this ruling also applied to rules of conduct designed to produce external effects, such as the 'Guidelines on the method of setting fines imposed pursuant to Article 15(2) of Regulation No 17 and Article 65 of the ECSC Treaty'.[36] The Court argued that '[i]n adopting such rules of conduct and announcing by publishing them that they will henceforth apply to the cases to which they relate, the institution in question imposes a limit on the exercise of its discretion and cannot depart from those rules under pain of being

---

[27] Case 92/78 *Simmenthal v Commission* [1979] ECR 777 at para. 40.

[28] More precisely, the provision which forms the subject of a challenge under Article 241 must be of general application, see Case T-251/02 *E v Commission* [2004] ECR II-1643, para. 122.

[29] Case 92/78 *Simmenthal v Commission* [1979] ECR 777, at paras 34 *et seq.*

[30] See C-301/02 P *Tralli v ECB* [2005] ECR I-4071.

[31] Case F-19/05 *Ferriz v Commission*, judgment 28 June 2006, para. 36.

[32] See Case T-351/02 *Deutsche Bahn v Commission* [2006] ECR II-1047, at para. 108, and Case C-86/03 *Greece v Commission* [2005] ECR I-10979, at para. 86. In both cases the Community Courts did not address the issue of the form of the act as Directive. See also M. Vogt, supra note 4, pp. 374–376.

[33] Case C-171/00 *Libéros v Commission* [2002] ECR I-451.

[34] Ibid., para. 35. The case concerned a Commission decision which laid down the criteria applicable to grade and step classification on recruitment of officials.

[35] Joined Cases C-189/02 P etc. *Dansk Rørindustri and Others v Commission* [2005] ECR I-5425, at paras. 214 and 237. See also Case T-329/01 *Archer Daniels Midland v Commission* [2006] ECR II-3255, at paras. 38–54 *et seq.* And in Case T-176/01 *Ferriere Nord v Commission* [2004] ECR II-3931, at para. 136, the CFI considered guidelines on state aid in relation to environmental protection as challengeable under Article 241.

[36] [1998] OJ C 9/3.

found, where appropriate, to be in breach of the general principles of law, such as equal treatment or the protection of legitimate expectations'.[37] It could therefore not be ruled out that such rules of general application might produce legal effects. Consequently, given their legal effects and their general application such guidelines could form the subject matter of a challenge under Article 241.[38] On the other hand, in *Guggenheim v Cedefop*[39] the Court considered a challenge to a note written by the Director of the European Centre for the Development of Vocational Training (Cedefop)[40] as inadmissible on the ground that the note did not produce any legal effects binding for the administration.

The Court justified its approach in *Simmenthal* by arguing that Article 241 expressed a general principle 'conferring upon any party to proceedings the right to challenge, for the purpose of obtaining the annulment of a decision of direct and individual concern to that party, the validity of previous acts of the institutions which form the legal basis of the decision which is being attacked, if that party was not entitled under Article 173 [now Article 230] of the Treaty to bring a direct action challenging those acts by which it was thus affected without having been in a position to ask that they be declared void'.[41]

This general principle has also been invoked in proceedings against a decision of the Board of Appeal of the Office for Harmonisation in the Internal Market (Trade Marks and Designs). The Court held that 'the fact that Regulation 40/94 on the Community trade mark[42] does not expressly mention the plea of illegality as a collateral legal remedy which persons bringing actions may use before the Court of First Instance when seeking the annulment or alteration of a decision of a Board of Appeal of the Office does not mean that they cannot raise such a plea in those actions'.[43] This means that an applicant who seeks review of a decision by a Board of Appeal of the Office can indirectly challenge the validity of Regulation 40/94. However, it can be argued that the invocation of the general principle set out in *Simmenthal* was unnecessary, as Article 241 merely refers to

---

[37] Joined Cases C-189/02 P etc. *Dansk Rørindustri and Others v Commission* [2005] ECR I-5425, para. 211.

[38] Ibid., at para. 237.

[39] Case T-373/04 *Guggenheim v Cedefop*, judgment of 25 July 2006, at para. 35.

[40] [1975] OJ L 39/1.

[41] Case 92/78 *Simmenthal v Commission* [1979] ECR 777, para. 39. See also Joined Cases T-93/00 and T-46/01 *Alessandrini and Others v Commission* [2003] ECR II-1635, at para. 76.

[42] [1994] OJ L 11/1.

[43] Case T-120/99 *Kik v OHIM* [2001] ECR II-2235, para. 21, upheld on appeal in Case C-361/01P *Kik v OHIM* [2003] ECR I-8283, at para. 76.

'proceedings in which a regulation [. . .] is at issue' provided the main action is brought in proceedings before the Community Courts.[44]

The rationale in *Simmenthal* could, however, be invoked to allow challenges to acts producing legal effects which are not adopted by institutions listed in Article 241, such as the European Parliament acting alone or the Court of Auditors, or other bodies, such as agencies. What is more, this principle could possibly also be employed to challenge acts which are not of general application, but could not have been challenged by individuals under Article 230(4), such as Decisions which are addressed to third parties and which are not of direct and individual concern to the applicant.[45]

On the other hand, the logic of the ruling in *Simmenthal* would exclude incidental challenges to acts which could have been challenged under Article 230(4) by an individual, but were not challenged within the time-limit laid down in Article 230(5). In *Wöhrmann and Lütticke v Commission*[46] the Court already pointed out that Article 241 did not allow the time limit laid down in Article 230(5) to be avoided. While such an approach is clearly justified in relation to acts of individual application, the clear wording of Article 241, comparisons with national law and considerations of judicial policy speak against this approach in relation to acts of general application.[47] This issue has assumed greater importance in preliminary references under Article 234 and will therefore be discussed in more detail below.[48]

The Lisbon Treaty would solve certain difficulties which the present wording of Article 241 EC presents. First, Article 277 TFEU would allow an indirect challenge to any act of general application, and not merely regulations. Second, Article 277 TFEU refers to institutions,[49] bodies, offices or agencies of the Union whose acts can be challenged under this provision. These innovations would allow a challenge to a wider range of acts than is currently the case.

---

[44] See the dictum in Joined Cases 31 and 33/62 *Wöhrmann and Lütticke v Commission* [1962] ECR 501, discussed above. The limitation in that case at p. 507 to 'some other provision in this Treaty', is too limited. Actions for judicial review of decisions of the Boards of Appeal of OHIM are based on Article 63 of Regulation 40/94 and not the EC Treaty. All the same, it is submitted that the decisive point is that the main proceedings are brought before the Community Courts, in this case the CFI.

[45] See T.C. Hartley, supra note 4, p. 392.

[46] Joined Cases 31 and 33/62 *Wöhrmann and Lütticke v Commission* [1962] ECR 501, at p. 507.

[47] See also M. Vogt, supra note 4, pp. 368–370.

[48] See, infra, pp. 216–217.

[49] The institutions of the Union are listed in Article 13(1) TEU (Lisbon).

Parties Able to Bring a Challenge

The statement of the Court in *Simmenthal* has even wider ramifications as it raises the question whether privileged applicants would be allowed to invoke Article 241. If the rationale of Article 241 is to ensure that a party which could not bring an action under Article 230 to challenge an act directly must be in a position to challenge such an act indirectly where it forms the legal basis of a measure which that party is entitled to challenge under Article 230, then privileged applicants cannot use Article 241 as they can challenge any reviewable act.[50] Article 241 could therefore only be invoked by private parties. This result could be justified by reference to the principle of legal certainty which would preclude privileged applicants from challenging acts the time-limit of which has already expired and which have therefore become definitive against them. If they were allowed to invoke Article 241 against acts which they failed to challenge within the time-limit of Article 230(5), privileged applicants could evade the time-limit under Article 230(5) and Community acts could be called in question indefinitely.[51] This might even encourage delaying tactics on the part of privileged applicants.[52]

However, several AGs have come out in favour of the right of privileged applicants to plead Article 241.[53] They have referred to the clear wording of Article 241 which allows 'any party' to challenge regulations even after the expiry of the time-limit laid down in Article 230(5).[54] The Treaty thereby 'undoubtedly opens up an additional possibility of review for privileged applicants who would have been able to institute proceedings for annulment as of right.'[55] They found that *Simmenthal* could not

---

[50] See Opinion of AG Jacobs in Case C-11/00 *Commission v ECB* [2003] ECR I-7147, at para. 193. See also G. Bebr, supra note 4; J. Usher, 'The Interrelationship of Article 173, 177 and 184 EEC' (1979) *ELRev* 36; R. Joliet, *Le droit institutionnel des Communautés européennes. Le contentieux* (1981), pp. 132 and 133.

[51] See Opinion of AG Jacobs in Case C-11/00 *Commission v ECB* [2003] ECR I-7147, at para. 192.

[52] Opinion of AG Jacobs, ibid., at para. 192.

[53] See AG Roemer in Case 32/65 *Italy v Council and Commission* [1966] ECR 389; AG Slynn in Case 181/85 *France v Commission* [1987] ECR 689; AG Mancini in Case 204/86 *Greece v Council* [1988] ECR 5323; AG Darmon in Case C-258/89 *Commission v Spain* [1991] ECR I-3977.

[54] See AG Roemer in Case 32/65 *Italy v Council and Commission* [1966] ECR 389, p. 414 *et seq.*; AG Slynn in Case 181/85 *France v Commission* [1987] ECR 689, at pp. 702–703. See also AG Mancini in Case 204/86 *Greece v Council* [1988] ECR 5323, at para. 6; AG Jacobs in Case C-11/00 *Commission v ECB* [2003] ECR I-7147, at para 194. See also A. Barav, supra note 4, pp. 366 *et seq.*; Dubois, 'L'exception d'illégalité devant la Cour de justice des Communautés européennes' (1978) *Cahier de droit européen* 411 *et seq.*

[55] Opinion of AG Darmon in Case C-258/89 *Commission v Spain* [1991] ECR I-3977, para. 26.

be invoked to justify the exclusion of privileged applicants from invoking Article 241.[56] In addition, they argued that defects in a general act usually come to light only after some time, when the act has been applied, and after the time limit for challenging it under Article 230 has expired.[57] Moreover, privileged applicants would otherwise have to challenge all general acts within the time limit of Article 230, a development that might not be desirable with regard to the case load of the Court.[58]

While strongly denying Member States the possibility of invoking Article 241 against decisions addressed to them,[59] the Court was initially reluctant to decide whether Member States and other privileged applicants could invoke Article 241. In *Italy v Council and Commission*,[60] the Court found that there was no link between the regulation which was the subject of the main proceedings and the regulation against which Italy invoked Article 241. The Court did however not pronounce on whether Article 241 could be invoked in principle in this situation. In *Commission v Germany*[61] the Court, without discussing the issue, allowed Germany to plead the illegality of a regulation in proceedings brought by the Commission under Article 226.

The Court finally decided the issue in *Commission v ECB*.[62] The Court confirmed its approach that decisions adopted by the Community institutions which have not been challenged within the time-limit laid down by Article 230(5) would become definitive against their addressees.[63] Similarly, a regulation could also become definitive against an individual in regard to whom it must be considered as individual decision where the individual could have undoubtedly challenged that act under Article 230. However, the Court found that this approach would not 'in any way affect the rule laid down by Article 241 EC, which provides that any party may, in proceedings in which a regulation of the kind referred to in Article 241 EC is at issue, plead the grounds specified in the second paragraph of Article 230 EC in order to invoke before the Court of Justice the inapplicability of

---

[56] See AG Slynn in Case 181/85 *France v Commission* [1987] ECR 689, at pp. 702–703. See also Opinion of AG Mancini in Case 204/86 *Greece v Council* [1988] ECR 5323, at para. 6; AG Darmon in Case C-258/89 *Commission v Spain* [1991] ECR I-3977, para. 27.

[57] Opinion of AG Mancini in Case 204/86 *Greece v Council* [1988] ECR 5323, at para. 6; Opinion of AG Darmon in Case C-258/89 *Commission v Spain* [1991] ECR I-3977, para. 30.

[58] Opinion of AG Darmon in Case C-258/89 *Commission v Spain* [1991] ECR I-3977, para. 30.

[59] See Case C-183/91 *Commission v Greece* [1993] ECR I-3131 at para. 10.

[60] Case 32/65 *Italy v Council and Commission* [1966] ECR 389.

[61] Case 116/82 *Commission v Germany* [1986] ECR 2519.

[62] Case C-11/00 *Commission v ECB* [2003] ECR I-7141.

[63] Ibid., para. 74.

that regulation'.[64] The Court found that the act was of a legislative nature and it could not be claimed that it 'should be treated as a decision or that the ECB would, in such a case, be the addressee thereof'.[65] Consequently, the ECB could invoke Article 241 against the regulation in issue. The Court has confirmed in *Spain v Council* that this approach is also applicable in respect of privileged applicants.[66]

Grounds of Review and Effect of Inapplicability

The grounds of review in a challenge under Article 241 are essentially the same as under Article 230.[67] In *Busacca,* the Court pointed out that 'the inapplicability of a regulation, found indirectly pursuant to Article 241 of the EC Treaty [. . .] in proceedings calling that regulation into question, is binding only between the parties to those proceedings'.[68] The effect of inapplicability of the regulation challenged under Article 241 is therefore only *inter partes* and not *erga omnes* as in case of proceedings under Article 230.

2. VALIDITY REVIEW

Article 234 EC provides the Court with the opportunity on a reference by a national court to review the validity of an act adopted by a Community institution.[69] As an indirect mechanism to review Community acts, Article 234 thereby provides an important complement to Article 241. While Article 241 only allows a challenge to Community acts of general application by way of an action against a Community implementing act in the Community Courts, Article 234 envisages the review of such acts where a national court is seized with an action against an implementing act adopted by a national authority. Given that the vast majority of Community acts of general application are implemented by national authorities, Article 234 assumes considerable importance for individuals to seek redress against Community acts of general application against which a direct challenge is usually not available. This is all the more so, as the Court has recently rejected attempts to abandon the *Plaumann* formula in favour of a broader interpretation of

---

[64] Ibid., para. 76.
[65] Ibid., para. 77.
[66] Case C-442/04 *Spain v Council,* judgment of 15 May 2008, at para. 22.
[67] See supra, pp. 106–150.
[68] Case C-434/98P *Council v Busacca and Others* [2000] ECR I-8577, at para. 26.
[69] See A. Ward, *Judicial Review and the Rights of Private Parties in EU Law* (OUP, 2nd edn., 2007), chapter 7.

individual concern in Article 230(4), which would allow private parties to challenge Community acts of general application directly in the Community Courts, and has expressly refused to grant standing in the Community Courts where an individual would not have a remedy in a national court.[70]

This section will set out the relevant features of validity review under Article 234 before returning to the debate on whether Article 234 constitutes an effective mechanism for review of Community acts.

Jurisdiction of the Court

Court or tribunal of a Member State

Article 234 EC provides that only a 'court or tribunal of a Member State'[71] can refer a question as to the validity of a Community act to the Court of Justice. The Court has consistently held that the question as to whether a body referring such a question to the ECJ is a 'court or tribunal' is 'governed by Community law alone'.[72] It is therefore irrelevant whether a body is regarded as court or tribunal under national law.[73]

The Court employs a number of different factors to assess whether the body referring the question is a 'court or tribunal'.[74] This rather pragmatic approach[75] has enabled a wide range of different bodies to make requests for a preliminary ruling. In particular, the Court takes into account whether the body is established by law,[76] whether it is permanent,[77] whether

---

[70] Joined Cases T-236/04 and T-241/04 *EEB and Another v Commission* [2005] ECR II-4945, at para. 67; Case T-369/03 *Arizona Chemical and others v Commission* [2005] ECR II-5839, at para. 95.

[71] The concept 'of a Member State' is determined by the geographical scope of application of the EC Treaty laid down in Article 299 EC, see Opinion of AG Jacobs in Case C-355/89 *Barr and Montrose Holdings* [1991] ECR I-3479, at paras. 6–10. It is doubtful that the term also includes international courts situated in a Member State, but see Case C-337/95 *Parfums Christian Dior* [1997] ECR I-6013, paras. 19–23.

[72] Case C-96/04 *Standesamt Stadt Niebüll* [2006] ECR I-3561, para. 12. See also Case 61/65 *Vaassen* [1966] ECR 261.

[73] See Case 246/80 *Broekmeulen* [1981] ECR 2311; Case C-111/94 *Job Centre Coop* [1995] ECR I-3361.

[74] Case 61/65 *Vaasen* [1966] ECR 261, Case C-111/94 *Job Centre* [1995] ECR I-3361, para. 9; Case C-54/96 *Dorsch Consult* [1997] ECR I-4961, at para. 23; Joined Cases C-110/98 to C-147/98 *Gabalfrisa and Others* [2000] ECR I-1577, at para. 33; Case C-53/03 *Syfait and Others* [2005] ECR I-4609, at para. 29; Case C-96/04 *Standesamt Stadt Niebüll* [2006] ECR I-3561, para. 12.

[75] For a critique of the Court's approach, see Opinion of AG Colomer in Case C-17/00 *Coster* [2001] ECR I-9445, at para. 14.

[76] Case 102/81 *Nordsee* [1982] ECR 1095, at para. 12. This excludes references made by an arbitration body appointed on the basis of a contractual provision agreed between private parties without state involvement, see Case 102/81 *Nordsee* [1982] ECR 1095, at paras. 9–13.

[77] Case C-416/96 *El-Yassini* [1999] ECR I-1209, at para. 20.

its jurisdiction is compulsory,[78] whether its procedure is *inter partes*,[79] whether it applies rules of law[80] and whether it is independent.[81]

The Court has emphasised that a reference is only admissible if a case is pending before the referring body which has to give judgment in proceedings of a judicial nature.[82] Consequently, the judicial nature of the proceedings will be lacking, where a body, even if it satisfies all other criteria, exercises administrative authority without deciding on a dispute.[83]

Reviewable acts

The Court has jurisdiction under Article 234(1)(b) EC to give preliminary rulings on the validity of acts of the institutions of the Community and the ECB.[84] The Court would therefore have jurisdiction to review acts adopted by the Council, the Commission, the European Parliament, the Court of Auditors and the European Central Bank.[85] On the other hand, preliminary rulings of the Court itself are not subject to review under Article 234.[86]

The jurisdiction of the Court under Article 234[87] clearly entails the review of Regulations, Directives[88] and Decisions.[89] However, the range

---

[78] Case 246/80 *Broekmeulen* [1981] ECR 2311, at paras. 15 and 17.

[79] *Inter partes* proceedings are often considered desirable, but references are accepted even in the absence of such proceedings, see Joined Cases C-277/91, C-318/91 and C-319/91 *Ligur Carni* [1993] ECR I-6621, at para. 16. See also Case C-111/94 *Job Centre* [1995] ECR I-3361, at para. 9; Case C-96/04 *Standesamt Stadt Niebüll* [2006] ECR I-3561, para. 13.

[80] Case C-393/92 *Almelo* [1994] ECR I-1477, at para. 23.

[81] Case C-24/92 *Corbiau* [1993] ECR I-1277, at paras. 14–16; Case C-54/96 *Dorsch Consult* [1997] ECR I-4961, at paras. 34–36. But compare Joined Cases C-110/98 and C-147/98 *Gabalfrisa and others* [2000] ECR I-1577, where the reference was considered admissible, with Case C-53/03 *Syfait* [2005] ECR I-4609, where the Court, in contrast to AG Jacobs, considered the reference as inadmissible.

[82] Case 138/80 *Borker* [1980] ECR 1975, at para. 4; Case 14/86 *Pretore di Salò* [1987] ECR 2545, at para. 7; Opinion of AG Jacobs in Case C-195/98 *Österreichischer Gewerkschaftsbund* [2000] ECR I-10497, at para. 35; Case C-165/03 *Längst*, judgment of 30 June 2005, at para. 25; Case C-96/04 *Standesamt Stadt Niebüll* [2006] ECR I-3561, para. 13.

[83] Case C-111/96 *Job Centre* [1995] ECR I-3361, at para. 11; Case C-165/03 *Längst* [2005] ECR I-5637, at para. 26; Case C-96/04 *Standesamt Stadt Niebüll* [2006] ECR I-3561, para. 14.

[84] While Article 225(3) provides jurisdiction for the CFI to hear and determine questions referred for a preliminary ruling under Article 234 in specific areas laid down by Statute, no such jurisdiction has yet been transferred.

[85] Article 267 TFEU widens the scope of review to include not only Union institutions, but also bodies, offices and agencies of the Union.

[86] Case 69/85 *Wünsche* [1986] ECR 947, at para. 16.

[87] Article 150 Euratom applies in the context of the European Atomic Energy Community.

[88] See 5/77 *Tedeschi v Denkavit* [1977] ECR 1555; Case 240/83 *Association de Defense des Brulers d'Huiles Usagees* [1983] ECR 531; Case C-331/88 *ex parte Fedesa* [1990] ECR I-4023; Case C-212/91 *Angelopharm* [1994] ECR I-200; Case C-51/93 *Meyhui v Schott* [1993] ECR I-3879.

[89] See Case 314/85 *Foto-Frost* [1987] ECR 4199; Case C-148/04 *Unicredito* [2005] ECR I-11137.

of reviewable acts under Article 234 is wider than that under Article 230. As the Court pointed out in *Grimaldi*, 'unlike Article 173 [now 230] of the EEC Treaty, which excludes review by the Court of acts in the nature of recommendations, Article 177 [now 234] confers on the Court jurisdiction to give a preliminary ruling on the *validity* and interpretation of all acts of the institutions of the Community without exception'.[90] This seems particularly relevant for Community measures which form part of proceedings leading to the adoption of a national act, but do not constitute reviewable acts under Article 230. In *Tillack*[91] the applicant challenged the referral by OLAF of information concerning suspicions of breach of professional secrecy and bribery to the national judicial authorities, which led to the search of the applicant's home and office and the seizure of professional documents and personal belongings. The CFI found that the referral could not be considered as reviewable act within the meaning of Article 230. However, in response to the suggestion that this would deprive the applicant of effective judicial protection, the CFI responded that 'the applicant also had the opportunity to request the national courts, which have no jurisdiction themselves to declare that the act by which OLAF forwarded information to the Belgian judicial authorities is invalid [. . .], to make a preliminary reference to the Court of Justice in that regard'.[92] On the other hand, the Court has no jurisdiction to review the validity of primary Community law. The Court has also made it clear that a failure to act by a Community institution cannot be reviewed within the context of a preliminary ruling.[93]

While neither the strict standing requirements of Article 230(4) EC nor the time-limit in Article 230(5) EC apply in cases of validity review under Article 234, the Court has found that 'a decision which has not been challenged by the addressee within the time-limit laid down in Article 173 [now Article 230] of the EC Treaty becomes definitive as against him'.[94] This means that the decision can no longer be called in question by a reference under Article 234. A decision can not only become definitive as against its addressee, but also against a third party, where that third party could undoubtedly have challenged that decision.[95] The Court held in *TWD*

[90] Case C-322/88 *Grimaldi* [1989] ECR 4407, para. 8. Emphasis added.

[91] Case T-193/04 *Tillack v Commission* [2006] ECR II-3995.

[92] Ibid., para. 80.

[93] Case C-68/95 *T. Port* [1996] ECR I-833, at para. 53.

[94] Case C-241/01 *National Farmers' Union v Secrétariat général du gouvernement* [2002] ECR I-9079, at para 36, where a Member State (France) failed to challenge an act under Article 230(2).

[95] See Case C-182/92 *TWD Textilwerke Deggendorf v Germany* [1994] ECR I-833; Case C-119/05 *Lucchini* [2007] ECR I-6199, at para. 55.

Textilwerke Deggendorf that in this case it was not possible 'to call in question the lawfulness of that decision before the national courts in an action brought against the measures taken by the national authorities for implementing that decision'.[96] A decision that is addressed to a third party can therefore be indirectly challenged in two situations. First, an indirect challenge is permissible where the applicant lacked standing due to the fact that the act did not concern him directly and individually.[97] Second, an indirect challenge has to be allowed where, even though the applicant was directly and individually concerned by the decision, it might not have been aware of it.[98] An indirect challenge against a Community act is, however, excluded whenever the applicant could have brought 'without any doubt' an action against that act.

This rationale for excluding indirect challenges applies also to regulations, even though the possibility that an individual could have challenged a regulation 'without any doubt' is rather the exception. Consequently, in *Accrington Beef*[99] the Court found that it was not obvious that the applicant would have been granted standing in a direct challenge under Article 230(4). Similarly, in *Eurotunnel*[100] the Court was not convinced that a direct challenge under Article 230(4) against a Directive would have been admissible. However, in *Nachi* the Court extended the approach adopted in *Textilwerke Deggendorf* to anti-dumping regulations by holding that also a regulation could become definitive against an individual 'in regard to whom it must be considered to be an individual decision and who could undoubtedly have sought its annulment under Article 230 EC'.[101] The Court's approach to determine the admissibility of an indirect challenge on the basis as to whether the applicant could have challenged the act under Article 230(4), is problematic because of the notorious uncertainties surrounding direct and individual concern under Article 230(4).[102]

---

[96] See Case C-182/92 *TWD Textilwerke Deggendorf v Germany* [1994] ECR I-833, para. 16. See also Case C-232/05 *Commission v France* [2006] ECR I-10071, para. 59; Joined Cases C-346/03 and C-529/03 *Atzeni and Others* [2006] ECR I-1875, para. 31; Case C-119/05 *Lucchini* [2007] ECR I-6199, at para. 55.

[97] See Joined Cases C-346/03 and C-529/03 *Atzeni and Others* [2006] ECR I-1875, at paras. 33–34.

[98] See Case 216/82 *Universität Hamburg* [1982] ECR 2771.

[99] Case C-241/95 *The Queen v Intervention Board for Agricultural Produce, ex p. Accrington Beef Co. Ltd. And Others* [1996] ECR I-6691, at para. 15.

[100] Case C-408/95 *Eurotunnel SA and Others v Sea France* [1997] ECR I-6315, at para. 29.

[101] Case C-239/99 *Nachi Europe GmbH v Hauptzollamt Krefeld* [2001] ECR I-1197, para. 37. See, however, Case C-351/04 *Ikea Wholesale* [2007] ECR I-7723, at para. 25; Case C-441/05 *Roquette Frères* [2007] ECR I-1993, at para. 48.

[102] See A. Arnull, 'Private Applicants and the Action for Annulment since Codorniu' (2001) 38 *CMLRev* 7–52, at p. 52; A. Ward, supra note 69, at p. 322–323; J. Usher 'Direct

The Court also has jurisdiction to review the validity of acts of the institutions of the Community adopted under Title IV of the EC Treaty subject to the considerations set out in Article 68 EC. Likewise, under the third pillar, Article 35(1) TEU provides the Court with jurisdiction to give preliminary rulings on the validity of framework decisions, decisions and measures implementing conventions established within the scope of Police and Judicial Co-operation in Criminal Matters.[103] The Court has ruled in relation to Article 35(1) TEU that 'the right to make a reference to the Court for a preliminary ruling must therefore exist in respect of all measures adopted by the Council, whatever their nature or form, which are intended to have legal effects in relation to third parties'.[104] While this generous interpretation of the scope of Article 35(1) TEU includes common positions which have such legal effects,[105] the protection of private parties under this provision falls well short of that provided under Article 234 ECT. It would only be with the entering into effect of the Lisbon Treaty that the restrictive provisions of Article 68 ECT and 35(1) TEU would be abolished allowing acts adopted in the area of freedom, security and justice[106] to fall under the regular regime of Article 267 TFEU, which would replace Article 234 EC. The Court would, however, continue to lack jurisdiction under Article 267 TFEU with regard to matters falling under the CFSP.

Question raised

Article 234 requires that a question be raised in national proceedings as to the validity of a Community act. While such a question can be raised by the parties to the proceedings or the national court of its own motion,[107] AG Jacobs argued in *UPA*[108] that access to national courts might often not be possible because the Community rules would not require any

---

and individual concern – an effective remedy or a conventional solution?' (2003) 28 *ELRev* 575–600, at p. 590.

[103] The Court's jurisdiction is, however, dependent on a declaration of the Member State to that effect. See Article 35(2) TEU.

[104] Case C-354/04 P *Gestoras Pro Amnistía and Others v Council* [2007] ECR I-1579, para. 52.

[105] Ibid., para. 53.

[106] Title V of the TFEU. See, however, Title VII of the Protocol of Transitional Provisions. For a transitional period of five years the powers of the Court of Justice remain those provided under the existing Title VI of the TEU in relation to acts of the Union adopted in the field of police co-operation and judicial co-operation in criminal matters which have been adopted before the Treaty of Lisbon (see Article 10(1) of the Protocol). The limitation does not apply to amendments of such acts (see Article 10(2) of the Protocol). Special provisions apply to the UK (see Article 10(4) and (5) of the Protocol).

[107] Case 126/80 *Salonia* [1981] ECR 1563, at para. 7.

[108] Case C-50/00 P *Unión de Pequeños v Council* [2002] ECR I-6677.

implementing act on the part of the national authorities or could only be obtained at the price of infringing the law.[109]

The Court has countered this criticism by imposing on the Member States a duty to provide an effective remedy to access national courts. In *UPA* the Court held that 'in accordance with the principle of sincere cooperation laid down in Article 5 [now Article 10] of the Treaty, national courts are required, so far as possible, to interpret and apply national procedural rules governing the exercise of rights of action in a way that enables natural and legal persons to challenge before the courts the legality of any decision or other national measure relative to the application to them of a Community act of general application, by pleading the invalidity of such an act'.[110] As one author made clear, this solution 'quite simply fails to deal with the situation where the applicant's legal situation is affected by a regulation which is not of direct and individual concern, as traditionally interpreted, and which has not received or required national implementation'.[111] It should be pointed out, however, that the facts in *UPA* seem to suggest that a remedy was available. The applicants could have applied for their usual subsidies and the refusal to grant them by the national authorities would have enabled them to bring an action in the national court.

All the same, this was not an option available to the applicants in *Jégo Quéré*.[112] Here the applicants claimed that they were only able to raise the issue of the validity of the Commission regulation if they were prepared to contravene the law first. The Court[113] on appeal rejected this suggestion:

> It is possible for domestic law to permit an individual directly concerned by a general legislative measure of national law which cannot be directly contested before the courts to seek from the national authorities under that legislation a measure which may itself be contested before the national courts, so that the individual may challenge the legislation indirectly. It is likewise possible that under national law an operator directly concerned by Regulation No 1162/2001 may seek from the national authorities a measure under that regulation which may be contested before the national court, enabling the operator to challenge the regulation indirectly.[114]

---

109 See also G. Mancini and D Keeling, 'Democracy and the European Court of Justice' (1994) 57 *MLR* 175, 188; Opinion of AG Tesauro in Case C-63/89 *Assurances du crédit v Council and Commission* [1991] ECR 1799, at para. 9.

110 Case C-50/00 P *Unión de Pequeños v Council* [2002] ECR I-6677, para. 42.

111 J. Usher, supra note 102, p. 584.

112 Case T-177/01 *Jégo Quéré v Commission* [2002] ECR II-2365.

113 Case C-263/02P *Jégo Quéré v Commission* [2004] ECR I-3425.

114 Ibid., para. 35.

In some Member States national courts have accommodated individuals' requests to challenge Community acts of general application, even without any national implementing acts having been adopted.[115] The English courts, for example, have accepted actions and made references to the Court in case of a Directive which had not been implemented[116] and a Regulation which did not require any national implementing measures.[117] The ruling in *Jégo Quéré* makes it clear that the duty of sincere co-operation only obliges national courts to provide an adequate remedy 'so far as possible'.[118] However, the ruling seems also to suggest that where national courts could not provide an adequate remedy under national law in the absence of a national implementing act, the Member State had to enact provisions which provide an individual with a remedy to access national courts to raise the invalidity of a Community act.

Decision must be necessary

Article 234 stipulates that a question can be referred to the Court if the national court considers that a decision on the question is necessary to enable it to give judgment. The assessment as to whether a decision is necessary is one for the national court to make.[119] The Court will, however, reject a reference where 'the appraisal of the validity of a rule of Community law sought by the national court bears no relation to the actual facts of the main action or its purpose'.[120] This approach seems to be more favourable to the applicant than the comparable approach under Article 241 where the Court requires a direct legal connection between the regulation and the contested act.[121] The Court will also declare the reference inadmissible, where the 'problem is hypothetical, or where the Court does not have

---

[115] See the references of English courts in Case C-74/99 *Imperial Tobacco and others* [2000] ECR I-8599; Case C-27/00 and C-122/00 *Omega Air and others* [2002] ECR I-2569; Case C-491/01 *British American Tobacco and Imperial Tobacco* [2002] ECR I-11453; Case C-344/04 *IATA and ELFAA* [2006] ECR I-403. See also J. Usher, supra note 102, p. 586; A. Ward, supra note 69, p. 348–349.

[116] See Case C-74/99 *Imperial Tobacco* [2000] ECR I-8599.

[117] Joined Cases C-27/00 and C-122/00 *Omega Air* [2002] ECR I-2569.

[118] See Case C-263/02P *Jégo Quéré v Commission* [2004] ECR I-3425, at para. 32. But see J. Temple-Lang, supra note 9, who argues, at p. 111, that national courts were under a duty to provide an appropriate remedy. See also A. Ward, supra note 69, at p. 349.

[119] See Case C-341/01 *Plato Plastik Robert Frank* [2004] ECR I-4883, at para. 26.

[120] Case C-296/03 *Glaxosmithkline* [2005] ECR I-669, para. 22. See also Joined Cases C-480/00 to 482/00, C-484/00, C-489/00 to C-491/00 and C-497/00 to C-499/00, *Azienda and Others* [2004] ECR I-2943, para. 72; Case C-341/01 *Plato Plastik Robert Frank* [2004] ECR I-4883, at para. 28; Case C-344/04 *IATA and ELFAA* [2006] ECR I-403, para. 25.

[121] On the question of direct link, see supra pp. 206–207.

before it the factual or legal material necessary to enable it to give a useful answer to the questions submitted to it'.[122]

Powers and Obligations of National Courts

Article 234 EC makes a distinction between courts against whose decisions there is a judicial remedy under national law and those against whose decisions no such remedy exists. The former have according to Article 234(2) EC a discretionary power to refer, while the latter are bound to make a reference under Article 234(3). The distinction is, however, mainly of relevance for preliminary references for the interpretation of Community law and of lesser importance for requests to rule on the validity of Community acts.

Limitations imposed by *Foto-Frost*

The Court held in *Foto-Frost*[123] that national courts, regardless of whether they fall under Article 234(2) or (3) EC, were precluded from declaring Community acts invalid. The Court found that this limitation on national courts was required to ensure the uniformity of Community law and the coherence of the system of judicial protection.[124] On the other hand, the ruling in *Foto-Frost* does not prevent national courts from examining the validity of Community acts. The Court found that national courts 'may consider the validity of a Community act and, if they consider that the grounds put forward before them by the parties in support of invalidity are unfounded, they may reject them, concluding that the measure is completely valid'.[125]

The Court expanded on this ruling in its judgment in *IATA*[126] in response to the question by the High Court as to whether under Article 234(2) a reference was necessary only where there is more than a certain degree of doubt as to the validity of a Community act. The Court made it clear that:

---

[122] Case C-341/01 *Plato Plastik Robert Frank* [2004] ECR I-4883, para. 28. See also Joined Cases C-480/00 to 482/00, C-484/00, C-489/00 to C-491/00 and C-497/00 to C-499/00, *Azienda and Others* [2004] ECR I-2943, para. 72; Case C-296/03 *Glaxosmithkline* [2005] ECR I-669, para. 22.

[123] Case 314/85 *Foto-Frost v Hauptzollamt Lübeck-Ost* [1987] ECR 4199, para. 15. See also Case C-119/05 *Lucchini* [2007] ECR I-6199, at para. 53.

[124] For a critical appraisal of these reasons, see A. Ward, supra note 69, pp. 352–354. For a defence of *Foto-Frost*, see S. Enchelmaier, 'No-One Slips Through the Net? Latest Developments and Non-Developments in the European Court of Justice's Jurisprudence on Article 230(4) EC' (2005) 24 *YEL* 173–221, p. 216.

[125] Case 314/85 *Foto-Frost v Hauptzollamt Lübeck-Ost* [1987] ECR 4199, para. 14.

[126] Case C-344/04 *IATA and ELFAA* [2006] ECR I-403.

> Article 234 EC does not constitute a means of redress available to the parties to a case pending before a national court and therefore the mere fact that a party contends that the dispute gives rise to a question concerning the validity of Community law does not mean that the court concerned is compelled to consider that a question has been raised within the meaning of Article 234 EC [. . .]. Accordingly, the fact that the validity of a Community act is contested before a national court is not in itself sufficient to warrant referral of a question to the Court for a preliminary ruling.[127]

The Court found that the national court 'may examine the validity of a Community act and, if they consider that the arguments put forward before them by the parties in support of invalidity are unfounded, they may reject them, concluding that the act is completely valid. On the other hand, where such a court considers that one or more arguments for invalidity, put forward by the parties or, as the case may be, raised by it of its own motion [. . .], are well founded, it is incumbent upon it to stay proceedings and to make a reference to the Court for a preliminary ruling on the act's validity.'[128]

While the ruling in *IATA* was clearly limited to national courts falling within Article 234(2), the recent judgment of the CFI in *Danzer*[129] seems to have extended this approach to last instance courts under Article 234(3).[130] It is submitted that this would leave the assessment as to the validity of a Community act entirely within the hands of national courts. The only means of redress for the individual would then consist in seeking redress from the Member State under *Francovich*.[131] As the recent judgment in *Köbler*[132] made clear, this remedy is available in principle where national courts of last instance have breached Community law, but it is unlikely to succeed in practice.

Power of national court to grant interim relief

The judgment in *Zuckerfabrik*,[133] while confirming the lack of competence for national courts to declare Community acts invalid, provided national courts[134] with the power to grant interim relief against such acts

127 Ibid., para. 28.

128 Ibid., paras. 29 and 30.

129 Case T-47/02 *Danzer v Council* [2006] ECR II-1779.

130 Ibid., at para. 37. The judgment seems to suggest that last instance courts are, however, subject to the limitations set out in Case 283/81 *CILFIT* [1982] ECR 3415 and Case C-495/03 *Intermodal Transports* [2005] ECR I-8151.

131 Joined Cases C-6/90 and C-9/90 *Francovich and Bonifaci v Italy* [1991] ECR I-5357.

132 Case C-224/01 *Köbler v Austria* [2003] ECR I-10239.

133 Joined Cases C-143/88 and C-92/89 *Zuckerfabrik Süderdithmarschen and Zuckerfabrik Soest* [1991] ECR I-415.

134 In contrast to national courts, national administrative authorities are not empowered to adopt interim measures, see Joined Cases C-453/03, C-11/04, C-12/04 and C-194/04 *ABNA*

in proceedings before them. The applicants in this case had challenged a decision by the national authorities which required the payment of a special elimination levy introduced by a Community regulation.[135] The national court, which on application had suspended the national decision, enquired about the power of national courts and the conditions for such a course of action. The Court pointed out that the legal protection guaranteed by Community law included 'the right of individuals to challenge, as a preliminary issue, the legality of Community regulations before national courts and to induce those courts to refer questions to the Court of Justice for a preliminary ruling'.[136] If individuals could not obtain a suspension of the effects of the disputed regulation, provided certain conditions were met, that right would be compromised. Since individuals who challenged a Community act directly in the Community Courts could obtain interim relief on the basis of Article 242 EC, the Court found that 'the coherence of the system of interim legal protection therefore requires that national courts should also be able to order suspension of enforcement of a national administrative measure based on a Community regulation'.[137] Moreover, as national courts could grant interim relief in disputes about the compatibility of national law with Community law, the Court stated that individuals must enjoy the same legal protection of Community law 'irrespective of whether they contest the compatibility of national provisions with Community law or the validity of secondary Community law, in view of the fact that the dispute in both cases is based on Community law itself'.[138]

In *Atlanta*[139] the Court held that this principle applied not only to the suspension of the enforcement of a national act adopted on the basis of a Community regulation, but also to the adoption of a positive order which provisionally disapplied that regulation.[140] The Court pointed out that the grant of a positive order 'does not as such have more radical consequences for the Community legal order than the mere suspension of enforcement of

---

and Others [2005] ECR I-10423, at paras. 108–110. Also the Court of Justice lacks jurisdiction to grant interim measures in preliminary-rulings proceedings, see Case C-186/01 R *Dory* [2001] ECR I-7823, at para. 13.

135 Council Regulation 1914/87, [1987] OJ L 183/5.

136 Joined Cases C-143/88 and C-92/89 *Zuckerfabrik Süderdithmarschen and Zuckerfabrik Soest* [1991] ECR I-415, para. 16.

137 Ibid., para. 18. See also Case C-465/93 *Atlanta Fruchthandelsgesellschaft and others* [1995] ECR I-3761, para. 22; Case C-68/95 *T. Port* [1996] ECR I-6065, para. 49.

138 Joined Cases C-143/88 and C-92/89 *Zuckerfabrik Süderdithmarschen and Zuckerfabrik Soest* [1991] ECR I-415, para. 20.

139 Case C-465/93 *Atlanta Fruchthandelsgesellschaft and others* [1995] ECR I-3761.

140 Ibid., paras. 26–28.

a national measure on the basis of a regulation'.[141] The effects of an interim measure had to be assessed in any event on the basis of a balancing of the Community interest with that of the individual concerned.

In its *Zuckerfabrik* ruling the Court also laid down the conditions under which the national court can adopt interim measures.[142] Interim measures can be adopted only where the national court is persuaded that 'serious doubts exist as to the validity of the Community regulation on which the contested administrative measure is based'.[143] The national court cannot merely refer the matter to the Court for a preliminary ruling, but must state the reasons for the invalidity of the Community act in the interim order.[144] When considering the invalidity of a Community act the national court has to take account of the discretion which the Community Courts accord the Community institutions in their decision-making.[145]

The Court also made it clear that interim relief granted by the national courts 'must retain the character of an interim measure'.[146] The national court can only grant interim relief until the Court has ruled on the validity of the act in question. The national court must therefore refer the question to the Court and must set out the reasons for the invalidity of the act.[147] This also means that interim relief can only be maintained 'for so long as the Court has not ruled that consideration of the questions referred for a preliminary ruling has disclosed no factor of such a kind as to affect the validity of the regulation in question'.[148]

The Court argues that the need for the uniform application of Community law in the Member States requires that uniform conditions as to the grant of interim relief are imposed restricting national autonomy to the making and examination of such relief.[149] The Court aligns the conditions for the grant of interim relief by national courts with those applicable in case of

---

[141] Ibid., para. 29.

[142] See also the clarifications in Case C-465/93 *Atlanta Fruchthandelsgesellschaft and others* [1995] ECR I-3761 and Joined Cases C-453/03, C-11/04, C-12/04 and C-194/04 *ABNA and Others* [2005] ECR I-10423.

[143] Joined Cases C-143/88 and C-92/89 *Zuckerfabrik Süderdithmarschen and Zuckerfabrik Soest* [1991] ECR I-415, para. 23. In light of the ruling in Case C-344/04 *IATA and ELFAA* [2006] ECR I-403 it should be sufficient that the national court considers the arguments as to the invalidity of the Community act well founded.

[144] Case C-465/93 *Atlanta Fruchthandelsgesellschaft and others* [1995] ECR I-3761, para. 36.

[145] Ibid., para. 37.

[146] Joined Cases C-143/88 and C-92/89 *Zuckerfabrik Süderdithmarschen and Zuckerfabrik Soest* [1991] ECR I-415, para. 24.

[147] Ibid., para. 24.

[148] Case C-465/93 *Atlanta Fruchthandelsgesellschaft and others* [1995] ECR I-3761, para. 38.

[149] Joined Cases C-143/88 and C-92/89 *Zuckerfabrik Süderdithmarschen and Zuckerfabrik Soest* [1991] ECR I-415, paras. 25 and 26.

interim relief adopted by the Community Courts under Articles 242 and 243.[150] Consequently, the application of the requirement of urgency by the national court has to follow the Court's case law adopted under these provisions.[151] The national court must examine the circumstances particular to the case and must consider 'whether immediate enforcement of the measure which is the subject of the application for interim relief would be likely to result in irreversible damage to the applicant which could not be made good if the Community act were to be declared invalid'.[152]

The national court is also obliged to ensure the full effect of Community law and must 'take account of the interest of the Community, namely that such regulations should not be set aside without proper guarantees'.[153] The national court must therefore examine whether 'the Community measure in question would be deprived of all effectiveness if not immediately implemented'.[154] The Court clarified this requirement in *Atlanta*, where it held that the national court must 'take account of the damage which the interim measure may cause the legal regime established by that regulation for the Community as a whole. It must consider, on the one hand, the cumulative effect which would arise if a large number of courts were also to adopt interim measures for similar reasons and, on the other, those special features of the applicant's situation which distinguish him from the other operators concerned'.[155] Finally, where interim relief constitutes a financial risk to the Community, the applicant must provide 'adequate guarantees, such as the deposit of money or other security'.[156]

In *Atlanta* the Court reminded the national court that in accordance with Article 10 EC it had to respect the decisions taken by the Court. Hence, where the ECJ[157] has dismissed an annulment action on the merits or has found in a preliminary ruling that the reference has not revealed any ground for the invalidity of the Community act in issue, the national court 'can no longer order interim measures or must revoke existing measures'.[158]

---

[150] Ibid., para. 27; Case C-465/93 *Atlanta Fruchthandelsgesellschaft and others* [1995] ECR I-3761, para. 39.

[151] Joined Cases C-143/88 and C-92/89 *Zuckerfabrik Süderdithmarschen and Zuckerfabrik Soest* [1991] ECR I-415, paras. 28 and 29.

[152] Ibid., para. 29.

[153] Ibid., para. 30.

[154] Ibid., para. 31.

[155] Case C-465/93 *Atlanta Fruchthandelsgesellschaft and others* [1995] ECR I-3761, para. 44.

[156] Joined Cases C-143/88 and C-92/89 *Zuckerfabrik Süderdithmarschen and Zuckerfabrik Soest* [1991] ECR I-415, para. 32.

[157] The same considerations apply for rulings of the CFI in annulment and plea of illegality cases, which have become final and binding.

[158] Case C-465/93 *Atlanta Fruchthandelsgesellschaft and others* [1995] ECR I-3761, para. 46.

The national court can, however, adopt interim measures where 'the grounds of illegality put forward before it differ from the pleas in law or grounds of illegality rejected by the Court in its judgment'.[159] In *Atlanta*, the Court had already ruled in an application for interim relief by Germany that a Member State could invoke in interim proceedings damage to a whole sector of its economy.[160] The national court had to accept the findings made by the Court in this respect as to the serious and irreparable nature of the damage, unless the applicant could distinguish himself from other operators in the sector.[161] The national court had to respect in particular 'the Court's assessment of the Community interest and the balance between that interest and that of the economic sector concerned'.[162]

Special regimes in Article 68 EC and Article 35 EU

National courts encounter more severe limitations on the possibility to refer under Article 68 EC. Article 68(1) limits the power of referring questions as to the validity of Community acts adopted under Title IV (Visas, Asylum and Immigration) to last instance courts.[163] The *Foto-Frost* doctrine is here particularly detrimental.[164] Courts other than those of last instance will not be in a position to grant applicants any remedy, as they are unable to set aside a Community act which they consider unlawful. Moreover, under the conditions set out in *Zuckerfabrik*, discussed above, these courts are also not able to grant interim relief, as they lack the power to refer the matter to the Court.[165] An individual would therefore have to appeal its case to a court against whose judgment there is no judicial remedy under national law, thereby considerably increasing the expense and delay of the proceedings. In order to avoid depriving individuals of effective judicial protection, it is submitted that either the *Foto-Frost* doctrine, which was established before the introduction of Article 68(1) EC, is considered not to apply in such cases and the national court is entitled to disapply the contested Community act, or to allow the national court to grant interim relief until such time as a reference can be made by a national court of last instance.

---

159 Ibid., para. 46.

160 See Case C-280/93 R *Germany v Council* [1994] ECR I-3667, at para. 27.

161 Case C-465/93 *Atlanta Fruchthandelsgesellschaft and others* [1995] ECR I-3761, para. 49.

162 Ibid., para. 50.

163 See J. Usher, supra note 102, p. 588.

164 See A. Ward, supra note 69, p. 352.

165 See also Communication from the Commission of 28 June 2006 on the adaptation of the provisions of Title IV of the Treaty establishing the European Community relating to the jurisdiction of the Court of Justice with a view to ensuring more effective judicial protection, COM (2006) 346 final, at p. 5.

Even worse is the position for private parties under the third pillar.[166] While direct actions against third pillar acts are not possible for individuals,[167] the jurisdiction of the Court to give preliminary rulings under Article 35(1) TEU on the validity of framework decisions and decisions, as well as measures implementing conventions, depends on the willingness of Member States to be subjected to such jurisdiction. Article 35(2) TEU states that the Court can only give a preliminary ruling where a Member State has accepted the jurisdiction of the Court to that effect.[168] Article 35(3) TEU gives Member States a choice as to whether to limit the possibility of making a reference to the national court of last instance or to allow any national court to make a reference.

The limitations imposed by Article 68 EC and Article 35 TEU would be eliminated by the Lisbon Treaty. Article 267 TFEU makes the preliminary rulings procedure available to acts adopted under Title IV TFEU, which brings the matters falling within the Area of Freedom, Security and Justice under one roof. This innovation would considerably strengthen the indirect mechanism of review under Article 267 TFEU as providing individuals with effective judicial protection.

Grounds of Review

Even though Article 234 differs from Article 230 in that the former entrusts the Court of Justice with the assessment of the validity of a Community act while the latter refers to the review of legality,[169] the case law of the Court does not seem to attach any significance to the difference in wording and employs the same grounds of review in Article 234 cases as it does in actions for annulment under Article 230.[170] These grounds have been discussed above.[171] The Court will, however, assess the validity of the Community act in issue only in light of the grounds referred to it by the national court.[172]

---

[166] See J. Usher, supra note 102, pp. 593–595.

[167] Article 35(6) TEU only allows Member States and the Commission to bring a direct action against decisions and framework decisions.

[168] For a list of Member States which have accepted the jurisdiction of the Court, see OJ [2005] L 327/19.

[169] The German government in Cases 73-74/63 *Handelsvereniging Rotterdam* [1964] ECR 1 suggested that a narrower interpretation had to be given to the term 'validity' in Article 234 than was applied in relation to 'legality' under Article 230.

[170] Joined Cases 21 to 24 *International Fruit and Others* [1972] ECR 1219, at para. 5. See also T.C. Hartley, supra note 4, p. 395; A. Ward, supra note 69, pp. 339–340.

[171] See supra pp. 106–150.

[172] Case C-305/05 *Ordre des barreaux francophones et germanophones and Others* [2007] ECR I-5305, at paras. 17–19.

Effects of judgment of the Court

A declaration of invalidity under Article 234 has binding effect not only on the national court which brought the matter before the Court, but, according to the Court's ruling in *ICC*[173] 'is sufficient reason for any other national court to regard that act as void for the purposes of a judgment which it has to give'.[174] The Court based this approach on the need for the uniform application of Community law, but also on 'imperative requirements concerning legal certainty'.[175] National courts are, however, not precluded from making references in relation to an act declared void by the Court, 'in particular if questions arise as to the grounds, the scope and possibly the consequences of the invalidity established earlier'.[176] It is also for the national courts to settle any disputes in relation to the effects of a Community act which has been declared void, such as the repayment of sums which were levied on the basis of an invalid Community act. As in the case of the invalidity of a national act which is contrary to Community law,[177] such disputes are governed by national procedural rules to the extent that Community rules do not determine the matter and subject to the principles of non-discrimination and effectiveness.[178]

A declaration of invalidity under Article 234 also has consequences for the Community institution responsible for the adoption of the act which has been declared void. It is incumbent on them to take all necessary measures to comply with the Court's ruling.[179] By analogy with Article 233[180] this does not only entail a negative duty to abstain from applying the act declared void, but also a positive duty to take certain measures 'to

---

173 Case 66/80 *International Chemical Corporation* [1981] ECR 1191.

174 Ibid., para. 13. See also J. Usher, 'Declarations of Invalidity Under Article 177 EEC: of General Effect?' (1984) 6 *ELRev* 284.

175 Case 66/80 *International Chemical Corporation* [1981] ECR 1191, para. 12.

176 Ibid., para. 14.

177 For a detailed comparison of the case law on the parity of treatment of the application of national procedural rules in the event of invalidity of a Community act and that of national law, see A. Ward, supra note 69, pp. 340–347, who comes to the conclusion, at p. 346, that 'the parity of treatment principle, which applied prior to the Court's 1980s interventionist challenge to domestic rules on remedies and procedures, continues to apply to validity claims'.

178 See Case 130/79 *Express Dairy Foods* [1980] ECR 1887, para. 12. See also Case 386/87 *Bessin et Salson* [1989] ECR 3551, para. 16, and the detailed discussion of various national procedural rules in Case C-212/94 *FMC and Others* [1996] ECR I-389.

179 See Joined Cases 117/76 and 16/77 *Ruckdeschel and Diamalt* [1977] ECR 1753, at para. 13; Case 4/79 *Providence Agricole de la Champagne* [1980] ECR 2823, at para. 44; Case 66/80 *International Chemical Corporation* [1981] ECR 1191, at para. 16.

180 On a detailed discussion on the duties arising under Article 233, see Chapter 1, pp. 155–164.

put an end to the illegality which has been found'.[181] It has, however, been observed that the Community institutions whose acts have been declared invalid under Article 234 do not always take the necessary measures in a timely manner.[182]

The Court has gradually established the principle that declarations of invalidity under Article 234 take retroactive effect, that is from the date on which the act entered into force, as in the case of an annulment under Article 230 EC.[183] The Court has, however, on occasion limited the temporal effects of a declaration of invalidity. In *Providence Agricole*[184] the Court found that, in the absence of any provisions in the EC Treaty on the effects of a declaration of invalidity, it was necessary to apply what is now Article 231(2) by analogy allowing the Court to 'state which of the effects of the regulation which it has declared void shall be considered as definitive, for the same reasons of legal certainty as those which form the basis of that provision'.[185] While it acknowledged the interest of the undertakings in recovering the sums paid but not owed due to the invalidity of the regulations adopted by the Commission, the Court argued that it was not possible to determine the economic disadvantages which resulted from the invalidity of the fixing of the monetary compensatory amounts under the system which the Commission had used for calculation 'without making assessments which that institution alone is required to make'.[186] Consequently, the Court limited the effects of the declaration of invalidity to the date of the judgment, thereby preventing the applicants from recovering the monetary compensatory amounts levied on them on the basis of the unlawful regulations.[187]

---

181 Opinion of AG Darmon in Case C-228/92 *Roquette Frères* [1994] ECR I-1445, para. 15. See also Joined Cases 117/76 and 16/77 *Ruckdeschel and Diamalt* [1977] ECR 1753, at para. 13.

182 See T. Vandamme, *The Invalid Directive: Legal Authority of a Union Act Requiring Domestic Law Making* (Groningen, European Law Publishing, 2005), pp. 71–72; A. Ward, supra note 69, p. 347.

183 See Case C-212/94 *FMC* [1996] ECR I-389, at para. 55. See also G. Bebr, 'Direct and Indirect Judicial Control of Community Acts in Practice: the Relation Between Arts 173 and 177 of the EEC Treaty', in *Michigan Law Review* (ed) 82 (1984), *The Art of Governance Festschrift zu Ehren von Eric Stein*, 1229; A. Ward, supra note 69, p. 354. After initial silence on the temporary effects of invalidity declarations (see Case 130/79 *Express Dairy Foods* [1980] ECR 1887), the Court implicitly acknowledged their *ex tunc* effect in Case 145/79 *Roquette Frères* [1980] ECR 2917.

184 See Case 4/79 *Providence Agricole de la Champagne* [1980] ECR 2823. See also Case 109/79 *Maïseries de Beauce* [1980] ECR 2883 and Case 145/79 *Roquette Frères* [1980] ECR 2917.

185 Case 4/79 *Providence Agricole de la Champagne* [1980] ECR 2823, para. 45.

186 Ibid., para. 45.

187 This also excluded the possibility of recovering the amounts by way of an action for compensation under Article 288(2), see Case 20/88 *Roquette Frères v Commission* [1989] ECR 1553.

While the Court's ruling encountered fierce criticism from the national courts concerned with repayment claims,[188] the Court's power to limit the temporal effects of a declaration of invalidity has generally received approval.[189] AG Darmon in his Opinion in *Roquette Frères* convincingly argued for the need to limit the effects of an invalidity declaration under Article 234.[190] First, unlike actions for annulment which are subject to strict time-limits, a preliminary reference to review the validity of a Community act can be brought many years after its adoption. A declaration of invalidity of the Community act can therefore expose a large number of legal relationships formed in good faith to illegality.[191] Secondly, AG Darmon opined that 'rules of Community law may affect especially sensitive sectors and declaring them invalid may entail significant consequences, including financial ones, which it is essential to be able to control'.[192] All the same, the limitation of a declaration of invalidity to the date of the judgment raises serious issues.[193] The limitation in time means that the regulation retains legal effects for some persons, but not for others. Moreover, individuals are prevented from relying on the unlawfulness of the Community act for the period before the date of the judgment. An *ex nunc* effect of an invalidity declaration should therefore remain the exception and be subject to strict conditions.[194] The Court must also take care to avoid the impression that 'less weighty considerations'[195] are employed to limit the effect of an invalidity declaration in relation to a Community act than in case of a ruling on the interpretation of Community law with legal effects in national law.

In later cases the Court moved away from its restrictive *ex nunc* approach. In *Pinna*[196] the Court limited the temporal effect of the declaration of inva-

---

188 See *Conseil d'Etat*, 2 June 1985 (1986) 22 *TRDE* 145; *Cour de Cassation*, 10 December 1985, (1986) 22 *RTDE* 159; Italian Constitutional Court in *Fragd v Amministraxione delle Finanze dello Stato*, (1989) *Rivista di diritto internazionale*, p. 103. See also G. Isaac, 'La modulation par la Court de Justice des Communautés européennes des effets dans le temps de ses arrêts d'invalidité' (1987) *CDE*, p. 444; D. Simon, 'L'effet dans le temps des arrêts préjudiciels de la Cour de justice des Communautés européennes: enjeu ou prétexte d'une nouvelle guerre des juges?', *Mélanges Pescatore* (Baden-Baden, 1987), p. 665.

189 See Opinion of AG Darmon in Case C-228/92 *Roquette Frères* [1994] ECR I-1445, at para.20. See also G. Bebr, supra note 183; C. Waelbroeck, 'May the Court of Justice Limit the Retrospective Operation of its Judgment?' (1981) 1 *YEL* 115; W. Alexander, 'The Temporal effects of Preliminary Rulings' (1988) 8 *YBEL* 11.

190 Opinion of AG Darmon in Case C-228/92 *Roquette Frères* [1994] ECR I-1445.

191 Ibid., at paras. 19 and 20.

192 Ibid., para. 20.

193 Ibid., para. 22.

194 Ibid., para. 25.

195 A. Ward, supra note 69, p. 356, comparing the considerations used in the MCA rulings with those entertained in Case 43/75 *Defrenne* [1976] ECR 455, in which the Court limited the temporal effects of the interpretation of what is now Article 141.

196 Case 41/84 *Pinna* [1986] ECR 1.

lidity to the date of the judgment with the exception of 'employed persons who have already brought legal proceedings or made an equivalent claim prior to the date of the judgment'.[197] The Court was rightly concerned that otherwise 'an economic agent such as the plaintiff in the main proceedings would thereby be deprived of its right to effective judicial protection in the event of a breach of Community law by the institutions, and the practical effect of Article 177 [now 234] of the Treaty would thereby be jeopardized'.[198] And in *Roquette Frères* the Court not only excluded those who had initiated judicial proceedings from the *ex nunc* effect of the invalidity declaration, but also 'traders who before the said date [date of the judgment declaring the act invalid] have submitted an administrative complaint, seeking reimbursement of the MCAs paid by them on the basis of such a regulation'.[199]

Article 234 as Effective Remedy

Validity review under Article 234 has recently come under attack by AG Jacobs in his Opinion in *UPA*, who argued that 'proceedings before national courts are not [. . .] capable of guaranteeing that individuals seeking to challenge the validity of Community measures are granted fully effective judicial protection'.[200] Even though it concedes that validity review under Article 234 does not grant individuals a right to a remedy,[201] the Court insists that 'the Treaty has established a complete system of legal remedies and procedures designed to ensure judicial review of the legality of acts of the institutions',[202] in which 'the reference for a preliminary ruling on the validity of an act and the action for annulment being the two mechanisms provided by the Treaty for reviewing the legality of legislation'.[203] Most academic commentators have rejected the idea that Article 234 provides effective judicial protection for individuals who wish to challenge acts of general application.[204] The remainder of this section

---

[197] Ibid., para. 30. See also Joined Cases C-38/90 and C-151/90 *Lomas* [1992] ECR I-1782, at para. 29; Case C-228/92 *Roquette Frères* [1994] ECR I-1445, at para. 28.

[198] Case C-228/92 *Roquette Frères* [1994] ECR I-1445, para. 27, following the Opinion of AG Darmon in this judgment.

[199] Ibid., para. 29.

[200] Opinion of AG Jacobs in Case C-50/00 P *Unión de Pequeños v Council* [2002] ECR I-6677, para. 41.

[201] Case C-344/04 *IATA and ELFAA* [2006] ECR I-403, para. 28.

[202] Case C-50/00 *Unión de Pequeños Agricultores v Council* [2002] ECR I-6677, para. 40.

[203] Case C-212/94 *FMC and Others* [1996] ECR I-389.

[204] See P. Ragolle, 'Access to justice for private applicants in the Community legal order: recent (r)evolutions' (2003) *ELRev* 90–101; J.M. Cortés Martin, 'Ubi Ius, Ibi Remedium? – *Locus Standi* of Private Applicants under Article 230(4) EC at a European Crossroads'

will explore to what extent AG Jacobs's criticism of Article 234 as effective remedy for individuals is justified and will argue that a more nuanced view might be preferable.[205]

Lack of competence of national courts

AG Jacobs's first criticism relates to the lack of competence of national courts to declare Community acts invalid under the Court's ruling in *Foto-Frost*.[206] Given the limitation of national courts to assess the validity of Community acts, he questioned whether national courts were the appropriate forum for such cases.

It should be pointed out in this respect that the Court has reduced the threshold at which national courts are competent and obliged to refer a Community act to the Court from serious doubts in *Foto-Frost* to whether arguments for the invalidity of the act are 'well founded' in *IATA*.[207] National courts therefore act as gatekeepers as to whether Community acts of general application are to be placed before the Court. Moreover, national courts, which have been entrusted with the interpretation and application of Community law, have become 'the ordinary courts of Community law'.[208] In the same way, they are entrusted to assess the validity of Community acts. Community law has become an integral part of national law and an assessment of the validity of Community acts is therefore no different from assessing the validity of national measures.

It is, however, a different matter as to whether the Court should reserve exclusive jurisdiction to declare Community acts invalid. It has been noted that the uniform application of Community law can be distorted just as much by allowing national courts to consider Community acts valid.[209] Moreover, the distortion of uniformity brought about by allowing a national court to declare an EC act invalid would be limited, in that such a declaration could, in contrast to the *erga omnes* effect of a declaration of invalidity by the Court, only take effect *inter partes*. The argument

(2004) *MJ* 233–261; C. Koch, '*Locus standi* of private applicants under the EU Constitution: preserving gaps in the protection of individuals' right to an effective remedy' (2005) *ELRev* 511–527, at p. 515; A. Ward, supra note 69, chapter 7.

[205] See also J. Usher, supra note 102; S. Enchelmaier, supra note 124, at pp. 199–220; J. Temple Lang, supra note 9.

[206] Opinion of AG Jacobs in Case C-50/00 *Unión de Pequeños Agricultores v Council* [2002] ECR I-6677, at para. 41.

[207] Case C-344/04 *IATA and ELFAA* [2006] ECR I-403, para. 30.

[208] Case T-219/95 R *Danielson v Council* [1995] ECR II-3051, para. 77. See also S. Enchelmaier, supra note 124, at pp. 202–203. On a critical discussion of the concept of 'legal subsidiarity', see also J.M. Cortés Martin, supra note 204, at pp. 251–253.

[209] A. Ward, supra note 69, p. 353. For the contrary view, see S. Enchelmaier, supra note 124, p. 216.

that national judges are capable of reviewing Community acts does not, however, imply that they should also be allowed to declare Community acts invalid. Community legislation in form enjoys a democratic legitimacy which is functionally comparable to that of parliamentary legislation in national legal systems.[210] This, however, only justifies the limitation of national courts to assess, but not to declare invalid, Community legislation in form, but not Community acts which only constitute legislation in substance. This point is made in Article 100 of the German Federal Constitution, which requires ordinary courts to refer Federal parliamentary acts, but not other acts of general application, which they consider unconstitutional to the German Constitutional Court, which is alone competent to declare such acts invalid.[211] All the same, to allow national courts to declare Community legislation in substance, but not form, invalid does not resolve the uncertainty as to the lawfulness of the act. Often, an appeal will follow and it would then only be the last instance court, which would have to refer the matter to the Court. This is undesirable in terms of cost and delay. The current system requires the national court which considers the EC act invalid to refer the matter to the Court allowing for a final settlement of the lawfulness of the act, and in case of a declaration of illegality with *erga omnes* effect.

Lack of remedy

AG Jacobs also points out that 'Article 234 is however not a remedy available to individual applicants as a matter of right'.[212] He argues that there is no guarantee that national courts, even after long delays on appeal, may refer the question to the Court. Moreover, it is for the national court to formulate the question, which entails that it is for them to determine the range of Community measures referred and the grounds on which they are considered invalid.

The Court conceded in *IATA* that 'Article 234 EC does not constitute a means of redress available to the parties to a case pending before a national court'.[213] And indeed individuals cannot force the national court to make a reference, where that court considers the act to be valid, or determine the scope and grounds for the reference. All the same, this does not mean that individuals are without a remedy. It is precisely the proceedings in the

---

[210] See A. Türk, *The Concept of Legislation in European Community Law – A Comparative Perspective* (Kluwer, 2006), p. 228.

[211] See also S. Enchelmaier, supra note 124, at p. 200.

[212] Opinion of AG Jacobs in Case C-50/00 P *Unión de Pequeños v Council* [2002] ECR I-6677, para. 42.

[213] Case C-344/04 *IATA and ELFAA* [2006] ECR I-403, para. 28.

national court which grant the individual the opportunity to have a court assess the validity of the Community act in issue.[214] And while it is true that national courts might refuse to refer on the ground that the Community act is valid,[215] individuals can avail themselves of appeal mechanisms under national law[216] and as a last resort would be able to rely on the Court's ruling in *Köbler*.

Problems in relation to effective judicial protection arise, however, under Articles 68 EC and Article 35(1) EU, where the national court, even though it considers the supranational act invalid, is not competent to refer the matter to the Court or to grant interim relief.[217] These limitations would, however, be removed with the entry into force of the Lisbon Treaty, as preliminary references under Article 267 TFEU would also be available in these areas.

Lack of access

A fault of the current system, in AG Jacobs's view, is also that in certain cases access to national courts might be difficult, or even impossible, where Community acts do not require any national implementing acts, which could form the basis for a challenge in national courts.[218] In this situation individuals would have to breach a Community act first before raising its invalidity in criminal or civil proceedings in national courts as a defence. This argument challenges the foundations of the Court's statement that the Community provides a comprehensive system of remedies. The Court's response, which imposes an obligation on national courts and national authorities to enable individuals to challenge Community acts of general application, should go some way to provide individuals with effective judicial protection.[219] While it currently results from the case-law of the Court, with the entering into force of the Lisbon Treaty this obligation would flow from Article 19(1)(2) of the Treaty of European Union.[220] Moreover, the reform of Article 230(4) EC in the Lisbon Treaty, discussed above,[221] which

---

[214] See also S. Enchelmaier, supra note 124, at p. 201.

[215] See the examples in A. Ward, supra note 69, pp. 350, 353.

[216] In Germany, the individual would also have the possibility to launch a constitutional complaint to the German Federal Constitutional Court under Article 101(1), second sentence, Grundgesetz against an unlawful refusal to refer. See S. Enchelmaier, supra note 124, p. 219.

[217] See J. Usher, supra note 102, pp. 588, 593–595.

[218] Opinion of AG Jacobs in Case C-50/00 P *Unión de Pequeños v Council* [2002] ECR I-6677, para. 43.

[219] See A. Ward, supra note 69, p. 364.

[220] Article 19(1)(2) TEU (Lisbon) reads: 'Member States shall provide remedies sufficient to ensure legal protection in the fields covered by Union law.'

[221] See Chapter 1, supra, at pp. 167–169.

allows a direct challenge in the Community Courts of regulatory acts which do not require any implementation at national level, would further reduce the potency of Jacobs's argument.

Disadvantages of validity review

AG Jacobs also pointed out that individual applicants suffer substantial additional delay and cost in comparison with direct actions.[222] Moreover, interim measures are within the discretion of national courts and are not applicable on a Community-wide basis.

The argument that individuals suffer greater delay and cost[223] in validity review proceedings in comparison with direct actions is questionable in its generality. Direct actions and preliminary proceedings take on average a similar length of time.[224] Proceedings which start in the national court will, however, on average, take longer, as the time of the national proceedings, in particular when the possibility of multiple levels of appeal is taken into account, would have to be added. All the same, if one includes an appeal from the CFI to the Court,[225] the length of time for a direct action to complete is on average just over three years. In comparison, it can be assumed proceedings in national courts, including a reference to the Court, will complete earlier, where the only issue at stake is the validity of a Community act of general application. In this case the national court of first instance which refers the matter to the Court will be able to provide a swift judgment after the Court, with no possibility of an appeal, has provided its preliminary ruling. Moreover, to avoid an appeal the national court will have to consider carefully the arguments of the applicant when making the reference to the Court.

While national courts are entitled to grant interim measures, the limited effect of such a measure within the national jurisdiction is indeed unsatisfactory.[226] The Court's refusal to grant interim relief in preliminary rulings proceedings[227] is, however, open to criticism. It is not readily apparent why

---

222 Opinion of AG Jacobs in Case C-50/00 P *Unión de Pequeños v Council* [2002] ECR I-6677, para. 44.

223 See, however, J. Usher, supra note 102, who points out, at pp. 591–592, that in direct actions the applicant has to be legally represented and risks having costs awarded against him, whereas in preliminary reference procedures no obligation to appear or to be legally represented before the Court exists and costs are a matter for the referring national court.

224 See section 8 of the Annual Report of the Court for 2006. In 2006 direct actions on average took 20 months to complete, while preliminary references lasted 19.8 months on average.

225 The average time for an appeal is 17.8 months.

226 See also A. Ward, supra note 69, p. 364. For a more balanced view, see S. Enchelmaier, supra note 124, p. 202.

227 See Case C-186/01 R *Dory* [2001] ECR I-7823, at para. 13.

the Court should lack jurisdiction, once a national court has referred the matter to the Court to grant interim relief against a Community act. The stipulation in Article 243 EC that the Court may 'in any cases before it' grant interim measures, does not *a priori* rule out such a course of action. Moreover, the repeated statements of the Court concerning the similarity between an action for annulment under Article 230 and validity review under Article 234 and its willingness to apply by analogy rules applicable to annulment actions seems to make it difficult to reject the argument that the adoption of interim measures be available not only in annulment proceedings but also in validity review proceedings under Article 234. Having said that, it is, however, not certain that the Court would show less reluctance in granting interim relief than national courts.[228]

Procedural limitations in 234 proceedings before the Court

AG Jacobs finally highlighted that validity review under Article 234 suffers from a number of procedural disadvantages in comparison with direct actions under Article 230.[229] Only in direct actions is the Community institution which adopted the act under review party to the proceedings from the beginning. Moreover, validity review only allows for a single round of written observations followed by oral observations, whereas direct actions involve a full exchange of pleadings.[230] Also, interested individuals will only be able to intervene in Article 234 proceedings if they have already intervened in the action before the national court. Even though the institution whose act is under review in preliminary rulings proceedings is not from the beginning a party to the proceedings, it is sufficiently protected under Community law. According to Article 23 of the Court's Statute the institution whose act is under review is notified and entitled to submit a written defence of the act and can refute any arguments submitted by other parties in the oral hearing. It should, however, be acknowledged that the intervention rights of interested individuals should be improved.

Finally, AG Jacobs emphasised that considerations of legal certainty make direct actions preferable, as the short time-limit of two months in Article 230(5) compares favourably with the open-ended nature of challenges under Article 234. This argument is also questionable. Firstly, swift clarity as to the validity of a Community act could only be achieved if individuals would be barred under a strict application of the *TWD*

---

[228] See S. Enchelmaier, supra note 124, p. 202.

[229] Opinion of AG Jacobs in Case C-50/00 P *Unión de Pequeños v Council* [2002] ECR I-6677, paras. 45–48.

[230] J. Usher, supra note 102, has remarked, at p. 592, that 'the balance of advantage depends on the perspective from which the matter is viewed'.

principle to challenge Community acts which they could have undoubtedly challenged under Article 230(4), but did not do so within the time-limit laid down in Article 230(5). It seems doubtful that AG Jacobs's interpretation of individual concern[231] provides greater clarity than the Court's *Plaumann* test. Given the continuing uncertainty as to the interpretation of individual concern under Article 230(4) it seems contradictory to improve the provision of effective judicial protection under Article 230(4) while at the same time eliminating the possibility of an indirect challenge against a Community act of general application under Article 234.[232] Moreover, such a strict application of the *TWD* principle would also have to be applied to indirect challenges under Article 241. Secondly, it is often difficult to assess the validity of acts of general application in the abstract and it is often after some time that faults of legislation emerge in individual cases. This is also why national legal systems which allow a direct challenge to acts of general application do usually not bar individuals from challenging such acts indirectly in actions against acts of individual application.

Viewed in this perspective the validity review under Article 234 compares favourably with an annulment action under Article 230. It is precisely the open-ended nature of the possibility of review without application of the admissibility requirements laid down in Article 230(4) and (5), which make validity review under Article 234 attractive to individuals. The possibility of imposing temporal limitations on the effects of an invalidity declaration by the Court will satisfy the need for legal certainty.[233] What is more, Article 234 also compares favourably with Article 230 in that the preliminary rulings procedure is not limited to reviewable acts in the meaning of Article 230.

Conclusion

Article 234 constitutes an important avenue for individuals to have Community legislation reviewed. While it is not a remedy for individuals in the traditional sense, Article 234 allows individuals to raise the unlawfulness of a wide range of Community measures years after their adoption in individual cases. National courts, while not empowered to invalidate a Community measure, have to assess the validity of Community acts and thereby act as screening panels for the Court. The inclusion of national

---

231 See Chapter 1, supra, pp. 96–97.

232 In his Opinion in Case C-50/00 P *Unión de Pequeños v Council* [2002] ECR I-6677, at para. 65, AG Jacobs himself seems to have been against such a bar on Article 234 references.

233 So also S. Enchelmaier, supra note 124, pp. 204–205.

courts in the process of judicial review of Community acts has become more prominent with the obligation to provide an effective remedy.

The dispute about widening the direct access to the Community Courts under Article 230(4) has had beneficial effects for individuals seeking indirect review of Community acts under Article 234. Access to national courts has been improved through the obligation on Member States to provide an effective remedy. Similarly, national courts can make a reference where they find arguments against a Community act well founded instead of having to have serious doubts. Over time the strict interpretation of temporal limitations of an invalidity declaration has also given way to a more flexible approach protecting the interests of individual applicants.

Nevertheless, there are still areas of concern. First, with *Nachi* the *TWD* principle seems to have reached its widest application and it is submitted that the principle should be limited to acts of individual application, but that acts of general application should be open to an indirect challenge under Article 234[234] as well as under Article 241. Second, while the limitation on the powers of national courts to invalidate Community acts can be justified, the *Foto-Frost* doctrine has particularly detrimental effects in the case of Article 68 EC and Article 35 TEU. At least in the case of Article 68 EC the case for allowing all national courts to refer a case to the Court for a validity review has become overwhelming. This issue would, however, become mute with the entry into force of the Lisbon Treaty, as Article 267 TFEU also applies in these areas without restrictions. Similarly, the limitation of the effects of interim relief granted by national courts invites a reconsideration of the refusal of the Court to grant interim relief in cases where a validity review under Article 234 is pending before it.

[234] See also Opinion of AG Jacobs in Case C-50/00 P *Unión de Pequeños v Council* [2002] ECR I-6677, at para. 65.

4 Non-contractual liability

Article 235 EC grants the Court jurisdiction in disputes which concern compensation for damage under the conditions set out in Article 288(2) EC.[1] The Court has understood the jurisdiction under Article 235 as exclusive, thereby excluding the national courts from hearing and determining actions for the non-contractual liability of the EC under Article 288(2).[2] In *First and Franex*,[3] the Court found that the exclusive jurisdiction of the Community Courts also includes the possibility 'to prescribe, with regard to one of the institutions of the European Community, any interim measure or measure of inquiry, such as commissioning an expert report whose purpose is to establish the role of that institution in the events which allegedly caused damage, for the purposes of an action which may be brought against the European Community to establish its non-contractual liability'.[4] The Court justified this approach with the need to ensure the uniform application of the system of non-contractual liability of the EC given that Member States apply different rules regarding the

---

[1] See generally, G. Roberts, 'Judicial Review of Legislative Measures: the European Court of Justice Breathes Life into the Second Paragraph of Article 215' (1988) 26 *Columbia Journal of Transnational Law* 245; H.G. Schermers, T. Heukels, and P. Mead (eds.), *Non-Contractual Liability of the European Communities* (Martinus Nijhoff, 1988); F. Schockweiler, G. Wivenes and J. Godart, 'Le régime de la responsibilité extra-contractuelle du fait d'actes juridiques dans la Communauté européenne' (1990) *RTDE* 27; F. Capelli and M. Migliazza, 'Recours en Indemnité et Protection des Intérêts Individuels: Quelles sont les Changements Possibles et Souhaitables?' (1995) *CDE* 585–640; T. Heukels and A. McDonnell (eds.), *The Action for Damages in Community Law* (Kluwer Law International, 1997); T. Tridimas, 'Liability for Breach of Community Law: Growing Up and Mellowing Down?' (2001) 38 *CMLRev* 301 (pp. 321–332); J. Wakefield, *Judicial Protection Through the Use of Article 288(2)* (Kluwer, 2002); P. Craig, *EU Administrative Law* (OUP, 2006), pp. 764–788; T.C. Hartley, *The Foundations of European Community Law* (OUP, 6th edn., 2007), chapter 16; T. Tridimas, *The General Principles of EU Law* (OUP, 2nd edn., 2006), chapter 10; A. Ward, *Judicial Review and the Rights of Private Parties in EU Law* (OUP, 2nd edn., 2007), chapter 8; P. Craig and G. DeBúrca, *EU Law – Text, Cases and Materials* (OUP, 4th edn., 2008), chapter 16. For a discussion of the contractual liability of the EC and on restitution, see T.C. Hartley, op. cit., pp. 421–428.

[2] Case C-275/00 *First and Franex* [2002] ECR I-10943, para. 43. See also Case 101/78 *Granaria* [1979] ECR 623, para. 14. See also Joined Cases 106/87 *Asteris and Others v Greece* [1988] ECR 5515, para. 15; Case C-55/90 *Cato v Commission* [1992] ECR I-2533, para. 17.

[3] Case C-275/00 *First and Franex* [2002] ECR I-10943.

[4] Ibid., para. 46.

submission of requests for interim measures and in relation to expert reports. National courts are therefore precluded from ordering expert reports for the purpose of establishing the non-contractual liability of the EC. On the other hand, the Court has made it recently clear that it does not have jurisdiction to entertain an action for damages under Title VI TEU.[5] With the entry into force of the Lisbon Treaty the Court would have jurisdiction under Article 268 TFEU to hear disputes in relation to compensation for damages as provided for by Article 340(2) and (3) TFEU, which contain few changes.[6]

Article 288(2) provides that 'in the case of non-contractual liability, the Community shall, in accordance with the general principles common to the Member States, make good any damage caused by its institutions or by its servants in the performance of their duties'. It is clear from this provision that an action cannot be brought against an institution of the Community itself, but against the Community represented by the institution or institutions whose action allegedly caused the damage.[7]

While not containing any substantive principles itself, Article 288(2) entrusts the Court of Justice with a creative mandate to develop such principles on the basis of a comparative approach. Given that it refers to common principles, the provision does not seem to require the Court to opt for rules which exist in most, or even all, Member States. In light of the differences in the national legal systems as to the rules on granting compensation for damage caused by public authorities, this would not be possible. Moreover, the special nature of the Community legal order would make it difficult to apply rules which have been developed in the context of constitutional states.

This provides the Court with considerable discretion in pursuing the task of establishing rules and principles of non-contractual liability which are suitable to the Community legal system. However, the relevance of such common principles reaches beyond the demands of Article 288(2), as the Court has used the principles established for non-contractual liability of the EC for the existence and conditions of Member State liability in the wake of the *Francovich* ruling.

---

[5] See Case C-354/04 P *Gestoras Pro Amnistía and Others v Council* [2007] ECR I-1579, at paras. 44–48.

[6] This jurisdiction apparently also includes, however, compensation for damage caused by acts currently adopted under the third pillar.

[7] See Case T-364/03 *Medici Grimm v Council* [2006] ECR II-79, at para. 47. See also Case T-209/00 *Lamberts v Ombudsman* [2002] ECR II-2203, at para. 48. In Cases 63-69/72 *Wehrhahn v Council and Commission* [1973] ECR 1229 the Court rejected the argument that, by analogy with Article 282 EC, the Commission should represent the Community in such proceedings. See also T.C. Hartley, supra note 1, p. 429.

On the basis of the mandate given to it under Article 288(2) the Court has established that 'Community responsibility depends on the coincidence of a set of conditions as regards the unlawfulness of the acts alleged against the institutions, the fact of damage, and the existence of a direct link in the chain of causality between the wrongful act and the damage complained of'.[8] These basic conditions have been developed in the case law of the Community Courts to form a comprehensive set of rules determining Community liability.

This chapter will discuss which acts can trigger the non-contractual liability of the EC under Article 288(2) and when they are attributable to the Community. The main focus of this chapter will be on the procedural and substantive problems which legal acts provide for establishing the non-contractual liability of the EC. This will be followed by considering the conditions of damage and causation. Finally, the time-limit within which an action under Article 288(2) has to be brought will be studied. The few changes brought about by Article 340(2) and (3) TFEU will be mentioned where they are relevant.

1. ATTRIBUTABLE ACT

Article 288(2) states that the Community is liable for an act that can be attributed to an EC institution or its civil servants in the performance of their duties. The concept of 'act' has been given a wide meaning and comprises 'measures or conduct attributable to a Community institution or body'.[9] The concept is therefore wider than the concept of reviewable act under Article 230. It includes a report by OLAF terminating an anti-fraud investigation,[10] press releases by OLAF,[11] the handling of a complaint by the Ombudsman,[12] the bringing of proceedings in the USA by the Commission,[13] and even physical acts, such as driving a car.[14] It can also comprise omissions, but 'only where the institutions have infringed a legal obligation to act under a provision of Community law'.[15] However,

---

[8] Case 153/73 *Holtz & Willemsen v Council* [1974] ECR 675 at para. 7.

[9] Case T-250/02 *Autosalone Ispra v EAEC* [2005] ECR II-5227, para. 41, for liability under Article 188(2) EA, which is similar in wording to Article 288(2).

[10] Case T-309/03 *Grau v Commission* [2006] ECR II-1173.

[11] See Case T-193/04 *Tillack v Commission* [2006] ECR II-3995, at para. 126.

[12] See Case C-234/02 P *European Ombudsman v Lamberts* [2004] ECR I-2803, at para. 63.

[13] Case C-131/03 P *Reynolds and Others v Council* [2006] ECR I-7795, para. 82.

[14] See Case 9/69 *Sayag v Leduc* [1969] ECR 329.

[15] Case T-196/99 *Area Cova SA and Others v Council and Commission* [2001] ECR II-3597, at para. 84. See also Case T-514/93 *Cobrecaf v Commission* [1995] ECR II-621 at para.

primary EC law cannot give rise to liability of the Community under Article 288(2). In *Dubois*[16] the applicant claimed compensation for damage due to the completion of the Internal Market on the basis of the Single European Act, which led to the abolition of the customs agency work in which he was involved in France. The CFI rejected the argument that primary EC law can give rise to the Community's liability, as '[t]he Single Act thus constitutes neither an act of the institutions nor an act of the servants of the Community. [. . .] Article 178 [now 235] and the second paragraph of Article 215 [now 288] of the Treaty, which govern the non-contractual liability of the Community, are also primary law. Under the hierarchy of rules, those provisions cannot be brought to bear on instruments belonging to an equivalent level where this is not expressly provided for.'[17]

Such an act must be attributable to an EC institution or to its servants in performance of their duties. EC liability arises therefore for acts of the European Parliament, Council, Commission and the Court of Auditors, which are referred to in Article 7(1) as Community institutions. In addition, Article 288(3)[18] provides that the Community is liable for damage caused by the ECB or its servants in the performance of their duties.[19] It is submitted that the Community is also liable for damage, at least in principle, by the European Court. First, the European Court is referred to in Article 7(1) as an EC institution. Secondly, in the light of the ruling in *Köbler*, where the Court held that Member States can be held liable for damage caused by a breach of Community law of their last instance courts, it would be difficult to reject the liability of the Community Courts. Moreover, the Court has emphasised on several occasions that the conditions governing Member State liability are also applicable to the Community.[20] The Community Courts have made it clear that they favour an expansive interpretation of the term 'institution', which goes beyond the institutions listed in Article 7(1). In *Lamberts v Ombudsman*[21] the CFI held that '[t]he term also covers, with regard to the system of non-contractual liability established by the Treaty, all other Community bodies established by the Treaty and intended to contribute to the achievement of the Community's objectives.

70; Joined Cases T-344/00 and T-345/00 *CEVA and Pfizer v Commission* [2003] ECR II-229, at para. 103, and the appeal in Case C-198/03 P *Commission v CEVA and Pfizer* [2005] ECR I-6357; Case T-195/00 *Travelex and Other v Commission* [2003] ECR II-1677, at para. 143.

[16] Case T-113/96 *Edouard Dubois v Council and Commission* [1998] ECR II-125.

[17] Ibid., para. 41.

[18] Under the Lisbon Treaty Article 340(3) TFEU will replace Article 288(3) EC with one that contains a wording similar to that used in Article 288(2).

[19] See also Case T-295/05 *Document Security Systems v ECB*, order of 5 September 2007, at para. 76.

[20] See C-352/98 P *Bergaderm and Goupil v Commission* [2000] ECR I-5291, at para. 41.

[21] Case T-209/00 *Lamberts v European Ombudsman* [2002] ECR II-2203.

Consequently, measures taken by those bodies in the exercise of the powers assigned to them by Community law are attributable to the Community, according to the general principles common to the Member States referred to in the second paragraph of Article 288 EC'.[22] On this basis the European Investment Bank[23] and the European Ombudsman[24] have been included within the term institution.

The Court's wide interpretation of the term 'institution' in Article 288(2) does not seem capable of including Community agencies which are set up by Community legislation and not the EC Treaty itself. The Community instruments establishing such agencies contain, however, a provision which provides that the agency shall be liable for any damage caused and confers jurisdiction on the Court in case of disputes.[25] It is submitted that also the Community, at least in a subsidiary manner, should incur liability for damage caused by bodies to which the Community has delegated powers, such as agencies.[26] The rationale for their inclusion would be that otherwise the Community 'could escape the consequences of the provisions of Article 178 [now 235] and the second paragraph of Article 215 [now 288] of the Treaty'.[27]

EC liability for acts of the servants of EC institutions can only be considered where they occurred in performance of their duties.[28] In *Sayag v Leduc*, the Court defined this as meaning 'acts which by virtue of their internal and direct relationship are the necessary extension of the tasks entrusted to the institution'.[29] The notion is fairly restrictive, since where a civil servant causes an accident with his private car the EC does not incur liability, even where the car is used to perform his duties. Where the EC is not liable, the servant can be sued in a national court in accordance

---

22 Ibid., para. 49, upheld on appeal in Case C-234/02 P *European Ombudsman v Lamberts* [2004] ECR I-2803, at paras. 43–48. See also Case C-370/89 *SGEEM v European Investment Bank* [1992] ECR I-6211, at para 15.

23 Case C-370/89 *SGEEM v European Investment Bank* [1992] ECR I-6211, at para 16. See also Case T-11/00 *Hautem v EIB* [2000] ECR II-4019.

24 See Case T-209/00 *Lamberts v European Ombudsman* [2002] ECR II-2203, upheld on appeal in Case C-234/02 P *European Ombudsman v Lamberts* [2004] ECR I-2803, at paras. 43–48.

25 The standard formulation is similar to that used in Article 288(2). See Article 17(2) Regulation 337/75 establishing a European Centre for the Development of Vocational Training, [1975] OJ L 39/1, as amended. See also Article 114 (3) and (4) of Regulation 40/94 on the Community trade mark, [1994] OJ L 11/1, as amended.

26 See T.C. Hartley, supra note 1, pp 433–434.

27 Case C-370/89 *SGEEM v European Investment Bank* [1992] ECR I-6211, at para 15.

28 For a discussion on why Article 288(2) provides separate categories for acts by the institutions and those of its servants, see T.C. Hartley, supra note 1, pp. 430–431. See also H.G. Schermers and C.R.A Swaak, 'Official Acts of Community Servants and Article 215(4) EC', in T. Heukels and A. McDonnell (eds.), supra note 1, pp. 167–178.

29 Case 9/69 *Sayag v Leduc* [1969] ECR 329 at 335f.

with national law. However, Article 12a of the Protocol on Privileges and Immunities of the European Communities guarantees EC civil servants immunity in national courts in respect of acts performed in their official capacity.[30] The concepts under Article 288(2) 'in performance of their duties' and Article 12a of the Protocol 'performed in their official capacities' are in principle distinct. However, in practice they will mostly coincide.

2. LIABILITY FOR ATTRIBUTABLE ACTS

Special considerations apply for legal acts. Here, the relationship between Article 288(2) and the other remedies provided by the EC Treaty, in particular Articles 230 and 234, has to be considered. Another difficult issue is whether the EC should incur liability for every legal error it commits in a legal act and therefore which standard of unlawfulness should be required in case of legal acts.

Autonomous Nature of Article 288(2)

Article 288(2) provides an attractive remedy for private parties only if the restrictive requirements of *locus standi* under Article 230(4) do not constitute a precondition of admissibility for this action. In *Plaumann*,[31] the Court ruled that in an action for compensation under Article 288(2) it could not nullify the legal effects of a decision which had not been annulled. In other words, it required that an act had first to be annulled under Article 230 before an action under Article 288(2) could be brought. This would have rendered Article 288(2) meaningless for a vast range of legislative acts. The Court soon overruled, however, this restrictive position in *Lütticke*, where it held that:

> the action for damages provided for by Article 178 [now 235] and the second paragraph of Article 215 [now 288] was established by the Treaty as an independent form of action with a particular purpose to fulfil within the system of actions and subject to conditions for its use, conceived with a view to its specific purpose. It would be contrary to the independent nature of this action as well as to the efficacy of the general system of forms of action created by the Treaty to regard as a ground of inadmissibility the fact that, in certain circumstances, an

---

[30] Such immunity is, however, to be waived unless the waiver is contrary to the interest of the Community, see Article 18 of the Protocol.

[31] Case 25/62 *Plaumann v Commission* [1963] ECR 95.

> action for damages might lead to a result similar to that of an action for failure to act under Article 175 [now Article 232].[32]

In *Zuckerfabrik Schöppenstedt*, the Court confirmed this ruling with regard to Article 230 and found that an action under Article 288(2) 'differs from an application for annulment in that its end is not the abolition of a particular measure, but compensation for damage caused by an institution in the performance of its duties'.[33] The position now is that where an applicant brings an action for damages under Article 288(2) the Court will not require the act that allegedly caused the damage first to be annulled under Article 230.[34] In other words, 'the fact that an application for annulment is inadmissible does not in itself render a claim for damages inadmissible.'[35] Consequently, where the Court dismisses an action under Article 230 as inadmissible because the act under review is not reviewable, this does not in itself affect the admissibility of an action for compensation.[36]

On the other hand, the Court might, as in *Cobrecaf v Commission*,[37] reject an action brought under Article 288(2) as inadmissible due to the inadmissibility of the annulment action, where 'the action for damages is actually aimed at securing withdrawal of an individual decision which has become definitive and would, if upheld, have the effect of nullifying the legal effects of that decision'.[38] In this case, the applicant requested additional payment of aid under a Council regulation, which the Commission due to a technical error had withheld. The applicant had, however, omitted to challenge under Article 230 within the required time the decision of the Commission granting the lesser amount of aid than requested. The decision became definitive and the additional amount could therefore not be demanded, neither under Article 230 nor under Article 288(2).

Similarly, in *Inpesca v Commission*[39] the Court stated that 'although a party may take action by means of a claim for compensation without

---

[32] Case 4/69 *Lütticke v Commission* [1971] ECR 325 at para 6.

[33] Case 5/71 *Zuckerfabrik Schöppenstedt v Council* [1971] ECR 975 at para 3; see also Case 9 and 11/71 *Grand Moulins v Commission* [1972] ECR 391, at para. 5; Case 43/72 *Merkur v Commission* [1973] ECR 1055 at para 4.

[34] See Case T-178/98 *Fresh Marine v Commission* [2000] ECR II-3331.

[35] Case T-514/93 *Cobrecaf v Commission* [1995] ECR II-621 para. 58.

[36] See Case T-309/03 *Grau v Commission* [2006] ECR II-1173, at paras. 78–79; Case T-193/04 *Tillack v Commission* [2006] ECR II-3995, at paras. 97 and 98.

[37] Case T-514/93 *Cobrecaf v Commission* [1995] ECR II-621.

[38] Ibid, at para 59. See also Case T-180/00 *Astipesca v Commission* [2002] ECR II-3985, at para. 139, Joined Cases T-44/01, T-119/01 and T-126/01 *Eduardo Vieira and Others v Commission* [2003] ECR II-1209, at para. 214; Case T-86/03 *Holcim v Commission* [2005] ECR II-1539, para. 50.

[39] Case T-186/98 *Inpesca v Commission* [2001] ECR II-557.

being obliged by any provisions of law to seek the annulment of the unlawful measure which causes him damage, he may not by those means circumvent the inadmissibility of an application which concerns the same instance of illegality and which has the same financial end in view'.[40] In contrast, where the applicant claims damages, which the annulment of the act could not have prevented, then the action under Article 288(2) is admissible, even if the applicant could have challenged the act under Article 230.[41]

Joint Liability and the Exhaustion of National Remedies

The structure of interaction between Community and national authorities in the adoption and application of Community law makes it likely that damage is caused to individuals not exclusively as a result of a Community act, but as a result of the co-operation between the Community and national authorities. Such joint liability might arise in a number of different circumstances.[42] It can occur where the Commission wrongfully authorises a Member State to take a certain course of action. This scenario was at issue in the early case of *Kampffmeyer v Commission*,[43] where the Commission unlawfully authorised the refusal by the German authorities to grant import permits to German grain dealers. Joint liability can also result from an unlawful instruction given by the Commission to a national authority. In *Krohn v Commission*,[44] the German authorities, on instructions by the Commission, refused to grant the applicant import licences for the import of manioc from Thailand. The joint liability of the Community and the Member State can also be established where the Community fails to supervise Member States adequately.[45] An important instance of joint liability is the application by Member States of Community legislation. This can be the case where the national authorities require individuals to make payments on the basis of an unlawful EC act. In *Haegeman v*

---

[40] Ibid., para. 76.

[41] Ibid., para. 76.

[42] See W. Wils, 'Concurrent Liability of the Community and a Member State' (1992) 17 *ELRev* 191; P. Oliver, 'Joint Liability of the Community and the Member States', in T. Heukels and A. McDonnell (eds.), supra note 1, pp. 285–309; M. de Visser, 'The Concept of Concurrent Liability and its Relationship with the Principle of Effectiveness: A One-way Ticket into Oblivion?' (2004) 11 *Maastricht Journal of European and Comparative Law* 4; T.C. Hartley, supra note 1, pp. 453–460.

[43] Joined Cases 5, 7, 13–24/66 *Kampffmeyer v Commission* [1967] ECR 245. See also Case C-80/04 P *DLD Trading v Council*, order of 12 April 2005 (not published).

[44] Case 175/84 *Krohn v Commission* [1986] ECR 753.

[45] See Case 4/69 *Lütticke v Commission* [1971] ECR 325. See, however, Joined Cases C-106/90, C-317/90 and C-129/91 *Emerald Meats v Commission* [1993] ECR I-209.

Commission,[46] the national authorities collected a countervailing charge imposed by Community regulations on imports of Greek wine into the Community. Equally, where the national authorities refuse to grant payments, licences or other measures, on the basis of an unlawful Community act, joint liability will exist. In *Compagnie d'approvisionnement and Grands Moulins v Commission*,[47] the applicants complained that the applicable Commission regulations fixed the subsidies to be granted by the national authorities on imports of common wheat and meslin from third countries at an inadequately low level. In *De Boer Buizen v Council and Commission*,[48] the national authorities refused to grant export licences for steel tubes and pipes to the USA on the basis of Community regulations implementing an arrangement between the Community and the USA. Joint liability also arises where the Member States implement Community Directives. In *Assurance v Council and Commission*[49] the applicants claimed that they suffered damage as a result of the exclusion of export credit insurance operations for the account of or guaranteed by the State from the scope of Council Directive 87/343. Even though the Directive had to be implemented by the Member States, the applicants brought a compensation claim under Article 288(2) against the Council and the Commission.

In cases of joint liability, the individual might have a remedy not only in the Court of First Instance, but also in a national court. In such instances, the question is where the applicant has to bring his action, in the national court or the Community Courts. The ECJ has made it clear that it has exclusive jurisdiction over compensation claims against the Community under Article 288(2). However, the Court has established the principle that applicants first have to exhaust remedies in the national courts before an

---

[46] Case 96/71 *Haegeman v Commission* [1972] ECR 1005. See also Case 26/74 *Roquette v Commission* [1976] ECR 677; Case 46/75 *IBC v Commission* [1976] ECR 65; Case 20/88 *Roquette v Commission* [1989] ECR 1553; Case C-282/90 *Vreugdenhil v Commission* [1992] ECR I-1937; Case T-167/94 *Detlef Nölle v Council and Commission* [1995] ECR II-2589; Case T-91/05 *Sinara Handel v Council and Commission* [2007] ECR II-245, at para. 79.

[47] Joined Cases 9 and 11/71 *Compagnie d'approvisionnement and Grands Moulins v Commission* [1972] ECR 391. See also Case 43/72 *Merkur v Commission* [1973] ECR 1055; Case 153/73 *Holtz & Willemsen v Council and Commission* [1974] ECR 675; Case 74/74 *CNTA v Commission* [1975] ECR 533; Case 99/74 *Grands Moulins v Commission* [1975] ECR 1531; Case 281/82 *Unifrex v Commission and Council* [1984] ECR 1969; Case C-119/88 *AERPO v Commission* [1990] ECR I-2189; Case C-55/90 *Cato v Commission* [1992] ECR I-2533.

[48] Case 81/86 *De Boer Buizen v Council and Commission* [1987] ECR 3677. See also Case 101/78 *Granaria* [1979] ECR 623; Case 12/79 *Wagner v Commission* [1979] ECR 3657; Joined Cases C-104/89 and C-37/90 *Mulder and others and Heinemann v Council and Commission* [1992] ECR I-3061; Case T-93/95 *Laga v Commission* [1998] ECR II-195; Case T-94/95 *Landuyt v Commission*, [1998] ECR II-213.

[49] Case C-63/89 *Assurances du Crédit and Compagnie Belge d'Assurance Crédit v Council and Commission* [1991] ECR I-1799. See also Case T-210/00 *Etablissements Biret v Council* [2002] ECR II-47; Case T-47/02 *Danzer v Council* [2006] ECR II-1779.

action for damages against the Community can be considered as admissible.[50] Where the application of a Community measure is left to the national authorities, the applicant has to contest the Community measure first in the national court, which can refer the question of the validity of the EC act to the Court under Article 234 EC.[51] However, after some uncertainty as to the extent of the obligation to exhaust national remedies, the Court made it clear in *Unifrex v Commission* that 'the existence of such means of redress will be capable of ensuring the effective protection of the individuals concerned only if it may result in making good the alleged damage'.[52]

Where the applicant has suffered loss for an amount unduly paid to the national authority, which requested the payment on the basis of an unlawful EC act, the Court would require the applicant to seek his remedy in the national court. Consequently, an action in the European Court is inadmissible, as the applicant should claim restitution in the national court.[53] This also includes 'ancillary questions', such as the payment of interest[54] or the reimbursement of legal costs.[55] On the other hand, where a ruling by the European Court on the invalidity of the EC act in issue would not have led to the recovery of the payment made in the national court, the action is admissible.[56] Similarly, where the damage consists of loss in addition to the payment of the duty demanded by the national authorities and does not constitute 'ancillary' damage, an action for compensation is admissible in the European Court as no national remedy would be available.[57]

The same principle applies where the national authority refuses to grant payment to an individual on the basis of an unlawful Community act.[58]

---

50 On the exhaustion of national remedies, see A. Ward, supra note 1, pp. 375–391.

51 Case T-47/02 *Danzer and another v Council* [2006] ECR II-1779, at paras. 31–33.

52 See Case 281/82 *Unifrex v Commission and Council* [1984] ECR 1969, para. 11. See also Case 175/84 *Krohn v Commission* [1986] ECR 763, at para. 27; Case T-195/00 *Travelex and Other v Commission* [2003] ECR II-1677, at para. 87; Case C-80/04P *DLD Trading v Council*, order of 12 April 2005 (not published), at para. 47.

53 Case 96/71 *Haegeman v Commission* [1972] ECR 1005, para. 16. See also Case 26/74 *Roquette v Commission* [1976] ECR 677, para. 11; Case 20/88 *Roquette v Commission* [1989] ECR 1553, para. 15; Case C-282/90 *Vreugdenhil v Commission* [1992] ECR I-1937, para. 12; Case T-167/94 *Detlef Nölle v Council and Commission* [1995] ECR II-2589, para. 36. See also Case T-429/04 *Trubowest Handel and Makarov v Council and Commission*, judgment of 9 July 2008, at paras. 70–71.

54 Case 26/74 *Roquette v Commission* [1976] ECR 677, para. 12.

55 Case T-167/94 *Detlef Nölle v Council and Commission* [1995] ECR II-2589, at para. 37. On the question of 'ancillary damage', see A. Ward, supra note 1, pp. 383–389.

56 Case 20/88 *Roquette v Commission* [1989] ECR 1553, para. 16.

57 Case 26/74 *Roquette v Commission* [1976] ECR 677; Case C-282/90 *Vreugdenhil v Commission* [1992] ECR I-1937, at paras 13–15.

58 This case should be distinguished from a situation where the national authority refuses to make a payment to which the applicant was entitled under EC law, but which is withheld

The Court considers that an action for 'payment of amounts due under Community regulations'[59] from the national authority, which refuses to comply with the request, is a matter for the national courts.[60] The applicant has normally an effective remedy in the national court only if the national court can, after the European Court has invalidated the unlawful Community act, grant the payment. This is usually the case where the Community institution replaces a previous act which contained a financially more favourable measure for the applicant.[61] On the other hand, and this is the normal case, the national authority is not in a position to grant the payment, even after the European Court would have annulled the unlawful Community act, as this would require some action on the part of the Community institution competent to act. In this case the individual does not have an effective remedy in the national court and can claim compensation directly in the European Court.[62] Similar considerations apply where the national authorities refuse a licence or other act on the basis of an unlawful Community act. Where the national court can grant the desired act after the unlawful Community act has been removed by the Community Court, the applicant is considered to have an effective remedy and an action in the European Court is inadmissible.[63] Where such a remedy does not exist in the national court, the action in the European Court is admissible.[64] Equally admissible is an action for damages in addition to loss sustained through the refusal to pay the requested amount or to grant the desired licence or other act, as in this case no national remedy would be available.[65]

Finally, where the loss sustained by the applicant is of a different kind from the one outlined above, an action in the European Court for

---

because the Community rules do not provide for reimbursement. See Case 99/74 *Grands Moulins v Commission* [1975] ECR 1531, where the Court held the action inadmissible.

[59] Joined Cases 64 and 113/76, 167 and 239/78, 27, 28 and 45/79 *Dumortier Frères v Council* [1979] ECR 3091 at para 6.

[60] Joined Cases 106 to 120/87 *Asteris v Greece* [1988] ECR 5515 at para 25; Case 281/82 *Unifrex v Commission and Council* [1984] ECR 1969 at para 11.

[61] Case 46/75 *IBC v Commission* [1976] ECR 65.

[62] Joined Cases 9 and 11/71 *Compagnie d'approvisionnement and Grands Moulins v Commission* [1972] ECR 391; Case 43/72 *Merkur v Commission* [1973] ECR 1055, at para. 6; Case 153/73 *Holtz & Willemsen v Council and Commission* [1974] ECR 675; Case 74/74 *CNTA v Commission* [1975] ECR 533; Case 281/82 *Unifrex v Commission and Council* [1984] ECR 1969 at para. 12; Opinion of AG Darmon in Case C-55/90 *Cato v Commission* [1992] ECR I-2533, at para. 23.

[63] Case 12/79 *Wagner v Commission* [1979] ECR 3657, at paras. 12–14.

[64] Case 81/86 *De Boer Buizen v Council and Commission* [1987] ECR 3677, para. 10; Joined Cases C-104/89 and C-37/90 *Mulder and others and Heinemann v Council and Commission* [1992] ECR I-3061, at para. 9.

[65] See Case 175/84 *Krohn v Commission* [1986] ECR 753; Case C-119/88 *AERPO v Commission* [1990] ECR I-2189.

compensation of such damage is admissible if an effective remedy does not exist in the national court.[66] However, where such additional loss resulted from a joint decision by the Community and the national authorities, as in *Kampffmeyer v Commission*,[67] the European Court will declare an action for compensation admissible, but will stay the proceedings to await the outcome of the compensation claim in the national court.

Substantive Test: Unlawful Act

The Community Courts have emphasised that the Community's liability can, in principle, only be engaged if the act which has caused the damage is unlawful. The grounds for such illegality are not mentioned in Article 288(2). As an action for liability does not have as its primary object the (objective) review of Community acts, but is intended to compensate for damage suffered by an individual in its (subjective) rights, it cannot be presumed that the grounds of review referred to in Article 230(2) are also applicable under Article 288(2). The latter provision rather suggests a comparative approach being used in establishing the unlawful nature of an act for the purposes of EC liability. Such an approach is, however, only useful if the rules developed in the Member States show a clear tendency for a specific solution, which can, moreover, be applied within the context of the Community. Finally, the Community Courts also need to ensure that whichever way they assess the unlawful nature of an act under Article 288(2) such an approach is consistent with that found in the context of Member State liability.

From the *Schöppenstedt* formula to *Bergaderm*

As the liability for administrative acts was recognised in the laws of the Member States and often did not require more than the wrongful conduct of the administration, Community liability in such cases was beyond doubt. More difficult to establish was whether the Community should incur liability for legislative measures and if so under what conditions. AG Roemer in *Zuckerfabrik Schöppenstedt*[68] discussed in detail as to whether the Community should incur liability for legislative measures, in the case in issue a Council regulation. In light of the silence of the wording of Article

---

[66] See Joined Cases 65 and 67-85/75 *Cotelle v Commission* [1976] ECR 391; Case 281/84 *Zuckerfabrik Bedburg v Council and Commission* [1987] ECR 49, para. 12; Case C-63/89 *Assurances du Crédit and Compagnie Belge d'Assurance Crédit v Council and Commission* [1991] ECR I-1799; Case T-210/00 *Établissements Biret v Council* [2002] ECR II-47, at paras 36–38.

[67] Joined Cases 5, 7, 13–24/66 *Kampffmeyer v Commission* [1967] ECR 245.

[68] Case 5/71 *Zuckerfabrik Schöppenstedt v Council* [1971] ECR 975.

288(2) on the matter, the AG found that several Member States provided for compensation for legislative measures, if understood in a wider meaning and not limited to legislation adopted by parliament.[69] AG Roemer argued that for a finding of EC liability it was not necessary that the principle was recognised in all Member States and emphasised that 'the particular objectives of the Treaty and the peculiarities of the Community structure must be taken into account'.[70] He justified the liability of Community measures of a legislative nature by reference to the weak parliamentary control in the E(E)C, the acknowledgment of liability for legislative measures under Article 34 ECSC, the possibility of indirect review of regulations under Articles 234 and 241 and the necessity not to interpret provisions dealing with the protection of rights too restrictively.[71] He concluded that 'although liability attaching to the administration resulting from legislative activity is not known in all Member States, it is justified to recognize the principle as part of Community law, because it is widely recognized and in certain cases even includes formal laws'.[72]

The Court in *Zuckerfabrik Schöppenstedt* followed AG Roemer and admitted liability in the case of legislative measures, but imposed more stringent requirements. The Court held that where 'legislative action involving measures of economic policy is concerned, the Community does not incur noncontractual liability for damage suffered by individuals as a consequence of that action, by virtue of the provisions contained in Article 215 [now 288], second paragraph, of the Treaty, unless a sufficiently flagrant violation of a superior rule of law for the protection of the individual has occurred'.[73]

In *Bayerische HNL*[74] AG Capotorti in his Opinion agreed that the Community should be liable in the case of legislative measures. In his analysis of the legal systems of the Member States he revealed that in some

---

[69] AG Roemer, ibid. at p. 989, remarked that most member states had excluded the review of legislative acts adopted by parliament. In his Opinion in Joined Cases 63 to 69/72 *Werhahn and others v Council* [1973] ECR 1229 AG Roemer distinguished between liability for 'normatives Unrecht' (legislation in a substantive sense), which was widely recognised in the Member States, and 'legislatives Unrecht' (legislation in the formal sense), which was rare.

[70] Ibid., at p. 989.

[71] Ibid., at p. 989.

[72] Ibid., at p. 990. AG Roemer made it clear in his Opinion in Joined Cases 63 to 69/72 *Werhahn and others v Council* [1973] ECR 1229 that this analysis was not affected by the entry of the United Kingdom, Ireland and Denmark, as, even though they did not recognise liability for legislative measures to the same extent, these countries showed 'a clear tendency to further development', ibid. p. 1260, in the field of state liability.

[73] Case 5/71 *Zuckerfabrik Schöppenstedt v Council* [1971] ECR 975, para. 11.

[74] Joined Cases 83 and 94/76, 4, 15 and 40/77 *HNL v Council and Commission* [1978] ECR 1209.

Member States it was impossible to obtain compensation for legislative acts adopted by parliament, whereas the situation was unclear in others. On the other hand, he found that liability for legislative measures adopted by the administration was generally accepted in the Member States. AG Capotorti found it difficult to determine whether Community regulations were more akin to legislative measures adopted by parliament (statutes) or the administration. He argued that Council regulations, in particular basic regulations and those involving choices of economic policy, were functionally similar to national statutes, in that they filled the framework laid down by the Treaty. He found, however, that the analogy with national statutes was flawed due to the structural differences between the national systems and the EC, in particular the absence of a parliamentary institution as legislator in the Community. This also explained the need for a more comprehensive system of review in the Community, which resembled therefore more that applicable to administrative acts in the Member States. After recalling the discussion on this point by AG Roemer in *Schöppenstedt*, AG Capotorti concluded that:

> in view of the extreme difficulty of making the hierarchy of the Community legislative measures coincide with that of the national legislative measures, it is logical that the more rigorous solution concerning the liability of the public authorities should be adopted with regard to the Council of the European Communities, which has the twofold capacity of legislature and administration without having the democratic mandate and the power to express the sovereignty of the people which may justify exempting the legislature from the general rules on liability.[75]

The Court in *Bayerische HNL* confirmed the position taken in *Schöppenstedt* that the Community can incur liability also for legislative measures, but emphasised the stringent conditions which had to be met in order to succeed with an action under Article 288(2) in such a case. The Court argued that the general principles of the Member States 'governing the liability of public authorities for damage caused to individuals by legislative measures'[76] had to be taken into account. The Court concluded from these principles that 'public authorities can only exceptionally and in special circumstances incur liability for legislative measures which are the result of choices of economic policy'.[77] The Court justified this restrictive approach by the consideration that 'the legislative authority [. . .] cannot always be hindered in making its decisions by the prospect of applications

[75] Opinion of AG Capotorti, ibid., p. 1229.
[76] Ibid, para. 5.
[77] Ibid, para. 5.

for damages whenever it has occasion to adopt legislative measures in the public interest which may adversely affect the interests of individuals'.[78] Consequently, the Court held that in the legislative sphere in which the institutions have wide discretion the Community would not be liable 'unless the institution concerned has manifestly and gravely disregarded the limits on the exercise of its powers'.[79]

The term 'legislation' in this context was understood by the Community Courts in a wide sense. The notion of legislative measures included not only basic regulations adopted by the Council, but also implementing acts by the Commission.[80] The Court made it clear in *Antillean Rice* that 'the fact that the contested measure is in the form of a decision, and hence in principle capable of being the subject of an action for annulment, is not sufficient to preclude its being legislative in character. In the context of an action for damages, that character depends on the nature of the measure in question, not its form.'[81] AG Darmon in *Vreugdenhil*[82] opined that such an approach did not accord with that found in the legal systems of the Member States, where liability for administrative action often only required a certain wrongful conduct whereas liability of the legislative authorities was subject to stricter rules or non-existent.[83] Nevertheless, the AG urged the Court not to adopt 'an organic distinction between measures adopted by the Council and those adopted by the Commission'. He pointed out that '[s]uch a distinction is often unrelated to the content of the measure and the way in which the institution exercises its power to adopt it'.[84] He suggested that the relevant criteria were, first, whether the act involves measures of economic policy and, secondly, the degree of discretion enjoyed by the Community institution.[85]

While the legislative nature of an act was still relevant for the application of the stricter *Schöppenstedt* formula to establish Community liability, the Court made it clear in *Brasserie du Pêcheur*[86] that the conditions for establishing the liability of Member States for a sufficiently serious breach

---

78 Ibid., para. 5.

79 Ibid., para. 6.

80 See Case 43/72 *Merkur v Commission* [1973] ECR 1055.

81 Case C-390/95P *Antillean Rice Mills and Others v Commission* [1999] ECR I-769, para. 60. See also Joined Cases T-481/93 and T-484/93 *Exporteurs in Levende Varkens and others v Commission* [1995] ECR II-2941, paras. 86–88. See also P. Craig and G. deBúrca, supra note 1, p. 578.

82 Case C-282/90 *Vreugdenhil v Commission* [1992] ECR I-1937.

83 See AG Darmon, ibid., at para. 43.

84 AG Darmon, ibid., para. 44.

85 AG Darmon, ibid., para. 45.

86 Joined Cases C-46/93 and C-48/93 *Brasserie du Pêcheur v Germany and the Queen v Secretary of State for Transport, ex parte Factortame* [1996] ECR I-1029.

of Community law were dependent on the degree of discretion which the national authorities enjoyed. Where it enjoyed wide discretion, a Member State could only be liable if it had manifestly and gravely disregarded the bounds of its discretion.[87] This anomaly between the stricter test for Member State liability, which was dependent on discretion, and that for Community liability, which was conditional on the legislative nature of the act, was difficult to sustain in the long run in particular as the Court in *Brasserie du Pêcheur* had emphasised that 'the conditions under which the State may incur liability for damage caused to individuals by a breach of Community law cannot, in the absence of particular justification, differ from those governing the liability of the Community in like circumstances'.[88] The Court justified this approach by arguing that the protection of rights which individuals enjoy could not differ as to whether a national or Community authority was responsible for the breach.[89]

In *Bergaderm and Goupil v Commission*[90] the Court finally took the opportunity to align the conditions for Member State and EC liability by making discretion also the decisive criterion for the standard to be applied in cases of EC liability. In the case the applicants had argued that by restricting the use of a chemical substance, which Bergaderm used in its sun oil, Bergasol, through the adoption of a Directive[91] which modified Annex II of the Cosmetics Directive,[92] the Commission was liable for compensation under Article 288(2). The applicants argued that the Commission Directive concerned exclusively Bergasol and was consequently an administrative act. The CFI considered the Directive to be of general application and required the breach of a higher-ranking rule of law for the protection of individuals. The CFI dismissed the action on the ground that the Commission had not infringed any such rule. On appeal the appellants challenged the CFI's analysis of the Commission's act as legislative. With reference to its dictum in *Brasserie du Pêcheur*, the Court on appeal pointed out that, save in justified cases, the conditions for Member State liability and those for Community liability for a breach of Community law could not differ.[93] The Community should therefore incur liability under the same conditions as a Member State: 'the rule of law infringed must be intended to confer rights on individuals; the breach must be sufficiently serious; and there must be a direct causal link between the breach of the obligation [. . .] and the damage

[87] Ibid., para. 45.
[88] Ibid., para. 42.
[89] Ibid., para. 42.
[90] Case C-352/98P *Bergaderm and Goupil v Commission* [2000] ECR I-5291.
[91] Commission Directive 95/34/EC, [1995] OJ L 167/19.
[92] Council Directive 76/768/EEC, [1976] OJ L 262/169, as amended.
[93] Ibid., para 41.

sustained by the injured party'.[94] The Court argued that where the institution enjoyed discretion, a breach of the law was sufficiently serious only in the case of a manifest and grave disregard of the law intended to confer rights on individuals. On the other hand, 'where the Member State or the institution in question has only considerably reduced, or even no, discretion the mere infringement of Community law may be sufficient to establish the existence of a sufficiently serious breach'.[95]

By aligning the conditions governing the liability of the Community with those employed for ascertaining Member State liability, the dictum in *Bergaderm* did not merely replace the *Schöppenstedt*[96] formula, but established a comprehensive test for Community liability for all areas of Community activity.[97] With discretion as the decisive factor justifying 'the stricter criterion of liability'[98] the nature of the act has become irrelevant. The Court consequently found in *Bergaderm* that 'the general or individual nature of a measure taken by an institution is not a decisive criterion for identifying the limits of the discretion enjoyed by the institution in question'.[99] It might well be that acts of general application are more likely to involve discretionary action, but it is equally clear that acts which have to be considered as decisions in substance can allow for discretion.[100] This means that provisions in legislative acts, the adoption of which does not provide for any or only reduced discretion, are now subject to the mere illegality test. On the other hand, administrative acts the adoption of which allows for discretion can now only lead to Community liability if they satisfy the stricter test for liability.

However, the synchronisation in *Bergaderm* of the conditions applicable for the liability of the Community with those applicable for Member State liability, has arguably led to a situation in which the system of Community liability has been out of step with the principles of liability prevalent in the legal systems of the Member States. In order to align the Community system with those of its Member States it has been argued that a distinction ought to be made between acts adopted under the co-decision and co-operation procedure, for which the more restrictive test

---

94 Ibid, at para 42.

95 Ibid, at para 44.

96 But see Case T-178/98 *Fresh Marine v Commission* [2000] ECR II-3331 and also Joined Cases T-344/00 and T-345/00 *CEVA and Other v Commission* [2003] ECR II-229, at para. 96, where the CFI still used the *Schöppenstedt* formula.

97 See also T. Tridimas (2006), supra note 1, p. 488.

98 Case C-390/95P *Antillean Rice Mills and Others v Commission* [1999] ECR I-769, para. 58.

99 Case C-352/98P *Bergaderm and Goupil v Commission* [2000] ECR I-5291, para. 46.

100 P. Craig and G. DeBúrca, supra note 1, p. 578.

could be applied, and all other Community acts, for which the normal test should be used.[101] Where the Court might have previously been deterred from employing the distinction made in national systems between parliamentary acts and administrative acts due to 'l'absence d'un réel contrôle démocratique exercé par un Parlement librement élu'[102] it has been claimed that this reason has lost force with the introduction of the co-operation and co-decision procedure.[103] It has been argued elsewhere that the functional equivalence in Community law of acts adopted in the co-decision and assent procedures with parliamentary laws in the Member States would justify a privileged position of such acts in the determination of non-contractual liability of the EC under Article 288(2).[104] It is suggested that with the constitutional development of the Community the arguments against an organic distinction, highlighted in particular by AG Darmon in *Vreugdenhil*, are no longer viable. The privileged position of acts adopted in the co-decision and assent procedures is not based on their content, but on the procedure in which these acts are adopted. Moreover, while there are valid arguments for aligning the conditions for Member State and Community liability, one also has to acknowledge that 'there are important disparities between the two'.[105] In addition, it should not be forgotten that Article 288(2) stipulates that the EC shall be liable for damage 'in accordance with the general principles common to the laws of the Member States'. While comparative studies on the liability of public authorities in the Member States are rare, it seems clear that discretion is not the decisive criterion for the application of stricter conditions for such liability.[106] Finally, there does not seem to be any reason to privilege non-legislative acts. The liability of the Community will only be incurred if such acts breach a rule of law intended to confer rights on individuals. As has already been discussed, where the Community institutions enjoy discretion in the adoption of such acts, the Community Courts have already reduced the intensity of review to manifest illegality.[107] It is difficult to see how a further restriction of the conditions for liability could be justified.

---

[101] See F. Capelli and M. Migliazza, supra note 1, at pp. 606–611.

[102] Ibid., pp. 620–621.

[103] Ibid., pp. 620–624.

[104] A. Türk, *The Concept of Legislation in European Community Law – A Comparative Perspective* (Kluwer, 2006), at pp. 234–235.

[105] T. Tridimas (2006), supra note 1, pp. 486f.

[106] See D. Fairgrieve, M. Andenas and J. Bell (eds.), *Tort Liability of Public Authorities in Comparative Perspective* (London, British Institute of International and Comparative Law, 2002).

[107] See Chapter 1, supra, pp. 146–147.

Breach of a rule of law

The *Bergaderm* ruling demands a breach of a 'rule of law', in contrast to *Schöppenstedt*, where the Court required the violation of a 'superior rule of law'. AG Capotorti in *Bayerische HNL*[108] argued that there could only be a sufficiently serious breach if the rule of law infringed was 'a principle or a rule which is of fundamental importance in the Community legal order'.[109] He considered that the importance of the rule had to be assessed 'within the system by reason of its content and function'.[110] In *Dumortier Frères*[111] the Court seemed to have confirmed this approach when it held that 'the principle of equality [. . .] occupies a particularly important place among the rules of Community law'.[112] Similar emphasis was placed on the importance of the rule infringed by AG Darmon in *Roquette Frères*[113] when he considered the principle of free movement of agricultural products in the Community as being of 'fundamental importance in Community law'.[114] All the same, even until *Bergaderm* these pronouncements did not seem to reflect a general trend in the case law, as the more important consideration in these cases was whether the rule breached was intended for the protection of the individual. It is therefore not surprising that many authors have come to the conclusion that the omission of the term 'superior' did not bring about any change.[115] This has recently been confirmed by the CFI in *Cofradia*,[116] where the CFI considered it 'unimportant whether or not the rule of law infringed constitutes a higher-raking rule of law'.[117] What is therefore relevant is not the importance of the rule breached, but whether it was binding on the author of the act.[118]

Rules intended to confer rights on individuals

In *Plaumann*[119] AG Roemer supported the Commission's argument that the liability of the Community could only be engaged if the rule breached was intended to protect the interests of the applicant. He pointed out that

---

108 Joined Cases 83 and 94/76, 4, 15 and 40/77 *Bayerische HNL and others v Council and Commission* [1978] ECR 1209.

109 Opinion of AG Capotorti, ibid., p. 1232.

110 Ibid.

111 Joined Cases 64 and 113/76, 167 and 239/78, 27, 28 and 45/79 *Dumortier Frères and others v Council* [1979] ECR 3091.

112 Ibid., para. 11.

113 Case 20/88 *Roquette Frères v Commission* [1989] ECR 1553.

114 Opinion of AG Darmon, ibid., para. 40.

115 See T.C. Hartley, supra note 1, pp. 444–445; T. Tridimas (2006), supra note 1, pp. 481, 489.

116 Case T-415/03 *Cofradia de pescadores v Council* [2005] ECR II-4355.

117 Ibid., para. 85.

118 T.C. Hartley, supra note 1, p. 445.

119 Case 25/62 *Plaumann v Commission* [1963] ECR 95.

this view was common to many Member States, in particular Germany, and that the Court had already adopted the same position in its case law under Article 40 ECSC.[120] Similarly, in *Lütticke*[121] AG Dutheillet de Lamothe argued that 'the rule which is alleged to have been infringed must be intended to protect the interests of those who have suffered the damage'.[122] In *Schöppenstedt*[123] the Court, which had already implicitly accepted the principle in *Kampffmeyer*,[124] integrated these demands into its formula applicable to legislative measures involving choices of economic policy by requiring the rule breached to have been intended to protect individuals. AG Capotorti noted in his Opinion in *Bayerische HNL*[125] that this had been restricted even further in 'the concept of a rule of law conferring personal rights on individuals'.[126] This would, in his view, exclude liability 'when a rule relating to the procedure or the form of legislative measures has been infringed'.[127] And AG Darmon in *Vreugdenhil*[128] argued that the laws of many Member States required that 'a *personal right* must be affected before the authorities can incur liability'.[129] Consequently, the Court's dictum in *Bergaderm* that the rule breached had to confer rights on individuals, despite its different wording and its application to all Community acts, is unlikely to have made a difference to the existing state of the law. This part of the *Bergaderm* test therefore expresses the idea that an individual cannot claim compensation for the violation of an objective rule of law, but needs to rely on a subjective right.[130]

The requirement that the rule breached must confer rights on individuals is distinct from the concept of direct effect. The principle of direct effect

---

[120] See Joined Cases 9 and 12/60 *Vloeberghs v High Authority* [1962] ECR 197. For a detailed discussion of the case, see T.C. Hartley, supra note 1, pp. 451–452. See also the Opinion of AG Gand in Joined Cases 5, 7 and 13 to 24/66 *Kampffmeyer v Commission* [1967] ECR 245, at p. 274.

[121] Case 4/69 *Lütticke v Commission* [1971] ECR 325.

[122] Opinion of AG de Lamothe, ibid., p. 345.

[123] Case 5/71 *Zuckerfabrik Schöppenstedt v Council* [1971] ECR 975, at para. 11.

[124] Joined Cases 5, 7 and 13 to 24/66 *Kampffmeyer v Commission* [1967] ECR 245.

[125] Joined Cases 83 and 94/76, 4, 15 and 40/77 *Bayerische HNL and others v Council and Commission* [1978] ECR 1209.

[126] Opinion of AG Caportoti, ibid., p. 1232.

[127] Ibid.

[128] Case C-282/90 *Vreugdenhil v Commission* [1992] ECR I-1937.

[129] Opinion of AG Darmon, ibid., para. 54. Emphasis added in the original. In his analysis Germany, Belgium, Italy and Denmark followed this principle.

[130] See E.-W. Fuss, 'La Responsabilité des Communautés européenes pour le comportement illégal de leurs organes', *RTDE* (1981) 1, at p. 9. The *Schutznormtheorie* is most clearly expressed in Article 34 of the German Federal Constitution, see I. Richter and G. F. Schuppert, *Casebook Verwaltungsrecht* (München, 2nd edn., 1995), at pp. 352–366. However, this principle is also applied in Belgium, Italy and Denmark. See the Opinion of AG Darmon in Case C-282/90 *Vreugdenhil v Commission* [1992] ECR I-1937, para. 54.

ensures that the legal effects that are brought about by Community acts are effectively enforced in the national legal system by imposing 'an obligation [on] a court or another authority to apply the relevant provisions of Community law, either as a norm which governs the case or as a standard for legal review'.[131] Individuals can invoke directly effective provisions of Community acts not only where they create rights, but also where they can show a direct interest in the enforcement of such provisions.[132] This is demonstrated by cases such as *CIA Security*[133] and *Unilever*,[134] where the Court found that persons that have a direct interest in the enforcement of an obligation imposed on a Member State by the directive in issue could invoke Community law provisions, even though the Court found that the directive in issue 'creates neither rights nor obligations for individuals'.[135] On the other hand, in *Francovich*,[136] the Court found that the directive in issue was not directly effective, as it was not possible to identify the person liable to provide the guarantee. However, for the purposes of State liability it was sufficient that the directive granted rights to individuals and that it was possible to identify the contents of the right based on the directive.

The term right in this context has to be understood as a Community term and its concept can therefore not depend on the preconceptions of any one legal system of the Member States, even though this does not exclude that the Community notion of right is informed by national considerations. However, the confusion about the meaning of right is caused not only by national assumptions as to its meaning, but also 'because the Court has never clearly indicated what it means by the term right and, moreover, it uses the term rather indiscriminately'.[137] The ambiguity in the Court's notion of rights has led to attempts to base the concept on sounder theoretical foundations. In this respect the Hohfeldian framework of correlatives, which subsumes under the concept of 'right' not only claim-rights, but also immunities, powers and privileges, seems to offer a solution.[138] However, it

---

131 S. Prechal, *Directives in European Community* Law (OUP, 2nd edn., 2005), p. 241.

132 See Case C-87 to 89/90 *Verholen and Others v Sociale Verzekeringsbank* [1991] ECR I-3757; Case C-345/89 *Stoeckel* [1991] ECR I-4047; Case C-118/94 *WWF and Others v Regione Veneto* [1996] ECR I-1223. See also M. Ruffert, 'Rights and Remedies in European Community Law: A Comparative View' (1997) 34 *CMLRev* 307, p. 315; S. Prechal, 'Does Direct Effect Still Matter?' (2000) 37 *CMLRev* 1047, p. 1050. W. Van Gerven, 'Of Rights, Remedies and Procedures' (2000) 37 *CMLRev* 501, pp. 506–509.

133 Case C-194/94 *CIA Security International SA v Signalson SA and Securital SPRL* [1996] ECR I-2201.

134 Case C-443/98 *Unilever Italia SpA v Central Food SpA* [2000] ECR I-7535.

135 Ibid., para. 51.

136 Case C-6 and 9/90 *Francovich and Bonifaci v Italy* [1991] ECR I-5357.

137 S. Prechal, supra note 132, p. 1057.

138 Each of these terms have correlatives: claim-rights correlate with duties, immunities with disabilities, powers with liabilities and privileges with no-rights, see C. Hilson and T.

has been pointed out that 'however helpful Hohfeld's analytical approach might be for a better understanding of legal relationships which may hide behind the term "right", as an analytical approach it does not provide answers to many other questions which may arise.'[139] The concept of right has therefore to be found in the case law of the Community Courts, which offers certain, albeit limited, indications as to when such a right exists. The concept of right is in particular discussed by the Community Courts in cases where the correct implementation of Community acts is in issue or as one of the preconditions for Member State liability. It is clear from the judgment in *Francovich* that rights exist where the beneficiary and the content of the right are sufficiently clearly defined by the terms of the Community act in issue. However, rights can also arise as a consequence of obligations imposed by a Community act on a Member State or another natural or legal person. This was already made clear with regard to rights created by the EC Treaty in *Van Gend* where the Court stated that 'rights arise not only where they are expressly granted by the Treaty, but also by reason of obligations which the Treaty imposes in a clearly defined way upon individuals as well as upon the Member States and upon the institutions of the Community'.[140] This statement is equally true for Community acts. However, in every case it has to be assessed for whom an obligation in a Community act creates corresponding rights. Cases such as *Enichem Base*[141] and *CIA* or *Unilever* show that not every obligation that is imposed on a Member State creates rights for individuals. It has been pointed out that the Community Courts determine the beneficiary of an obligation by reference to a protective interest of the Community act.[142] Where a Community act, more precisely any of its provisions, is enacted with the intention of protecting an individual interest, then an obligation can create a corresponding right.[143] In this respect it has been pointed out that the protective interest that is relevant for the creation of a right is not the same as the direct interest required for the enforcement of a Community act through the concept of direct effect.[144]

Rules of law which protect the interests of individuals can be found in

---

Downes, 'Making Sense of Rights: Community Rights in E.C. Law' (1999) 24 *ELRev* 121, at p. 122.

139 S. Prechal, supra note 132, p. 1058.

140 Case 26/62 *Van Gend en Loos v Nederlandse Administratie der Belastingen* [1962] ECR 1, p. 12.

141 Case 380/87 *Enichem Base v Commune di Cinisello Balsamo* [1989] ECR 2491.

142 S. Prechal, supra note 131, pp. 115–124. On the interest theory of rights, see J. Coppel, 'Rights, Duties and the End of Marshall' (1994) 57 *MLR* 859, pp. 864 *et seq.*

143 M. Ruffert, supra note 132, pp. 324 *et seq.*; S. Prechal, supra note 131, pp. 118–124.

144 See C. Hilson and T. Downes, supra note 138, pp. 132 *et seq.*

statutory provisions.[145] In *Kampffmeyer*[146] the Commission disputed that Article 22 of Regulation 19/62,[147] which the Commission infringed when it authorised Germany to retain in force protective measures against importers of maize and other products, was intended to protect the interests of the applicants. AG Gand in his Opinion dismissed the Commission's argument by pointing out that it was not necessary that 'the disputed provisions should be intended exclusively to serve the interest of importers; it is sufficient that they also contribute to the defence of their interests',[148] which the AG found was the case. The Court agreed with its AG and held that the fact that Article 22 and other provisions of Regulation 19/62 protected interests of a general nature 'does not prevent their including the interests of individual undertakings such as the applicants which as cereal importers are parties engaged in intra-Community trade'.[149] The Court made it clear that even though the application of these provisions was not of direct and individual concern to the applicants, this did not preclude the possibility that those rules were intended to protect their interests.[150] It is therefore sufficient that the rule infringed has also been adopted in the interest of individuals, even though it pursues other aims.

The Community Courts have also recognised that the general principles of non-discrimination,[151] proportionality,[152] legitimate expectations,[153]

---

[145] This is in particular, but not exclusively, the case when such provisions constitute the expression of a general principle of law. See Joined Cases T-481/93 and T-484/93 *Exporteurs in Levende Varkens and others v Commission* [1995] ECR II-2941, at para. 103, and Joined Cases T-480/93 and T-483/93 *Antillean Rice Mills and Others v Commission* [1995] ECR II-2305, at para. 189, in relation to provisions which embody the principle of proportionality.

[146] Joined Cases 5, 7 and 13 to 24/66 *Kampffmeyer v Commission* [1967] ECR 245.

[147] [1962] OJ, p. 933.

[148] Joined Cases 5, 7 and 13 to 24/66 *Kampffmeyer v Commission* [1967] ECR 245, Opinion of AG Gand, pp. 274–275.

[149] Ibid., p. 262.

[150] Ibid., p. 262.

[151] Case T-57/00 *Banan-Kompaniet and Another v Council and Commission* [2003] ECR II-607, at para. 64; Joined Cases T-481/93 and T-484/93 *Vereniging van Exporteurs in Levende Varkens and others v Commission* [1995] ECR II-2941, at para. 102; Case T-120/89 *Stahlwerke Peine-Salzgitter v Commission* [1991] ECR II-279, at para. 92; Joined Cases 64 and 113/76, 167 and 239/78, 27, 28 and 45/79 *Dumortier Frères and others v Council* [1979] ECR 3091, at para. 11; Joined Cases 83 and 94/76, 4, 15 and 40/77 *Bayerische HNL and others v Council and Commission* [1978] ECR 1209, at para. 5.

[152] Joined Cases 63 to 69/72 *Werhahn and Others v Council* [1973] ECR 1229, at para. 18; Joined Cases T-481/93 and T-484/93 *Vereniging van Exporteurs in Levende Varkens and others v Commission* [1995] ECR II-2941, at para. 102; Case T-489/93 *Unifruit Hellas v Commission* [1994] ECR II-1201, at para. 42.

[153] Case 74/74 *CNTA v Commission* [1975] ECR 533, at para. 44; Case C-152/88 *Sofrimport v Commission* [1990] ECR I-2477, at para. 26; Joined Cases C-104/89 and C-37/90 *Mulder and Others v Council and Commission* [1992] ECR I-3061, at para. 15; Joined Cases T-481/93 and T-484/93 *Vereniging van Exporteurs in Levende Varkens and others v*

the right to be heard[154] and the prohibition of unjust enrichment[155] confer rights on individuals. Similarly, in *Tillack*,[156] the CFI found that the protection of family life, the freedom of the press, the principle of the presumption of innocence and the right to a fair trial are fundamental rights, which confer rights on individuals. Moreover, in *Grau*[157] the CFI held that 'the requirement of impartiality [. . .] is intended, as well as ensuring that the public interest is respected, to protect the persons concerned and confers on them a right as individuals to see that the corresponding guarantees are complied with'.[158] In addition, the Court has found that the misuse of power constitutes a rule intended to protect individuals.[159]

On the other hand, where an institution violates the division of powers between the Council and the Commission, it will not incur liability, as such a division is only to uphold the institutional balance, but not to protect the individual.[160] The Community Courts have also rejected claims that WTO rules should be considered as conferring rights on individuals.[161]

Similarly, the requirement to state reasons under Article 253 does not seem to be amongst the rules conferring rights on individuals. In *Kind*[162] the Court held that 'any inadequacy in the statement of the reasons on which a measure contained in a regulation is based is not sufficient to make the Community liable'.[163] This seems at first glance surprising. The Court acknowledged in this case that the requirement of the statement of reasons

---

Commission [1995] ECR II-2941, at para. 102; Case T-489/93 *Unifruit Hellas v Commission* [1994] ECR II-1201, at para. 42.

154 Joined Cases T-481/93 and T-484/93 *Vereniging van Exporteurs in Levende Varkens and others v Commission* [1995] ECR II-2941, at para. 102.

155 Case T-133/03 *Masdar v Commission* [2006] ECR II-4377, at para. 94.

156 Case T-193/04 *Tillack v Commission* [2006] ECR II-3995, at para. 121.

157 Case T-309/03 *Grau v Commission* [2006] ECR II-1173.

158 Ibid., para. 102.

159 Case C-119/88 *AERPO and Others v Commission* [1990] ECR I-2189, at para. 19; Case T-489/93 *Unifruit Hellas v Commission* [1994] ECR II-1201, at para. 40; Joined Cases T-481/93 and T-484/93 *Vereniging van Exporteurs in Levende Varkens and others v Commission* [1995] ECR II-2941, at para. 102.

160 Case C-282/90 *Vreugdenhil v Commission* [1992] ECR I-1937. See also Joined Cases T-64/01 and T-65/01 *Afrikanische Frucht-Compagnie GmbH and Another v Council and Commission* [2004] ECR II-521, at para 116 and Case T-19/01 *Chiquita Brands International and Others v Commission* [2005] ECR II-315, at para 181.

161 Case T-52/99 *T. Port v Commission* [2001] ECR II-981, at para 51. See also Joined Cases T-64/01 and T-65/01 *Afrikanische Frucht-Compagnie GmbH and Another v Council and Commission* [2004] ECR II-521, at paras 139–141, where the CFI rejected the argument that the EC can incur liability for an infringement of a DSB decision. Similarly, see Case T-69/00 *FIAMM and another v Council and Commission* [2005] ECR II-5393, at paras. 110 *et seq.*

162 Case 106/81 *Kind v European Economic Community* [1982] ECR 2885.

163 Ibid., para. 14. See also Case C-119/88 *AERPO and Others v Commission* [1990] ECR I-2189, at para. 20; Case T-489/93 *Unifruit Hellas v Commission* [1994] ECR II-1201, para. 41.

'is designed to enable the Court to exercise its powers of review of the legality of such measures in the context of Article [230] for the benefit of individuals to whom that remedy is made available by the Treaty'.[164] Moreover, the Court has acknowledged in other cases that the requirement to state reasons 'is not taking mere formal considerations into account but seeks to give an opportunity to the parties of defending their rights'.[165] The Court seemed to have based the exclusion of the requirement to state reasons from amongst the rules conferring rights on individuals on the legislative nature of the adopted act.[166] This can be justified on the ground that acts of general application can be 'confined to indicating the general situation which led to its adoption, on the one hand, and the general objectives which it intended to achieve on the other',[167] rather than being concerned with the specific situation of individuals. All the same, the Community Courts seemed to have extended the exclusion of the requirement to state reasons from the rules intended to confer rights on individuals also to administrative measures. Despite the limitation to regulations in previous cases, the CFI in *Exporteurs* held that 'according to settled case-law of the Court of Justice and the Court of First Instance, the obligation to state reasons [. . .] is not a superior rule of law for the protection of individuals'.[168] The Court seemed to have confirmed this position in its ruling in *Eurocoton*,[169] when it held that 'although proceedings in respect of anti-dumping duties are similar in several respects to an administrative procedure [. . .] an inadequate statement of reasons for an act bringing such proceedings to an end is also not of itself sufficient to cause the Community to incur liability'.[170]

Finally, the principle of sound administration does not, at least not as such, confer rights on individuals.[171] The principle of sound administration

---

[164] Case 106/81 *Kind v European Economic Community* [1982] ECR 2885, para. 14.

[165] Case 24/62 *Germany v Commission* [1963] ECR 63, p. 69. See Also A. Arnull, 'Liability for Legislative Acts', in T. Heukels and A. McDonnell (eds.), supra note 1, pp. 129–151, at p. 138.

[166] See Case C-76/01P *Eurocoton v Council* [2003] ECR I-10091, at para. 98.

[167] Case 5/67 *Beus* [1968] ECR 83, p. 95. See also Case T-13/99 *Pfizer Animal Health v Council* [2002] ECR II-3305, para. 510; Case T-70/99 *Alpharma v Council* [2002] ECR II-3495, para. 394; Case C-304/01 *Spain v Commission* [2004] ECR I-7655, para. 51; Case C-184/02 *Spain and Finland v European Parliament and Council* [2004] ECR I-7789, para. 79; Case C-342/03 *Spain v Council* [2005] ECR 1975, para. 55.

[168] Joined Cases T-481/93 and T-484/93 *Vereniging van Exporteurs in Levende Varkens and others v Commission* [1995] ECR II-2941, para. 104.

[169] Case C-76/01P *Eurocoton v Council* [2003] ECR I-10091.

[170] Ibid., para. 99. However, see Case T-193/04 *Tillack v Commission* [2006] ECR II-3995, where the CFI, at para. 127, named the obligation to give reasons for decisions as conferring specific rights on individuals.

[171] See Case T-196/99 *Area Cova and Others v Council and Commission* [2001] ECR II-3597, at para. 43; Case T-193/04 *Tillack v Commission* [2006] ECR II-3995, at para. 127.

can, however, be considered as conferring rights on individuals where it 'constitutes the expression of specific rights'.[172]

Sufficiently serious breach

In *Bergaderm v Commission*,[173] the Court made it clear that the EC can only incur liability for legal acts if the breach of the law was sufficiently serious. Where the institution has only considerably reduced, or even no, discretion the *Bergaderm* formula seems to suggest that the mere infringement of Community law is sufficient to establish a sufficiently serious breach. On the other hand, where the EC institution enjoys discretion the breach is only sufficiently serious in the case of a manifest and grave disregard of the law.[174] In contrast to the *Schöppenstedt* formula, under the test in *Bergaderm* the requirement of a sufficiently serious breach applies regardless of whether the institution has discretion or not. Moreover, under the *Bergaderm* test the discretion available to the institution would determine the conditions necessary to be met to establish a sufficiently serious breach and not the legislative nature of the act, as prescribed under the *Schöppenstedt* formula. The Court found in *Bergaderm* that 'the general or individual nature of a measure taken by an institution is not a decisive criterion for identifying the limits of the discretion enjoyed by the institution in question'.[175]

Discretionary acts: manifest and grave disregard Where the institution enjoys discretion, the requirement of the *Schöppenstedt* formula is in fact similar to the condition in *Bergaderm*, as both demand a manifest and grave disregard of the law.[176] It therefore appears that the cases prior to *Bergaderm* will be most relevant for establishing the meaning of 'manifest and grave disregard'. However, given the alignment of the requirements for Community liability with the liability of the Member States in the

---

See also H.P. Nehl, *Principles of Administrative Procedure in EC Law* (OUP, 1999), at p. 37, who rejects the binding effect of the principle of sound administration.

[172] Case T-193/04 *Tillack v Commission* [2006] ECR II-3995, para. 127. EC liability can also exist where the institution does not act with due diligence, see Case T-160/03 *AFCon Management Consultants v Commission* [2005] ECR II-981, at para. 75.

[173] Case C-352/98P *Bergaderm and Goupil v Commission* [2000] ECR I-5291.

[174] See Case C-312/00P *Camar and Others v Commission* [2002] ECR I-11355, at para. 56, and Case T-4/01 *Renco v Council* [2003] ECR II-171, at para. 73. On the relevance of whether the EC institution had discretion, see Case C-198/03 P *Commission v CEVA Santé animale and another* [2005] ECR I-6357, at paras. 66–69 and 89.

[175] Case C-352/98P *Bergaderm and Goupil v Commission* [2000] ECR I-5291, at para. 46. Compare with the Opinion of AG Fennelly in this case and the judgment of the CFI in Case T-199/96 *Bergaderm and Goupil* v *Commission* [1998] ECR II-2805.

[176] See P. Craig, supra note 1, pp. 769–772.

Bergaderm judgment, it will be necessary to assess the continued relevance of the pre-*Bergaderm* case law.

AG Roemer in *Plaumann*[177] made it clear that for legislative measures, in addition to a requirement of fault, the Court should follow the restrictive approach taken in French administrative law and should only accord compensation for 'abnormal specific and direct damage'.[178] As AG Mayras in *Grands Moulins*[179] pointed out, the test required that the damage had to be 'particular to one or more persons' and 'so serious as to exceed the duties imposed on each citizen by the requirements of life in a community',[180] without the measure having been adopted in the interests in public order. In addition, the breach had to be considered as 'clear infringement'[181] or 'particularly clear breach'.[182] AG Reischl summed this position up by stating that compensation for legislative measures required 'an obvious and serious disregard'[183] of rules of law.

Even though in *CNTA*[184] it granted compensation to the applicants, the Court gave little indication as to whether it wanted to follow this approach. In this case the applicants alleged damage caused by the withdrawal of the monetary compensatory amounts applicable for colza and rape seeds by Commission Regulation 189/72.[185] After having confirmed that the *Schöppenstedt* test was to apply in the present case, the Court held the Community liable, as the Commission had breached the applicants' legitimate expectations when it terminated, in the absence of an overriding matter of public interest, 'with immediate effect and without warning the application of compensatory amounts in a specific sector without adopting transitional measures'.[186]

It was only in *Bayerische HNL*[187] that the Court elucidated in greater detail the meaning of 'sufficiently serious breach', which it had established in the *Schöppenstedt* formula. The Court was concerned with an action for

---

177 Case 26/62 *Plaumann v Commission* [1963] ECR 95.

178 Opinion of AG Roemer, ibid., at p. 121.

179 Joined Cases 9 and 11/71 *Grands Moulins v Commission* [1972] ECR 391. AG Mayras made it clear that he wanted to see the test applied only in the absence of illegality.

180 Opinion of AG Mayras, ibid., p. 423. See also AG Roemer in Joined Cases 63 to 69/72 *Werhahn v Council* [1973] ECR 1229, at p. 1260, where he saw the test satisfied if a 'smaller circle of specially affected parties' is affected in 'the very core of their existence'.

181 AG Roemer in Joined Cases 63 to 69/72 *Werhahn v Council* [1973] ECR 1229, p. 1261.

182 AG Reischl in Case 153/73 *Holtz & Willemsen v Council* [1974] ECR 675, p. 704.

183 Ibid.

184 Case 74/74 *CNTA v Commission* [1975] ECR 533.

185 [1972] OJ L 24/25.

186 Case 74/74 *CNTA v Commission* [1975] ECR 533, para. 43.

187 Joined Cases 83 and 94/76, 4, 15 and 40/77 *Bayerische HNL v Council and Commission* [1978] ECR 1209.

compensation concerning Council Regulation 563/76,[188] which provided for the compulsory purchase of skimmed-milk powder held by intervention agencies by producers for use in feeding-stuffs. In a number of earlier cases,[189] the Court had declared the regulation invalid on the ground that it had violated the principles of equality and proportionality. AG Capotorti argued that for a breach to be considered as sufficiently serious the rule of law breached must be of 'fundamental importance in the Community legal order'.[190] On the other hand, the AG found that a subjective element of blame, that is whether the breach was excusable, was not required.[191] Moreover, the assessment by the Court of the act as unlawful already included a finding that the measure could not be justified. Similarly, he rejected the seriousness of the damage as criterion.[192] The AG also denied that requirements of public interest might justify an exclusion of compensation of damage affecting wide categories of persons. He argued that it would be logical that 'the person whose right has been infringed to be the person entitled to claim for damages regardless of the number of other persons whose rights have similarly been infringed'.[193]

In contrast, as AG Capotorti put it in a later case, the Court in its judgment 'was influenced by the "restrictive view" taken by the legal systems of the Member States concerning the liability of the public authorities for damage caused to individuals by legislative measures'.[194] In other words, the Court had followed the suggestion to apply the restrictive test applied in French administrative law for legislative measures. The Court found that:

> individuals may be required [. . .] to accept within reasonable limits certain harmful effects on their economic interests as a result of a legislative measure without being able to obtain compensation from public funds even if that

---

[188] [1976] OJ L 67/18.

[189] Case 114/76 *Bela-Mühle* [1977] ECR 1211; Case 116/76 *Granaria* [1977] ECR 1247; Joined Cases 119 and 120/76 *Ölmühle Hamburg and Firma Kurt A. Becher* [1977] ECR 1269.

[190] Joined Cases 83 and 94/76, 4, 15 and 40/77 *Bayerische HNL v Council and Commission* [1978] ECR 1209, Opinion of AG Capotorti, at p. 1232.

[191] The AG referred in this respect to the legal systems of Italy, the Netherlands, Belgium and Luxembourg, which seemed to favour this solution with regard to the liability for unlawful administrative acts, see Opinion of AG Capotorti, ibid, at p. 1233.

[192] This had been raised by AG Roemer in his Opinion in Joined Cases 63 to 69/72 *Werhahn v Council* [1973] ECR 1255, at p. 1260, in which he found that the act threatened the very existence of the applicants. However, this position was refuted by AG Reischl in his Opinion in Case 153/73 *Holtz & Willemsen v Council* [1974] ECR 697, at p. 700.

[193] Joined Cases 83 and 94/76, 4, 15 and 40/77 *Bayerische HNL v Council and Commission* [1978] ECR 1209, Opinion of AG Capotorti, p. 1236.

[194] See Opinion of AG Capotorti in Case 238/78 *Ireks Arkady v Council and Commission* [1979] ECR 2955, at p. 2992.

> measure has been declared null and void. In a legislative field, such as the one in question, in which one of the chief features is the exercise of a wide discretion essential for the implementation of the Common Agricultural Policy, the Community does not, therefore, incur liability unless the institution concerned has manifestly and gravely disregarded the limits on the exercise of its powers.[195]

In the view of the Court, such a manifest and grave disregard was not present. First, the measure affected very wide categories of traders and consequently the effects on individual undertakings were considerably lessened. Secondly, the price increase caused by the regulation was small in comparison to other factors. Therefore, the effects of the measure on profits 'did not ultimately exceed the bounds of the risks inherent in the activities of the agricultural sector'.[196]

The test of 'manifest and grave disregard' made it difficult to succeed in compensation cases. Nevertheless, in *Dumortier*,[197] the applicants satisfied the test. The case concerned a Council regulation[198] that had abolished production refunds for maize groats and meal ('gritz'), whereas those for maize starch were not abolished. The Court in an earlier case had annulled the discriminatory measure.[199] Subsequently, the Council restored the refunds,[200] but only from the date of the Court's judgment annulling its regulation. The applicants claimed compensation for the period between the application of the regulation and the day it was annulled. The Court ruled that the Council's measure constituted a manifest and grave disregard of the law, as a 'limited and clearly defined group of commercial operators' was concerned and the loss went 'beyond the bounds of the economic risks normally inherent in the activities in the sector concerned'.[201] Finally, the Court emphasised the fact that the Council had terminated the equality of treatment with maize starch producers without objective justification. This latter aspect made it clear that in addition to 'the special and serious

---

195 Joined Cases 83 and 94/76, 4, 15 and 40/77 *Bayerische HNL v Council and Commission* [1978] ECR 1209, para. 6.

196 Ibid., para. 7.

197 Case 64 and 113/76, 167 and 239/78, 27, 28 and 45/79 *Dumortier Frères v Council* [1979] ECR 3091. See also Case 238/78 *Ireks Arkady v Council and Commission* [1979] ECR 2955; Joined Cases 241, 242, 245–250/78 *DGV v Council and Commission* [1979] ECR 3017; Joined Cases 261 and 262/78 *Interquell Stärke-Chemie v Council and Commission* [1979] ECR 3045.

198 Council Regulation 665/75, [1975] OJ L 72/14.

199 See Joined Cases 124/76 *S.A. Moulins* [1977] ECR 1795.

200 See Council Regulation 1125/78, [1978] OJ L 142/21 and Council Regulation 1127/78, [1978] OJ L 142/24.

201 Case 64 and 113/76, 167 and 239/78, 27, 28 and 45/79 *Dumortier Frères v Council* [1979] ECR 3091, para. 11.

nature of the damage',[202] the Court also considered the 'actual nature of the unlawfulness'.[203]

This made it clear that a certain gravity of the breach was required. In *Amylum*,[204] the Court took the opportunity to elucidate this point further. The applicants had claimed compensation for damage suffered by the imposition of a production levy on isoglucose by Council Regulation 1111/77.[205] The regulation, which the Court had in an earlier ruling[206] declared in breach of the principle of equality, affected a small group of producers and its economic impact on those producers has been described as 'little short of catastrophic'.[207] However, the Court rejected the application on the ground that the errors committed by the Council in the contested regulation 'were not errors of such gravity that it may be said that the conduct of the defendant institution in this respect was verging on the arbitrary'.[208] The latter requirement of an arbitrary breach diminished the already reduced chances of claimants for compensation even further. What is more, it created uncertainty as to the gravity of the breach necessary to obtain compensation.

It is therefore not surprising that over the following years, the Court and its Advocates-General differed in the assessment as to whether a sufficiently serious breach had occurred. In *Roquette*,[209] AG Darmon came to the conclusion that the illegality of Commission Regulation 652/76,[210] which the Court had already established in an earlier ruling,[211] was verging on the arbitrary.[212] The Court, on the other hand, found that the fixing of the monetary compensatory amounts by the Commission 'resulted from a technical error which [. . .] cannot be considered to constitute a serious breach of a superior rule of law for the protection of the individual or a manifest and grave disregard by the Commission of the limits of its discretion'.[213] Similarly, in *Assurances du Crédit*,[214] AG Tesauro found

---

202 Opinion of AG Darmon in Case C-282/90 *Vreugdenhil v Commission* [1992] ECR I-1937, para. 48.

203 Opinion of AG Darmon, ibid., para. 49.

204 Case 116 and 124/77 *Amylum v Council and Commission* [1979] ECR 3497. See also Case 143/77 *KSH v Council and Commission* [1979] ECR 3583.

205 [1977] OJ L 134/4.

206 See Joined Cases 103 and 145/77 *Royal Scholten Honig* [1978] ECR 2037.

207 T.C. Hartley, supra note 1, p. 449.

208 Case 116 and 124/77 *Amylum v Council and Commission* [1979] ECR 3497, para. 19.

209 Case 20/88 *Roquette Frères v Commission* [1989] ECR 1553.

210 [1976] OJ L 79/4.

211 Case 145/79 *Roquette Frères* [1980] ECR 2917.

212 Opinion of AG Darmon in Case 20/88 *Roquette Frères v Commission* [1989] ECR 1553, at paras. 35–50.

213 Case 20/88 *Roquette Frères v Commission* [1989] ECR 1553, para. 26.

214 Case C-63/89 *Assurances du Crédit v Council and Commission* [1991] ECR I-1799.

that Council Directive 87/343,[215] by excluding the public sector from financial guarantees imposed on private sector insurance companies, constituted a particularly flagrant infringement of the principle of equal treatment.[216] The AG stated that the Council had committed a manifest and grave disregard of the limits of its powers, as it had 'arbitrarily extended for an indefinite period discriminatory rules which had already been in force for too long'.[217] In contrast, the Court dismissed the action on the ground that 'the Council and Commission cannot be found to have acted unlawfully'.[218]

On the other hand there were also signs of a more liberal approach to granting compensation in this respect. In *Sofrimport*[219] the applicants claimed compensation for damages which they alleged to have suffered as a result of the suspension of import licences for Chilean apples by various Commission regulations.[220] In this case the Court followed AG Tesauro, who had concluded that the Commission had manifestly and gravely disregarded the limits on its discretion and that the measure exceeded the risks inherent in the sector concerned. The Court held that the Commission committed a sufficiently serious breach 'by failing completely to take account of the position of traders such as Sofrimport, without invoking any overriding public interest'.[221] The Court also found that 'the damage [. . .] goes beyond the limits of the economic risks inherent in the business in issue inasmuch as the purpose of that provision is precisely to limit those risks with regard to goods in transit'.[222] It is noteworthy that neither AG Tesauro nor the Court discussed whether the breach was 'verging on the arbitrary'. It is submitted that the decisive point in the analysis for establishing whether the breach was manifest is that it occurred without any public interest justification. The requirement of verging on the arbitrary was finally abolished by the Court in *Peine-Salzgitter*,[223] where it held that 'the concept of arbitrary conduct [. . .] does not provide a basis for holding that a finding of conduct verging on the arbitrary represents a necessary condition or formulation for the Community to be rendered

---

215 [1987] OJ L 185/72.

216 Opinion of AG Tesauro in Case C-63/89 *Assurances du Crédit v Council and Commission* [1991] ECR I-1799, at para. 18.

217 Opinion of AG Tesauro, ibid., para. 18.

218 Case C-63/89 *Assurances du Crédit v Council and Commission* [1991] ECR, para. 28.

219 Case C-152/88 *Sofrimport v Commission* [1990] ECR I-2477.

220 See Commission Regulation 962/88, [1988] OJ L 95/10, Commission Regulation 984/88, [1988] OJ L 98/37, Commission Regulation 1040/88, [1988] OJ L 102/23.

221 Case C-152/88 *Sofrimport v Commission* [1990] ECR I-2477, para. 27.

222 Ibid., para. 28. Compare with Joined Cases T-480/93 and T-483/93 *Antillean Rice and others v Commission* [1995] ECR II-2305, at para. 205.

223 Case C-220/91 P *Stahlwerke Peine-Salzgitter v Commission* [1993] ECR I-2393.

liable'.[224] The second notable point in the judgment is that the Court did not discuss whether the measure affected a limited and clearly defined group.

And it was in relation to this latter point that the Court showed a more generous approach in *Mulder II*.[225] The Court had already found in *Mulder I*[226] that Council Regulation 857/84[227] breached the principle of the protection of legitimate expectations of milk producers who, on the basis of an undertaking given under Regulation 1078/77,[228] had ceased the production of milk. The Council corrected this regulation in a subsequent act,[229] which was equally declared invalid.[230] The Court found that compensation should be awarded for the damage caused by the first regulation 'in so far as it failed completely, without invoking any higher public interest, to take account of the specific situation of a clearly defined group of economic agents'.[231] Moreover, the Court stated that 'the total and permanent exclusion of the producers concerned [. . .] cannot be regarded as foreseeable or as falling within the bounds of the normal economic risks inherent in the activities of a milk producer'.[232] The interesting fact of the case was that the number of producers affected was rather large and that the Court, therefore, did not seem any longer to insist on the group being small.[233] With regard to the second regulation the Court found that the measure could not be considered as a manifest and grave disregard of the law, even though it was illegal, as the Council in correcting the earlier regulation could invoke a public interest by balancing the various interests involved.

This indicates that the Court, in addition to the requirement that the measure affects a clearly defined group and constitutes an extraordinary risk, demands that the measure is more than just illegal, but that the breach of Community law need not reach the level of 'verging on the arbitrary', as required in *Amylum*. The level of illegality necessary to establish Community liability still remains, however, a considerable obstacle to succeeding in compensation cases. This can be seen in *Nölle*,[234] where

---

224 Ibid., para. 51.
225 Case C-104/89, C-37/90 *Mulder v Council and Commission* [1991] ECR I-3061.
226 Case 120/86 *Mulder v Minister van Landbouw en Visserij* [1988] ECR 2321.
227 [1989] OJ L 84/2, as supplemented by Commission Regulation 1371/84, [1984] OJ L 132/11.
228 [1977] OJ L 131/1.
229 Council Regulation 764/89, [1989] OJ L 84/2.
230 See Case C-189/89 *Spagl v Hauptzollamt Rosenheim* [1990] ECR I-4539.
231 Case 120/86 *Mulder v Minister van Landbouw en Visserij* [1988] ECR 2321, para. 16.
232 Ibid., para. 17.
233 See T.C. Hartley, supra note 1, pp. 450–451.
234 See Case T-167/94 *Nölle v Council and Commission* [1995] ECR II-2589.

the CFI held that 'in so far as the Community institutions did not fail completely in the duty of care and proper administration which they owed to the applicant but simply failed properly to appreciate the extent of their obligations under that principle, the breach of the principle of care cannot in this case be regarded as a sufficiently serious breach or a manifest and grave disregard'.[235]

The judgments adopted after *Bergaderm* do not provide a clear picture as to whether the Community Courts intend to follow the criteria for assessing whether an institution has committed a manifest and grave disregard, set out above. *Banan-Kompaniet*,[236] a post-*Bergaderm* judgment, is an example where the CFI was willing to follow the pre-*Bergaderm* criteria. The applicants, category A importers of bananas from Colombia and Costa Rica, claimed compensation for the damage allegedly caused by Council Decision 94/800[237] and Commission Regulation 478/95.[238] In *Council v Germany*[239] the Court had declared Article 1(1) of Council Decision 94/800 invalid, as the Council had breached the principle of non-discrimination by approving in that decision the conclusion of a Framework Agreement,[240] which exempted Category B operators from the export licence system. For similar reasons the Court in *T. Port*[241] had also annulled Commission Regulation 478/95. The CFI found that under the *Bergaderm* test the institutions could only have committed a sufficiently serious breach if they had 'manifestly and gravely disregarded the limits of their discretion'.[242] Given the complex economic assessments necessary, the CFI found that the justification of the difference in treatment of the various operators was not 'manifestly unreasonable'.[243] The CFI also argued that the measure was not adopted 'with the intention of placing an unwarranted burden on Category A and C operators'.[244] The CFI, while referring to the

---

235 Ibid., para. 89.

236 Case T-57/00 *Banan-Kompaniet and Other v Council and Commission* [2003] ECR II-607.

237 [1994] OJ L 336/1.

238 [1995] OJ L 49/13.

239 Case C-122/95 *Germany v Council* [1998] ECR I-973.

240 The Community had concluded a Framework Agreement with Colombia, Costa Rica, Nicaragua and Venezuela, which allocated to these states a quota for importing bananas into the Community. These states could deliver for up to 70% of their quota special export certificates which were a precondition of the grant of import certificates by the Community to Category A and C operators.

241 Joined Cases C-364/95 and C-365/95 *T. Port* [1998] ECR I-1023.

242 Case T-57/00 *Banan-Kompaniet and Other v Council and Commission* [2003] ECR II-607, para. 65.

243 Ibid., para. 67.

244 Ibid., para. 68.

Court's ruling in *Bayerische HNL*,[245] also considered that 'the measure affected very broad categories of operators'[246] and the damage 'could not be viewed as going beyond the bounds of the economic risks inherent in the banana trade'.[247]

While the CFI's assessment as to the absence of a manifest breach can be reconciled with earlier cases discussed in this section, it is much more difficult to agree with the CFI's analysis of the gravity of the breach. First, the CFI seemed to have ignored that the Court, while using the term 'very wide categories of traders' in *Bayerische HNL*,[248] in later cases employed the more liberal test of 'a clearly defined group'.[249] Moreover, the number of persons affected[250] in *Banan-Kompaniet* seems to have been considerably smaller than those affected in *Mulder II*. Second, it is difficult to see how an increase of some 33 per cent for bananas from the third countries concerned as a result of the export licence system could be considered within the bounds of economic risks inherent in the trade. In *Bayerische HNL*, by comparison, the measure in issue led to a price rise of little more than 2 per cent.[251]

Other cases of the post-*Bergaderm* era make it less clear as to which criteria are relevant to assess whether the institution has manifestly and gravely disregarded the limits of its discretion. In *Camar*[252] the Court on appeal found that the CFI, which had given its ruling shortly before the adoption of the *Bergaderm* judgment, wrongly considered the administrative nature of the Commission decision as decisive for determining the liability of the Community.[253] The Court noted that the Commission enjoyed broad discretion when it considers whether transitional measures are necessary under Article 30 of Regulation 404/93.[254] Consequently, the Community could only be liable for compensation if the Commission manifestly and gravely disregarded the limits of its discretion and not just committed any

---

245 Joined Cases 83/76, 94/76, 4/77, 15/77 and 40/77 *Bayerische HNL v Council and Commission* [1978] ECR 1209.

246 Case T-57/00 *Banan-Kompaniet and Other v Council and Commission* [2003] ECR II-607, para. 69.

247 Ibid., para. 70. See also Case T-193/04 *Tillack v Commission* [2006] ECR II-3995, at para. 131.

248 See Joined Cases 83/76, 94/76, 4/77, 15/77 and 40/77 *Bayerische HNL v Council and Commission* [1978] ECR 1209, at para. 7.

249 Case 120/86 *Mulder v Minister van Landbouw en Visserij* [1988] ECR 2321, para. 16.

250 The CFI noted that in 1996 there were 704 Category A operators and 2,981 Category C operators.

251 See Joined Cases 83/76, 94/76, 4/77, 15/77 and 40/77 *Bayerische HNL v Council and Commission* [1978] ECR 1209, at para. 7.

252 Case C-312/00 P *Commission v Camar and Tico* [2002] ECR I-11355.

253 Ibid., at para. 55.

254 [1993] OJ L 47/1.

infringement, as the CFI held. On the basis of the findings of the CFI, the Court came, however, to the conclusion that the Commission committed a manifest and grave disregard when it refused to adopt such transitional measures.[255] The CFI had argued that the Commission had committed a manifest error of appraisal when assessing the applicant's difficulties and that the only way to overcome these difficulties was for the Commission to adopt transitional measures. This ruling raises several questions. First, it is not clear on what basis the Court assesses whether an institution has discretion. The Commission had only broad discretion in the abstract, but in the situation in hand the Court's reasoning seems to suggest that the Commission's hands were bound, in that it did not have any discretion as to whether to adopt transitional measures or not. Second, it is not clear on the basis of which criteria the Court regarded the breach as manifest and grave.

In *AFCon*[256] the CFI had to decide on a claim for compensation for damages which the applicants allegedly suffered as a result of irregularities in the tendering procedure for a project financed by the TACIS programme. The CFI found that the Commission made a manifest error of assessment when it failed to investigate a conflict of interests between a member of the evaluation committee and one of the tendering companies. The CFI argued that the Commission did not act with due diligence and thereby breached the principle of sound administration and equal treatment. The CFI considered that given the circumstances of the conflict of interests and the risk of fraud 'the Commission's omission is of a manifest and serious nature and is thus such as to cause the Community to incur liability'.[257] The manifest nature of the breach seems to be evident in the case. Similarly, the damage went beyond the normal risks inherent in the sector and the breach affected a clearly defined group of companies.[258]

In *Grau*[259] the CFI undertook a more thorough analysis of the concept of 'manifest and grave disregard'. The case concerned a report by the European Anti-Fraud Office (OLAF) on the investigation concerning the

---

[255] Case C-312/00 P *Commission v Camar and Tico* [2002] ECR I-11355, at para. 60.

[256] Case T-160/03 *AFCon Management and others v Commission* [2005] ECR II-981.

[257] Ibid., para. 93.

[258] Ibid., para. 102, where the CFI discussed the risk which tenderers have to accept in connection with the requirement of damage.

[259] Case T-309/03 *Grau v Commission* [2006] ECR II-1173. Compare with Case T-193/04 *Tillack v Commission* [2006] ECR II-3995, where the CFI noted that an OLAF press release which had been considered as an act of maladministration by the Ombudsman could not be regarded as a sufficiently serious breach. See also Case T-209/00 *Lamberts v European Ombudsman* [2002] ECR II-2203, in which the CFI held that the Ombudsman had not committed a flagrant and manifest breach; upheld on appeal in Case C-234/02P *European Ombudsman v Lamberts* [2004] ECR I-2803.

Institute for European-Latin American Relations (IRELA). The CFI had to decide whether the report, which implicated the applicant in financial irregularities that had occurred at IRELA and recommended the initiation of disciplinary proceedings against the applicant, constituted a sufficiently serious breach of the principle of impartiality. The CFI found that the content and conclusions of OLAF's report did not satisfy the principle of impartiality, given that the effective and significant part played by an OLAF official who had a conflict of interests led to a biased and one-sided report. After a careful analysis of the facts, the CFI stated that OLAF had committed a serious and manifest breach of the requirement of impartiality.[260]

Non-discretionary acts Where the institution in question has only a considerably reduced, or even no, discretion the *Bergaderm* formula suggests that the mere infringement of Community law might be sufficient to establish the existence of a sufficiently serious breach.[261] The apparently strict liability for non-discretionary acts under the *Bergaderm* ruling coincides with the previously applicable test established in *Lütticke*,[262] which applied to acts falling outside the *Schöppenstedt* formula.

The application of the *Lütticke* test, even though designed as general rule, remained exceptional.[263] The *Lütticke* test could theoretically have been applied to legislative measures which did not involve any discretionary choices,[264] but it has proven difficult to find examples in the case-law.[265] In addition, the wide definition of the concept of legislative measures, which comprised all acts of general application, limited the scope of application of the *Lütticke* test to Community acts of individual application. Such administrative acts remained, however, the exception, as the direct administration of Community rules was mainly carried out by the Member States.[266] In 1997, Van der Woude identified four areas in which the *Lütticke* test was applied: the exercise of supervisory powers, factual conduct, public procurement and Community funding.[267]

The expansion of Community tasks in the direct and indirect administration of Community rules beyond those areas has increased the possibility

---

260 Case T-309/03 *Grau v Commission* [2006] ECR II-1173, para. 141.

261 See P. Craig, supra note 1, pp. 773–775.

262 Case 4/69 *Alfons Lütticke v Commission* [1971] ECR 325.

263 M.H. Van der Woude, 'Liability for Adminsitrative Acts under Article 215(2) EC', in T. Heukels and A. McDonnell (eds.), supra note 1, pp. 110–112.

264 Ibid., at pp. 112–115.

265 See J. Wakefield, supra note 1, p. 83.

266 See M.H. Van der Woude, supra note 263, p. 110.

267 Ibid., p. 117.

of Community liability for administrative acts. On the other hand, the focus of the *Bergaderm* formula on discretion as the relevant criterion for determining the standard of Community liability has removed those administrative tasks from the scope of the strict test which have hitherto fallen under the *Lütticke* test.[268] In *Lütticke*, while assessing the exercise of the Commission's supervisory powers, the Court emphasised that 'a discretion to appraise the factors which the state has taken into consideration, is conferred upon the Commission in pursuance of the second paragraph of Article 97'.[269] Under the *Bergaderm* formula, such discretion would have ruled out the strict standard for liability. Similarly, in *AFCon*[270] the CFI assessed a claim for compensation for damage which the applicants allegedly suffered as a result of irregularities in a tendering procedure on the basis of whether a manifest and grave disregard of the Commission's discretion had occurred. And in *Camar*, despite the fact that the CFI had characterised the measure as administrative,[271] the Court on appeal found that the decisive element was the discretion of the Commission under Article 30 of Regulation 404/93[272] and decided the case on the basis of whether there had been a manifest and grave disregard of the limits of that discretion.[273] It is therefore apparent that also in the administrative area a careful assessment as to the discretion of the Community institution is necessary. In the competition area, the CFI held in *Holcim* that the Commission enjoys discretion only where the Commission has to make complex economic appraisals, but is otherwise subject to a comprehensive review as to whether the conditions set out in Article 81(1) EC are met, in particular the existence of conduct contrary to that provision.[274]

Conversely, recent case law has made it clear that there are instances where the institution in the adoption of legislative acts has no or only reduced discretion. The institution has no discretion where the adoption of the act is a 'purely arithmetical exercise'.[275] In *Comafrica*[276] the CFI therefore held that the Commission under the applicable rules had no discretion as to whether and how to fix a reduction/adjustment coefficient for

---

[268] See also Opinion of AG Stix-Hackl in Case C-312/00 P *European Commission v Camar* [2002] ECR I-11355, at para. 133.

[269] Case 4/69 *Alfons Lütticke v Commission* [1971] ECR 325, para. 14.

[270] Case T-160/03 *AFCon Management and others v Commission* [2005] ECR II-981.

[271] Joined Cases T-79/96, T-260/97 and T-117/98 *Camar and Tico v Commission* [2000] ECR II-2193, at para. 206.

[272] [1993] OJ L 47/1.

[273] Case C-312/00 P *Commission v Camar* [2002] ECR I-11355, at para. 58.

[274] Case T-28/03 *Holcim v Commission* [2005] ECR II-1357, para. 95.

[275] See AG Slynn in Case 64/82 *Tradax v Commission* [1984] ECR 1359, at p. 1381.

[276] Joined Cases T-198/95, T-171/96, T-230/97, T-174/98 and T-225/99 *Comafrica and Dole v Commission* [2001] ECR II-1975, at para. 137.

the purposes of the Community's market regime in bananas, even though the adoption of such measures had been considered to be an act of general application and hence legislative in nature.[277] Also in areas where the institutions generally have discretion in the adoption of legal acts, it is necessary to determine whether such discretion exists under the specific provision which forms the legal basis for the action. In *Fresh Marine* AG Stix-Hackl found that, even though the Community institutions generally have broad discretion in anti-dumping matters, Article 8(10) of the basic regulation[278] as the applicable provision in the case accorded the Commission only reduced discretion.[279] Consequently, where the Community Courts have to assess whether the institution has complied with a clear obligation under the applicable rules, the standard for the determination of liability will be a strict one, even though other elements of those rules provide it with discretion.

Even where the Community institution has no or reduced discretion in the exercise of its powers, Community liability will not necessarily follow from a mere infringement of Community law. This does not result from a different meaning of the term infringement, which is employed in the *Bergaderm* ruling instead of illegality or unlawfulness as used under the *Lütticke* test.[280] These terms seem to be used synonymously.[281] The assumption develops rather from the fact that already under the *Lütticke* test the Community could incur liability only where fault as an additional requirement was satisfied.[282] The approach under Article 288(2) seems to be therefore modelled on the one adopted under Articles 34 and 40 ECSC.[283] Fault was thereby established when the illegality committed by the institution was inexcusable.[284] In *Richez-Parise* Community liability

---

[277] See Case C-73/97 P *France v Comafrica and Others* [1999] ECR I-185, at para. 38.

[278] Council Regulation 384/96, [1996] OJ L 56/1.

[279] Opinion of AG Stix-Hackl in Case C-472/00 P *Commission v Fresh Marine* [2003] ECR I-7541, at paras. 76 and 80.

[280] On the question as to whether sound administration is sufficient for Community liability where the conduct of the institution does not amount to illegality, see J. Wakefield, supra note 1, at pp. 186–193.

[281] See Case T-390/94 *Schröder and Thamann v Commission* [1997] ECR II-501, at para. 51, where the CFI uses the terms unlawful conduct and illegality as synonymous concepts. See also Case T-28/03 *Holcim v Commission* [2005] ECR II-1357, at para. 86, where the CFI held that unlawfulness is one of the requirements for Community liability under Article 288(2).

[282] See J. Wakefield, supra note 1, at p. 146 and pp. 154 *et seq.* See also M. H. Van der Woude, supra note 263, pp. 109–128, at p. 110.

[283] See J. Wakefield, supra note 1, at pp. 148–152.

[284] See ibid., p. 145. On the question as to whether fault constitutes a subjective or objective test, see Opinion of AG Tesauro in Joined Cases C-46/93 and C-48/93 *Brasserie du Pêcheur and Factortame* [1996] ECR I-1019, at para. 90, who rejects the relevance of fault as a subjective concept and J. Wakefield, supra note 1, at pp. 145 and 152–154, who argues that fault constitutes subjective illegality, but is measured objectively. See also AG Capotorti

was not established on the basis of the provision of incorrect information by the Commission to the applicants about their rights on retirement, even though the Commission requested them to contact the competent departments to obtain the information, but resulted from the inexcusable delay in correcting the information.[285] In *Oberthür*, the Court considered the Community liable, as no justification could be found as to why the Commission had not drawn up the periodic report to which the applicant as official was entitled.[286] In *Adams*, the Court found that the Commission had acted imprudently by handing over photocopies which could identify the applicant as its informant in an anti-trust case and led to his arrest and conviction in a criminal trial in Switzerland.[287] As the Commission had not taken the necessary steps to warn the applicant, the Community was liable under Article 288(2). In *Grifoni*[288] the Court found that the Community was liable under Article 188 EAEC,[289] as the Commission failed to show 'due diligence'[290] with regard to the safety measures necessary to prevent the accident which befell the applicant on the Commission's premises. In *Cobrecaf*[291] the Commission had erroneously declared the applicant's costs for fishing nets as ineligible for Community aid. The CFI made it clear that 'the Commission committed an administrative fault of a kind for which it incurs non-contractual liability in failing to rectify, within a reasonable time, the error which it accepts that it made. The fact that it took 15 months to rectify a manifest error shows obvious lack of care on its part'.[292]

This approach has been followed also after the Court's ruling in *Bergaderm*. In *Comafrica*,[293] the CFI found that 'in particular, a finding of an error which, in analogous circumstances, an administrative authority exercising ordinary care and diligence would not have committed, will

---

in Joined Cases 83 and 94/76, 4, 15 and 40/77 *Bayerische HNL and others v Council and Commission* [1978] ECR 1209, p. 1233, who argued that 'Community law accepts [. . .] that the undoubtedly voluntary nature of the acts adopted by the institutions is sufficient and that that nature gives rise to a presumption of blame when an unlawful measure is enacted.'

285 Case 19, 20, 25 and 30/69 *Richez-Parise and others v Commission* [1970] ECR 325, at paras. 32–42. See also Case 79/71 *Heinemann v Commission* [1972] ECR 579, at paras. 11 and 12. Compare with Case T-203/96 *Embassy Limousines & Services v European Parliament* [1998] ECR II-4239.

286 See Case 24/79 *Oberthür v Commission* [1980] ECR 1743, at paras. 8–11.

287 Case 145/83 *Adams v Commission* [1985] ECR 3539, at para. 40.

288 Case C-308/87 *Grifoni v EAEC* [1990] ECR I-1203.

289 The provision is similar to Article 288(2) EC.

290 Case C-308/87 *Grifoni v EAEC* [1990] ECR I-1203, para. 14.

291 Case T-514/93 *Cobrecaf and Klipper v Commission* [1995] ECR II-621.

292 Ibid., para. 70. On the question whether the conduct of the Commission amounted to illegality, see J. Wakefield, supra note 1, at p. 188.

293 Joined Cases T-198/95, T-171/96, T-171/97, T-174/98 and T-225/99 *Comafrica and Dole v Commission* [2001] ECR II-1975.

support the conclusion that the conduct of the Community institution was unlawful in such a way as to render the Community liable under Article 215 [now Article 288] of the Treaty'.[294] This means that a mere error or irregularity on the part of an institution is not sufficient in itself to attract the non-contractual liability of the Community 'unless that error or irregularity is characterised by a lack of diligence or care'.[295] Moreover, the *Bergaderm* ruling seems to allow the Community Courts to consider additional factors for the assessment of Community liability. In *Holcim*[296] the CFI, after having found that the Commission had only reduced discretion, held that additional factors, such as 'the complexity of the situations to be regulated and also the difficulties in the application or interpretation of the texts'[297] can be taken into account to assess whether a sufficiently serious breach has occurred.

Substantive Test: Lawful Act

Applicants who have suffered substantial damage as a result of Community acts will often not succeed in their attempt to meet the conditions which the Community Courts have imposed in order to obtain compensation for unlawful Community acts, in particular when the institution had discretion in their adoption. Therefore, applicants turned their attention early on to concepts of liability which did not involve any unlawfulness on the part of public authorities. In *Compagnie d'Approvisionnement*[298] the applicants claimed that the Community should incur liability even in the absence of illegality as they suffered 'unusual and special damage'.

Given the silence of Article 288(2) EC on the matter,[299] support for Community liability for lawful acts can be derived from the liability regimes of a number of Member States.[300] It has been argued that the

---

[294] Ibid., para. 134.

[295] Ibid., para. 144. Consequently, the Commission cannot be held liable for any infringement of Community law, where it correctly implements an allegedly unlawful Council regulation, see Case T-94/98 *Alferink v Commission*, judgment of 26 June 2008.

[296] Case T-28/03 *Holcim v Commission* [2005] ECR II-1357.

[297] Ibid., para 101; upheld on appeal in Case C-282/05P *Holcim v Commission* [2007] ECR I-2941, at para. 51. See also Case T-364/03 *Medici Grimm v Council* [2006] ECR II-79, at para. 87.

[298] Joined Cases 9 and 11/71 *Compagnie d'Approvisionnement and Grands Moulins v Commission* [1972] ECR 391.

[299] On 'absolute liability' under the EAEC Treaty, see L. Hancher, 'Issues of Non-Contractual Liability Under the EAEC Treaty', in T. Heukels and A. McDonnell (eds.), supra note 1, pp. 41–69, at pp. 45–49.

[300] See the analysis of the Dutch, French, Belgian, German and Spanish law by H.J. Bronkhorst, 'The Valid Legislative Act as a Cause of Liability of the Communities', in T. Heukels and A. McDonnell (eds.), supra note 1, pp. 153–165, at pp. 155–158.

German '*Sonderopfer*'[301] theory and the French principle of '*égalité devant les charges publiques*'[302] are 'expressions of the principle of equality when applied to the duty of private persons to contribute to the financial burden of the administration: the principle of equal treatment includes the obligation for the administration not to hold a limited number of private individuals financially responsible for the consequences of acts taken in the general interest'.[303]

While acknowledging the existence of these principles,[304] most Advocates-General remained, however, sceptical as to their acceptance in the Community legal order.[305] Until recently, this approach was also shared by the Community Courts, which left the question as to whether Community liability for lawful conduct could be accepted in principle open.[306] In a series of cases the CFI abandoned this approach and firmly recognised that the non-contractual liability of the EC could be engaged in principle even where the action of the Community could not be considered as illegal.[307] In these cases the applicants argued that the Community should be liable for damage

---

301 A claim based on the 'Sonderopfer' theory of the German *Bundesgerichtshof* (BGH) requires that certain individuals or groups bear a special burden in comparison to others (see BGHE 6, 270, at 276) and that the burden, even though not severe, exceeds a certain threshold (see BGHZ 50, 93, at 98f.).

302 See the case law of the French *Conseil d'Etat* in Couitéas, Recueil Lebon 1923, 789.

303 H.J. Bronkhorst, supra note 300, p. 156. See also Principle II of Recommendation No. R (84) 15 of the Committee of Ministers of the Council of Europe, Council of Europe, *Recommendations to Member States 1984* (Strasbourg, 1985).

304 See Opinion of AG Lamothe in Joined Cases 9 and 11/71 *Compagnie d'Approvisionnement and Grands Moulins v Commission* [1972] ECR 391, at pp. 422; Opinion of AG Roemer in Joined Cases 63-69/72 *Werhahn v Council* [1973] ECR 1229, at pp. 1273–1274; Opinion of AG Capotorti in Joined Cases 83 and 94/76, 4, 15 and 40/77 *Bayerische HNL and others v Council and Commission* [1978] ECR 1209, at pp. 1234.

305 See Opinion of AG Mayras in Joined Cases 9 and 11/71 *Compagnie d'Approvisionnement and Grands Moulins v Commission* [1972] ECR 391, at pp. 422–423; Opinion of AG Roemer in Joined Cases 63-69/72 *Werhahn v Council* [1973] ECR 1229, at pp. 1274–1275, who explored the acceptance of the principle of liability in the absence of fault; Opinion of AG Verloren van Themaat in Case 26/81 *Oleifici Mediterranei v EEC* [1982] ECR 3057, at pp. 3088–3090; Opinion of AG Lenz in Joined Cases 279, 280, 285 and 286/84 *Rau v Commission* [1987] ECR 1069, at paras. 187 and 188, who wanted to limit such liability to cases where the very existence of the applicant was threatened.

306 Case 59/83 *Biovilac v EEC* [1984] ECR 4057, at para. 28; Case 267/82 *Développement and Clemessy v Commission* [1986] ECR 1907, at para. 33; Case T-184/95 *Dorsch Consult v Council and Commission* [1998] ECR II-667, at para. 80; Case T-170/00 *Förde-Reederei GmbH v Council and Commission* [2002] ECR II-515; at para. 56; Case T-195/00 *Travelex and Other v Commission* [2003] ECR II-1677, at para. 161; Joined Cases T-64/01 and T-65/01 *Afrikanische Frucht-Compagnie GmbH and Another v Council and Commission* [2004] ECR II-521, at para. 150. See, however, Case 81/86 *De Boer Buizen v Council and Commission* [1987] ECR 3677, at para. 17.

307 Case T-151/00 *Le Laboratoire du Bain v Council and Commission* [2005] ECR II-23, at paras 146–149; Case T-69/00 *FIAMM and another v Council and Commission* [2005] ECR II-5393, at paras. 157–159 and Case T-383/00 *Beamglow v European Parliament, Council and*

which they suffered as a result of an increase in customs duties by the USA on the basis of an authorisation by the WTO's Dispute Settlement Body, which followed a finding that the Community's market regime for bananas was incompatible under WTO rules. The CFI found that, even though the applicants could not base their claim on the unlawfulness of the conduct of the Community institutions, 'that does not mean that undertakings which, as a category of economic operators, are required to bear a disproportionate part of the burden resulting from a restriction of access to export markets can in no circumstances obtain compensation by virtue of the Community's non-contractual liability'.[308] The CFI pointed out that the wording of Article 288(2) did not restrict liability to unlawful conduct and that national laws, albeit with variations, allowed individuals to obtain compensation even in the absence of unlawful action. The CFI therefore concluded that '[w]hen damage is caused by conduct of the Community institution not shown to be unlawful, the Community can incur non-contractual liability if the conditions as to sustaining actual damage, to the causal link between that damage and the conduct of the Community institution and to the unusual and special nature of the damage in question are all met'.[309]

However, on appeal in *FIAMM and FIAMM Technologies v Council and Commission* the Court of Justice stated in emphatic terms that 'as Community law currently stands, no liability regime exists under which the Community can incur liability for conduct falling within the sphere of its legislative competence in a situation where any failure of such conduct to comply with the WTO agreements cannot be relied upon before Community courts'.[310] While the narrow scope of the ruling, limited as it is to non-compliance of the Community legislator with WTO rules, might suggest that the Court did not want to rule out the possibility of liability of the Community under article 288(2) for all lawful acts, the reasoning of the Court, nevertheless, makes it clear that such liability will not arise for legislative action or inaction. This leaves the possibility open that the Community could be liable under Article 288(2) for lawful administrative conduct.

Commission [2005] ECR II-5459, at para. 174; Case T-333/03 *Masdar v Commission* [2006] ECR II-4377, at para. 93.

[308] Case T-383/00 *Beamglow v European Parliament, Council and Commission* [2005] ECR II-5459, at para. 171.

[309] Case T-151/00 *Le Laboratoire du Bain v Council and Commission* [2005] ECR II-23, at para. 149; Case T-69/00 *FIAMM and another v Council and Commission* [2005] ECR II-5393, at para. 160 and Case T-383/00 *Beamglow v European Parliament, Council and Commission* [2005] ECR II-5459, at para. 174.

[310] Joined Cases C-120/06 P and C-121/06 P *FIAMM and FIAMM Technologies v Council and Commission*, judgment of 9 September 2008, para. 176.

In contrast to the doubts as to the existence of Community liability for lawful acts, the conditions of 'unusual and special damage', which the CFI imposed in these judgments, were based on established case law of the Community Courts, which had already clarified the conditions which had to be met were the principle of Community liability for lawful acts to be accepted in Community law.[311] In *Förde-Reederei*,[312] the CFI, without acknowledging the existence of such a principle, stated that 'in the event of the principle of Community liability for a lawful act being recognised in Community law, a precondition for such liability would in any event be the existence of unusual and special damage'.[313] The damage will be characterised as unusual 'when it exceeds the limits of the economic risks inherent in operating in the sector concerned and, second, special when it affects a particular circle of economic operators in a disproportionate manner by comparison with other operators'.[314]

It is apparent from the case law that these conditions are difficult to meet and it is therefore not surprising that to date no claim has been successful. In *Clemessy*[315] the Court rejected the claim on the basis that the alleged damage was 'merely the result of the ordinary risk taken by any tenderer taking part in a tendering procedure'.[316] In *Biovilac*,[317] the Court found that 'the forseeability of the risks inherent in the market conditions at the time when the applicant began to manufacture and market those

---

311 Joined Cases 54-60/76 *Compagnie Industrielle du Comité de Loheac v Council and Commission* [1977] ECR 645, where the Court dismissed a claim for Community liability for lawful conduct on the ground that 'direct, special and abnormal damage' could not be substantiated. See also Opinion of AG de Lamothe in Joined Cases 9 and 11/71 *Compagnie d'Approvisionnement and Grands Moulins v Commission* [1972] ECR 391, at pp. 423, with reference to the Opinion of AG Roemer in Case 25/62 *Plaumann v Commission* [1963] ECR 95, at p. 121.

312 Case T-170/00 *Förde-Reederei GmbH v Council and Commission* [2002] ECR II-515.

313 Ibid., para. 56. See also Case T-184/95 *Dorsch Consult v Council and Commission* [1998] ECR II-667, at para. 80, upheld on appeal in Case C-237/98 P *Dorsch Consult v Council and Commission* [2000] ECR I-4549, at para. 18; Case T-196/99 *Area Cova and Others v Council and Commission* [2001] ECR II-3597, at para. 171; Case T-195/00 *Travelex and another v Commission* [2003] ECR II-1677, at para. 161; Joined Cases T-64/01 and T-65/01 *Afrikanische Frucht-Compagnie GmbH and Another v Council and Commission* [2004] ECR II-521, at para. 150.

314 Case T-151/00 *Le Laboratoire du Bain v Council and Commission* [2005] ECR II-23, para. 183; Case T-69/00 *FIAMM and another v Council and Commission* [2005] ECR II-5393, para. 202; Case T-383/00 *Beamglow v European Parliament, Council and Commission* [2005] ECR II-5459, para. 208. See also Case T-170/00 *Förde-Reederei GmbH v Council and Commission* [2002] ECR II-515, para 56; Joined Cases T-64/01 and T-65/01 *Afrikanische Frucht-Compagnie GmbH and Another v Council and Commission* [2004] ECR II-521, para. 151.

315 Case 267/82 *Développement and Clemessy v Commission* [1986] ECR 1907.

316 Ibid., para. 33.

317 Case 59/83 *Biovilac v EEC* [1984] ECR 4057.

products excludes the possibility of any recompense for the loss of competitiveness which it has suffered', as those risks 'form part of the economic risks inherent in the activities of an industrial and commercial undertaking in this sector'.[318] In *Dorsch Consult*[319] the CFI held that the damage which the applicant suffered as a result of a trade embargo imposed by the Community on Iraq following its invasion of Kuwait was not unusual,[320] as it lay within the economic risks inherent in the sector concerned. The CFI found that 'the economic and commercial risks deriving from the possible involvement of Iraq in renewed warfare with neighbouring countries and the suspension of payment of its debts for reasons associated with its foreign policy constituted foreseeable risks inherent in any provision of services in Iraq'.[321] Moreover, the damage could not be considered as special, as the applicant was not 'part of a category of economic operators whose property interests were affected in a manner which set them apart from all other economic operators whose claims became irrecoverable as a result of imposition of the Community embargo'.[322] Similarly, in *Förde Reederei*[323] the CFI made it clear that the damage allegedly caused by the abolition of the duty-free regime for passenger transport by sea between Member States could not be considered as unusual as such a development 'was objectively foreseeable'.[324] Also, the damage was not special, as the applicant was concerned 'only in its objective capacity as an economic operator which [. . .] could engage in an economic activity [. . .] in the same way as all the other economic operators within the Community carrying on the same activity'.[325] The ruling in *Afrikanische Frucht-Compagnie*[326] makes it clear that where the Community institutions enjoy considerable discretion, as in case of the organisation of the market regimes, the applicants do not suffer unusual damage where their activities entail the risk that the institutions adjust current arrangements for trade with third states to meet changes in the economic situation. And in *Beamglow*[327] the CFI found that the damage

---

318 Ibid., para 29.

319 Case T-184/95 *Dorsch Consult v Council and Commission* [1998] ECR II-667.

320 Note that the CFI does not follow the normal definition, set out above, but classifies unusual damage as 'special' and special damage as 'unusual'.

321 Ibid., para. 83.

322 Ibid., para. 82.

323 Case T-170/00 *Förde-Reederei GmbH v Council and Commission* [2002] ECR II-515.

324 Ibid., para. 59.

325 Ibid., para. 57. See also Joined Cases T-64/01 and T-65/01 *Afrikanische Frucht-Compagnie GmbH and Another v Council and Commission* [2004] ECR II-521, at para. 153.

326 Joined Cases T-64/01 and T-65/01 *Afrikanische Frucht-Compagnie GmbH and Another v Council and Commission* [2004] ECR II-521, at para. 154

327 Case T-383/00 *Beamglow v European Parliament, Council and Commission* [2005] ECR II-5459.

which the applicants suffered as a result of an increase in customs duties by the USA on the basis of an authorisation by the WTO's Dispute Settlement Body, which followed a finding that the Community's market regime for bananas was incompatible under WTO rules, was not unusual. The CFI argued that 'the possibility [. . .] of tariff concessions being suspended as provided for by the WTO agreements is among the vicissitudes inherent in the current system of international trade. Accordingly, the risk of this vicissitude has to be borne by every operator who decides to sell his products on the market of one of the WTO members'.[328]

Damage

It has been argued that the Community Courts decide on a case by case basis as to what constitutes damage in the sense of Article 288(2), rather than with the help of general principles.[329] While initially the case law did not offer any fundamental insights as to the notion of damage in the context of Article 288(2), the rapidly expanding jurisprudence of the Community Courts now provides more ample guidance in this area.[330]

The assessment of damages which an applicant will obtain in case of non-contractual liability of the Community is determined by the function which the notion of damage fulfils. The Court made it clear in *Mulder* that 'compensation for the loss suffered is intended so far as possible to provide restitution for the victim of the unlawful conduct of the Community institutions'.[331] While the principle of restitution can sometimes also be achieved through non-pecuniary redress,[332] such as the annulment of the unlawful act,[333] the restoration of the victim will usually be achieved through pecuniary compensation, which will consist not only

---

[328] Ibid., para. 211. See also Case T-151/00 *Le Laboratoire du Bain v Council and Commission* [2005] ECR II-23, para 186; Case T-69/00 *FIAMM and another v Council and Commission* [2005] ECR II-5393, at para. 205. Cf. Opinion of AG Maduro of 20 February 2008 in Joined Cases C-120/06 P and C-121/06 P *FIAMM and FIAMM Technologies v Council and Commission*, at paras. 71–83.

[329] T.C. Hartley, supra note 1, p. 434.

[330] See J. Wakefield, supra note 1, at pp. 202–213; A.G. Toth, 'The concepts of Damage and Causality as Elements of Noncontractual Liability', in T. Heukels and A. McDonnell, supra note 1, pp. 179–198.

[331] Joined Cases C-104/89 and C-37/90 *Mulder and Others v Council and Commission* [2000] ECR I-203, at para. 63. See also Case C-308/87 *Grifoni v EAEC* [1994] ECR I-341, at para. 40.

[332] See also J. Wakefield, supra note 1, pp. 205–206.

[333] See Case T-416/04 *Kontouli v Council*, judgment of 27 September 2006, at para. 187, where the CFI stated that 'except in special circumstances, the annulment of an act challenged by an official constitutes appropriate and, generally, sufficient reparation for the harm which he may have suffered'.

in compensation for material damage, but also non-material damage and interest. As 'the object of compensation is to restore the assets of the victim to the condition in which they would have been apart from the unlawful act',[334] the restoration of material damage is hypothetical in nature and 'often entails a certain degree of approximation'.[335] The principle of restitution also means that compensation will be reduced where the applicant could make good the losses suffered or obtained any benefit as a result of the unlawful act. Moreover, the duty of mitigation might oblige the applicant to reduce the damage.

The applicant must prove[336] that the damage sustained is 'actual and certain'.[337] The damage must also be quantifiable.[338] Therefore, 'purely hypothetical and indeterminate damage'[339] will not lead to compensation. This means that the applicant has to specify the nature and extent of the alleged damage in the application instituting the proceedings.[340]

The Community Courts considered themselves, however, not prevented from declaring the Community liable 'for imminent damage foreseeable with sufficient certainty even if the damage cannot yet be precisely assessed'.[341] The Court has justified this approach in *Kampffmeyer* by holding that 'to prevent even greater damage it may prove necessary to bring the matter before the Court as soon as the cause of damage is certain.'[342] In such a case, the applicant can reserve the right to specify the

---

334 Opinion of AG Capotorti in Case 238/78 *Ireks-Arkady v Council and Commission* [1979] ECR 2955, at p. 2999.

335 Ibid.

336 See A.G. Toth, supra note 330, at pp. 184 and 185; J. Wakefield, supra note 1, at pp. 214 and 216. See also Case 26/74 *Roquette Frères v Commission* [1976] ECR 677, at paras. 22–23.

337 Case T-415/03 *Cofradia v Council* [2005] ECR II-4355, para. 110. See also Joined Cases T-3/00 and T-337/04 *Pitsiorlas v Council and ECB*, judgment of 27 November 2007, at paras. 293, 319–320. For cases where the action was considered as premature as the damage could not yet be assessed with certainty, see Joined Cases 9 and 25/64 *FERAM v High Authority* [1985] ECR 311, at pp. 320–321, and Case T-478/93 *Wafer Zoo v Commission* [1995] ECR II-1479, at paras. 49 and 50.

338 Case T-415/03 *Cofradia v Council* [2005] ECR II-4355, para. 110.

339 Ibid., para. 110.

340 See Case T-13/96 *TEAM v Commission* [1998] ECR II-4073, at paras. 27–29. This is necessary to satisfy Article 38(1)(c) of the Court's Rules of Procedure, [1991] OJ L 176/7 as amended, and Article 44(1)(c) of the Court of First Instance's Rules of Procedures, [1991] OJ L 136/1 as amended. However, in the interest of procedural economy and in complex cases, the Court is prepared to reserve the nature and extent of the damage for a later stage, see A.G. Toth, supra note 330, at p. 185.

341 Joined Cases 56–60/74 *Kampffmeyer v Commission* [1976] ECR 711, at para. 6. See also Case 44/76 *Milchkontor v Council and Commission* [1977] ECR 393, at para. 8; Case T-99/98 *Hameico Stuttgart and Others v Council and Commission* [2003] ECR II-2195, at para. 63.

342 Joined Cases 56–60/74 *Kampffmeyer v Commission* [1976] ECR 711, para. 6.

amount of the damage and can ask the Court for a declaration as to the liability of the Community in principle.

The first type of damage for which compensation can be obtained constitutes material loss. Such loss is said to include a reduction in assets (*damnum emergens*), but also the loss of an increase in assets (*lucrum cessans*), which includes loss of profit.[343] However, the distinction between those categories is often difficult in practice.[344] Moreover, as both categories fall within the notion of damage under Article 288(2), the distinction seems of little practical relevance.[345] The Court has accepted in *Kampffmeyer*[346] that the payment of an import levy which was illegally imposed[347] as well as the penalties for the repudiation of contracts[348] could be regarded as damage. The Court also awarded compensation for loss of profit, but only to those companies that had concluded contracts when the Commission adopted the illegal act and only 10 per cent of the profits that could have been made. On the other hand, the Court rejected the argument of applicants who gave up the proposed transaction after they were refused the import licence they had applied for as 'the imports in which there was a mere intention to engage lack any substantial character capable of giving rise to compensation for loss of profits'.[349] In *Roquette*[350] the Court found that the applicant's assertion that the monetary compensatory amounts which the applicant had to pay provided more favourable market conditions to its foreign competitors was not sufficient to prove 'actual damage which it has specifically suffered in the course of its business'.[351] In *CNTA*[352]

---

343 See Opinion of AG Capotorti in Case 238/78 *Ireks-Arkady v Council and Commission* [1979] ECR 2955, at p. 2998. See also A.G. Toth, supra note 330, at p. 187, and J. Wakefield, supra note 1, at p. 203, who distinguishes between immediate loss and consequential economic loss.

344 AG Capotorti in Case 238/78 *Ireks-Arkady v Council and Commission* [1979] ECR 2955, at p. 3003, leaves it open whether the abolition of refunds for quellmehl and gritz should be categorised as *damnum emergens*, *lucrum cessans* or even as being of a hybrid nature. While J. Wakefield, supra note 1, at p. 207, classifies such loss as loss of earning (*damnum emergens*), the point can easily be made that such damage should be considered as loss of profit, and therefore as *lucrum cessans*, see AG Capotorti, ibid., at p. 3003. See also the difference in classification in Joined Cases C-104/89 and C-37/90 *Mulder and others v Council and Commission* [1992] ECR I-3061, in which the Court, at para. 26, regarded the damage as loss of earning, while AG Van Gerven, at para. 46, considered it as loss of profit.

345 It has, however, been noted that the Court shows a more conservative approach in quantifying *lucrum cessans*, see J. Wakefield, supra note 1, p. 205, A.G. Toth, supra note 330, p. 187.

346 Joined Cases 5, 7, 13–24/66 *Kampffmeyer v Commission* [1967] ECR 245.

347 Ibid., at pp. 263 and 264. However, the Court, at p. 264, made compensation by the Community subject to the exhaustion of national remedies.

348 Ibid., p. 265.

349 Ibid., pa. 267.

350 Case 26/74 *Roquette Frères v Commission* [1976] ECR 677.

351 Ibid., para. 23.

352 Case 74/74 *CNTA v Commission* [1975] ECR 533.

the Court made it clear that the applicant could not 'legitimately expect under all circumstances to make the profits which would have accrued to it from the contract under the system of compensatory amounts'.[353] Instead the Court limited compensation to the loss 'which the unforeseeable abolition of compensatory amounts caused to the applicant, owing to the fact that, in the performance of transactions irrevocably undertaken by it it was re-exposed to the exchange risk against which it was entitled to consider itself covered by the system of these amounts'.[354] In *TEAM*[355] the Court pointed out that even though 'charges and expenses incurred by a tenderer in connection with his participation in a tendering procedure cannot in principle constitute damage which is capable of being remedied by an award of damages',[356] compensation must be provided 'in cases where an infringement of Community law in the conduct of the tendering procedure has affected a tenderer's chances of being awarded the contract'.[357] The CFI in *AFCon*[358] therefore considered the Community liable for damage when the Commission by disregarding its duty to act impartially in the tendering procedure 'directly prejudiced AFCon's chances'.[359] The damage comprised the loss relating to the costs incurred in participating in the procedure, including costs for the preparation of the tender and costs spent in the defence of its interests.[360] On the other hand, in *TEAM* the CFI held that loss of profit in a tendering procedure could only be recognised if 'the applicant was entitled to be awarded the contract',[361] which given the broad discretion of the Commission in the matter was not a certainty. Consequently, the damage was judged to be merely hypothetical, not real.[362]

---

[353] Ibid., para. 45.

[354] Case 74/74 *CNTA v Commission* [1976] ECR 797, para. 6.

[355] Case T-13/96 *TEAM v Commission* [1998] ECR II-4073.

[356] Ibid., para. 71.

[357] Ibid., para. 72; upheld on appeal in Case C-13/99P *TEAM v Commission* [2000] ECR I-4671, at para. 56.

[358] Case T-160/03 *AFCon Management Consultants and others v Commission* [2005] ECR II-981.

[359] Ibid., para. 102.

[360] Ibid., paras. 103–109. It should, however, be noted that the Court held in Case C-331/05 P *Internationaler Hilfsfonds v Commission* [2007] ECR I-5475, at paras. 25–29, that, in contrast to costs incurred by the applicant to institute legal proceedings against the Commission, costs incurred in submitting complaints to the Ombudsman could not be regarded as being caused by the institution in question.

[361] Case T-13/96 *TEAM v Commission* [1998] ECR II-4073, para. 76. See also Case T-160/03 *AFCon Management Consultants and others v Commission* [2005] ECR II-981, at para. 112.

[362] Case T-13/96 *TEAM v Commission* [1998] ECR II-4073, para. 76. See also Case T-267/94 *Oleifici Italiani v Commission* [1997] ECR II-1239, at para. 73, in which the CFI considered the applicant's claim to loss of profit as hypothetical and indeterminate.

In *Grifoni*[363] the Court recognised as damage financial loss resulting from an accident. The financial loss comprised expenditure caused by the accident (mainly medical expenses). The Court also accepted as damage the total and partial loss of earnings (as a result of temporary and permanent invalidity). In line with the restitution principle the Court found that it was necessary 'to determine what the applicant's income would have been if he had not suffered the accident'.[364] Such a hypothetical assessment also had to be undertaken in *Dumortier Frères*,[365] where the Court considered the damage to lie 'in the abolition by the Council of the refunds which would have been paid to the gritz producers if equality of treatment with the producers of maize starch had been observed'.[366] While the amount of those refunds therefore constituted the starting point for the calculation of the damage, the Court made it clear that if any loss from the abolition of the refunds had actually been passed on in the prices the amount of compensation would have to be reduced accordingly.[367] Similarly, in *Mulder*[368] the Court assessed the damage on the basis of 'loss of earnings consisting in the difference between, on the one hand, the income which the applicants would have obtained in the normal course of events from the milk deliveries which they would have made if [. . .] they had obtained the reference quantities to which they were entitled and, on the other hand, the income which they actually obtained from milk deliveries made during that period in the absence of any reference quantity, plus any income which they obtained, or could have obtained, during that period from any replacement activities.'[369] The hypothetical assessment of the loss of earnings required a comparator which the Court found in 'the profitability of a farm representative of the type of farm run by each of the applicants'.[370] Moreover,

---

[363] See Case C-308/87 *Grifoni v EAEC* [1994] ECR I-341.

[364] Ibid., para. 20.

[365] Joined Cases 64 and 113/76, 167 and 239/78, 27, 28 and 45/79 *Dumortier Frères and others v Council* [1979] ECR 3091. See also Case 238/78 *Ireks-Arkady v Council and Commission* [1979] ECR 2955; Joined Cases 241, 242 and 245–250/78 *DGV v Council and Commission* [1979] ECR 3017; Joined Cases 261 and 262/78 *Interquell Stärke-Chemie v Council and Commission* [1979] ECR 3045.

[366] Ibid., para. 14. On the hypothetical nature of such an approach, see also Opinion of AG Capotorti in Case 238/78 *Ireks-Arkady v Council and Commission* [1979] ECR 2955, at p. 2999.

[367] Joined Cases 64 and 113/76, 167 and 239/78, 27, 28 and 45/79 *Dumortier Frères and others v Council* [1979] ECR 3091, para. 15. See also Joined Cases 256, 257, 265, 267/80, 5 and 51/81 and 282/82 *Birra Wührer v Council and Commission* [1984] ECR 3693, at paras. 26–33; Case 256/81 *Paul's Agriculture v Council and Commission* [1983] ECR 1707, at paras. 8–13; Case T-56/00 *Dole v Council and Commission* [2003] ECR II-577, at paras. 85 and 86. For a critical assessment of this approach, see A.G. Toth, supra note 330, pp. 189–190.

[368] Joined Cases C-104/89 and C-37/90 *Mulder and others v Council and Commission* [1992] ECR I-3061.

[369] Ibid., para. 26.

[370] Ibid., para. 32.

the complexity of the hypothetical evaluation of the damage led the Court to assume that it was entitled to broad discretion in the calculation of the damage.[371] Given the function of compensation as restitution for loss suffered the Court found that income from any replacement activities had to be deducted from such hypothetical income.[372] This included not only income which the applicants did actually make from replacement activities, but also 'income which they could have obtained had they reasonably engaged in such activities'.[373] The Court justified this approach by reference to the general principle that 'the injured party must show reasonable diligence in limiting the extent of his loss or risk having to bear the damage himself'.[374] In *Fresh Marine*[375] the CFI considered the applicant's damage as the loss of profit which it suffered as a result of the suspension of its exports to the Community during a certain period following the imposition of provisional anti-dumping duties by the Commission on its products. The CFI found that the damage consisted in the profit which the applicant would have made if it had continued to export to the Community in that period.[376] The CFI enquired, however, also whether the applicant complied with its duty to mitigate the loss by showing 'reasonable diligence in limiting the extent of the damage'.[377] The CFI held that the applicant, contrary to the Commission's assertion, did not have to obtain a bank guarantee and continue its exports, as 'it would have run an unusual commercial risk, beyond the level of risks inherent in any commercial enterprise'.[378] It is doubtful that this approach imposed a greater responsibility to mitigate on the applicant than the requirement of reasonable diligence envisaged in *Mulder*.[379] Rather than constituting 'a new requirement to balance risks'[380] the CFI's position could simply be understood as assessing whether the applicant acted with reasonable diligence when it chose not to set up a bank guarantee.

---

[371] See Joined Cases C-104/89 and C-37/90 *Mulder and others v Council and Commission* [2000] ECR I-203, at para. 79. See also J. Wakefield, supra note 1, at p. 206 and M. Ruffert, Case Annotation, 38 *C.M.L.Rev.* (2001) 781, at 789.

[372] See also Case 229/84 *Sommerlatte v Commission* [1986] ECR 1805, at para. 28.

[373] Joined Cases C-104/89 and C-37/90 *Mulder and others v Council and Commission* [1992] ECR I-3061, para. 33.

[374] Ibid., para. 33. On this basis the Court refused to accept that operating losses which arose as a result of such replacement activities could be taken into account. The Court had already recognised this principle in staff cases, see Case 58/78 *Sergy v Commission* [1976] ECR 1139, at para. 46.

[375] Case T-178/98 *Fresh Marine v Commission* [2000] ECR II-3331.

[376] Ibid., para. 109.

[377] Ibid., para. 121.

[378] Ibid., para. 124.

[379] J. Wakefield, supra note 1, at p. 213.

[380] Ibid., p. 213.

The second type of damage for which the Community Courts have awarded compensation comprises non-material damage. In staff cases,[381] the Court awarded non-material damage in *Algera*,[382] as the applicants were confronted with the prospect of a dismissal, which caused them shock, disturbance and uneasiness.[383] In *Vainker*[384] the CFI granted compensation for suffering due to the considerable delay in the EP's procedure for the recognition of the applicant's occupational illness.[385] In *Hautem*[386] the CFI held that the European Investment Bank's express refusal to comply with a previous judgment,[387] in which the CFI had annulled the applicant's dismissal, involved non-material damage, as it 'placed the applicant in a prolonged state of uncertainty and anxiety with regard to the recognition of his rights and his professional future, whilst the indeterminate nature of his present work status has also caused him difficulties in finding employment'.[388] And in *Grau*[389] the CFI established non-material damage on the basis that the applicant, 'by reason of the accusations, the findings and the recommendations made against him by OLAF, had his honour and professional reputation impaired and suffered difficulties in his living conditions'.[390]

The Court has accepted non-material damage also in cases of personal injury. In *Grifoni*[391] the Court found that 'the victim of an accident must be compensated, irrespective of any financial loss, for any personal damage which may cover physical and mental suffering'.[392] On the other hand, the Court seems to be more reluctant to award compensation for non-material damage in commercial cases.[393] In *TEAM*[394] the CFI left it open as to whether harm to a tenderer's image could constitute non-material damage,

---

381 See A.G. Toth, supra note 330, p. 190.

382 Joined Cases 7/56, 3/57 to 7/57 *Algera and others v Common Assembly of the European Coal and Steel Community* [1957] ECR 39.

383 Ibid., at p. 66. See also Case 61/76 *Geist v Commission* [1977] ECR 1419, para. 49, in which the Court granted non-material damages, as the absence of periodic reports put the applicant 'in an uncertain and anxious state of mind with regard to his professional future'.

384 Case T-48/01 *Vainker v European Parliament* [2004] ECR II-197.

385 Ibid. at para. 178.

386 Case T-11/00 *Hautem v EIB* [2000] ECR II-4019.

387 Case T-140/97 *Hautem v EIB* [1999] ECR II-897.

388 Case T-11/00 *Hautem v EIB* [2000] ECR II-4019, para. 52.

389 Case T-309/03 *Grau v Commission* [2006] ECR II-1173.

390 Ibid., para. 162.

391 Case C-308/87 *Grifoni v Euratom* [1994] ECR I-341.

392 Ibid., para. 37.

393 See J. Wakefield, supra note 1, pp. 209–210.

394 Case T-13/96 *TEAM v Commission* [1998] ECR II-4073, at para. 77. See also Case T-160/03 *AFCon Management Consultants and others v Commission* [2005] ECR II-981, at paras. 126 and 127.

as it found that the applicant had failed to establish a causal link between the Commission's conduct and the damage.

Finally, in the third group the Community Courts have established various types of interest as part of a compensation award. The award of interest logically follows from the restitution principle. Since 'compensation for the loss suffered is intended so far as possible to provide restitution for the victim of the unlawful conduct of the Community institutions',[395] compensation must be provided for 'the adverse consequences resulting from the lapse of time '.[396]

The Community Courts distinguish between two types of interest, default interest and compensatory interest. This distinction, which was initially developed in staff cases,[397] is now firmly established in damages actions under Article 288(2).[398] Default interest has been defined as 'interest which is due by reason of a delay in complying with an obligation to pay, irrespective of its contractual or non-contractual nature'.[399] Default interest is usually awarded from the date at which the obligation for compensation is certain, even though the precise amount is not yet known.[400] Default interest is therefore awarded from the date of the judgment which establishes the obligation to make good the damage, usually the interlocutory judgment.[401]

Compensatory interest, which the Community Courts award in addition to any default interest, has been described as 'supplementary damage which is always connected with the temporal factor, but only indirectly

---

395 Joined Cases C-104/89 and C-37/90 *Mulder and Others v Council and Commission* [2000] ECR I-203, at para. 63.

396 Ibid., para. 51. See A. van Casteren 'Article 215(2) EC and the Question of Interest', in T. Heukels and A. McDonnell (eds.), supra note 1, pp. 199–216, at pp. 199–200.

397 See Case 158/79 *Romengous Carpentier v Commission* [1985] ECR 39, at paras. 8–14; C-136/92 P *Brazelli Lualdi v Commission* [1994] ECR I-1981, at para. 35. See also A. van Casteren, supra note 396, at p. 206.

398 Case C-308/87 *Grifoni v EAEC* [1994] ECR I-341, at paras. 39–43; Joined Cases C-104/89 and C-37/90 *Mulder and others v Council and Commission* [2000] ECR I-203, at para. 55; Case T-160/03 *AFCon and others v Commission* [2005] ECR II-981, at paras. 130–133.

399 A. van Casteren, supra note 396, p. 207.

400 Ibid., p. 213.

401 See Joined Cases 64 and 113/76, 167 and 239/78, 27, 28 and 45/79 *Dumortier Frères and others v Council* [1979] ECR 3091, at para. 25. See also Case 238/78 *Ireks-Arkady v Council and Commission* [1979] ECR 2955, at para. 20; Joined Cases 241, 242 and 245–250/78 *DGV v Council and Commission* [1979] ECR 3017, at para. 22; Joined Cases 261 and 262/78 *Interquell Stärke-Chemie v Council and Commission* [1979] ECR 3045, at para. 23; Case C-308/87 *Grifoni v EAEC* [1994] ECR I-341, at para. 43; Joined Cases C-104/89 and 37/90 *Mulder and others v Council and Commission* [1992] ECR I-3061, at para 35; Case T-160/03 *AFCon and others v Commission* [2005] ECR II-981, at para. 133. See, however, Case T-48/01 *Vainker v European Parliament* [2004] ECR II-197, at para. 191, where the CFI chose an earlier date.

caused by the belated payment'.[402] Compensatory interest is therefore relevant where the damage consists in a 'loss of purchasing power or of the possibility of investment, or monetary depreciation, caused by the elapse of time'.[403] In *Grifoni*, the Court accepted that the compensation to be paid to the victim of an accident must 'take account of inflation since the event occasioning the loss'.[404] In *Mulder* the Court pointed out that 'the fall in the value of money'[405] had to be taken into account when determining compensation from the event occasioning the loss. The event occasioning the loss is more difficult to determine where omission on the part of the responsible institution establishes the liability of the Community. Perhaps this might explain why the CFI in *AFCon* awarded compensatory interest for the loss which the applicant suffered 'from the first day of the month following the month in which AFCon last took steps prior to commencing proceedings'.[406]

While the Community Courts initially set the amount of interest autonomously at various arbitrary rates,[407] the amount of interest seems now to be calculated by reference to 'the rate fixed by the European Central Bank for its principal refinancing operations, in force during the period concerned'.[408] In *AFCon* the CFI established the amount of compensatory and default interest on the basis of this rate increased by two percentage points.[409]

Causation

The Court requires as a third element a causal link between the unlawful act and the damage suffered.[410] The Community Courts employ different formulations to express this requirement. In some cases the Community Courts demand a 'direct causal nexus between the fault committed by the

402 A. van Casteren, supra note 396, p. 207.

403 Ibid., p. 207.

404 Case C-308/87 *Grifoni v EAEC* [1994] ECR I-341, at para. 40.

405 Joined Cases C-104/89 and C-37/90 *Mulder and others v Council and Commission* [2000] ECR I-203, at para. 51.

406 Case T-160/03 *AFCon Management Consultants v Commission* [2005] ECR II-981, at para. 130.

407 See Van Casteren, supra note 396, pp. 202–203.

408 Case T-160/03 *AFCon Management Consultants v Commission* [2005] ECR II-981, para. 132. See also Case T-48/01 *Vainker v European Parliament* [2004] ECR II-197, at para. 192.

409 Case T-160/03 *AFCon Management Consultants v Commission* [2005] ECR II-981, at paras 132 and 133.

410 See A.G. Toth, 'The concepts of Damage and Causality as Elements of Noncontractual Liability', in T. Heukels and A. McDonnell, supra note 330, pp. 179–198.

institution concerned and the injury pleaded',[411] while in others a 'direct link of cause and effect between the unlawfulness of the conduct and the damage alleged'[412] is necessary. Despite the difference in wording the decisive point is that the Community can only incur liability where the damage is 'a sufficiently direct consequence of the unlawful conduct'[413] of the EC institution. The burden of proof rests with the applicant.[414]

The Community Courts have denied a direct causal link where the loss results from the independent action of a Member State.[415] In *Exportation des Sucres*[416] the Court found that the refusal by the French authorities to grant an exemption from the monetary compensatory amounts for certain contracts concluded by the applicant 'arose from an independent decision by those authorities'.[417] Even though it could object to the grant of an exemption in individual cases, the Commission had merely informed the national authorities by telex about its objection to contracts not related to the case in issue. Similarly, in *Tillack*[418] the CFI denied the Community's liability for the forwarding of information by OLAF (European Anti-Fraud Office) to national judicial authorities. On the basis of the information received, which included suspicions of breach of professional secrecy and bribery committed by the applicant, the authorities had opened criminal investigations against the applicant, in the course of which the applicant's home was searched and his professional documents and

---

411 Case T-149/96 *Coldiretti and 110 farmers v Council and Commission* [1998] ECR II-3841, para. 101. See also Case T-383/00 *Beamglow v European Parliament, Council and Commission* [2005] ECR II-5459, at para. 193, where the CFI required a 'sufficiently direct causal nexus'; Case T-304/01 *Perez and Others v Council and Commission* [2006] ECR II-4857, at para. 101.

412 Case T-146/01 *DLD Trading v Council* [2003] ECR II-6005, para. 72. See also Case T-220/96 *EVO v Council and Commission* [2002] ECR II-2265, at para. 41; Case T-226/01 *CAS v Commission* [2006] ECR II-2763, at para. 37; Case T-193/04R *Tillack v Commission* [2004] ECR II-3575, at para. 54.

413 Joined Cases 64 and 113/76, 167 and 239/78, 27, 28 and 45/79 *Dumortier Frères v Council* [1979] ECR 3091 at para 21. See also Case T-175/94 *International Procurement Services v Commission* [1996] ECR II-729, at para. 55; Case T-7/96 *Perillo v Commission* [1997] ECR II-1061, at para. 41; Case T-226/01 *CAS v Commission* [2006] ECR II-2763, at para. 40; Case T-333/01 *Meyer v Commission* [2003] ECR II-117, at para. 32; Case T-28/03 *Holcim v Commission* [2005] ECR II-1357, at para. 119; see also Joined Cases T-3/00 and T-337/04 *Pitsiorlas v Council and ECB*, judgment of 27 November 2007, at para. 292.

414 See Case 253/84 *GAEC v Council and Commission* [1987] ECR 123, at para. 21; Case T-194/94 *Blackspur and Others v Council and Commission* [1995] ECR II-2627, at para. 40; Case T-146/01 *DLD Trading v Council* [2003] ECR II-6005, at para. 73; Case T-367/03 *Ticaret v Council and Commission* [2006] ECR II-873, at para. 57.

415 Case T-571/93 *Lefebvre v Commission* [1995] ECR II-2379 at para. 65.

416 Case 132/77 *Société pour l'Exportation des Sucres v Commission* [1978] ECR 1061.

417 Ibid., para. 27. See also Joined Cases 89 and 91/86 *L'Etoile commerciale and CNTA v Commission* [1987] ECR 3005, at para. 19.

418 Case T-193/04 *Tillack v Commission* [2006] ECR II-3995.

personal belongings were seized. The CFI excluded a direct causal link, as the conduct of the national authorities, which acted 'in the context of their own prerogatives',[419] caused the applicant's harm.

On the other hand, the Community Courts would consider a direct causal link to exist where a Member State acts on the instruction of an EC institution.[420] In *Krohn*[421] the Court made it clear that the alleged damage was attributable to the Commission which sent telex messages to the German authorities in the exercise of its competences 'to instruct the Bundesanstalt to refuse the import licences at issue'[422] and thereby caused the alleged damage.[423] A direct causal link can also be established where the Commission's failure to exercise its supervisory duty allowed a Member State to cause harm to individuals.[424] The EC is, however, not liable where it does not bring proceedings against a Member State that is in breach of EC law.[425]

Uncertainty as to the existence of a direct causal link exists in cases where a Community institution authorises a Member State to take a particular course of action. The Court's ruling in *Kampffmeyer*[426] established that the unlawful authorisation by the Community of a national measure would result in the joint liability of the Community and the Member State. This ruling has recently been called in question by the CFI's judgment in *DLD Trading*.[427] The applicant argued that as a result of Council Regulation 2744/98,[428] which extended Austria's exemption from turnover tax and excise duty on imports in international travel beyond 1 January 1998, the Austrian government could maintain its customs allowance of ECU 75 instead of ECU 175, the amount applicable in the rest of the EU. The applicant, who sells duty-free goods in the Czech Republic close to

---

419 Ibid., para. 122.

420 See Joined Cases 89 and 91/86 *L'Etoile commerciale and CNTA v Commission* [1987] ECR 3005, at para. 19.

421 Case 175/84 *Krohn v Commission* [1986] ECR 753.

422 Ibid., para. 22.

423 Case 175/84 *Krohn v Commission* [1987] ECR 97, at para. 24.

424 See Joined Cases 9 and 12/60 *Vloeberghs v High Authority* [1961] ECR 197, judgment at p. 216 and Opinion of AG Roemer at p. 240; Joined Cases 326/86 and 66/88 *Francesconi and others v Commission* [1989] ECR 2087; Case T-304/01 *Perez and Others v Council and Commission* [2006] ECR II-4857, in which the CFI, at para. 155, rejected the claim that 'the alleged failures by the Commission and the Council in their surveillance and monitoring obligations in the field of public health were decisive in the appearance of BSE in Spain'. See also A.G. Toth, supra note 330, p. 194–5.

425 Case T-571/93 *Lefebvre v Commission* [1995] ECR II-2379 at paras. 60 and 61.

426 Joined Cases 5, 7 and 13 to 24/66 *Kampffmeyer and others v Commission* [1967] ECR 245, at pp. 263 *et seq*. See also A.G. Toth, supra note 330, at p. 195.

427 Case T-146/01 *DLD Trading v Council* [2003] ECR II-6005; upheld on appeal in Case C-80/04 *DLD Trading v Council*, order of 12 April 2005 (not published), at paras. 44–45.

428 [1998] OJ L 345/9.

the Austrian border, claimed that as a result it suffered loss of income. The CFI rejected a causal link between Council Regulation 2744/98 and the applicant's alleged damage, as it regarded the Council Regulation as 'a mere power, free of any obligation, for the national authorities'[429] to adopt minimum allowance amounts which were below those imposed by the Community. This means that the CFI did not consider the Community liable as the Regulation was not the exclusive cause of the damage. It is submitted that this approach is unnecessarily restrictive. First, it is clear that without the Regulation Austria was not allowed to maintain its lower customs allowance. In contrast to *Exportation des Sucres* the Regulation in issue in *DLD Trading* was *conditio sine qua non* for the alleged damage. Second, the CFI's approach in *DLD Trading* is out of step with the case-law on direct concern under Article 230(4). Although it is designed to determine the standing of individuals, the concept of direct concern also deals with the question of causality. It might be remembered that the case law on direct concern considers an applicant directly concerned by a Community act which authorises a Member State, where the requesting Member State has made it clear, expressly or implicitly, that it intends to make use of the authorisation.[430] On the expiry of the exemption on 31 December 1997 Austria maintained its lower customs allowance and it was only the retroactive effect of the Regulation which legalised this approach.

The ruling in *DLD Trading* also contrasts with the CFI's more liberal approach in *Beamglow*,[431] in which the applicant had asserted that the Community was liable for damage it had suffered when the United States increased its customs duties as a result of an authorisation by the WTO's Dispute Settlement Body (DSB), which had found the Community regime covering the imports of bananas in breach with WTO rules. The CFI believed that a direct causal link existed between the Community's banana regime and the alleged damage despite the fact that the USA was merely authorised, but not obliged, by the DSB to increase its customs duties and that it did so in the exercise of its discretion.[432] All the same the CFI argued that had it not been for the Community's bananas regime and the finding of its incompatibility with WTO rules by the DSB, the USA could not have sought authorisation from the DSB to suspend its tariff concessions.[433] The

---

429 Case T-146/01 *DLD Trading v Council* [2003] ECR II-6005, para. 79.

430 See Chapter 1, pp. 56–58.

431 Case T-383/00 *Beamglow v European Parliament, Council and Commission* [2005] ECR II-5459.

432 Ibid., at paras. 194 and 195.

433 Ibid., at para. 196.

CFI found that the increase in customs duties was 'a consequence resulting objectively, in accordance with the normal and foreseeable operation of the WTO dispute settlement system accepted by the Community, from the retention in force by the defendant institutions of a banana import regime incompatible with WTO agreements'.[434] Consequently, the unilateral decision by the USA did not break the chain of causation and the conduct of the defendant institution was the immediate cause for the US measures.[435] This was in particular so, as the USA had already indicated that they were to impose the increased customs duties and had already published a provisional list of affected products to that effect.

The judgment in *Beamglow* is all the more remarkable, as the Community Courts have in other instances ruled out a direct causal link where the alleged damage was not exclusively attributable to the Community, but a third party.[436] In *EVO*[437] the CFI found that the non-payment of a sum owed to the applicant by Iraq was due to the compliance by Iraq with United Nations Security Council Resolutions freezing Iraqi funds and not Council Regulation 2340/90,[438] which established a trade embargo by the Community. Similarly, in *Hassan*[439] the CFI held that the applicant's loss was attributable to the United Nations Security Council Resolutions requesting the states to freeze the applicant's funds and not the Council Regulation[440] which gave effect to that request.

It is equally clear from the case law that the Community Courts will reduce or even reject a claim for damages where it was the conduct of the applicant that led to the loss suffered. In personal injury and staff cases the Community Courts seem to be inclined to reduce the claim for compensation where the applicant's conduct, because of negligence or lack of diligence, was also responsible for the damage.[441] In other instances, however, the Community Courts have dismissed the claim for damages entirely where the alleged damage was not exclusively attributable to the

---

[434] Ibid., para. 198.

[435] Ibid., at paras. 199 and 200.

[436] See Case 33/82 *Murri Frères v Commission* [1985] ECR 2759, at para. 36; Case T-7/96 *Perillo v Commission* [1997] ECR II-1061, at para. 42. See also Case T-429/04 *Trubowest Handel and Makarov v Council and Commission*, judgment of 9 July 2008, para. 113.

[437] Case T-220/96 *EVO v Council and Commission* [2002] ECR II-2265, at paras. 41–46.

[438] [1990] OJ L 213/1.

[439] Case T-49/04 *Hassan v Council and Commission* [2006] ECR II-52, at para. 145.

[440] Council Regulation 881/2002, [2002] OJ L 139/9.

[441] Case 58/75 *Sergy v Commission* [1976] ECR 1139, at para. 46; Case 145/83 *Adams v Commission* [1985] ECR 3539, at para. 53; Case C-308/87 *Grifoni v Euratom* [1990] ECR I-1203, at para. 17; Case T-36/89 *Nijman v Commission* [1991] ECR II-699, at para. 43; Joined Cases T-3/00 and T-337/04 *Pitsiorlas v Council and ECB*, judgment of 27 November 2007, at para. 318. See also J. Wakefield, supra note 1, p. 221.

Community. In *Compagnie Continentale France*[442] the Court found that by adopting a resolution with the object of informing and guiding commercial operators, the Council should have expressed reservations as to its possible application. All the same, the Court found that there was no chain of causation between the Council's conduct and the alleged damage, as the conduct could not have caused any error in the mind of the applicant as 'prudent exporter, fully informed of the conditions of the market'.[443] This might require the applicant to pursue a certain course of action before being able to claim damages from the Community. In *International Procurement*[444] the CFI made it clear that a successful tenderer for a contract financed by the European Development Fund could not claim that the Commission's action caused it damage if that tenderer had not attempted to settle its dispute with the awarding State on an amicable basis or by arbitration. On the other hand, whether the applicant has to make use of other judicial remedies, be it in the national or the Community Courts, is not a question of causation, but of the admissibility of the action under Article 288(2).[445]

A direct causal link is also excluded where other determining factors might have caused the damage.[446] In *Dumortier Frères*[447] the applicants claimed that the abolition of refunds for maize gritz by the Council led to the closure of factories by two companies and the initiation of insolvency proceedings by another. The Court found that 'even if it were assumed that the abolition of the refunds exacerbated the difficulties encountered by those applicants, those difficulties would not be a sufficiently direct consequence of the unlawful conduct of the Council'.[448] Similarly, the Commission cannot be liable for wrongful conduct in the procedure for

---

442 Case 169/73 *Compagnie Continentale France v Council* [1975] ECR 117.

443 Ibid., para. 28. See also Case 26/82 *Oleifici Mediterranei v EEC* [1982] ECR 3057, at paras. 22–24; Case T-514/93 *Cobrecaf v Commission* [1995] ECR II-621, at para. 67; Case T572/93 *Odigitria v Council and Commission* [1995] ECR II-2025, at para. 69–71; Case T-143/97 *van den Berg v Council and Commission* [2001] ECR II-277, at para. 49; Case T-1/99 *T.Port v Commission* [2001] ECR II-465, at para., 80; Case T-28/03 *Holcim v Commission* [2005] ECR II-1357, at para. 123; Case T-367/03 *Ticaret v Council and Commission* [2006] ECR II-873, at para. 60. See, however, Case T-178/98 *Fresh Marine Company v Commission* [2000] ECR II-3331, at para. 91, where the CFI did not exclude, but merely reduced the applicant's claim for compensation, despite the fact that the applicant's negligence contributed to the damage.

444 Case T-175/94 *International Procurement Services v Commission* [1996] ECR II-729, at para. 58.

445 See A.G. Toth, supra note 330, pp. 196–198.

446 Case T-226/01 *CAS v Commission* [2006] ECR II-2763; Case T-367/03 *Ticaret v Council and Commission* [2006] ECR II-873, at para. 59.

447 Joined Cases 64 and 113/76, 167 and 239/78, 27, 28 and 45/79 *Dumortier Frères and others v Council* [1979] ECR 3091.

448 Ibid., para. 21.

the award of a contract or grant, where the award might have been denied for other reasons.[449]

Time-limit

Article 46 of the Protocol on the Statute of the Court[450] provides a time limit of five years for proceedings against the Community in cases of non-contractual liability from the occurrence of the event giving rise to compensation.[451] The date when the act in question was declared invalid is irrelevant.[452] The time bar has to be invoked by the defendant, as the Court will not of its own motion raise the issue of time limitation.[453]

Interlocutory Judgment

In several cases, the Court has only adopted an interlocutory judgment, in which it laid down 'the criteria whereby the Court considers that the applicants must be compensated, leaving the amount of the compensation to be determined either by agreement between the parties or by the Court in the absence of such agreement.'[454]

---

449 See Case T-478/93 *Wafer Zoo v Commission* [1995] ECR II-1479, at para. 49; Case T-13/96 *TEAM v Commission* [1998] ECR II-4073, at paras. 73–76; Case T-40/01 *Scan Office Design v Commission* [2002] ECR II-5043, at paras. 109–121; Case T-333/01 *Meyer v Commission* [2003] ECR II-117, at para. 41.

450 [2001] OJ C 80, as amended.

451 Joined Cases 256/80, 257/80, 265/80, 267/80 and 5/81 *Birra Wührer and Others v Council and Commission* [1982] ECR 85 at para. 10. See also Case T-261/94 *Schulte v Council and Commission* [2002] ECR II-441, at para. 59. In Case C-51/05 P *Commission v Cantina sociale di Dilanova and Others*, judgment of 17 July 2008, the Court stated that the limitation period does not start until the damaging effects of a measure have occurred and therefore the persons concerned had suffered certain damage. However, the Court made it clear that 'the rules on limitation periods which govern actions for compensation in respect of that damage may be based only on strictly objective criteria' (para. 59) and that the 'subjective appraisal of the reality of the damage cannot therefore be taken into consideration' (para. 61).

452 Case T-20/94 *Hartmann v Council and Commission* [1997] ECR II-595 at para. 126.

453 Case 20/88 *Roquette v Commission* [1989] ECR 1553 at para. 12.

454 Joined Cases 64 and 113/76, 167 and 239/78, 27, 28 and 45/79 *Dumortier Frères v Council* [1979] ECR 3091 at para. 23.

5 Interim relief

Community acts enjoy the presumption of validity and their effects will be realised in full until such time as they are set aside. As Article 242 EC makes clear, actions brought before the Community Courts do not have suspensory effect. A system of judicial review, in order to provide effective protection, must therefore take account of the delay which occurs before final judgment is rendered.[1] The effects of a successful completion of an action for judicial review can be considerably diminished or even prove illusive if the applicant's interests cannot be protected against damage until such judgment is rendered.[2] Such protection is all the more necessary given the increasingly long time-frames for completion of actions before the Community Courts.

The Community Courts have acknowledged the need for effective judicial protection[3] as a basis for interim measures. According to settled case law 'the purpose of the procedure for interim relief is to guarantee the full effectiveness of the definitive future decision, in order to ensure that there is no lacuna in the legal protection provided by the Community Courts'.[4] Articles 242 and 243 EC provide the Community Courts with the possibility of granting interim measures where an action for judicial review is pending before them. While Article 242 EC allows the Community Courts to adopt an order suspending the application of a contested act, Article 243 EC provides for the prescription of any necessary interim measures. Under the Lisbon Treaty Articles 242 and 243 would remain substantially unchanged and become Articles 278 and 279 TFEU respectively.

---

[1] See F.C. de la Torre, 'Interim Measures in Community Courts: Recent Trends' (2007) *CMLRev* 273–353, at pp. 273–274.

[2] See also Case C-313/90 R *CIRFS and Others v Commission* [1991] ECR I-2557, para. 24.

[3] For a comparative analysis, see S. de la Sierra, 'Provisional Court Protection in Administrative Disputes in Europe: The Constitutional Status of Interim Measures Deriving from the Right to Effective Court Protection. A Comparative Approach' (2004) *ELJ* 42–60.

[4] Case T-384/06 R *IBP and International Building Products France* [2007] ECR II-30*, at para. 53. See also Opinion of AG Tesauro in Case C-213/89 *Factortame* [1990] ECR I-2433; Case C-393/96 P(R) *Antonissen v Council and Commission* [1997] ECR I-441, para. 36; Case T-306/01 R *Aden et al. v Council and Commission* [2002] ECR II-2387, para. 45.

The provision of interim protection in the Community Courts forms the focus of this chapter.[5] The scope of application of Articles 242 and 243 will be discussed in section one, while the requirements for granting interim measures will be set out in section two. Section three will briefly touch upon procedural issues.

1. SCOPE OF APPLICATION OF ARTICLES 242 AND 243

Suspension of Operation of the Act under Article 242

Article 242 allows the Community Courts to order that the application of the contested act be suspended. An application under Article 242 for the suspension of the operation of a measure adopted by a Community institution requires that the applicant challenge that measure in proceedings before the Court.[6] An application for suspension under Article 242 can therefore only be brought where the main action is brought against an act adopted by a Community institution.

Such an action is in most cases one for the annulment of an act under Article 230. Interim measures are unlikely to occur in connection with other proceedings, such as Articles 232, 288(2) and 241. The suspension under Article 242 presupposes a positive act. This excludes the application of Article 242 in the context of an action under Article 232, where the inaction of a Community institution is under review. Even though the Court has not ruled out the application of Article 242 in damages actions under Article 288(2),[7] the aim of actions under Article 288(2) is not the review of the lawfulness of an act, but the award of damages. This justifies the autonomous nature of a damages claim. Where an act is contested indirectly by use of Article 241, it should be capable of suspension under Article 242.[8]

---

[5] For a discussion of interim relief granted by national courts against Community measures which are challenged in an action before the national courts, see Chapter 3, supra, pp. 222–226.

[6] See Article 83(1) of the ECJ Rules ([1991] OJ L 176/7, as amended) and Article 104(1) of the CFI Rules ([1991] OJ L 136, as amended). The provision for which suspension is requested must be the same as the one challenged in the main action.

[7] Cases C-51/90 R and C-59/90 R *Comos Tank and Others v Commission* [1990] ECR I-2167, at para. 33.

[8] The Community Courts have, however, been reluctant to comply with such requests. See Case T-306/01 R *Aden et al. v Council and Commission* [2002] ECR II-2387, at paras. 44–46; Case T-369/03 R *Arizona Chemicals v Commission* [2004] ECR II-205, at para. 66.

Other Interim Measures under Article 243

Where the suspension of an act under Article 242 proves inadequate, applicants can rely on Article 243 to request the Court to adopt any necessary measures in cases before them. The application under Article 243 can be made by a party to a case before the Court provided the application relates to that case.[9] The wider scope of Article 243 allows the Court considerable discretion in the adoption of interim measures. While a judgment in the main proceedings concerned with judicial review cannot contain injunctions against the institution concerned, orders under Article 243 are not subject to such restrictions.[10] Interim measures can include the suspension of acts not challenged before the Court.[11] The Court can also require a party to take positive measures[12] or even substitute its decision for that of the institution.[13]

Interim measures under Article 243 are available not only in relation to actions against Member States, but also in judicial review proceedings against acts of the institutions. In annulment actions, interim measures under Article 243 form a useful complement to the possibility of having the contested act suspended under Article 242. Even though the Community Courts have accepted the possibility of interim measures under Article 243 in the context of an action for failure to act,[14] such measures are rare. Interim measures in the form of an advance payment are even possible in damages actions under Article 288(2).[15] On the other hand, the Court does not have jurisdiction to adopt interim measures in the context of the preliminary ruling procedure under Article 234.[16]

---

9 See Article 83(1)(2) ECJ Rules and Article 104(1)(2) CFI Rules.

10 See F.C. de la Torre, supra note 1, pp. 341–342.

11 See Case 18/65 R *Gutmann v Commission* [1966] ECR 135. It is, however, necessary that the act emanates 'from one and the same institution and that institution is a party to the proceedings', see Case 133/87 R *Nashua v Commission* [1987] ECR 2883, para. 7.

12 See Joined Cases 160, 161, 170/73 R II *Miles Druce v Commission* [1974] ECR 284; Case 118/83 R *CMC v Commission* [1983] ECR 2583, at para. 53; Case 65/87 R *Pfizer International v Commission* [1987] ECR 1691; Case T-203/95 R *Connolly v Commission* [1995] ECR II-2919, para. 25, where a request to remind the institution to observe the existing rules was considered as admissible.

13 Case T-44/98 R II *Emesa Sugar v Commission* [1999] ECR II-1427, where the CFI authorised the applicant to import sugar subject to stringent conditions.

14 See Case C-68/95 *T. Port* [1996] ECR I-6065, at para. 60; Case C-43/98 P(R) *Camar v Commission and Council* [1998] ECR I-1815, para. 44.

15 Case C-393/96 P(R) *Antonissen v Council* [1997] ECR I-441.

16 See Case C-186/01 R *Dory* [2001] ECR I-7823, at para. 6.

Limits on the Scope of Interim Measures

Interim measures under Articles 242 and 243 are provisional. Consequently, such measures lapse at the latest[17] when the judgment in the main action is rendered.[18] Moreover, the order 'must not prejudge the points of law or fact in issue or neutralize in advance the effects of the decision subsequently to be given in the main action'.[19] The Community Courts are therefore reluctant to adopt interim measures which have definitive effects. In exceptional cases, however, the Community Courts are prepared to adopt interim measures, even though their effects might lead to irreversible consequences.[20]

In addition the Community Courts have made it clear that interim measures are 'ancillary in the sense that they must only seek to safeguard, during the course of the procedure before the Court, the interests of one of the parties to the proceedings in order to prevent the judgment in the main proceedings from being rendered illusory by being deprived of any practical effect'.[21] The application for interim measures requires that the main action has been lodged before the Court.[22] An application for interim measures to prevent the adoption of a future decision can therefore only be entertained 'in cases where the unidentifiable or future decisions in issue would immediately create rights for third parties and produce irreversible effects'.[23] Similarly, the application for interim relief becomes devoid of purpose if the main action is rejected by the Court.[24]

Limitations on the scope of interim measures can also result from the scope of the main action.[25] The Community Courts are reluctant to adopt

---

17 The order can prescribe a shorter period.

18 Consequently, on appeal a new order has to be sought. See Case T-191/98 R II *Cho Yang Shipping v Commission* [2000] ECR II-2551, para. 41.

19 Case C-149/95 P(R) *Commission v Atlantic Container Line* [1995] ECR I-2165, para. 22; Case C-393/96 P(R) *Antonissen v Commission and Council* [1997] ECR I-441, para. 27; Case T-37/04 R *Azores v Council* [2004] ECR II-2153, para. 104. See also Case T-164/97 R *Moccia Irme v Commission* [1996] ECR II-2261, para. 29; Case T-61/97 R *Carlsen v Council* [1998] ECR II-485, paras. 54 and 55. See also Article 39 of the Statute of the Court; Article 86(4) of the ECJ Rules and Article 107(4) of the CFI Rules.

20 See Case T-179/96 R *Antonissen v Commission and Council* [1997] ECR II-425, para. 22; Case C-393/96 P(R) *Antonissen v Commission and Council* [1997] ECR I-441, para. 41. In these cases the Court imposed, however, stricter standards for the fulfilment of the conditions for interim relief.

21 Case T-610/97 R *Carlsen and Others v Council* [1998] ECR II-485, para. 55.

22 The application for interim relief can be made at the same time as that for the main action.

23 See Case T-395/94 R II *Atlantic Container v Commission* [1995] ECR II-2893, para. 49. See also Cases 160, 161 and 170/73 R II *Miles Druce v Commission* [1974] ECR 281 and Case 118/83 R *CMC v Commission* [1983] ECR 2583.

24 F.C. de la Torre, supra note 1, p. 277.

25 Ibid., pp. 339–340.

interim measures which go beyond the limitations of judicial review in the main action, where the Community Courts cannot give the institutions specific directions as to how to comply with the judgment.[26] This is particularly the case where the institution whose action is under scrutiny has wide discretion in the exercise of its powers.[27] The Community Courts are only prepared to override the discretion of the institution in exceptional circumstances[28] to compel them to take a specific course of action[29] or to prevent them from exercising their powers in the course of an administrative or legislative procedure.[30] Obviously, the Community Courts will not order any interim measures which exceed the powers of the institution.[31] This reluctance can be contrasted with the apparent greater readiness of the Court to grant orders against Member States in the context of an action under Article 226. Even though judgments under Article 226 are merely declaratory in nature, the Court has not hesitated to adopt interim measures which suspend the operation of the national measures in issue[32] or even impose specific limitations.[33]

Finally, the Community Courts have refused to grant interim measures against individuals who are not parties to the proceedings.[34] Similarly,

---

[26] Ibid., pp. 339–340. See Case C-313/90 *CIRFS and Others v Commission* [1991] ECR I-2557; Case T-543/93 R *Gestevisión Telecinco v Commission* [1993] ECR II-1409; Opinion of AG Elmer in Case C-68/95 *T. Port* [1996] ECR I-6068, at para. 52; Case T-86/96 R *Arbeitsgemeinschaft Deutscher Luftfahrt-Unternehmen and Hapag Lloyd Fluggesellschaft v Commission* [1998] ECR II-641Case T-369/03 R *Arizona Chemicals v Commission* [2004] ECR II-205, para. 67.

[27] See Case T-213/97 R *Eurocoton v Council* [1997] ECR II-1609, at para. 40.

[28] See F.C. de la Torre, supra note 1, pp. 342–344.

[29] See Case T-310/97 R *Netherlands Antilles v Council* [1998] ECR II-455, para. 65; Case T-350/00 R *Free Trade Foods v Commission* [2001] ECR II-493, para. 48; Case T-37/04 *Azores v Council* [2004] ECR II-2153, para. 138.

[30] See Case T-395/94 R II *Atlantic Container and Others v Commission* [1995] ECR II-2893, para. 39; Case T-52/96 *Sogecable v Commission* [1996] ECR II-797, paras. 40–41; Case T-216/01 R *Reisebank v Commission* [2001] ECR II-3481, para. 52; Case T-422/03 R II *Enviro Tech v Commission* [2004] ECR II-2003, para. 55.

[31] See Case T-107/96 R *Pantochim v Commission* [1996] ECR II-1361, para. 42; Case T-164/96 R *Moccia Irme v Commission* [1996] ECR II-2261, para. 30; Joined Cases T-107/01 R and T-175/01 R *Sacilor v Commission* [2002] ECR II-3139, para. 61.

[32] Case 61/77 R *Commission v Ireland* [1977] ECR 1411; Case 293/85 R *Commission v Belgium* [1985] ECR 3521; Case C-195/90 R *Commission v Germany* [1990] ECR I-3351; Case C-87/94 R *Commission v Belgium* [1994] ECR I-1395; Case C-320/03 R *Commission v Austria* [2003] ECR I-11665. Interim measures are also granted in the context of state aid cases, see Joined Cases 31 and 53/77 *Commission v United Kingdom* [1977] ECR 921; Case 171/83 R *Commission v France* [1983] ECR 2621. For the possibility of obtaining interim relief in the context of Article 228, see Joined Cases 24 and 97/80 R *Commission v France* [1980] ECR 1319.

[33] See Case 42/82 R *Commission v France* [1982] ECR 841.

[34] See Case T-543/93 R *Gestevisión Telecinco v Commission* [1993] ECR II-1409, para. 25; Case T-322/94 R *Union Carbide v Commission* [1994] ECR II-1159, para. 28; Case T-353/94 R *Postbank v Commission* [1994] ECR II-1141, para. 33.

orders against Member States which are not parties to the proceedings will be rejected.[35] An order against an EC institution which is not a party to the proceedings will also be rejected[36] unless the institution is represented in the proceedings and agrees to the order.[37] Moreover, the Community Courts have made it clear that 'where the interim measures applied for may seriously affect the rights and interests of third parties, which, not being parties to the proceedings, have not been able to have their views heard, such measures can be justified only if it appears that, without them, the applicants would be exposed to a situation liable to endanger their very existence'.[38]

2. REQUIREMENTS FOR THE GRANT OF INTERIM MEASURES

The Community Courts will adopt interim measures if the applicant can establish a *prima facie* case, show urgency in the sense that the order is necessary to avoid serious and irreparable damage, and can convince the judge that the balance of interests involved is favourable to the applicant.[39] The judge hearing the application for interim measures will necessarily have to examine these requirements summarily due to the time constraints involved. While all three requirements have to be met, the weight that is attached to them might depend on the circumstances of the case and the effects an order will have. The grant of an order will often depend on an overall assessment of the case, which provides the judge hearing the application with considerable discretion.

Prima facie case

The Community Courts are reluctant to assess the admissibility of the main action, as 'the judge in the interim proceedings must not prejudge

[35] See Cases T-107/01 R and T-175/01 R *Sacilor v Commission* [2002] ECR II-3139, at paras. 59 and 60.

[36] See Case 133/87 R *Nashua v Commission* [1987] ECR 2883, para. 8.

[37] See Case 23/86 R *United Kingdom v European Parliament* [1986] ECR 1085, para. 23.

[38] Case T-96/92 R *CCE de la Société Générale des Grandes Sources and others v Commission* [1992] ECR II- 2579, para. 40. See also Case 243/78 R *Simmenthal v Commission* [1978] ECR 2391, para. 6; T-12/93 R *CCE Vittel and CE Perval v Commission* [1993] ECR II-785, para. 20; Case T-339/00 R *Bactria v Commission* [2001] ECR II-1721, para. 113. See, however, Case T-114/06 R *Globe v Commission* [2006] ECR II-2627, paras. 150–152.

[39] The first two requirements are laid down in Article 83(2) ECJ Rules and Article 104(2) CFI Rules, whereas the third requirement is the result of case law.

questions relating to the admissibility of the main action which are within the jurisdiction of the Court hearing the main action'.[40] All the same, the judge hearing the application for interim measures cannot avoid dealing with the admissibility of the main action.[41] Where it is claimed that the main action is manifestly inadmissible, the judge has to establish 'grounds for concluding prima facie that the admissibility of the main application cannot be completely ruled out'.[42] The Community Courts have therefore, exceptionally, refused interim measures where the main action was considered inadmissible.[43] As the assessment of the judge hearing the application for interim measures cannot prejudge the main action, the court in the main proceedings is free to take a different view of the admissibility.[44]

The judge hearing the application for interim relief also has to examine whether the applicant has a *prima facie* case in relation to the substance of the claim. The Court in *Atlantic Container Line* noted that 'a number of different forms of wording have been used in the case law to define the condition relating to the establishment of a prima facie case, depending on the individual circumstances'.[45] It has, however, been argued[46] that the standard of the test has undergone a change from earlier rulings which required a stronger *prima facie* case.[47] The more recent case law presents a more relaxed approach in that the court is to enquire whether 'the application does not appear to be prima facie wholly unjustified'.[48] The essential aspect

---

[40] Case 75/72 R *Perinciolo v Council* [1972] ECR 1201, para. 7. See also Case 23/86 R *United Kingdom v Parliament* [1986] ECR 1085, para. 21; Case 65/87 R *Pfizer International v Commission* [1987] ECR 1691, para. 15; Case T-168/95 R *Eridania v Council* [1995] ECR II-2817, para. 27.

[41] See Case 118/83 R *CMC v Commission* [1983] ECR 2583, para. 37.

[42] Case 221/86 R *Group of the European Right and National Front Party v European Parliament* [1986] ECR 2969, para. 19. See also Case 160/88 R *Fedesa v Council* [1988] ECR 4121, para. 22; Case T-168/95 R *Eridania v Council* [1995] ECR II-2817, para. 27; Case C-240/96 R *United Kingdom v Commission* [1996] ECR I-4475, para. 37. For a less cautious approach, see Case C-300/00 P(R) *Federación de Cofradías de Pescadores de Guipúzcoa and Others v Council* [2000] ECR I-8797, para. 34; Case T-398/02 *Linea GIG v Commission* [2003] ECR II-1139, para. 44; Case T-34/05 R *Makhteshim-Agan and Others v Commission* [2005] ECR II-1465; Case T-41/08 R *Vakakis v Commission*, order of 25 April 2008, at para. 34.

[43] See Case 160/88 R *Fedesa v Council* [1988] ECR 4121; Case C-300/00 P(R) *Federación de Cofradías de Pescadores de Guipúzcoa and Others v Council* [2000] ECR I-8797; Case T-85/03 R *Cayman Islands v Commission*, order of 26 March 2003, para. 62.

[44] Case C-258/05 P(R) *Makhteshim-Agan and Others v Commission*, order of 29 October 2005 (not published), para. 21.

[45] Case C-149/95 P(R) *Commission v Atlantic Container Line and Others* [1995] ECR I-2165, para. 26.

[46] F.C. de la Torre, supra note 1, p. 284.

[47] See Cases 43, 44 and 45/59 *Von Lachmüller and Others v Commission* [1960] ECR 489, at p. 492; Case 42/82 R *Commission v France* [1982] ECR 841, at para. 13.

[48] Case C-280/93 R *Germany v Council* [1993] ECR I-3667, para. 21. See also Case 56/89 R *Publishers Association v Commission* [1989] ECR 1693, para. 31; Case C-149/95 P(R)

of a *prima facie* case seems to be that 'the arguments put forward by the applicant cannot be dismissed at that stage in the procedure without a more detailed examination'.[49] This is in particular relevant where the case presents complex legal issues.[50] On the other hand, more recent orders will not shy away from expressing an opinion on the strength or weakness of the case.[51]

The Court pointed out in *Le Pen* that 'the strength or weakness of the pleas relied on to show a *prima facie* case may be taken into consideration by the judge in his assessment of urgency and, if appropriate, of the balance of interests'.[52] However, even though a strong *prima facie* case might be relevant for the assessment of urgency,[53] it cannot 'make up for a complete failure to demonstrate urgency'.[54] On the other hand, in some cases a strong *prima facie* case is indispensable for the order to be granted.[55] This is in particular so where the order produces irreversible effects[56] or in case of an appeal against an interim relief order of the CFI.[57]

Urgency

The Court has pointed out that in order to guarantee the effectiveness of the definitive future decision 'urgency must be assessed in the light of the need for an interlocutory order in order to avoid serious and irreparable damage to the party seeking the interim relief'.[58] This rationale of urgency makes it difficult to demonstrate that its conditions are met. First, the requirement of urgency demands that interim measures are necessary.

Commission v Atlantic Container Line and Others [1995] ECR I-2165, para. 26; Case C-208/03 R *Le Pen v European Parliament* [2003] ECR I-7939, para. 100.

49 Case C-149/95 P(R) *Commission v Atlantic Container Line and Others* [1995] ECR I-2165, para. 26.

50 Case C-280/93 R *Germany v Council* [1993] ECR I-3667, at para. 21; Case C-180/96 R *United Kingdom v Commission* [1996] ECR I-3903, para. 81.

51 See F.C. de la Torre, supra note 1, p. 285.

52 Case C-208/03 R *Le Pen v European Parliament* [2003] ECR I-7939, para. 110. See also Case C-481/01 P(R) *NDC Health v IMS Health and Commission* [2002] ECR I-3401, para. 63.

53 Case C-445/00 R *Austria v Council* [2001] ECR I-1461, para. 110; Case T-114/06 R *Globe v Commission* [2006] ECR II-2627, para. 140.

54 Case T-69/96 R *Aughinish Alumina v Commission* [2006] ECR II-58, para. 84. For exceptions to this rule in cases of manifest breach of essential rules of Community law, see F.C. de la Torre, supra note 1, p. 286.

55 See F.C. de la Torre, supra note 1, pp. 287–288.

56 See Case C-393/96 P(R) *Antonissen v Council and Commission* [1997] ECR I-441, para. 41; Case T-139/01 R *Comafrica v Commission* [2001] ECR II-2415, para. 98; Case T-207/01 R *Gibraltar v Commission* [2001] ECR II-3915, para. 115; Case T-37/04 R *Azores v Council* [2004] ECR II-2153, para. 138.

57 Case C-404/04 P(R) *Technische Glaswerke Ilmenau v Commission* [2004] ECR I-3539, paras. 18–20.

58 Case C-39/03 P(R) *Commission v Artegodan and Others* [2003] ECR I-4485, para. 41.

Secondly, the applicant needs to show that the damage must be certain and that the contested act caused the damage. Thirdly, while urgency presupposes serious and irreparable harm, the Community Courts are more demanding in whether those conditions are met where the applicants are private parties rather than public authorities. Finally, where the order for interim relief reaches the limits of judicial intervention, urgency must be clear and manifest.

Necessity for interim measures

Interim measures are only necessary to avoid that the final judgment will be illusory. Urgency will therefore be rejected if it is foreseeable that the final judgment will be delivered before the damage occurs.[59] Similarly, interim measures will be rejected if alternative avenues exist to avert the damage.[60] In *Sison v Commission*,[61] the President of the CFI denied urgency, as the applicant whose assets had been frozen under EC anti-terrorism legislation could obtain funds by applying to the national authorities.[62] Conversely, where the alleged damage has already occurred, an order granting interim relief to prevent such damage will come too late and will therefore be rejected.[63]

Nature of damage

The Community Courts have consistently held that the damage must be certain.[64] This means that 'damage which is purely hypothetical in so far

---

[59] Case T-322/94 R *Union Carbide v Commission* [1994] ECR II-1159, at para. 35. While it does not *per se* exclude urgency (see Case T-392/02 R *Solvay v Commission* [2003] ECR II-1825, at para. 104), the use of the expedited procedure will make it more unlikely that damage will occur before judgment in the main action is rendered, see F.C. de la Torre, supra note 1, pp. 3124–315 and E. Barbier de la Serre, 'Accelerated and Expedited Procedures before the EC Courts: a Review of the Practice' (2006) *CMLRev* 783–815, at pp. 808–811.

[60] Cases in which Community law was considered to provide a sufficient alternative: Case T-37/04 R *Azores v Council* [2004] ECR II-2153, para. 157; Case T-310/06 R *Hungary v Commission* [2007] ECR II-15, para. 67. Cases in which the applicant could rely on remedies in national courts: see Case 310/85 R *Deufil v Commission* [1986] ECR 537, para. 22; Case T-34/02 R *B v Commission* [2002] ECR II-2803, at para. 93; Case T-417/05 R *Endesa v Commission* [2006] ECR II-18, at para. 50. However, see Case T-198/01 R *Technische Glaswerke Ilmenau v Commission* [2002] ECR II-2153, para. 58; upheld on appeal in Case C-232/02 P(R) *Commission v Technische Glaswerke Ilmenau* [2002] ECR I-8977, at paras. 31–36. On contractual safeguards, see Case T-201/04 *Microsoft v Commission* [2004] ECR II-4463, para. 268.

[61] Case T-47/03 R *Sison v Council and Commission* [2003] ECR II-2047.

[62] See Case T-47/03 R *Sison v Council and Commission* [2003] ECR II-2047, at paras. 34 and 35.

[63] Case C-445/00 R *Austria v Council* [2001] ECR I-1461, para. 113; C-480/01 *Commerzbank v Commission* [2002] ECR I-2129.

[64] Case C-174/94 R *France v Commission* [1994] ECR I-5229, para. 32; Case T-322/94 R *Union Carbide v Commission* [1994] ECR II-1159, at para. 35

as it is based on the occurrence of future and uncertain events cannot justify granting the interim measures'.[65] While absolute certainty is not required, the damage has to occur with a 'sufficient degree of probability'.[66] Consequently, the occurrence of damage remains hypothetical where it depends 'not on the act suspension of whose operation is sought, but on the possible taking of a decision by a Member State'.[67] Closely related is the requirement that the damage must be imminent[68] for which 'it is sufficient that the harm in question, particularly when it depends on the occurrence of a number of factors, should be foreseeable with a sufficient degree of probability'.[69] The Community Courts have held that damage is not sufficiently imminent where the national authorities have not yet adopted any measures implementing a decision ordering the recovery of state aid which was declared incompatible with the Common Market.[70]

The applicant must also demonstrate that the contested act constituted the cause of the damage.[71] The Court noted in *United Kingdom v Commission*[72] that the applicant had not shown that the principal cause of the damage for British beef producers and exporters resulted from Commission Decision 96/239[73] banning all exports of beef from the UK. The Court found that the fall in demand for beef was prompted, a week before the Commission's decision was adopted, by the announcement by the national scientific advisory committee, and by the United Kingdom Government itself, of a likely link between BSE and a variant of Creutzfeldt-Jakob disease. Moreover, even before the adoption of the Commission's Decision other Member States and a number of non-member countries had adopted bans. The Court was not convinced 'at

---

65 Case T-422/03 R *Enviro Tech v Commission* [2004] ECR II-469, para. 65. See also Case C-149/95 P(R) *Commission v Atlantic Container Line and Others* [1995] ECR I-2165, para. 38; Case T-241/00 R *Le Canne v Commission* [2001] ECR II-37, para. 37; Case C-180/01 P(R) *Commission v NALOO* [2001] ECR I-5737, para. 57.

66 Case C-39/03 P(R) *Commission v Artegodan and Others* [2003] ECR I-4485, para. 42.

67 Case T-420/05 R *Vischim v Commission* [2006] ECR II-34, para. 71. See also Case C-39/03 P(R) *Commission v Artegodan and Others* [2003] ECR I-4485.

68 On the link between certainty and imminence, see F.C. de la Torre, supra note 1, pp. 310–311.

69 Case C-149/95 P(R) *Commission v Atlantic Container Line and Others* [1995] ECR I-2165, para. 38. See also Case C-310/04 R *Spain v Council*, order of 18 January 2005, at para. 37.

70 See Case T-34/02 R *B v Commission* [2002] ECR II-2803, at paras. 88 and 89; Case T-416/05 R *Olympiakes Aerogrammes v Commission* [2206] ECR II-45, at para. 52.

71 Case C-399/02 P(R) *Marcuccio v Commission* [2002] ECR I-1417, at para. 26; Case T-303/04 R *European Dynamics v Commission* [2004] ECR II-3889, at para. 60.

72 Case C-180/96 R *United Kingdom v Commission* [1996] ECR I-3903, at para. 87. See also Case T-76/96 R *The National Farmers' Union v Commission* [1996] ECR II-815, at para. 99.

73 [1996] OJ L 78/47.

the present stage in the proceedings, that Decision 96/239 significantly magnified the damage caused by those measures or that, in the absence of such a decision, demand for United Kingdom beef would have recovered in the other Member States or in non-member countries, given the media coverage of the issue and increasing health awareness among consumers'.[74] The Community Courts will also deny causality where the applicant could reduce the damage thereby imposing a duty of diligence.[75]

Serious and irreparable harm

An application for interim relief will only satisfy the requirement of urgency if it can show that the damage is serious as well as irreparable.[76] The tendency in the recent case law to consider the seriousness of the damage independent from whether the damage is irreparable has not been undisputed.[77] It has been argued that in light of the need to ensure effective protection of the applicant irreparable damage is to be considered as serious.[78] The assessment of damage as 'serious in the sense of whether or not there is much at stake for the applicant is, consequently, arguably inadequate for examining urgency'[79] and should, instead, form part of the balancing of interests.

When determining whether damage is serious the Community Courts seem to apply a *de minimis* approach.[80] Damage which is inherent in the activity in the market will not be considered as sufficiently serious.[81] The judge hearing the application for interim relief will apply, however, not an absolute threshold but will take account of the size of the undertaking in determining the seriousness of the damage.[82] While it seems to be clear that the demand for urgency is satisfied where damage is irreparable, it is less

---

74 Case C-180/96 R *United Kingdom v Commission* [1996] ECR I-3903, at para. 87.

75 See Case C-377/98 R *Netherlands v European Parliament and Council* [2000] ECR I-6229, at para. 57.

76 See Case C-51/90 R and C-59/90 R *Comos Tank and Others v Commission* [1990] ECR I-2167; Case C-377/98 R *Netherlands v European Parliament and Council* [2000] ECR I-6229; Case T-195/05 R *Deloitte v Commission* [2005] ECR II-3485; Case T-114/06 R *Globe v Commission* [2006] ECR II-2627.

77 See F.C. de la Torre, supra note 1, pp. 292–293.

78 Ibid., pp. 292–293. See AG Capotorti in Joined Cases 24 and 97/80 *Commission v France* [1980] ECR 1319, at p. 1341, who considered that serious damage meant irreparable damage.

79 F.C. de la Torre, supra note 1, p. 293.

80 Ibid., p. 293.

81 Case T-342/00 R *Petrolessence and SG2R v Commission* [2001] ECR I-67, at para. 44; Case T-195/05 R *Deloitte v Commission* [2005] ECR II-3485, at para. 150.

82 Case C-51/90 R *Comos Tank and Others v Commission* [1990] ECR I-2167, at para. 26; Case T-201/04 R *Microsoft v Commission* [2004] ECR II-4463, para. 257; Case T-195/05 R *Deloitte v Commission* [2005] ECR II-3485, at para. 156.

clear why independently from irreparability urgency also requires damage to be serious. The seriousness of such damage seems therefore more relevant within the framework of balancing the interests of the parties.

Serious and irreparable harm for private parties

Private parties can only claim that the damage is serious and irreparable in relation to their own interests. Private parties can therefore not invoke the interests of third parties[83] or general interests[84] to establish urgency. Such interests can be considered only when the balance of interests involved is examined.[85] Associations can invoke the interests which they are called upon to protect.[86]

The Community Courts have pursued a strict line in relation to financial damage.[87] In *Arizona Chemical*[88] the President of the CFI pointed out that 'it has consistently been held that damage of a purely financial nature cannot, save in exceptional circumstances, be regarded as irreparable, or even as being reparable only with difficulty, if it can ultimately be the subject of financial compensation'.[89] The President explained that this approach assumes that financial damage which is not made good by the judgment in the main action constitutes economic loss for which the applicant can be compensated in an action under Article 288(2).[90] It has been

---

[83] Case 22/75 R *Küster v European Parliament* [1975] ECR 278, para. 8; Case T-70/99 *Alpharma v Council* [1999] ECR II-2027, para. 146; Case T-417/05 R *Endesa v Commission* [2005] ECR II-18, at paras. 37–40; Case T-420/05 R *Vischim v Commission* [2006] ECR II-34, paras. 73 and 74; Case T-69/06 R *Aughinish v Commission* [2006] ECR II-58, para. 80.

[84] Case T-213/97 R *Eurocoton and Others v Council* [1997] ECR II-1609, at para. 46; Case T-417/05 R *Endesa v Commission* [2005] ECR II-18, at paras. 59 and 60. However, see Case T-326/99 R *Olivieri v Commission* [2000] ECR II-1985, para. 135.

[85] Case T-13/99 R *Pfizer v Council* [1999] ECR II-1961, para. 136; Case T-69/06 R *Aughinish v Commission* [2006] ECR II-58, para. 80.

[86] See Case T-213/97 R *Eurocoton and Others v Council* [1997] ECR II-1609, at para. 46; Case T-86/96 R *Arbeitsgemeinschaft Deutscher Luftfahrtunternehmen and Hapag Lloyd v Commission* [1998] ECR II-641, at para. 63.

[87] For a detailed examination of the requirements for urgency in different areas, such as tenders, anti-trust, anti-dumping and State Aid, see F.C. de la Torre, supra note 1, at pp. 304–309.

[88] Case T-369/03 R *Arizona Chemical and Others v Commission* [2004] ECR II-205.

[89] Ibid., para. 75. See also Case C-213/91 R *Abertal SAT v Commission* [2001] ECR I-5109, para. 24; Case T-230/97 R *Comafrica and Dole v Commission* [1997] ECR II-1589, para. 32; Case T-339/00 R *Bactria v Commission* [2001] ECR II-1721, para. 94. This approach is also pursued in case of pecuniary damage suffered by natural persons, see Case T-47/03 R *Sison v Council and Commission* [2003] ECR II-2047, at paras. 29–31; see also F.C. de la Torre, supra note 1, p. 303.

[90] Case T-369/03 R *Arizona Chemical and Others v Commission* [2004] ECR II-205, at para. 75. See also Case T-230/97 R *Comafrica and Dole v Commission* [1997] ECR II-1589, at para. 38; Case T-169/00 R *Esedra v Commission* [2000] ECR II-2951, at para. 47; Case C-404/01 P(R) *Commission v Euroalliages and Others* [2001] ECR I-10367, at para. 70; Case T-148/04 R TQ3 *Travel Solutions Belgium v Commission* [2004] ECR II-3027, at para.

pointed out that the consideration of Article 288(2) as means of redress for any damage suffered is a more recent phenomenon in the case law.[91] As previously discussed,[92] compensation under Article 288(2) is difficult to obtain where the institution enjoys wide discretion. The President of the CFI in *Euroalliages v Commission*[93] found that given the wide discretion which the Commission enjoyed in the adoption of the contested measure it was not certain whether the applicants would obtain compensation under Article 288(2) and consequently accepted urgency.[94] On appeal, the President of the Court set the ruling aside on the ground that 'by taking exclusively the uncertainty of success in any action for damages, in view of the nature of the contested decision, as a ground for finding that the damage is irreparable and thus for granting interim measures, the contested order is vitiated by an error in law'.[95] The President of the Court argued that it was by necessity uncertain whether the applicant would obtain damages in an action under Article 288(2) and an action for interim measures was not designed to remove such uncertainty. The President rejected the wide discretion of the Commission as relevant on the ground that 'if that criterion were applied systematically, the irreparable nature of the injury would depend on the characteristics of the contested measure and not on the applicant's individual circumstances'.[96]

The appeal ruling calls for a few observations. First, it should be noted that since the Court's ruling in *Bergaderm* it is no longer the nature of the act which is relevant, but the discretion which the institution has in adopting it. Secondly, the President of the CFI rightly pointed out that where the institution has wide discretion, an application for damages will depend on whether the institution manifestly and gravely disregarded the limits of its discretion. While an automatic exclusion of compensation under Article 288(2) can therefore not follow from the discretion of the institution alone, a *prima facie* assessment of whether the institution manifestly and gravely disregard the limits of its discretion seems, however, unavoidable.

45; Case T-195/05 R *Deloitte v Commission* [2005] ECR II-3485, at para. 141; Case T-114/06 R *Globe v Commission* [2006] ECR II-2627, at para. 115. On the other hand, the Community Courts seem to be more reluctant to consider damages actions in national courts, see Case T-184/01 R *IMS Health v Commission* [2001] ECR II-3193, at para. 119.

[91] F.C. de la Torre, supra note 1, p. 293. For the earlier approach, see AG Capotorti in Joined Cases 24 and 97/80 R *Commission v France* [1980] ECR 1319, at p. 1341. See also Case 113/77 R *NTN Toyo Bearing and Others v Council* [1977] ECR 1721 and Case 232/91 R *Agricola Commerciale Olio v Commission* [1981] ECR 2193.

[92] See supra Chapter 4, pp. 264–274.

[93] Case T-132/01 R *Euroalliages and Others v Commission* [2001] ECR II-2307.

[94] Ibid., at paras. 73–77.

[95] Case C-404/01 P *Commission v Euroalliages and Others* [2001] ECR I-10367, para. 75.

[96] Ibid., para. 74.

Where such an assessment leads to the conclusion that damage will not be compensated, and given the exceptional nature of a finding of manifest and grave disregard this seems the most likely outcome, then the damage should be considered as irreparable. The only error which the President of the CFI therefore committed was that he did not undertake such an assessment.

The possibility of obtaining compensation under Article 288(2) is also doubtful if the damage is difficult to quantify. In *Deloitte*[97] the President of the CFI considered the exclusion of the applicant from a tender as damage which consisted in the loss of the opportunity to be awarded the contract in the tendering procedure. The President found, however, that it was 'very difficult, or even impossible, to quantify that opportunity and therefore to evaluate the damage resulting from its loss'[98] and therefore considered the damage as irreparable.[99]

Exceptionally, financial damage, even if it could be compensated, is regarded as irreparable if it threatens the undertaking's very existence.[100] The fact that an undertaking might have to apply for the commencement of bankruptcy proceedings may constitute such a threat, but each case must be assessed on a case-by-case basis.[101] The Community Courts have made it clear that 'in considering the financial viability of an applicant, an assessment of its financial situation may be made, in particular, by taking into consideration characteristics of the group to which its shareholders belong'.[102] This approach has been justified on the ground that 'the

---

97 Case T-195/05 R *Deloitte v Commission* [2005] ECR II-3485.

98 Ibid., para. 147.

99 Ibid., paras. 147 and 148. See also Joined Cases C-51/90 R and C-59/90 R *Comos Tank and Others v Commission* [1990] ECR I-2167, para.; Case T-41/97 R *Antillean Rice Mills v Council* [1997] ECR II-447, para. 47; Case T-65/98 R *Van den Bergh Foods v Commission* [1998] ECR II-2641, para. 65; Case T-114/06 R *Globe v Commission* [2006] ECR II-2627, at paras. 117 and 118. For a critical evaluation of this approach, see F.C. de la Torre, supra note 1, at pp. 299–301.

100 Case C-152/88 R *Sofrimport v Commission* [1988] ECR 2931, at paras. 31 and 32; Case T-11/99 R *Van Parys and Others v Commission* [1999] ECR II-1355, para. 62; Case C-474/00 P(R) *Commission v Bruno and Others* [2001] ECR I-2909, at paras. 106 and 107; T-53/01 R *Poste Italiane v Commission* [2001] ECR II-1479, at para. 120; Case T-198/01 *Technische Glaswerke Ilmenau v Commission* [2002] ECR II-2153, at para. 99. On the evidence required, see F.C. de la Torre, supra note 1, p. 296.

101 See Case C-335/99 P(R) *HFB and Others v Commission* [1999] ECR I-8705, at paras. 56 and 57; Case T-181/02 R *Neue Erba Lautex v Commission* [2002] ECR II-5081, at paras. 88 and 89. For an assessment of the threat of closure of production sites, see Case T-13/99 R *Pfizer Animal Health v Council* [1999] ECR II-1961, at paras. 140 *et seq.*

102 Case T-241/00 *Le Canne v Commission* [2001] ECR II-37, para. 39. See also Case C-12/95 P *Transacciones Marítimas and Others v Commission* [1995] ECR I-467, para. 12; Case T-13/99 R *Pfizer Animal Health v Council* [1999] ECR II-1961, para. 155, upheld on appeal in Case C-329/99 P *Pfizer Animal Health and Others v Commission and Others* [1999] ECR I-8343, para. 67; Case T-181/02 R *Neue Erba Lautex v Commission* [2002] ECR II-5081,

objective interests of the undertaking concerned are not distinct from the interests of the natural or legal persons who control it, and that the serious and irreparable nature of the alleged damage must therefore be assessed at the level of the group composed by those persons. That coincidence of interests constitutes a ground for, in particular, not assessing the interests of the undertaking concerned in surviving independently of the interests which the persons who control it have in its survival'.[103] Similarly, the Community Courts when assessing damage to an association of undertakings will take into account the financial situation of its members 'where the objective interests of the association are not independent of those of the member undertakings'.[104]

The Community Courts have also recognised that where the implementation of a contested measure 'may cause irreversible market developments on a market in which the applicant is already present, the losses which would thereby ensue for the applicant, though financial in nature, may nevertheless exceptionally be regarded as irreparable for the purposes of granting interim relief'.[105] This is in particular the case where without the order the applicant would be in a situation where its market share would be irreparably modified. However, in order to demonstrate that their market shares are irremediably affected, applicants have to demonstrate that 'they would be confronted with obstacles of a structural or legal nature that could prevent them from regaining a significant proportion of those market shares following the introduction, in particular, of appropriate publicity measures'.[106]

The reluctance displayed in the case law to accept urgency is not limited to pecuniary damage, but can also be found in cases dealing with other

---

para. 92; Case T-369/03 R *Arizona Chemical and Others v Commission* [2004] ECR II-205, para. 87; Case T-420/05 R *Vischim v Commission* [2006] ECR II-34, para. 81; Case T-69/06 R *Aughinish Alumina v Commission* [2006] ECR II-58, para. 69.

[103] Case T-241/00 *Le Canne v Commission* [2001] ECR II-37, para. 40.

[104] Case T-245/03 R *FNSEA and Others v Commission* [2004] ECR II-271, para. 84.

[105] Case T-139/01 R *Comafrica and Dole Fresh Fruit Europe v Commission* [2001] ECR II-2415, para. 94. See also Joined Cases 76, 77 and 91/89 *RTE and Others v Commission* [1989] ECR 1141, para. 18; Case T-395/94 R *Atlantic Container Line and Others v Commission* [1995] ECR II-595, para. 55; Case T-260/97 R *Camar v Commission and Council* [1997] ECR II-2357, para. 42; Case T-13/99 R *Pfizer Animal Health v Council* [1999] ECR II-1961, para. 138; Case T-342/00 R *Petrolessence and SG2R v Commission* [2001] ECR I-67, at paras. 47 and 48, in which the applicant was not present on the market; Case T-310/06 R *Hungary v Commission* [2007] ECR II-15, at para. 52.

[106] Case T-369/03 R *Arizona Chemical and Others v Commission* [2004] ECR II-205, para. 84. See also Case C-471/00 P(R) *Commission v Cambridge Healthcare* [2001] ECR I-2865, at para. 111; Case T-392/02 R *Solvay v Council* [2003] ECR II-1825, paras. 118 and 119; Case T-291/04 R *Enviro Tech Europe and Enviro Tech International v Commission* [2005] ECR II-475, at para. 83; Case T-420/05 R *Vischim v Commission* [2006] ECR II-34, para. 76.

types of damage to commercial rights and interests.[107] On the other hand, the Community Courts seem to be more generous in cases which concern damage to non-commercial interests.[108]

Serious and irreparable harm for public authorities

Interests claimed In contrast to private parties, public authorities can rely on the general interest in demonstrating the urgency of their claim.[109] In *Germany v Council (bananas)*[110] the Court pointed out that 'the Member States are responsible for interests, in particular those of an economic and social nature, which are regarded as general interests at national level and are therefore entitled to defend such interests before the courts. They may therefore invoke damage affecting a whole sector of their economy, in particular when the contested Community measure may entail unfavourable repercussions on the level of employment and the cost of living'.[111] On the other hand, a Member State cannot rely on the damage to specific undertakings unless it affects the state itself.[112] In *Austria v Commission*[113] the Court accepted that a Member State can base urgency on considerations of environmental protection, in the particular case nuisance caused by traffic density. Member States can even rely 'on the damage which would arise from expenditure being incurred contrary to the rules governing the powers of the Community and its institutions'.[114] On the other hand, an

---

[107] See Case T-184/01 R *IMSHealth v Commission* [2001] ECR II-3193, paras. 126–131, and Case T-201/04 R *Microsoft v Commission* [2004] ECR II-4463, at paras. 250–251, on damage to intellectual property rights; Case T-201/04 R *Microsoft v Commission* [2004] ECR II-4463, at paras. 253 and 267–274, on harm caused by the disclosure of secret business information; Case C-7/04 P(R) *Commission v Akzo and Akcros* [2004] ECR I-8739, paras. 38–44, on damage to professional privilege; Case T-201/04 R *Microsoft v Commission* [2004] ECR II-4463, at para. 292 on harm to business freedom in general.

[108] See Case T-17/00 R *Rothley and Others v European Parliament* [2000] ECR II-2085 on the harm to the immunity of Members of the European Parliament. See also Case T-203/95 R *Connolly v Commission* [1995] ECR II-2919, at para. 44, on harm to the applicant's reputation, but see Case T-47/03 R *Sison v Council and Commission* [2003] ECR II-2047, at paras. 40–41; see also Case 118/83 R *CMC v Commission* [1983] ECR 2583, para. 51, and Case T-148/04 R *TQ3 Travel Solutions Belgium v Commission* [2004] ECR II-3027, at para. 53, where the Court did not consider the elimination of a tenderer as in itself prejudicial to his reputation.

[109] See F.C. de la Torre, supra note 1, pp. 290–291.

[110] Case C-280/93 R *Germany v Council* [1993] ECR I-3667.

[111] Ibid., para. 27. See also Case C-180/96 R *United Kingdom v Commission* [1996] ECR I-3903, para. 85.

[112] Case 142/87 R *Belgium v Commission* [1987] ECR 2589, at para. 24; Case C-356/90 R *Belgium v Commission* [1991] ECR I-2423, at para. 24; Joined Cases C-182/03 R and C-217/03 R *Belgium and Forum 187 v Commission* [2003] ECR II-6887, paras. 130 *et seq.*

[113] Case C-296/02 R *Austria v Commission* [2002] ECR I-9159, para. 91. See also Case C-445/00 R *Austria v Council* [2001] I-1461, at para. 103.

[114] Case C-239/96 R *United Kingdom v Commission* [1996] ECR I-4475, para. 66.

abstract allegation of damage to fundamental rights is not sufficient.[115] It should be noted that also regional and municipal authorities will be able to invoke the general interest, albeit limited to the territory for which they are responsible.[116] Finally, a Community institution will also be able to rely on a wide range of general interests.[117]

Serious and irreparable damage The level of scrutiny by the Community Courts of whether material damage is serious and irreparable seems to vary, but seems to be generally lower when invoked by public bodies, such as Member States or EC institutions.[118] In *Germany v Council*[119] the Court merely stated that the Community measure 'may entail unfavourable repercussions on the level of employment and the cost of living'[120] without assessing whether such damage was serious and irreparable. In *United Kingdom v Commission*[121] the Court asserted without further examination that in connection with the BSE crisis 'severe damage has been caused in the United Kingdom and that operators, particularly beef producers and exporters, are currently in a very difficult situation; moreover, it cannot be ruled out that the harm will, in part, be irreparable'.[122] In contrast, in *Netherlands v European Parliament and Council*[123] the President of the Court after a detailed examination did not consider the damage serious and irreparable.

Damage to health and the environment is generally considered as irreparable.[124] In *Commission v Austria*,[125] the President of the Court pointed

---

[115] Case C-377/98 R *Netherlands v European Parliament and Council* [2000] ECR I-6229, para. 45.

[116] See Case T-310/97 R *Netherlands Antilles v Council* [1998] ECR II-455; Joined Cases T-195/01 R and T-207/01 R *Gibraltar v Commission* [2001] ECR II-3915; Case T-37/04 R *Azores v Council* [2004] ECR II-2153; T-85/05 R *Dimos Ano Liosion and others v Commission* [2005] ECR II-1721.

[117] In judicial review cases this has mainly been relevant where the institution appealed the grant of interim measures: see Case C-345/90 P(R) *European Parliament v Hanning* [1991] ECR I-231; Case C-180/01 P(R) *Commission v NALOO* [2001] ECR I-5737; Case C-156/03 P(R) *Commission v Laboratoires Servier* [2003] ECR I-6575.

[118] See F.C. de la Torre, supra note 1, p. 309.

[119] Case C-280/93 R *Germany v Council* [1993] ECR I-3667.

[120] Ibid., para. 27.

[121] Case C-180/96 R *United Kingdom v Commission* [1996] ECR I-3903.

[122] Ibid., para. 86. See also Joined Cases C-182/03 R and C-217/03 R *Belgium and Forum 187 v Commission* [2003] ECR I-6887, at para. 135, in which the President of the Court merely referred to the likelihood of significant problems.

[123] Case C-377/98 R *Netherlands v European Parliament and Council* [2000] ECR I-6229, at paras. 49–65. See also Case C-296/93 R *France v Commission* [1993] ECR I-4181, at paras. 26–30.

[124] Case C-445/00 R *Austria v Council* [2001] ECR I-1461, at para. 106; Case C-459/00 P(R) *Commission v Trenker* [2001] ECR I-2823, at para. 113; Case C-296/02 R *Austria v Commission* [2002] ECR I-9159, at paras. 91 and 92.

[125] Case C-320/03 R *Commission v Austria* [2003] ECR I-11665.

out that '[h]arm caused to such interests is generally irreversible since, more often than not, damage to the environment or to health cannot, by reason of its nature, be eliminated retroactively'.[126] Similarly, it has been argued that a manifest breach of essential rules of the Community legal order will reduce, albeit not eliminate, the need for demonstrating urgency.[127]

On the other hand, the Community Courts have rejected urgency based on the 'general assertions concerning the practical or administrative difficulties which immediate compliance with the judgment under appeal would create for the working of the Commission'.[128]

Manifest urgency As pointed out above,[129] the Community Courts are more reluctant to grant interim relief, where the order has a definitive nature, where it interferes with the discretion of other institutions or where it prevents another institution from exercising its powers. As in these instances they reach the limits of judicial intervention, the Community Courts will require a higher degree of urgency to justify interim measures.[130] Only manifest or clear urgency will then satisfy an order for interim measures.[131]

Balance of Interests

The balance of interests as part of the assessment as to whether interim relief be granted finds its basis exclusively in the case law of the Court.[132] The judge seized with an application for interim measures would have to balance the applicant's interests in the suspension of the contested act or other interim relief being granted against the interests of other parties in having the act maintained and would have to consider whether the former

---

126 Ibid., para. 92.

127 See F.C. de la Torre, supra note 1, p. 310.

128 Case C-180/01 P(R) *Commission v NALOO* [2001] ECR I-5737, para. 57. See also Case T-155/96 R *City of Mainz v Commission* [1996] ECR II-1655.

129 See supra, pp. 301–303.

130 See F.C. de la Torre, supra note 1, p. 317.

131 See Case C-393/96 P(R) *Antonissen v Council and Commission* [1997] ECR I-441, at para. 41; Case C-363/98 P(R) *Emesa Sugar v Council* [1998] ECR I-8787, at para. 55; Case T-350/00 R *Free Trade Foods v Commission* [2001] ECR II-493, at para. 48; Case T-207/01 R *Gibraltar v Commission* [2001] ECR II-3915, para. 115; Case T-37/04 R *Azores v Council* [2004] ECR II-2153, at para. 138.

132 For an explanation as to the nature of the condition, see B. Pastor and E. Van Ginderachter, 'La procédure en référé' (1989) *RTDE* 561–621 and J.L. de la Cruz Vilaça, 'La procédure en référé comme instrument de protection jurisdictionelle des particuliers in droit communautaire', *Mélanges F. Mancini* (Giuffré, 1998), at p. 257, who consider it as expression of the principle of proportionality.

outweigh the latter. When assessing the interests in granting interim relief, the Community Courts will not only take account of the damage which might result for the applicant if interim relief is not granted, but also damage to the public interest[133] and damage to third parties directly affected by the interim measure.[134] On the other side of the scales, the judge has to consider the damage to the interests of the other party if interim relief is granted, but also public interests, and prejudice to the interests of third parties.

The Community Courts have understood public interest in a broad sense[135] and will consider under this heading, amongst others, the protection of public health,[136] the environment,[137] public safety,[138] the internal market, legal certainty,[139] the right to property,[140] EC competition rules[141] and the Community's financial interest.[142] Some of these public interests carry considerable weight in the balancing process. In *Commission v Trenker* the President of the Court pointed out that, 'in principle, the requirements of the protection of public health must unquestionably be given precedence over economic considerations'.[143] Similarly, the President

---

133 This is mainly relevant for private parties, who cannot invoke damage to the general interest at the stage of the assessment of urgency, see Case T-65/98 R *Van den Bergh Foods v Commission* [1998] ECR II-2641, at para. 74.

134 See Case T-339/00 R *Bactria v Commission* [2001] ECR II-1721, at para. 111.

135 See F.C. de la Torre, supra note 1, p. 319.

136 See Case C-180/96 R *United Kingdom v Commission* [1996] ECR I-3903, at para. 93; Case C-329/99 P(R) *Pfizer Animal Health v Council* [1999] ECR I-8343, at para. 102. On the level of risk to be demonstrated, see Case T-70/99 R *Alpharma v Council* [1999] ECR II-2027, at paras. 155–166; Case C-365/03 P(R) *Industrias Químicas del Vallés v Commission* [2003] ECR I-12389, para. 23.

137 See Case C-320/03 R *Commission v Austria* [2003] ECR I-11665, at para. 91.

138 See Case C-87/94 R *Commission v Belgium* [1994] ECR I-1395, at paras. 40–41.

139 See Joined Cases C-182/03 R and C-217/03 R *Belgium and Forum 187 v Commission* [2003] ECR I-6887, para. 134.

140 See Case C-151/01 R *Duales System Deutschland v Commission* [2001] ECR II-3295, at para. 220.

141 See Case 56/89 R *Publishers Association v Commission* [1989] ECR I-1693, at para. 35; Case T-88/94 R *Société commerciale des potasses et de l'azote and Entreprise minière et chimique v Commission* [1994] ECR II-401, at para. 32; Case T-322/94 R *Union Carbide v Commission* [1994] ECR II-1159, at para. 36, concerning the public interest in implementation of decisions adopted under the merger regulation; Case T-53/01 R *Poste Italiane v Commission* [2001] ECR II-1479, at para. 130, concerning the enforcement of decisions adopted under Article 86(3); Case T-198/01 R *Technische Glaswerke Ilmenau v Commission* [2002] ECR II-2153, at para. 113, concerning the enforcement of state aid rules; Case T-217/03 R *FNCBV v Commission* [2004] ECR II-239, para. 92, concerning 'the public interest in preserving the effectiveness of Community competition rules and the deterrent effect of fines imposed by the Commission'.

142 See Case T-141/01 R *Entorn v Commission* [2001] ECR II-3123, at para. 55; Case T-398/02 R *Linea GIG v Commission* [2003] ECR II-1139, para. 62; Case T-11/06 R *Romana Tabacchi v Commission* [2006] ECR II-2491, at para. 136.

143 Case C-459/00 P(R) *Commission v Trenker* [2001] ECR I-2823, para. 109. See also Case T-392/02 R *Solvay v Council* [2003] ECR II-1825, at para. 125. Considerations of public

of the CFI made it clear in *Technische Glaswerke Ilmenau v Commission*[144] that 'the Community interest must normally, if not always, take precedence over the interest of the aid recipient in avoiding enforcement of the obligation to repay it before judgment is given in the main proceedings'.[145] Moreover, it has been remarked that 'it is rarely the case that damage to the public interest is examined with a high degree of detail' and 'it is not necessary, for public interest to be examined in the balance of interests, to conclude that it is irreparably harmed'.[146]

The Community Courts will also have to consider the interests of third parties whose rights and interests are affected by the envisaged measure.[147] In *Bayer v Commission*[148] the President of the CFI was asked to suspend a Commission decision which stated that the applicant had infringed Article 81 by concluding with their wholesalers in Spain and France, in the context of continuing commercial relations, an agreement whose purpose was to prohibit the export of a medicinal product, Adalat, to other Member States. When considering the interests involved the President found that the applicant's interests had to be weighed against 'the interest of wholesalers in Spain and France in increasing the volume of their exports to the United Kingdom in the context of a unified market, and, secondly, the interest of the NHS [National Health Service] and of United Kingdom consumers and taxpayers in a reduction of Adalat prices on the national market'.[149] But

health also outweigh, in principle, those of animal health, see Case T-392/02 R *Solvay v Council* [2003] ECR II-1825, at para. 127.

[144] Case T-198/01 R *Technische Glaswerke Ilmenau v Commission* [2002] ECR II-2153.

[145] Ibid., para. 114. See also case T-181/02 R *Neue Erba Lautex v Commission* [2002] ECR II-5081, para. 119. In exceptional circumstances interim relief may, however, be granted, see Case T-198/01 R *Technische Glaswerke Ilmenau v Commission* [2002] ECR II-2153, at paras. 115 and 116; Joined Cases C-182/03 R and C-217/03 R *Belgium and Forum 187 v Commission* [2003] ECR I-6887, paras. 142–147.

[146] F.C. de la Torre, supra note 1, p. 323.

[147] See Case T-13/99 R *Pfizer Animal Health v Council* [1999] ECR II-1961, at para. 166, concerning the interests of the interveners; Case T-339/00 R *Bactria v Commission* [2001] ECR II-1721, at para. 113; Case T-37/04 R *Azores v Council* [2004] ECR II-2153, at para. 135. See also F.C. de la Torre, supra note 1, pp. 322–323.

[148] Case T-41/96 R *Bayer v Commission* [1996] ECR II-381.

[149] Ibid., para. 60. See also Case T-96/92 R *CCE des Grandes Sources and Others v Commission* [1992] ECR II-2579, para. 39; Case T-88/94 R *Société Commerciale des Potasses et de l'Azote et Entreprise Minière et Chimique v Commission* [1994] ECR II-263, para. 44; Case T-322/94 R *Union Carbide v Commission* [1994] ECR II-1159, para. 36; Case T-342/00 R *Petrolessence and SG2R v Commission* [2001] ECR II-67, para. 51; Case C-481/01 P(R) *NDC Health v IMS Health and Commission* [2002] ECR I-3401, at para. 84, where the President of the Court considered that the interests of competing undertakings could not be excluded from the aim pursued by Article 82, in contrast to the order given in Case T-184/01 R *IMS Health v Commission* [2001] ECR II-3193, at para. 145.

not only will the interests of private parties be considered, but also those of Member States.[150]

The Community Courts have pointed out that when balancing the various interests involved they would have to determine 'whether the possible annulment of the contested decision by the Court seised of the main action would allow the situation brought about by its immediate implementation to be reversed and, conversely, whether suspension of the operation of that decision would be such as to prevent its being fully effective in the event of the main application being dismissed'.[151] Consequently, they will have to consider the importance of the interests involved and the irreversible nature of the damage.[152]

It should, however, not be forgotten that the balancing of interests is an overall assessment and gives the judge hearing the application for interim relief considerable discretion in considering all elements of the case, which are regarded as relevant.[153] The Community Courts will also take account of the merit of the *prima facie* case,[154] of the diligence of the parties in averting the damage,[155] and of the limits of their judicial competence in granting interim relief.[156]

3. PROCEDURE

An application for interim relief can only be brought once the main action has been lodged.[157] While this does not exclude the application for interim

---

150 See Case T-53/01 R *Poste Italiane v Commission* [2001] ECR II-1479, at para. 134; C-208/03 P(R) *Le Pen v European Parliament* [2003] ECR I-7939, at para. 106.

151 Case C-180/96 R *United Kingdom v Commission* [1996] ECR I-3903, para. 89. See also Case C-149/95 P(R) *Commission v Atlantic Container Line and Others* [1995] ECR I-2165, para. 50.

152 See Joined Cases C-182/03 R and C-217/03 R *Belgium and Forum 187 v Commission* [2003] ECR I-6887, at paras. 142–147; Case C-208/03 P(R) *Le Pen v European Parliament* [2003] ECR I-7939, at para. 106; Case T-114/06 *Globe v Commission* [2006] ECR II-2627, at paras. 150–154.

153 See F.C. de la Torre, supra note 1, pp. 324–325.

154 See Case C-208/03 R *Le Pen v European Parliament* [2003] ECR I-7939, at para. 110; Case C-481/01 P(R) *NDC Health v IMS Health and Commission* [2002] ECR I-3401, para. 63. Where an order for interim measures is appealed, on appeal the balance of interests will be affected by an intervening judgment of the CFI in the main action, see Case C-208/03 R *Le Pen v European Parliament* [2003] ECR I-7939; C-404/04 P(R); Case C-404/04 P(R) *Technische Glaswerke Ilmenau v Commission* [2004] ECR I-3539; Case C-326/05 P(R) *Industrias Químicas del Vallés v Commission*, order of 15 December 2005.

155 Joined Cases C-182/03 R and C-217/03 R *Belgium and Forum 187 v Commission* [2003] ECR II-6887, para. 147.

156 See supra, pp. 301–303.

157 Applicants in the main action can therefore request interim relief. On the position of interveners to lodge an application for interim relief, see F.C. de la Torre, supra note 1, pp. 329–330.

relief and the main action being made at the same time, the former must be made by a separate document[158] and in the language of the case in the main action.[159] The application must state the subject-matter of the proceedings, the circumstances giving rise to urgency and the pleas of fact and law establishing a *prima facie* case for the interim measures applied for.[160] In addition, the application for interim relief must comply with the general rules for applications and documents.[161] The relief sought has to be specific and an application containing a 'general request for the adoption of any further interim measures which the President might deem necessary or appropriate'[162] would be considered inadmissible.

The application is served on the other party and the President will set a short time period within which that party can make written or oral submissions.[163] However, in cases of extreme urgency the President can grant the application even before such submissions have been made.[164] On many occasions the submission of written observations is followed by an oral hearing.[165] It is, however, clear from the case law that 'the question whether to hear oral argument from the parties is a matter which falls within the discretion of the court dealing with the application for interim measures'.[166]

The decision will be taken by the President[167] unless the President refers the matter to the court.[168] It is not unusual for the judge hearing

---

[158] See Article 83(3) of the ECJ Rules and Article 104(3) of the CFI Rules. Otherwise, the application is considered as inadmissible, see Case T-107/94 *Kik v Council and Commission* [1995] ECR II-1717, at para. 38.

[159] See Case T-417/05 R *Endesa v Commission* [2006] ECR II-18, at para. 13.

[160] See Article 83(2) of the ECJ Rules and Article 104(2) of the CFI Rules.

[161] See Articles 37 and 38 of the ECJ Rules and Articles 43 and 44 of the CFI Rules. See for more detail, M. Brealey and M. Hoskins, *Remedies in EC Law* (Sweet & Maxwell, 2nd edn., 1998), pp. 382–384 and F.C. de la Torre, supra note 1, pp. 327–329.

[162] Case T-228/95 *Lehrfreund v Council and Commission* [1996] ECR II-111, para. 58. See also Case T-422/03 R II *Enviro Tech v Commission* [2004] ECR II-2003, para. 59.

[163] Article 84(1) of the ECJ Rules and Article 105(1) of the CFI Rules.

[164] Article 84(2)(2) of the ECJ Rules and Article 105(2)(2) of the CFI Rules.

[165] Sometimes only oral observations will be heard.

[166] Case C-393/96 P(R) *Antonissen v Council and Commission* [1997] ECR I-441, para. 22; Case C-65/99 P(R) *Willeme v Commission* [1999] ECR I-1857, at para. 47. Consequently where that court considers that it has all the information necessary to determine the application for interim measures, there is no need first to hear oral argument from the parties, see Case C-393/96 P(R) *Antonissen v Council and Commission* [1997] ECR I-441, para. 24; Case C-65/99 P(R) *Willeme v Commission* [1999] ECR I-1857, at para. 48.

[167] See Article 85 of the ECJ Rules and Article 106 of the CFI Rules. Where the President is absent or prevented from attending another judge will decide the application. See Article 85, second sentence, in combination with Article 11 of the ECJ Rules; Article 106 of the CFI Rules. On the issue of whether the judge hearing the application for interim relief should also hear the main action, see F.C. de la Torre, supra note 1, at footnote 399.

[168] This possibility only exists for the Court of Justice, see Article 85, first sentence, of the ECJ Rules. Such a referral is, however, rare.

the application to propose a settlement solution before proceeding to a formal decision.[169] The decision is taken in the form of a reasoned order.[170] Where it does not state a specific date, the order will lapse on the date of the final judgment.[171] Where the order has been rejected the applicant can make a further application on the basis of new facts.[172] At any time a party can make an application to have the order varied or cancelled in case of a change of circumstances.[173] The Court in *Commission v Artegodan*[174] found that the term change in circumstances covered 'the occurrence of any factual or legal matter such as to call into question the assessment by the judge who heard the application with regard to the conditions [. . .], which are to be met if the operation of an act is to be suspended or other interim relief is to be granted'.[175] On the one hand, such an order differs from an application based on new facts in that it is 'not limited to the coming to light of circumstances of a factual nature',[176] but can also be based on 'fresh considerations of a legal nature'.[177] On the other, it can be distinguished from an appeal in that it can be made at any time and is solely intended to make the judge 'to reconsider, for the future only, an order granting interim relief, including, where appropriate, with regard to the assessment of the pleas of fact and of law which established a prima facie case for the grant of that relief'.[178]

An appeal against any decision made by the CFI concerning interim measures lies with the Court and is subject to the mandatory time limit of two months.[179] The Court has characterised the appeal as being 'designed to set aside retroactively the order appealed against, following a judicial review which, albeit limited to questions of law, is full'.[180] The appeal will be heard and determined in accordance with the same procedure which applies in the case of a direct application for interim relief to the Court.[181]

---

169 See F.C. de la Torre, supra note 1, p. 331.

170 Article 86(1) of the ECJ Rules and Article 107(1) of the CFI Rules. For the content of an order for interim relief, see Section 2, above.

171 Article 86(3) of the ECJ Rules and Article 107(3) of the CFI Rules.

172 Article 88 of the ECJ Rules and Article 109 of the CFI Rules.

173 Article 87 of the ECJ Rules and Article 108 of the CFI Rules.

174 Case C-440/01 P(R) *Commission v Artegodan* [2002] ECR I-1489.

175 Ibid., para. 63.

176 Ibid., para. 64.

177 Ibid., para. 65.

178 Ibid., para. 65.

179 Article 57(2) of the Court's Statute.

180 Case C-440/01 P(R) *Commission v Artegodan* [2002] ECR I-1489, para. 65.

181 Article 57(3) of the Court's Statute. The Court can dismiss the appeal, set aside the order of the CFI and either refer the matter back to the CFI or decide the application itself.

Conclusion

The Lisbon Treaty does not revolutionise the system of judicial review in the EU, but its amendments reflect a more cautious evolution of the existing system. The most important improvement in this respect is that measures currently adopted under the third pillar would no longer be subject to a different regime of judicial review and could be challenged directly in the Union courts.[1] It should also be noted that the Lisbon Treaty allows challenges to acts adopted by the European Council and removes the uncertainty as to whether remedies are also available against agencies and other Union bodies by including them as defendants in the various actions available under Union law. In annulment actions, Article 263(4) TFEU would make it easier for private parties to bring an action against regulatory acts which do not require implementing measures. If, as has been argued in this book, regulatory acts should be understood as non-legislative acts of general application, private parties would still have to show direct and individual concern when they challenge legislative acts. The introduction of an express hierarchy of norms in the Lisbon Treaty reflects the transformation that the European Community has undergone from an economic endeavour based on international law to a constitutional Union with comprehensive competences. As a result the Lisbon Treaty envisages that Union legislation, as a functional equivalent to national legislation, can only be directly challenged in exceptional circumstances. In this respect the situation in the EU would still be more favourable than in most Member States, where direct actions against legislative acts in the formal sense[2] are not available. The elimination of individual concern as a requirement to challenge regulatory acts which do not require implementing measures would remove, however, the criticism that private parties are denied an effective remedy when challenging acts of general application. On the other hand, Article 263 TFEU still provides an important role for national courts and the validity review

[1] This is, however, subject to the provisions of Title VII of the Protocol on Transitional Provisions.

[2] Legislation in the formal sense is here understood as acts adopted in the legislative procedure provided for by the Constitution or by constitutional principle. On the notion of legislation in form, see A. Türk, *The Concept of Legislation in European Community Law* (Kluwer, 2006), pp. 63–65.

process under Article 267 TFEU. National courts would still provide the ordinary forum for private parties to challenge indirectly legislative acts of the Union and non-legislative acts of general application which require implementing measures or are not of direct concern to the applicant. The role of national courts in judicial review of Union acts would therefore continue to be a key aspect of the EU's judicial architecture. This role would be strengthened by the removal of the special regimes for validity references in Article 68 EC and Article 35 TEU. All in all, the Lisbon Treaty would make it easier for the Union courts to claim that 'the Treaty has established a complete system of legal remedies and procedures designed to ensure judicial review of the legality of acts of the institutions, and has entrusted such review to the Community Courts [. . .]'.[3]

This does, however, not mean that all issues have been solved and it is not difficult to predict that existing problems would persist under the new regime. In annulment actions, the continued relevance of the notion of reviewable act would make it necessary to iron out certain inconsistencies in its interpretation. While reviewable acts should be defined as those which produce legal effects, the insistence that such effects have to exist in relation to the applicant should be reconsidered. It seems incoherent to require in some cases that the measure brings about a distinct change in the applicant's legal position, but in others to be content with the fact that the measure produces legal effects for some persons, but not for the applicant.[4] What is more, it is submitted that the relationship between the act and the applicant should be determined by the relevant standing requirements obviating the need for such a link when considering whether the act is reviewable. Otherwise the notion of reviewable act becomes indistinguishable from the assessment of direct concern. The concept of reviewable act also poses problems when assessing Community acts which are part of a composite procedure which involves contributions by Community institutions, committees and agencies, as well as national administrations in the decision-making process.[5] Community measures which contribute towards a decision by national authorities will often not be reviewable, as they are regarded as preparatory or merely as providing an opinion, leaving the applicant to challenge such measures in the national courts or to bring an action for damages under Article 288(2).[6]

---

[3] Case C-50/00 *Unión de Pequeños Agricultores v Council* [2002] ECR I-6677, para. 40.

[4] See, supra, at pp. 37–40.

[5] See S. Cassese, 'European Administrative Proceedings' (2004) 68 *Law and Contemporary Problems* 21–36; E. Chiti, 'Forms of European Administrative Action' (2004) 68 *Law and Contemporary Problems* 37–57.

[6] See Case T-309/03 *Grau v Commission* [2006] ECR II-1173.

Also the issue of standing in annulment actions would continue to pose challenges for the Union courts after the entry into force of the Lisbon Treaty. Regional authorities would still be forced to comply with the standing requirements for natural and legal persons under Article 263(4) TFEU despite their often constitutional status in the Member States. Such regional authorities should have been included amongst the semi-privileged applicants in Article 263(3) TFEU. In the absence of such inclusion their only hope rests with a more liberal interpretation of the notion of individual concern by the Union courts. In the same way, the standing of interest associations continues to be regulated by the provisions applicable for private parties and the case law developed in this respect. While the need for an interpretation of the term 'regulatory act' in Article 263(4) TFEU arises entirely as a result of the amendments included by the Lisbon Treaty, the interpretation of the concepts of direct and individual concern in this provision will no doubt be inspired by existing case law. The interpretation of whether a measure concerns the applicant directly has created difficulties for the Community Courts mainly in case of Community decisions relating to Community funding. It is submitted that rulings, such as *Dreyfus*[7] and *Interhotel*[8] on the one hand, and the judgment in *Greenpeace*[9] and the rulings concerning EAGGF and ERDF funding on the other hand, seem to be difficult to reconcile.[10] Divergence across different areas in the case law can also be discerned in the current interpretation of individual concern. The difference in treatment of applicants who constitute 'parties concerned' in competition proceedings, state aid proceedings and anti-dumping proceedings[11] is difficult to explain. The right to participate as 'interested party' seems to be sufficient in antitrust cases to satisfy individual concern.[12] In state aid cases participation rights of 'parties concerned' are only sufficient for individual concern where the Commission decides under Article 88(3) EC not to open an investigation under Article 88(2) EC and then only to protect procedural guarantees under Article 88(2) EC. Where a challenge of the merits of a state aid decision is brought, individual concern will only be satisfied where the applicant's position on the market is substantially affected.[13] Finally, in anti-dumping proceedings the Community Courts distinguish various categories of applicants for the

---

[7] Case C-386/96 P *Dreyfus v Commission* [1998] ECR I-2309.

[8] Case C-291/89 *Interhotel v Commission* [1991] ECR I-2257.

[9] Case C-321/95P *Greenpeace Council and Others v Commission* [1998] ECR I-1651.

[10] See, supra, pp. 59–63.

[11] See, supra, pp. 77–85.

[12] Joined Cases T-528/93, T-542/93, T-543/93 and T-546/93 *Metropole télévision SA and Others v Commission* [1996] ECR II-649.

[13] Case C-260/05 P *Sniace v Commission* [2007] ECR I-10005, para. 60.

purpose of individual concern. In the case of complainants their role in the anti-dumping proceedings and their position in the market are the relevant criteria for establishing individual concern,[14] but participation alone is not sufficient. The rationale for these differences in treatment is not apparent. It is submitted that individual concern should be granted where Community legislation has laid down specific procedural guarantees for a person in an administrative procedure at Union level. A person should therefore be individually concerned where 'Community law has made provision for a special procedure prior to the adoption of the contested act, in which those individuals may participate and submit their observations'.[15] In addition, despite their repeated claim that the availability of a remedy in the national courts is irrelevant for the interpretation of individual concern,[16] the Community Courts give the impression that in certain cases they are prepared to consider just that. How else should one explain cases such as *Les Verts*, *Codorniu* and *Extramet*. All three cases have remained unique in their interpretation of the *Plaumann* formula and can be seen as a desire of the Court to provide 'justice' for the applicants. It should not surprise the Community Courts when applicants expect them to make an exception in their case as well. It is of course a different matter whether the Community Courts will continue to interpret individual concern in accordance with the *Plaumann* formula. This will depend to a large extent on whether the Union courts are prepared to break the link between the nature of the act as decision and individual concern. It has been submitted that the Community Courts have already loosened that connection but have not entirely abandoned it.[17] Strictly speaking the *Plaumann* formula only requires individuals to distinguish themselves. The restrictive nature of the formula is less due to its formulation than the desire of the Community Courts to maintain a close link with the nature of the act as decision in substance. A further disassociation between individual concern and the nature of the act will, however, force the Community Courts to provide a different rationale for the formula or abandon it altogether. It is submitted that Article 263(4) TFEU might hold out an answer in this respect. Precisely because it removes the requirement of individual concern for regulatory acts which do not entail implementing measures, the provision seems to suggest that the requirement of individual concern can be more easily satisfied in the case of acts of individual application. Article

---

[14] Case 264/82 *Timex v Council and Commission* [1985] ECR 849.

[15] Opinion of AG Cosmas in Case C-321/95P *Greenpeace v Commission* [1998] ECR I-1651, para. 79.

[16] See Case C-50/00 *Unión de Pequeños Agricultores v Council* [2002] ECR I-6677, para. 43.

[17] See, supra, pp. 98–100.

263(4) TFEU thereby maintains the link between individual concern and the nature of the act as decision in substance. It is submitted that the distinction between acts of general and those of individual application would therefore continue to be of relevance under Article 263(4) TFEU.

Even though the grounds of review remain unchanged in Article 263(2) TFEU, the amendments in the TEU (Lisbon) and the TFEU alter the substantive law against which the legality of Union acts would have to be judged. On the one hand, the changes brought about by the Lisbon Treaty might help to reduce potential areas of conflict between the Union institutions. In particular the European Parliament would have finally achieved the status in the law-making process it has always aspired to. On the other hand, disputes between the Union and its Member States about competence issues might well increase, not least because of the reinforced principle of subsidiarity.[18] A new factor in the review of Union action would be the application of the Charter of Fundamental Rights, which should provide a standard of review on the basis of Article 6(1) TEU (Lisbon).[19] As a final point it is submitted that the new hierarchy of norms could exert an influence over the intensity of judicial review. A more detached review of legislative acts, at least those adopted in the ordinary legislative procedure, can be justified on ground of their enhanced legitimacy. For other Union acts, the case law does provide some indication as to where the Union courts would operate a more or less intense review. It would, however, be helpful if the rationale(s) for reduced or enhanced review could be made clear and then applied consistently across the range of Union law.

The interpretation of Articles 264 and 266 TFEU, which determine the consequences of a ruling of illegality, would follow in the footsteps of the case law developed under Articles 231 and 233 EC. The continued absence of a remedy of declaratory relief in Union law and the lack of power of the Union courts to give directions to Union institutions under Article 266 TFEU would make a strict interpretation of the obligations of the institution whose act has been declared void under Article 266 TFEU paramount.

The action for failure to act in Article 265 TFEU has remained virtually unchanged. Certain problems which have emerged in the application of Article 232 EC would therefore persist and continue to make this remedy unattractive. First, where the procedure for the adoption of a Union act consists of various steps before a final decision is adopted, the case law

---

[18] See the Protocol on the Application of the Principles of Subsidiarity and Proportionality.

[19] Article 263(2) TFEU includes as ground of review the 'infringement of the Treaties' thereby including the TEU.

requires the applicant 'to bring a series of actions for failure to act, to produce a useful result',[20] where the institution remains inactive. Where the institution adopts the necessary preparatory measure, but not with the content the applicant requested, the institution will have defined its position and thereby terminated its failure to act. All the same, as it is merely preparatory such a measure cannot be reviewed in an action for annulment. What makes matters worse is that the institution can define its position even after an action for failure to act has been brought in the Union courts. It has been submitted that recent arguments in defence of this approach are not entirely convincing.[21] Secondly, concerns have been raised as to the imposition of the requirement that actions for failure to act have to be brought within a reasonable time. The requirement is difficult to justify as a matter of principle and has left applicants with uncertainty as to when the time-limit starts and as to what constitutes a reasonable period of time. Thirdly, Article 265(3) TFEU, which deals with the standing of private parties, does not incorporate the approach of the Community Courts to grant standing where the requested act would not be addressed to the applicant, but would be of direct and individual concern to him.[22] There can, however, be little doubt that the provision would continue to be interpreted in this way.

The Court's claim that 'the Treaty has established a complete system of legal remedies and procedures designed to ensure judicial review of the legality of acts of the institutions'[23] will be strengthened if the Lisbon Treaty enters into force. The abolition of the special regimes of judicial review in Article 68 EC and Article 35 EU, the liberalisation of Article 263(4) TFEU for regulatory acts which do not entail implementing measures and the obligation in Article 19(1)(2) TEU (Lisbon) for Member States to provide remedies to ensure legal protection would enhance the judicial protection of private parties against Union acts considerably. All the same, the comprehensive nature of remedies for judicial review would depend to a large extent on the effectiveness of incidental review of Union acts either in the Union courts through Article 277 TFEU or in the national courts through Article 267 TFEU.

The availability of indirect review against acts of general application in Article 277 TFEU reinforces the view that direct challenges in the Union courts would mainly be available against acts of individual application

---

[20] Opinion of AG Tesauro in Case C-282/95 *Guérin automobiles v Commission* [1997] ECR I-1503, at para. 33.

[21] See, supra, pp. 191–193.

[22] Case C-107/91 *ENU v Commission* [1993] ECR I-599.

[23] Case C-50/00 *Unión de Pequeños Agricultores v Council* [2002] ECR I-6677, para. 40.

and, exceptionally, against regulatory acts which do not require implementing measures. It is, however, in respect of these latter acts that the current case law might exacerbate already existing problems. The Court's dictum in *Simmenthal*[24] that incidental review under Article 241 EC should be provided to those who could not bring a direct challenge under Article 230 EC, would imply that regulatory acts which do not entail implementing measures would become immune to incidental review under Article 277 TFEU where they could have been challenged under Article 263(4) TFEU, but an action was not brought within the time-limit in Article 263(6) TFEU. This problem would arise with equal force under Article 267 TFEU, if the *TWD*[25] principle, in accordance with which a validity reference under Article 234 EC is inadmissible, where the applicant could have 'undoubtedly' challenged a Community act directly under Article 230(4) EC, is continued to be applied under the Lisbon Treaty also in the case of acts of general application.[26] This approach would mean that validity review for regulatory acts which do not entail implementing measures is no longer available for those who were 'undoubtedly' directly concerned by the act, but did not bring a direct challenge under Article 263(4) TFEU within the time-limit of Article 263(6) TFEU. This would lead to the unwelcome situation that the increase in judicial protection under Article 263(4) TFEU would be cancelled out by the reduction in protection under Article 267 TFEU.

It is submitted that a bar to incidental review, be it under Article 277 TFEU or Article 267 TFEU, should be limited to Union acts of individual application. This would also provide a more rational basis for allowing privileged applicants to challenge Union acts of general application, but not those of individual application, indirectly under Article 277 TFEU.

While this author has advocated a more balanced view as to the merits of Article 234 EC as effective remedy,[27] validity review under Article 267 TFEU would certainly be capable of improvement. First, the Union courts might be asked to assess the continued relevance of the *Foto-Frost* doctrine. While the limitation of the doctrine to legislative acts could be envisaged, it is by no means certain that a relaxation in this respect would be desirable, not least because the Union would still not have an appeal system from national courts to the European courts. Secondly, national judges would need to be aware and trained in assessing the validity of Union acts. Where, after careful consideration, they find a challenge well-founded and

---

[24] Case 92/78 *Simmenthal v Commission* [1979] ECR 777.
[25] Case C-182/92 *TWD Textilwerke Deggendorf v Germany* [1994] ECR I-833.
[26] See Case C-239/99 *Nachi Europe GmbH v Hauptzollamt Krefeld* [2001] ECR I-1197.
[27] See, supra, pp. 231–237.

are therefore preparing a reference, they should take care to consider the grounds on which such a reference is made. Thirdly, the availability of interim relief should be revisited. While the ruling in *Zuckerfabrik*[28] would allow national courts to grant such interim relief, it is submitted that the Union courts should consider requests for interim relief once a preliminary reference has been made.

As Article 340(2) TFEU contains only cosmetic changes in comparison with Article 288(2) EC, the Union courts would have to confront the same legal issues also under the new regime for non-contractual liability of the Union. The Union courts would have to continue to deal with the issues of joint liability of Union and Member State action and the doctrine of exhaustion of remedies. With a move towards a more functionally integrated European administration, these issues would increase in importance. The application of the *Bergaderm*[29] test under the regime of Article 340(2) TFEU would lead to an increased alignment of the principles applicable to Member State liability and those governing Union liability. However, it has been submitted in this book[30] that such an alignment might not necessarily be justified. Instead of focusing on discretion as the relevant factor for different tests of liability, the Union courts ought to consider the nature of the act as relevant factor. The explicit hierarchy of norms under the Lisbon Treaty would allow a distinction to be made between legislative acts, at least those adopted in the ordinary legislative procedure, for which a more restrictive test could be applied and non-legislative acts, which should be subject to a less restrictive test. This would then also be more in line with the general principles common to the laws of the Member States applicable in case of non-contractual liability of public authorities.

Under the Lisbon Treaty, the application of the *Bergaderm* test for discretionary acts would have to make it clearer as to which criteria are to be used to establish a manifest and grave disregard of an institution's discretion and what role, if any, the previous case law developed in the wake of the *Schöppenstedt*[31] formula could play. Also the dictum in the *Bergaderm* test that any breach is sufficiently serious in the case of non-discretionary acts, would require further clarification in light of recent case law. And it would have to be seen whether the Union courts are prepared to accept in principle the liability of the Union for lawful acts in cases which fall outside a WTO context.

---

[28] Joined Cases C-143/88 and C-92/89 *Zuckerfabrik Süderdithmarschen and Zuckerfabrik Soest* [1991] ECR I-415.

[29] C-352/98 P *Bergaderm and Goupil v Commission* [2000] ECR I-5291.

[30] See, supra, pp. 255–256.

[31] Case 5/71 *Zuckerfabrik Schöppenstedt v Council* [1971] ECR 975.

Finally, the regime applicable to the grant of interim relief by the Union courts under Articles 278 and 279 TFEU would remain unchanged. The dispute over the restrictive interpretation of serious and irreparable harm, and in particular the availability of compensation for non-contractual liability as relevant factor for denying that damage of a purely financial nature is irreparable, would continue under the Lisbon Treaty.

Measured against the criticism levelled at the remedies available for individuals to bring a direct challenge against Community and, even more so, Union acts under the current regime of the EC and EU Treaties, and the aspirations for reform, the Lisbon Treaty, much like the Constitutional Treaty, will come to be seen by many as a disappointment. Such criticism is often, implicitly at least, based on the idea of a centralised provision of judicial review in the Community courts alone. The Community's and, with the entry into force of the Lisbon Treaty, the Union's judicial architecture, is more to be perceived as integrated administration of justice, in which the national courts play an important part. Seen in this light, the Lisbon Treaty reinforces merely the existing trend towards a more integrated nature of European governance.

Bibliography

A. Adinolfi, 'Admissibility of Action for Annulment by Social Partners and "Sufficient Representativity" of European Agreements' (2000) 25 *ELRev* 165.

A. Albors-Llorens, 'The Standing of Private Parties to Challenge Community Measures: Has the European Court Missed the Boat?' (2003) *CLJ* 72–92.

A. Albors-Llorens, *Private Parties in European Community Law* (1996).

A. Arnull, *The European Union and its Court of Justice* (OUP, 2nd edn., 2006).

W. Alexander, 'The Temporal Effects of Preliminary Rulings' (1988) 8 *YBEL* 11.

M. Andenas, A. Türk (eds.), *Delegated Legislation and the Role of Committees in the EC* (Kluwer, 2000).

A. Arnull, 'Challenging EC Anti-dumping Regulations' (1992) 13 *ELRev* 73–81.

A. Arnull, 'Liability for Legislative Acts', in T. Heukels and A. McDonnell (eds.), *The Action for Damages in Community Law* (Kluwer Law International, 1997).

A. Arnull, 'Private Applicants and the Action for Annulment since Codorniu' (2001) 38 *CMLRev* 7–52.

A. Arnull, 'Private Applicants and the Action for Annulment under Art. 173 of the EC Treaty' (1995) 32 *CMLRev* 7.

D. Bailey, 'Standard of Proof in EC Merger Proceedings: A Common Law Perspective' (2003) *CMLRev* 845.

A. Barav, 'Considerations sur la Spécificité du Recours en Carence' (1975) *RTDE* 53.

A. Barav, 'The Exception of Illegality in Community Law: A Critical Analysis' (1974) 11 *CMLRev* 366.

A. Barav, 'Direct and Individual Concern: An Almost Insurmountable Barrier to the Admissibility of Individual Appeal to the EEC Court' (1974) 11 *CMLRev* 191–198.

E. Barbier de la Serre, 'Accelerated and Expedited Procedures before the EC Courts: a Review of the Practice' (2006) *CMLRev* 783–815.

G. Bebr, 'Direct and Indirect Judicial Control of Community Acts in Practice: the Relation Between Arts 173 and 177 of the EEC Treaty', in Michigan Law Review Association (ed) *The Art of Governance Festschrift zu Ehren von Eric Stein* (Ann Arbor, 1984).

G. Bebr, 'Judicial Remedy of Private Parties against Normative Acts of the European Communities: The Role of the Exception of Illegality' (1966) 4 *CMLRev* 7.

U. Bernitz and J. Nergelius, *General Principles of European Community Law* (Kluwer, 2000).

E. Berry and S. Boyes, 'Access to Justice in the Community Courts: A Limited Right?' (2005) *Civil Justice Quarterly* 224–245

C. Bergström, *Comitology, Delegation of Powers in the European Union and the Committee System* (OUP, 2005).

F. Bignami, 'Three Generations of Participation Rights before the European Commission' (2004) 68 *Law and Contemporary Problems* 61–83.

M. Brealey and M. Hoskins, *Remedies in EC Law* (Sweet & Maxwell, 2nd edn., 1998).

H.J. Bronkhorst, 'The Valid Legislative Act as a Cause of Liability of the Communities', in T. Heukels and A. McDonnell (eds.), *The Action for Damages in Community Law* (Kluwer Law International, 1997).

L.N. Brown and J.S. Bell, *French Administrative Law* (Clarendon Press Oxford, 4th edn., 1993).

F. Capelli and M. Migliazza, 'Recours en Indemnité et Protection des Intérêts Individuels: Quelles sont les Changements Possibles et Souhaitables?' (1995) *CDE* 585–640.

S. Cassese, 'European Administrative Proceedings' (2004) 68 *Law and Contemporary Problems* 21–36.

D. Chalmers, C. Hadjiemmanuil, G. Monti, A. Tomkins, *European Union Law* (CUP, 2006).

E. Chiti, 'Forms of European Administrative Action' (2004) 68 *Law and Contemporary Problems* 37–57.

T. Christiansen and T. Larsson, *The Role of Committees in the Policy Process of the European Union* (Edward Elgar Publishing, 2007).

J. Coppel, 'Rights, Duties and the End of Marshall' (1994) 57 *MLR* 859–879.

J.M. Cortés Martin, 'Ubi Ius, Ibi Remedium? – *Locus Standi* of Private Applicants under Article 230(4) EC at a European Crossroads' (2004) *MJ* 233–261.

P. Craig, 'Legality, Standing and Substantive Review in Community Law' (1994) 14 *OJLS* 507.

P. Craig, 'Constitutions, Constitutionalism, and the European Union' (2001) *ELJ* 125–150.

P. Craig, 'Standing, Rights and the Structure of Legal Argument' (2003) 9 *EPL* 493.

P. Craig, *EU Administrative Law* (OUP, 2006).
P. Craig and G. DeBúrca, *EU Law – Text, Cases and Materials* (OUP, 4th edn., 2008).
J.L. de la Cruz Vilaça, 'La Procédure en Référé Comme Instrument de Protection Jurisdictionelle des Particuliers in Droit Communautaire' *Mélanges F. Mancini* (Giuffré, 1998).
S. de la Sierra, 'Provisional Court Protection in Administrative Disputes in Europe: The Constitutional Status of Interim Measures Deriving from the Right to Effective Court Protection. A Comparative Approach' (2004) *ELJ* 42–60.
F.C. de la Torre, 'Interim Measures in Community Courts: Recent Trends' (2007) *CMLRev* 273–353.
O. De Schutter, 'Public Interest Litigation Before the European Court of Justice' (2006) *MJ* 9–34.
De Smith, Woolf and Jowell, *Judicial Review of Administrative Action* (Sweet & Maxwell, 5th edn., 1995).
M. de Visser, 'The Concept of Concurrent Liability and its Relationship with the Principle of Effectiveness: A One-way Ticket into Oblivion?' (2004) 11 *Maastricht Journal of European and Comparative Law* 4.
G. DeBúrca, 'The Principle of Proportionality and its Application in EC Law' (1993) 13 *YEL* 105.
R. Dehousse, 'Misfits: EU Law and the Transformation of European Governance', in: C. Joerges and R. Dehousse, *Good Governance in Europe's Integrated Market* (OUP, 2002).
B. Dubey, 'Administration Indirecte et Fédéralisme d'Exécution en Europe', (2003) *CDE* 87–133.
Dubois, 'L'exception D'illégalité Devant la Cour de Justice des Communautés européennes' (1978) *Cahier de Droit Européen* 411.
P. Eeckhout, *External Relations of the European Union – Legal and Constitutional Foundations* (OUP, 2004).
E. Ellis (ed.) *The Principle of Proportionality* (Hart, 1999).
N. Emiliou, *The Principle of Proportionality in European Law* (Kluwer, 1996)
S. Enchelmaier, 'No-One Slips Through the Net? Latest Developments and Non-Developments in the European Court of Justice's Jurisprudence on Article 230(4) EC' (2005) 24 *YEL* 173–221.
A. Estella, *The EU Principle of Subsidiarity and its Critique* (OUP, 2002).
D. Fairgrieve, M. Andenas and J. Bell (eds.), *Tort Liability of Public Authorities in Comparative Perspective* (London, British Institute of International and Comparative Law, 2002).
E.-W. Fuss, 'La Responsabilité des Communautés Européennes pour le Comportement Illégal de Leurs Organes' (1981) *RTDE* 1.

R. Gavison, 'The Role of Courts in Rifted Democracies' (1999) 33 *Israel Law Review* 216.

R. Greaves, 'Locus Standi under Article 173' (1986) 11 *ELRev* 119–133.

L. Hancher, 'Issues of Non-Contractual Liability Under the EAEC Treaty', in T. Heukels and A. McDonnell (eds.), *The Action for Damages in Community Law* (Kluwer Law International, 1997).

C. Harding, 'The Private Interest in Challenging Community Action' (1980) 5 *ELRev* 354–361.

C. Harlow, 'Towards a Theory of Access for the European Court of Justice' (1992) 12 *YEL* 213–248.

T.C. Hartley, *The Foundations of European Community Law* (OUP, 6th edn., 2007).

M. Hedemann-Robinson, 'Article 173 EC, General Community Measures and *Locus Standi* for Private Persons: Still a Cause for Individual Concern?' (1996) 2 *EPL* 127.

T. Heukels and A. McDonnell (eds.), *The Action for Damages in Community Law* (Kluwer Law International, 1997).

C. Hilson and T. Downes, 'Making Sense of Rights: Community Rights in E.C. Law' (1999) 24 *ELRev* 121.

H. Hofmann, 'Administrative governance in state aid policy', in H. Hofmann and A. Türk (eds.) *EU Administrative Governance* (Edward Elgar Publishing, 2006), at pp. 185–214.

H. Hofmann and A. Türk (eds.), *EU Administrative Governance* (Edward Elgar Publishing, 2006).

H. Hofmann and A. Türk, 'The Development of Integrated Administration in the EU and its Consequences' (2007) 13(2) *ELJ* 253–271.

G. Isaac, 'La modulation par la Court de Justice des Communautés européennes des effets dans le temps de ses arrêts d'invalidité' (1987) *CDE*, p. 444.

F.G. Jacobs 'Recent Developments in the Principle of Proportionality in European Community Law', in E. Ellis (ed.) *The Principle of Proportionality* (Hart, 1999).

C. Joerges and E. Vos (eds.), *EU Committees: Social Regulation, Law and Politics* (Hart, 1999).

R. Joliet, *Le droit institutionnel des Communautés européennes. Le contentieux* (1981).

C. Koch, 'Locus Standi of Private Applicants under the EU Constitution: Preserving Gaps in the Protection of Individuals' Right to an Effective Remedy' (2005) *ELRev* 511–527.

K. Lenaerts, 'Some Reflections on the Separation of Powers in the European Community' (1991) 28 *CMLRev* 11–35.

K. Lenaerts, 'Regulating the Regulatory Process: "Delegation of Powers" in the European Community' (1993) *ELRev* 22.

K. Lenaerts and J. Vanhamme, 'Procedural Rights of Private Parties in the Community Administrative Process' (1997) *CMLRev* 531.

P.L. Lindseth, 'Democratic Legitimacy and the Administrative Character of Supranationalism: The Example of the European Community' (1999) *Columbia Law Review* 628.

G. Mancini and D. Keeling, 'Democracy and the European Court of Justice' (1994) 57 *MLR* 175.

H.P. Nehl, *Principles of Administrative Procedure in EC Law* (OUP, 1999).

M. Nettesheim, 'Article 173 of the EC Treaty and Regulations: Towards the Development of Uniform Standing Requirements', in W. Micklitz and N. Reich (eds.), *Public Interest Litigation Before European Courts* (1996) 225.

P. Nihoul, 'La Recevabilité des Recours en Annulation' (1994) 30 *RTDE* 171–194.

D. Obradovic, 'EC Rules on Public Participation in Environmental Decision-Making Operating at the European and National Levels' (2007) *ELRev* 839–859.

D. O'Keeffe and A. Bavasso (eds.), *Judicial Review in European Union Law* (Kluwer Law International, 2000).

P. Oliver, 'Joint Liability of the Community and the Member States', in T. Heukels and A. McDonnell (eds.), *The Action for Damages in Community Law* (Kluwer Law International, 1997).

B. Pastor and E. Van Ginderachter, 'La procédure en référé' (1989) *RTDE* 561–621.

S. Prechal, 'Does Direct Effect Still Matter?' (2000) 37 *CMLRev* 1047.

S. Prechal, *Directives in European Community* Law (OUP, 2nd edn., 2005).

P. Ragolle, 'Access to Justice for Private Applicants in the Community Legal Order: Recent (R)evolutions' (2003) *ELRev* 90–101.

H. Rasmussen, 'Why is Article 173 Interpreted against Private Plaintiffs?' (1980) 5 *ELRev* 112.

I. Richter and G. F. Schuppert, *Casebook Verwaltungsrecht* (München, 2nd edn., 1995).

G. Roberts, 'Judicial Review of Legislative Measures: the European Court of Justice Breathes Life into the Second Paragraph of Article 215' (1988) 26 *Columbia Journal of Transnational Law* 245.

M. Ruffert, 'Rights and Remedies in European Community Law: A Comparative View' (1997) *CMLRev* 307.

M. Ruffert, Case Annotation, (2001) 38 *CMLRev* 781.

H.G. Schermers and C.R.A Swaak, 'Official Acts of Community Servants and Article 215(4) EC', in T. Heukels and A. McDonnell (eds.), *The Action for Damages in Community Law* (Kluwer Law International, 1997).

H.G. Schermers and D.F. Waelbroeck, *Judicial Protection in the European Union* (Kluwer, 6th edn., 2001).

H.G. Schermers, T. Heukels, and P. Mead (eds.), *Non-Contractual Liability of the European Communities* (Martinus Nijhoff, 1988).

F. Schockweiler, G. Wivenes and J. Godart, 'Le Régime de la Responsabilité Extra-Contractuelle du fait D'actes Juridiques dans la Communauté Européenne' (1990) *RTDE* 27.

S. Schonberg, *Legitimate Expectations in Administrative Law* (OUP, 2000).

J. Schwarze, *European Administrative Law* (Sweet & Maxwell, 1992).

M. Shapiro, 'The Giving Reasons Requirement' (1992) *University Chicago Legal Forum* 179.

D. Simon, 'L'effet dans le Temps des Arrêts Préjudiciels de la Cour de Justice des Communautés Européennes: Enjeu ou Prétexte d'une Nouvelle Guerre des Juges?', *Mélanges Pescatore* (Baden-Baden, 1987), p. 665.

D. Sinaniotis, 'The Plea of Illegality in EC Law' (2001) *EPL* 103.

J. Steiner, 'Subsidiarity under the Maastricht Treaty', in D. O'Keeffe and P.M. Twomey (eds.) *Legal Issues of the Maastricht Treaty* (Chancery, 1994).

J. Temple Lang, 'Actions for Declarations that Community Regulations are Invalid: The Duties of National Courts under Article 10 EC' (2003) *CMLRev* 102.

A.G. Toth, 'The Concepts of Damage and Causality as Elements of Noncontractual Liability', in T. Heukels and A. McDonnell (eds.), *The Action for Damages in Community Law* (Kluwer Law International, 1997).

A.G. Toth, 'A Legal Analysis of Subsidiarity', in D. O'Keeffe and P.M. Twomey (eds.), *Legal Issues of the Maastricht Treaty* (Chancery, 1994).

T. Tridimas, 'Liability for Breach of Community Law: Growing Up and Mellowing Down?' (2001) 38 *CMLRev* 301.

T. Tridimas, 'Proportionality in European Community Law: Searching for the Appropriate Standard of Scrutiny' in E. Ellis (ed.) *The Principle of Proportionality* (Hart, 1999).

T. Tridimas, *The General Principles of EC Law* (OUP, 2nd edn., 2006).

A. Türk, 'Judicial Review of Integrated Administration', in H.C.H. Hofmann and A. Türk (eds.), *Legal Challenges in EU Administrative Law: Towards an Integrated Administration* (Edward Elgar Publishing, forthcoming).

A. Türk, 'The Concept of the "Legislative" Act in the Constitutional Treaty' (2005) *German Law Journal* 1555–1570.

A. Türk, 'The role of the European Court of Justice in the area of comitology', in T. Christiansen and T. Larsson, *The Role of the Committees in the Policy Process of the European Union* (Edward Elgar Publishing, 2007).

A. Türk, *The Concept of Legislation in European Community Law – A Comparative Perspective* (Kluwer, 2006).

J. Usher 'Direct and Individual Concern – An Effective Remedy or a Conventional Solution?' (2003) 28 *ELRev* 575–600.

J. Usher, 'Declarations of Invalidity Under Article 177 EEC: of General Effect?' (1984) 6 *ELRev* 284.

J. Usher, 'Individual Concern in General Legislation – 10 Years On' (1994) *ELRev* 636.

J. Usher, 'The Interrelationship of Article 173, 177 and 184 EEC' (1979) *ELRev* 36.

J. Usher, *General Principles of EC Law* (Longman, 1998).

A. van Casteren 'Article 215(2) EC and the Question of Interest', in T. Heukels and A. McDonnell (eds.), *The Action for Damages in Community Law* (Kluwer Law International, 1997).

M.H. Van der Woude, 'Liability for Administrative Acts under Article 215(2) EC', in T. Heukels and A. McDonnell (eds.), *The Action for Damages in Community Law* (Kluwer Law International, 1997).

W. Van Gerven, 'Of Rights, Remedies and Procedures' (2000) 37 *CMLRev* 501–536.

W. Van Gerven, 'The Effect of Proportionality on the Actions of Member States of the European Community: National Viewpoints from Continental Europe', in E. Ellis (ed.) *The Principle of Proportionality* (Hart, 1999).

T. Vandamme, *The Invalid Directive: Legal Authority of a Union Act Requiring Domestic Law Making* (European Law Publishing, Groningen, 2005).

B. Versterdorf, 'Certain Reflections on Recent Judgments Reviewing Commission Merger Control Decisions', in M. Hoskins and W. Robinson (eds.), *A True European, Essays for Judge David Edward* (Hart, 2003), chapter 10.

M. Vogt, 'Indirect Judicial Protection in EC Law – The Case of the Plea of Illegality' (2006) *ELRev* 364–377.

A. von Bogdandy and J. Bast, '*La loi europeénne*: Promise and Pretence', in D. Curtin, A.E. Kellermann and S. Blockmans (eds.), *The EU Constitution: The Best Way Forward?* (T.M.C. Asser Press, The Hague, 2006), pp. 171–181.

C. Waelbroeck, 'May the Court of Justice Limit the Retrospective Operation of its Judgment?' (1981) 1 *YEL* 115.

C. Waelbroeck, *Encyclopédie Dalloz*, 'Failure to Act', No. 26 and No. 27.

J. Wakefield, 'The Plight of the Regions in a Multi-Layered Europe' (2005) *ELRev* 406.

J. Wakefield, *Judicial Protection Through the Use of Article 288(2)* (Kluwer, 2002).

A. Ward, '*Locus Standi* under Article 230(4) of the EC Treaty: Crafting a Coherent Test for a "Wobbly Policy"' (2003) *YEL* 45–77.

A. Ward, *Judicial Review and the Rights of Private Parties in EU Law* (OUP, 2nd edn., 2007).

J.H.H. Weiler, *The Constitution of Europe* (CUP, 1999).

J.H.H. Weiler and N.J.S. Lockhart, '"Taking Rights Seriously" Seriously: the European Court and its Fundamental Rights Jurisprudence' (1995) 32 *CMLRev* 51.

W. Wils, 'Concurrent Liability of the Community and a Member State' (1992) 17 *ELRev* 191.

J.A. Winter, 'The Rights of Complainants in State Aid Cases: Judicial Review of Commission Decisions Adopted under Article 88 (ex 93) EC' (1999) 36 *CMLRev* 521–568.

Index